The American 1890s

□□□ **The**

American 1890s

Life and Times of a Lost Generation

Larzer Ziff

New York · The Viking Press

VIKING COMPASS EDITION
Issued in 1968 by The Viking Press, Inc.
625 Madison Avenue, New York, N. Y. 10022

Distributed in Canada by
The Macmillan Company of Canada Limited

Library of Congress catalog card number: 66-15885
Printed in U.S.A.

Second printing October 1968

Time and facilities for the preparation of this book were provided by grants-in-aid from the American Council of Learned Societies and the Newberry Library.

—L.Z.

For Sara and Isidore Ziff

CONTENTS

The American 1890s

Land of Contrasts

Chicago, the filthy Indian village on the shores of Lake Michigan, had grown within a generation to be the second largest city in America, and even New Yorkers, bored to the point of bad digestion by Chicago's brag, were secretly admitting that the future —railroads, the produce of the Great Plains, the business of buying and selling the world's foodstuffs—belonged to Chicago. Bostonians, already resigned to New York's pushy ways, could only repeat incredulously the Chicagoan's remark that they didn't yet have culture in his city but that when they got some they would make it hum.[1] But the Congress saw Chicago as the new world of the nineteenth century and granted it the exclusive right to hold the fair that would commemorate the four-hundredth anniversary of the discovery of America. In the spring of 1890 President Benjamin Harrison signed the act providing for the World's Columbian Exposition of "arts, industries, manufactures, and the products of the soil, mine, and sea." [2]

Within a year of President Harrison's invitation, over six million dollars had been appropriated for projects at the fair, and forty-four nations together with twenty-eight colonies and provinces were engaged in plans that kept six thousand workers employed at the Jackson Park site in the summer of 1891. The Exposition was to have its panoramic and theatrical displays, its continental cafés, and a staggering abundance of devices and appliances for comfort, instruction, and amusement. The visitors who didn't like the model of Saint Peter's would be delighted with the Hungarian Orpheum. Those who had been dazzled by the Rue de Caire at the Paris Exposition of 1889 would find it surpassed by the Chicago version of a street in Cairo, complete with the wrigglings of Little Egypt. The living representatives of savage, civilized, and semi-civilized nations were to occupy models of their native villages—Dahoman, Indian, Chinese, Turkish, German. Here there would be an ice railway, a Moorish palace, a Japanese bazaar, a Bohemian glass factory, and an exhibition of Irish lacemaking. Towering above all would be the huge revolving wheel designed and constructed for the occasion by George Washington Gale Ferris.

Those who came to see the Exposition would also see Chicago, and that young city, if it had no past to display, was at least equipped to give visitors a glimpse into the future and show them how things were done in a wide-awake commercial fashion. One Chicago commentator, after pointing out that the Dahomans were a cruel and brutal people, piously added, "It is to be hoped that they will carry back to their West African home some of the influences of civilization with which they were surrounded in Jackson Park." [3] It was also hoped that less barbarous visitors would carry home some sense of the effect a growing United States would inevitably have on their economies and on their political positions. The Krupp firm displayed its newest and biggest cannon at the Exposition.

Another European firm that took the hint of the promise of the fair was that of Karl Baedeker, Publishers, of Leipzig. In 1890 that house assigned to an extremely perceptive young Englishman, James F. Muirhead, the vital task of providing a handbook for English-speaking travelers to the United States. The Exposition was thus to bring the United States into the company of places on the habitable globe which Baedeker considered worthy of the patronage of discriminating tourists.

Muirhead's results were impressive. With skill and intelligence he mastered the extremes of climate, the divergence of customs in various sections of the country, and the mysteries of the American table, and produced an equable, shrewd, and sympathetic guide for the use of the touring Englishman. He began where all tourism begins, with money, and explained that in America one would find gold coins worth $20, $10, $5, $2.50, and $1; silver coins worth $1, a half-dollar, a quarter-dollar, and 10 cents; a nickel coin worth 5 cents; and bronze coins worth 2½ cents and 1 cent. The pounds, shillings, and pence equivalents followed in parentheses. He ended some five hundred pages later with a side tour to Mexico which finally deposited the traveler in Vera Cruz, where "commerce has declined since the opening of railway communication with the United States," but from which a side trip could be made to Jalapa. His parting words were, "The women of Jalapa are distinguished for their beauty." [4]

The world of the tourist is one of an infinite number of novelties held tightly in control by certain standards of comfort and cost in eating, sleeping, and traveling. Baedeker's *United States* thus explored the country with a willing curiosity and yet with an iron and inescapable yardstick, and in it Americans were made to measure up in ways less equivocal than those which had been invoked by the glittering procession of literary and scientific visitors of the past: Mrs. Trollope, Alexis de Tocqueville, Charles Dickens, Matthew Arnold, and others.

The United States, the Baedeker reports, is an expensive country. Even with the most rigid economies, a visit there will cost from one-fourth to one-third more than would comparable travel on the continent—without counting the cost of the initial voyage. This voyage can be accomplished in from seven to ten days on an extremely well-run ship. A good first-class cabin can be secured for $100, and some might even find a second-class cabin bearable at a rate as low as $40. Neither case is at an extreme, because the boat offers a de luxe suite of cabins for $500, and in its steerage it carries hundreds and hundreds of immigrants for $20 a head.

The Baedeker puts one at ease immediately about the language. Americans do speak English; you will be understood and can make yourself understood, despite all the jokes you have heard about their native tongue. Of course, you will never be able to understand the names of towns through which the railway (in America called railroad) passes as they are shouted out by the train guard (in America called conductor except in the South and West, where he is addressed as "Captain"), but this minor inconvenience can be overcome by the aid of the excellent brochures most railroad companies give away. You will be amused to learn that hot tea rolls are, in America, called biscuits; you will be chilled to find that the word chicken is used for "fowl of any age."

The first attempt to deal directly with an American cannot be postponed beyond the custom house, where a much more minute examination of your goods will take place than is usual in Europe. The Baedeker does not say why; it passes on to assure you of the courtesy of the guard even as he conducts his scrupulous search. But elsewhere in the book you are told to bring everything you will need with you, since prices in America are higher for all items of clothing and personal use save cotton garments and shoes. If you have the faintest inkling of political economy, you will realize you are encountering the famous American protective tariff.

All Presidents since the Civil War, save one, have been Republicans. Though the Baedeker gives a brief course in United States history, it does not quote the humorist who said, "Whenever you see a newspaper picture of a man with a full beard and a sort of have-tried-two-bottles-of-your-medicine-and-been-benefited look about the eyes you are to know that there is another Ohio candidate in the field." [5] That was Eugene Field, the same humorist who was somewhat short with Mrs. Humphry Ward—who was, admittedly, dreadfully serious even for a member of the Arnold family —when she asked him if he did not find that the social atmosphere in Chicago was too crude to furnish him with intellectual companionship. "Really, Mrs. Ward," Field said, "I do not consider myself competent to give an opinion on the matter. Please bear in mind that up to the time Barnum captured me and took me to Chicago to be civilized I had always lived in a tree in the wilds of Missouri." [6]

The Baedeker warns against such American familiarities in a

less dramatic way. Number one among the general hints is that the traveler "should from the outset reconcile himself to the absence of deference or servility on the part of those he considers his social inferiors; but if ready himself to be courteous on a footing of equality he will seldom meet any real impoliteness." This applies in hotels, for instance, where, outside of New York, the waiter will not expect a tip and will resent a patronizing tone. But don't relax too fully in the presence of easy speech, the Baedeker cautions: "Restaurants which solicit the patronage of 'gents' should be avoided." [7]

Dining in America presents no real problems even outside of New York, so long as you fit yourself to the rhythm of dinner at midday. Wine, however, when you can get it, is outrageously expensive and very bad at that, since Americans set great store by imported wine, though they import only the worst. Indeed, on this matter the Baedeker urges a polite instructing of the citizenry: "It is much to be regretted that, outside of California, the native vintages, which are often superior to the cheap imported wines, seldom appear on the wine-list; and travellers will do good service by making a point of demanding Californian wines and expressing surprise when they cannot be furnished." [8] Meals, however, can be secured at moderate prices, and, while some hotels are dear, as a general rule the comfort of an American hotel is much more likely to be in direct ratio to its charges than is the case in Europe.

America is so expensive (you must count on spending about $10 a day) largely because of its peculiar railroad system. The facts and figures on rail travel are impressive, but their most impressive aspect is the cost to you. In America the railroads are owned by private corporations, more than 20 of them, which employ some 900,000 persons in their systems of 170,000 miles of rails, the estimated value of which is $10 billion. But rates differ in different parts of the country so that it is difficult to arrive at an average cost of travel, though three to four cents a mile is a best guess, and this, compared to European state railways, is high.

Moreover, in spite of the large number of corporations operating trains, should you wish first-class accommodations or a sleeping berth, you must deal with yet another corporation which is not a railroad at all: the Pullman Palace Car Company. At least you are saved the trouble of carrying a traveling rug; the railroad coaches are heated to a point of discomfort, just as are American homes, where temperatures as high as from 70 to 75 degrees Fahrenheit are maintained. Ladies are well advised, even in winter, to plan to wear silk rather than woolen garments.

Though James Muirhead's Baedeker was published in 1893, in time for travelers to the Exposition to benefit from it, he was then no more done with America than the user of his guide was done with Chicago after he had glanced at pages 279-86 in his hotel room, preparatory to descending into Wabash Avenue. The trip Muirhead had made to America to gather material for the book had proved absorbing to the extent of his taking a Bostonian for a wife, and his notebooks contained speculations for which the admirable standards of the Leipzig publishing house had no tolerance. Accordingly, he wrote a second work, based on his travels in the United States from 1890 to 1893, and since it was built on the thousand and one contradictions he had met, he decided the book was best titled *The Land of Contrasts*.

The work is marked by a blithe good cheer which refuses to complain about the countless anti-Toryisms encountered by, even deliberately inflicted upon, an Englishman. England, to many an American businessman in the nineties, was the enemy, holding its world market as an army holds a fortress, while to many an American farmer it was the source of the degenerate refinements which were being aped in the big cities to the destruction of urban morals and at the cost of a fair price for his products. Muirhead had a formula with which to meet these and the many other antagonisms which sprang actually or supposedly from what he called "the events of 1776." When you think of these differences between the Americans and us, he urges his English readers, be like Dr. Johnson, "who dreamed that he had been worsted in a conversation, but reflected when he awoke that the conversation of his adversary must also have been his own." [9] He could even go farther and laugh at himself, trapped in the path of democracy rampant: "I have hailed with delight the democratic spirit displayed in the greeting of my friend and myself by the porter of a hotel as 'You fellows,' and then had the cup of pleasure dashed from my lips by being told by the same porter that 'the other *gentleman* would attend to my baggage.' " [10] Yet he could observe, "Such questions as socialism and the labour movement seldom receive so fair and sympathetic treatment as in the English press." [11]

Some contrasts were delightful in their geographical balance: "From New York to Buffalo I am whisked through the air at a rate of fifty or sixty miles an hour; in California I travelled on a train on which the engineer shot rabbits from the locomotive, and the fireman picked them up in time to jump on the baggage car at the rear end of the train." [12] Others approached the antic: "If an Englishman has a mile to go to an appointment he will take his leisurely way twenty minutes to do the distance, and then settle his business in two or three dozen sentences; an American is much more likely to devour the ground in five minutes, and then spend an hour or more in lively conversation not wholly pertinent to the matter in hand." [13] And still others achieved the zany: "It is a solemn fact that what would appear in England as 'No spitting allowed in this car' is translated in the electric cars of Boston into: 'The Board of Health hereby adjudges that the deposit of sputum in street-cars is a public nuisance.' " [14]

Muirhead cheerfully declined to expand on the significance of these contrasts. The gilt message of the Boston Board of Health and the careless democracy of the porter's vocabulary spoke of one kind of gulf in American life, a social one. His offhand observation that office buildings and apartment houses rose higher than church spires spoke of another, the commercial. But he did not pry into them. He was amused by them as he was amused to observe: "It is in America that I have over and over again heard language to which the calling a spade a spade would seem the most delicate allusiveness; but it is also in America that I have summoned a blush to the cheek of conscious sixty-six by an incautious though innocent reference to the temperature of my morning tub." [15] Here the happy Englishman had gamboled to the verge of a literary gulf, the immense canyon which yawned in American culture between private experience and public admission, tempting a generation that came of age in the nineties to bridge it or to bleach their bones in its depths. Again, Muirhead was not impelled to draw conclusions.

Indeed, why should he have been? Accounting for these formations in the American spiritual landscape was the task of those who would account for America itself, who would reconcile the speed of a New York train with that of one in California, who would move from the $500 de luxe suite to the steerage with ease, who would look up to the church spire from the street or down on it from the broker's office, who would be consciously careless about whom they called gentlemen, who would find a way of saying what all adults knew privately so that it became their public possession and their common experience. It was the task, then, of the American writer.

And yet no writer was going to take it on consciously. It had about it the deadly odor of the Great American Novel, that hypothetical work which was to express the life of a nation but which, by definition, was so unachievable that to pursue it was to die a literary death.

One such living death was being endured in New York in 1890 by Herman Melville. In a marvelous decade before the Great American Novel had ever been heard of, the 1850s, he had nevertheless put forth his candidate, *Moby-Dick,* within two years of his friend Hawthorne's *The Scarlet Letter.* Then Emerson had been inspiring the contradictions of American life with a unitary spirit, and although Melville had differed with Emerson he had differed with a deep-rooted romantic conviction that unity was possible. In that decade before a war that came as the price of insisting on unity, he had embarked his cast of characters on a ship which, trusting to omens, slew a right whale and hung its head over one side, while the head of a sperm whale was hung over the other. This, the superstitions of the sea said, would assure that the ship could never be sunk, and Melville went on to demonstrate that his book was freighted with two whales' heads also—the transcendental romanticism of Kant on one side and the empirical science of Locke on the other. But for all that Captain Ahab did —indeed, because of all that Captain Ahab did—the *Pequod* sank, and Ishmael alone escaped to tell the tale. So did *Moby-Dick* sink its author's reputation, and if he escaped to tell further tales he was soon silenced. A volume of poems in each of the decades since the fifties was the muted announcement that he was still alive.

Few noticed the announcement. Whaling was a dead industry; kerosene was more economical than whale oil, and electricity was even surpassing that. Echoes of neither Kant nor Locke could be heard above the shouts of the scientific popularizers. The trick was to hoist Darwin up on one side of the locomotive and the Bible on the other and run a railroad that would never go bankrupt. The seventy-six-year-old custom-house worker died in 1891, an event briefly noted by *The New York Times*. Barrett Wendell, Harvard professor and guide to many a literary aspirant in the nineties, mentioned Melville in his *Literary History of America* (1900), observing that "Herman Melville with his books about the South Seas, which Robert Louis Stevenson is said to have declared the best ever written, and with his novels on maritime adventure, began a career of literary promise, which never came to fruition." [16] The Stevenson hallmark was worth something; it meant that reading could be good clean fun, not the dirty business that Zola's novels represented at the century's end, and Herman Melville passed into literary history as a minor purveyor of healthy adventure, decently removed from all association with social criticism.

Still alive also in 1890 was Melville's great contemporary, a man who had consciously attempted the Great American Novel, although he thought of it as a poem, and who worked upon it on his deathbed in 1892. Walt Whitman had eagerly seized on America as a land of contrasts and made it his theme: "ONE'S-SELF I sing, a simple separate person,/Yet utter the word Democratic, the word En-Masse." [17] "Yet" was the key word. There was a tension in America between the opportunity the young democracy offered each person, however plain, to realize himself in response to his own bent, and the Americans' nervous herding together that was an inevitable consequence of their being cast loose from the protections of inherited class, fidelity to a royal house, and membership in an established national church. This was the main strain on the integrity of the country, though other pressures were noticeable in sectional differences, occupational differences, cultural differences, and sexual differences.

What was to hold these centrifugal elements together? asked Whitman in the fifties and the sixties. Either men crowded together in colorless conformity or they flew off, each on his own tangent. How was the American to derive his identity, his sense of sharing a particular experience available only in America and better than any in the history of the world, and yet not yield up his individuality, his simple separateness? He could not derive it from his priests, bound to conflicting outworn creeds, nor from his statesmen—the President, Whitman proudly sang, took off his hat to the people, not they theirs to him. Where all offices and institutions failed, there, Whitman insisted in 1855, the poet would serve:

> Of all nations the United States with veins full of poetical stuff most needs poets and will doubtless have the greatest and use them the greatest. Their Presidents shall not be their common referee so much as their poets shall. Of all mankind the great poet is the equable man. Not in him but off from him things are grotesque or eccentric or fail of their sanity. Nothing out of its place is good and nothing in its place is bad. He bestows on every object or quality its fit proportions neither more nor less. He is the arbiter of the diverse and he is the key.[18]

In the seventies Whitman considered the threat to the poet of a mob vulgarity which seemed to follow from the extension of the vote. Culture, many felt, was sure to sink to the level of a backwoods river bottom. But Whitman refused to be dismayed; literature was adequate to save the day:

Our fundamental want to-day in the United States, with closest, amplest reference to present conditions, and to the future, is of a class, and the clear idea of a class, of native authors, literatuses, far different, far higher in grade than any yet known, sacerdotal, modern, fit to cope with our occasions, lands, permeating the whole mass of American mentality, taste, belief, breathing into it a new breath of life, giving it decision, affecting politics far more than the popular superficial suffrage, with results inside and underneath the elections of Presidents or Congresses—radiating, begetting appropriate teachers, schools, manners, and, as its grandest result, accomplishing, (what neither the schools nor the churches and their clergy have hitherto accomplish'd, and without which this nation will no more stand, permanently, soundly, than a house will stand without a substratum,) a religious and moral character beneath the political and productive and intellectual bases of the States.[19]

By 1881, however, Whitman could not gloss over the evidence that his timetable was inaccurate. His countrymen still clung to the fantasies of a deceased world, asking only these of literature, and increasingly built their moral bases, the substratum of the American house, from the materials of modern business. He now had to force his will into a belief that America's writers could realize the promise he claimed for them in 1855. And by 1888 he was content to congratulate himself on the simple fact that he and his poems, though generally ignored, had managed simply to survive: "My Book and I—what a period we have presumed to span! those thirty years from 1850 to '80—and America in them! Proud, proud indeed may we be, if we have cull'd enough of that period in its own spirit to worthily waft a few live breaths of it to the future!"[20] The exclamation marks are embarrassing flags of false cheer. Indeed, on his deathbed in 1892, Whitman himself was a national embarrassment. A young iconoclast who might well have been attracted to his work as he turned in disgust from the teapot poets of the seventies and eighties complained that the cult which had formed around Whitman to protect him in his advanced years also blocked access to him by serious new writers who might learn from him. That cult's "slush, hash, obscurity, morbid eroticism, vulgarity and preposterous mouthings," James Huneker said, "well nigh spoil one's taste for what is really great in *Leaves of Grass*." [21]

By the beginning of the nineties Whitman's dream was bankrupt, and Melville saved himself the pain of speaking out. What had intervened to guarantee them loneliness in their old age was a wholesale commercialization of life. It did not deny literature. Rather, it granted literature a place and in so doing reduced it far more than organized denial could have done. Before the Civil War the critic could ask whether American culture was to be symbolized by a Grecian nymph who would modestly occupy her pedestal in a pantheon of sisters: American industry, American agriculture, American fisheries, etc.; or whether American culture would be the expression of all these and inseparable from them. The years since the war had answered the question. Culture was to have her own pedestal and mind her own business.

What business? The business of beauty; the business of idealizing daily actualities to make the American scene one with the court of Arthur and the Palestine of Jesus; the business of adding "est" to verbs in poetry so as to render American speech poetic; the business of elevating the American landscape to a distinction equal to that of the Alps and the Nile—the business of decoration. The American of the day grew mutton-chop whiskers or Piccadilly weepers and wore a stiff hat when he dressed up, while his lady carried a lace-trimmed parasol. His house wore its whiskers and lace in its towers, cupolas, and bay windows.[22] And his literature decorated his life in the same fashion.

Such a milieu, moreover, encouraged a national habit of carelessness about the rights of the author. Literature was to be beautiful as the setting sun is beautiful, and it was, ideally, to be just as accessible to those who cared to enjoy it. This notion lay behind the failure of the Congress to subscribe to an international copyright law that would give native writers an equal chance to be published in their own country. With the products of British pens free for the taking in the United States, few publishers would risk an American book for which they would have to pay royalties.

On November 28 and 29, 1887, in Chickering Hall in New York, a benefit reading for the American Copyright League took place, and here, before large and enthusiastic audiences, appeared the chief representatives of American literature: James Russell Lowell, Oliver Wendell Holmes, John Greenleaf Whittier, Samuel Langhorne Clemens, Dr. Edward Eggleston, Richard Henry Stoddard, Henry Cuyler Bunner, George Washington Cable, Richard Malcolm Johnston, George William Curtis, and James Whitcomb Riley. One observer reported, and his comment was widely seconded, that "no more remarkable gathering of literary men had ever appeared in America." [28]

Lowell, Holmes, and Whittier were the representatives of the continuity of all that was cherished in American letters. Together with Bryant, Longfellow, Emerson, and Hawthorne, their faces had appeared in the long narrow strips of photographs lovingly framed in gilt or colored cardboard and hung on the walls of cultured homes in the seventies and eighties as a votive offering to both literature and decorative art. Now here they stood, sixty-eight, seventy-eight, and eighty years old respectively. The verve of their reading was surpassed by that of the younger men, but their appearance served a higher function than that of mere entertainment or edification. Their pre-eminence was an item of national faith, and their presence unified and sanctified their fellow readers. Whitman was not there, a contemporary explained, because he "no longer wrote, his adherents were few, and the morality that colored all our literary judgments was too strong to

assure him a place in the group." [24] But the New England trium-
virate continued to write for a wide audience and did so with
unimpeachable moral purpose.

Johnston, Curtis, and Stoddard were their juniors by some
years; they had been born in the twenties, Curtis and Stoddard in
New England in the great days of its literature. They were entirely
familiar with their function on this occasion. They had basked
before in the presence of such as the great three: Curtis had taken
part in the Brook Farm experiment; Stoddard had been befriended
by Hawthorne and was one of the few literary men in 1887 who
still talked with Melville. Curtis had moved from charming essays
on travel to other informal topics in his widely admired books,
and from his position as editor of *Harper's Weekly* continued the
reforming zeal of his youth, supporting women's rights and civil-
service reform. Through newspaper criticism and editorial work,
Stoddard too was a cultural arbiter, who was to bring out a volume of Poe's poetry and yet attack his character. He was author of
Songs of Summer, among other volumes noted for their ravishing
melodic lines. Johnston, a Georgian, had developed the pseudonymous Southerner Philemon Perch, through whose person he
told tales of Georgia country life, hastening reunification after the
war with sketches of the charming and quaint ways of the folks
down South.

Clemens and Eggleston had been born in the thirties, both in
the Midwest, and both, like Johnston, had come to eminence by
sketching the scenes and incidents of specific regions. Dr. Eggleston was a Methodist minister and an expert editor of church
journals as well as the author of novels of backwoods Indiana,
most notably *The Hoosier Schoolmaster* (1871). Clemens' well-
known pictures of boyhood in Missouri were, in the popular mind,
outdistanced by the pseudonymous character of their author,
Mark Twain, from whose mouth, it appeared, nothing unfunny
could possibly issue.

The representatives born in the forties carried on in the tradition of exposing the charms of their native regions. Cable's pic-

tures of New Orleans and his uncanny ability to communicate the lilt of Creole dialect on the printed page as well as from the lecture platform had brought him in 1887 to the peak of his fame, a fame which was exceeded only by that of his contemporary, Riley, singer of Hoosier songs and Hoosier sentiments. These two were the stars at the Chickering Hall readings.

Henry Cuyler Bunner, the young man of the group, born in 1855, was a hopeful glimpse of things to come in American letters. A cute hand at familiar verse, he now occupied the editorship of *Puck* and was sketching New York City with the same loving eye for color and sentiment that his elders had brought to more rural regions.

Would these men of the twenties, thirties, and forties become the subjects of group portraits suitable for framing in the American home? Even their enthusiastic audience in 1887 would have thought not. It was not their fault. They had the moral force of the New England immortals and they had their dedication to American culture. But, their followers would have argued, the country had sprawled since the 1850s. Even though Lowell, Holmes, and Whittier spoke in New England accents of New England things, in their day they had been speaking from an acknowledged cultural center to a people related to them in ancestry and therefore quick to share the content of their works. Now New England, like Johnston's Georgia or Cable's bayous, was but a region; even New York was best treated, as Bunner was showing, as a particular locality. The geographical spread, a Chickering Hall auditor would have said, prevented any of the authors on the platform from achieving a national tone; even though they were equal in talent to the older authors, the very extent of their native land in 1887 prevented them from attaining equal force.

As James F. Muirhead and many another observer of America had noted, however, the American spread was not geographical alone. Steerage passengers were outnumbering the users of Baedeker; Chicago and New York were developing standards different from those of the prairie hamlet and the Maine village, not as the result of their locations but as the result of the density of their populations; the interests of Eastern capital were distinctly diverging from those of Western agriculture. But although Stoddard's verse preserved the genteel use of "thee" and "thy" while Riley's was folksy, they did not offer opposing views of life. Both upheld the same values. Both were laborers in the vineyard of beauty, growing the vines that were to decorate American life, idealizing the experiences conventionally supposed to be available to Americans. Actualities which resisted idealization, they and their companions judged to be unliterary, and they avoided them. Sentiments which were presumed to be shared by all—the Indiana farmer's wife loved her baby even as the New York lawyer's wife loved hers—were made themes that could be enjoyed by all.

By and large, then, the kind of literature represented on the platform of Chickering Hall in November of 1887 was one which was regional in its tone and setting but national in its moral purpose and in its shared sentiments. The admission of geographical differences inherent in the exploitation of local color had developed into an ignoring of deeper social differences. Insofar as these differences were a subject for literature, the burden was the underlying goodhearted humanity of all men, regardless of background, when faced with the important matters of courtship, children, and age.

Whitman had scorned the producers of such a literature:

We see in every polite circle, a class of accomplish'd, good-natured persons, ("society," in fact, could not get on without them,) fully eligible for certain problems, times and duties—to mix egg-nog, to mend the broken spectacles, to decide whether the stew'd eels shall precede the sherry or the sherry the stew'd eels, to eke out our Mr. A. B.'s parlor-tableaux with monk, Jew, lover, Puck, Prospero, Caliban, or what not, and to generally contribute and gracefully adapt their flexibilities and talents, in those ranges, to the world's service. But for real crises, great needs and pulls, moral or physical, they might as well never have been born.[25]

Some were to live into the nineties to challenge this characterization in their social actions if not in their writings, but in 1887 they fitted the picture well. The disparities noted by Muirhead were not their subject matter.

Just as the defeated old Whitman complained of them, so the untried youngster Ellen Glasgow, surveying the state of letters at the outset of her career, said, "The trouble was that I thought of them as old gentlemen, and they thought of themselves as old masters." [26]

Looking back on the literary geniality of the old gentlemen, she explained:

They were important and they knew it, but they were also as affable as royalty; and no one who valued manners could help liking them. Life had been easy for them, and literature had been easier. They had created both the literature of America and the literary renown that embalmed it. They constituted the only critical judgment, as well as the only material for criticism. When they were not, as Charles Lamb once remarked of a similar coterie, "encouraging one another in mediocrity," they were gravely preparing work for one another to praise. For this reason, no doubt, they impressed me with a kind of evergreen optimism. They were elderly, but they were not yet mature. One and all, in their sunny exposure, they had mellowed too quickly. And this ever-green optimism spread over the whole consciousness of America. That, also, had mellowed too quickly; that, also, had softened before it was ripe.[27]

Miss Glasgow's contemporaries, the aspiring writers who were to seek outlet in the 1890s, would have agreed with her, though most would have substituted "rotted" for "softened" in describing what had prematurely overtaken the American consciousness. Raised amid the facts of post-Civil-War America, they saw little significance in the regional gaps when they compared them with the social gaps and the chasm which yawned between private experience and public literature.

Indeed, what the old, in the person of Whitman, and the young, in the person of Ellen Glasgow, found missing from the literary expression of the day was also to evade the physical embodiment of the American spirit at the great Columbian Exposition of 1893. Here the machine age was being ushered in and American commercial and technological superiority was being announced to the world. But the architectural focus of the fair was the White City, where the mirror-like pool of the Court of Honor reflected the massive Greek temples which surrounded it. In column, portico, and caryatid the White City provided the central aesthetic experience for a large majority of visitors. Here, overnight, as it were, an enthralling reality of classical grandeur had been constructed. Hundreds and thousands of Americans who visited it proudly felt that their culture had come of age. They were showing the world that they shared the timeless aesthetic dream in spite of the raw youth and bustle of their civilization. Even a world-weary and sophisticated Henry Adams was impressed. He sat in the Court of Honor to ponder with a willed optimism the miracle of continuity which allowed a flexible metropolis like Chicago to overleap the centuries and root its future, as it seemed to him, in ancient Greece; to settle its contradictions in the measured rhythms of classical unity.[28]

Certain European commissioners, however, were not so happy.[29] Convinced already of American commercial and technical superiority, they had come to Chicago to learn how this modern spirit was to embody itself in form, and they found, instead, uninteresting imitations of the ruins of the old world. Business was everywhere at the fair, displaying its products and profiting from every amusement booth and refreshment counter. Yet the architecture expressed none of this. The White City was a fantasy decoration perched atop the ill-disguised actualities of the American spirit, rather than an organic outgrowth of them.

One disappointed foreigner pushed his inquiry to a point of satisfaction, however. He said:

At the Columbian Fair in Chicago, in the midst of the whiteness of this *carton pâté* city, where the imitation (*pasticcio*) of Greek and Latin antiquity were mingled with those of the Italian Renaissance —a curious gathering of columns, porticoes in severe lines with rococo *campanillas*,—a fantastic construction attracted us; its walls covered with vermilion appeared to the eye as a bloody spot upon the field of snow. It was architecture of a primary character, of studied roughness; a cyclopean and barbarous conception, but certainly not a common one. One could see in it a seeking after the strange and enormous, a dream of new forms which would harmonize with the tumultuous and brutal genius of the human collectivity acting in Chicago, that monstrous city, forced as a precocious vegetation upon the marshes of Lake Michigan.[30]

In the back yard of the exhibition, the French visitor had at last come across the Transportation Building, the sole architectural attempt at expressing the American spirit in the final decade of the nineteenth century. Its architect was a thirty-eight-year-old devotee of Walt Whitman named Louis Sullivan, and the fact that his building struck a discordant note with the main design of the fair represented a major defeat dealt him by the forces of the ideal. The view which prevailed over Sullivan's was expressed by another architect, Daniel Burnham: "The influence of the Exposition architecture will be to inspire a reversion to the pure ideal of the ancients."[31]

Daniel Burnham was chief architect of the fair. Unlike Sullivan, he and other supporters of the "ideal" had grown up in pre-Civil-War America. In their adult lifetime the population of the country had doubled and America had changed from a country of rural villages into an industrial nation. Every third American, at the time of the Exposition, lived in a city, and the average family wealth of city dwellers was $9000, while that of country residents was $3250. In 1890 the number of foreign-born inhabitants of Chicago was almost equal to the total number of inhabitants in the city ten years before.[32] Most men who had seen this happen in their adult lifetimes had come from young manhoods of rural

calm and Christian teaching, and though they could not turn back
the clock and relive the barnyard idyl of their adolescence, they
nevertheless yearned to impose upon the whirl of late-nineteenth-
century America the dream of stasis, an ideal and all-covering
beauty. For Burnham's generation the great crisis in American
life had been sectional war, not class differences, and national
reunion overshadowed all and gave them the key to unity. When
Daniel Burnham told his mother of the magnificent consensus in
the capitalists and artists who cooperated in the Exposition to
create the beauty of the White City, she told him that she saw
in it a vision of the New Jerusalem, the wonder that shall be
when all men work in harmony.[33]

Sullivan, however, had known no other America than that of
strident acceleration, and he wanted his architecture to express
its spirit and, like the poetry of his hero, Whitman, unify its contradictions in New American terms. The dream of ideal form
feeding on a sentimental nostalgia was, for him, pure escapist
fantasy.

The parallel between Burnham and the literary men of the day
was obvious at Chickering Hall in 1887 and was published and
illustrated in America every month of the years between then and
1893. Static idealization of the human condition seemed to be
the answer to the impossibly unaesthetic whirl of social conditions.
Diminishing all seeming difficulties was the feeling that the nation was again united and those in each part of it could appreciate their kinship with the other parts. This feeling was not shared,
however, by a number of young writers absent from Chickering
Hall who were to parallel in literature Sullivan's concern and reject the verbal equivalents of the Greek temple in favor of what
the polychrome stridency of the Transportation Building represented. They were concerned with the difference in texture between rural life and urban life, and with the resulting difference
in morality. They were not so impressed by reunification after the
war as they were by the legacy of violence left by the war. As

Sullivan lost the battle for architectural influence, so they lost the battle for literary influence. But just as, in the twentieth century, modern architecture developed out of the ideas of Sullivan, which had been denied in his day, so modern American literary men were to look to the defeated of the nineties as their true precursors.

Literary Hospitality:

William Dean Howells

The acknowledged leader of American letters did not take part in the Chickering Hall readings. William Dean Howells was passionately committed to the principles of international copyright and was completely at home in company with the men on the platform. But he was a poor reader, and his acute consciousness of this fact made him even a poorer one. His influence was spread so widely by his novels, his monthly editorial essays, his book reviews, his comprehensive correspondence, and his conscientious advice to visitors that he had learned to do almost without whatever small influence (and considerable income) might have been added by his cultivating a platform manner. His daughter's illness required his frequent presence in northern New York state that winter of 1887, and he made no special effort to attend the readings.[1]

In 1887 Howells was in his second year of occupancy of the "editor's study" of *Harper's Monthly,* whence he had come from editorial posts on the *Atlantic.* In that same year, he was also arranging to publish his novels and essays with the firm of Harper's rather than with the illustrious old Boston house of Ticknor & Company. The fifty-year-old native of Ohio was, in short, beginning the transition which, in 1889, would bring him bodily as well as commercially to New York. When he did make that move, then the nation accepted as accomplished fact what until then had been only trend: New York had succeeded Boston as the cultural center of the country.

Till the time of his move to New York, Howells' career had been the model success story of American letters, and his deserved eminence argued the strength of the tradition he represented. The son of a small-town Ohio printer and country journalist, he had schooled himself in literature while learning to set type, and in the evenings, the shop swept and the press oiled, he had turned up his lamp to teach himself German, Italian, and Spanish. In the silent print shop the New England of Emerson, Hawthorne, Lowell, and Holmes loomed before him as the capital of all that was meaningful in American culture; the Yankee voices were heard as clearly and as movingly in the Ohio fields as in the New England towns. The evening parties Howells attended in his adolescence were enlivened by boys and girls reading the poetry of Longfellow or Lowell to one another, and the newest issue of the *Atlantic* was handed about like a good long letter from home, though the youngsters had never strayed from southern Ohio.

As Howells developed from father's helper through independent newspaperman to correspondent at the state capital, he pursued his ambition of appearing in the *Atlantic*. Finally the editor, James Russell Lowell, accepted a poem, but not until after a silence of months, during which interval Lowell, suspecting the poem to be a translation from Heine, tried to locate the original. The young Westerner had learned technique as well as grammar when he studied the foreign languages.

In 1860 William Dean Howells, twenty-three years of age, visited Boston en route to a consular post in Venice. He had won the appointment through his efforts on behalf of Abraham Lincoln, the successful presidential candidate, for whom he had written a campaign biography. Now his excitement at going abroad was postponed in favor of the greater wonder of being able not only to see Boston but to visit with the lordly writers in the vicinity. His appearance in the *Atlantic* had made him, in an infinitesimal way, part of their company, and their letters had given him advance assurance that they would receive him with the reserved cordiality typical of them and of their region.

Howells was not disappointed in his meetings. There was, of

course, the expected chill in the air, born not of hostility or indifference so much as of the loftiness of the plane from which the
New Englanders viewed life. "They surround themselves with a
subtle ether of potential disapprobation," Howells wrote, "in which,
at the first signs of unworthiness in you, they helplessly suffer
you to gasp and perish; they have good hearts, and they would
probably come to your succor out of humanity, if they knew how,
but they do not know how." [2] But he was not found wanting;
indeed, in the card of introduction Emerson sent to Hawthorne
for him, the Concord sage had written that he found this young
man worthy.

Moreover, Howells was delighted to find that his interviews
were not one-sided. All the men with whom he spoke made it
clear that they felt there was something more American about
the West, and they drew Howells out about the life there. Hawthorne, especially, was emphatic on that point, saying that he
would like to see some portion of the country over which the
damned shadow of Europe had not fallen. Finally, at a gathering
at the Parker House, Holmes remarked to Lowell that lunching
with Howells was the laying on of hands, the insuring of the
apostolic succession. The great men acknowledged not only
Howells' individual merit but the fact that the country was growing up and taking more of its tone from the West, so that the
mantle of literary authority must pass to a Westerner—but one
who was raised in a West thoroughly imbued with a sense of
its continuity with the New England standards.

The symbolic gesture of 1860 became fact in 1867 when
Howells, after his European service, became an assistant on the
Atlantic. From 1867 to 1881 he wrote over four hundred and
fifty book reviews; in 1871 he succeeded Lowell as editor-in-chief.
When he left the editorship in 1881, he continued to contribute
to the *Atlantic*, as well as to *Harper's* and the *Century*. And in his
social life he supplied Boston with precisely the flavor which had
been anticipated by Holmes and Hawthorne in 1860. He was a
polite and sympathetic sharer of the city's cultural ideals, but he

tempered them with a Western egalitarianism. Although a graduate only of the print shop, he was welcome, for instance, at the Cambridge meetings of the Dante Club, where, canto by canto, as he composed it, Longfellow was presenting his translation of *The Divine Comedy*. Typical of the difference between Howells' literary commitment and that of the older men was that fact that he could share this experience with them, aware that their knowledge of Italian exceeded his from the point of view of Romance philology, but also that he must restrain himself from correcting their many mispronunciations in conversation, since his Venetian experience had led him to a far greater practical command of the language than they possessed.

A year after he became editor of the *Atlantic,* Howells published his first novel, *Their Wedding Journey* (1872), and books of fiction followed at the rate of almost one a year, along with occasional volumes of travel, criticism, and poetry. In his fiction he most clearly realized the promise detected by his elders in 1860, for here he carried into post-Civil-War America a sense of the sturdy morality which sinewed American life. True to his Western origins, however, he did so by concentrating far more closely on the daily actualities of middle-class American life than did the New Englanders. Emerson saw the American democracy as a splendid ground for the individual's realization of the noble purposes which unified humanity, but he spoke of the possibilities in an essentially unhistorical fashion. As John Jay Chapman was to note:

> The ethical assumption that all men are exactly alike permeates his work. In his mind, Socrates, Marco Polo, and General Jackson stand surrounded by the same atmosphere, or rather stand as mere naked characters surrounded by no atmosphere at all. He is probably the last great writer who will fling about classic anecdotes as if they were club gossip.[3]

Howells, with his incredibly detailed sense of the present historical moment—so much so that he was always vulnerable to attacks that he dealt in the petty—did, nevertheless, take his note from Emerson.

The Concord philosopher, unhistorical as he may have been, had called for other writers to bring his ideals to bear on American realities:

> What would we really know the meaning of? The meal in the firkin; the milk in the pan; the ballad in the street; the news of the boat; the glance of the eye; the form and the gait of the body;—show me the ultimate reason of these matters; show me the sublime presence of the highest spiritual cause lurking, as always it does lurk, in these suburbs and extremities of nature; let me see every trifle bristling with the polarity that ranges it instantly on an eternal law; and the shop, the plough, and the ledger referred to the like cause by which light undulates and poets sing;—and the world lies no longer a dull miscellany and lumber-room, but has form and order; there is no trifle, there is no puzzle, but one design unites and animates the farthest pinnacle and the lowest trench.[4]

The emphasis here is not on the realities; rather, Emerson asks the writer to take them up in order to reveal their transcendental purpose. His immediate followers responded in different ways: Thoreau, for instance, attempted to peel the triviality away from daily life in order to show a core that was one with the life of the Greek heroes and the Hindu gods; while Whitman attempted to pick up every bead of reality and arrange it on a transcendental string of unity.

Howells' novels, with their bickering newlyweds and middle-aged visitors to summer hotels, appeared at some remove from Emerson. He seemed concerned with the meal and the milk in themselves rather than with their animating design. But he only appeared so. The trivialities with which he concerned himself were polarized also, but the polarizing force had changed, had been enfeebled and yet made more flexible by its contact with its materials.

Howells' greatest fictional success in his Boston days was *The Rise of Silas Lapham* (1885), the story of a newly rich vulgarian's social downfall. At one point in this novel Lapham and his young Brahmin employee, Corey, are on an excursion steamer to Nantasket, crowded with specimens of middle- and lower-class Americans out for a good time. Howells looks at them and says:

> The greater part of the crowd on board—and, of course, the boat was crowded—looked as if they might not only be easily but safely known. There was little style and no distinction among them; they were people who were going down to the beach for the fun of it. . . . In face they were commonplace, with nothing but the American poetry of vivid purpose to light them up, where they did not wholly lack fire.[5]

"The American poetry of vivid purpose" is Howells' equivalent to Emerson's "animating design," and he details the commonplace in order to reveal its underlying purpose as the great unifier in national life.

At the close of the novel Silas Lapham, his scarcely won social status and his commercial winnings tumbling about him to ruin, meets with an opportunity to stem his losses. It will involve a swindle in which a well-heeled and impersonal corporation will be the loser, but in which Lapham will be legally free of any wrongdoing. He resists the temptation and continues his commercial and social descent, but in so doing he achieves a moral rise. That this hearty vulgarian could make such a decision is believable, Howells demonstrates, because commercialism and social climbing merely form a patina on American life. Scratch the patina and, as in Lapham's case, you find the sturdy, honest country boy who will give no quarter in a fair fight, but who will not take mean advantage of even those who can afford to lose.

Lapham himself had looked at the crowd on the boat on which the author had commented and had said, "But you take faces now! The astonishing thing to me is not what a face tells, but what it don't tell. When you think of what a man is, or a woman is, and what most of 'em have been through before they get to be thirty, it seems as if their experience would burn right through.

But it don't." [6] Because it doesn't burn right through, Howells is attracted to it. For him the novelist's task is to reveal in action what the commonplace face does not reveal when glanced at. Thus he will reveal the spiritual cause which lurks in the "suburbs and extremities of nature."

If editorship of the *Atlantic* and undisputed leadership in the field of fiction, capped by *Silas Lapham* in 1885, were not sufficient evidence that the obvious play on his name was justified, that Howells was indeed the Dean of American letters, more was to come: literary Boston extended its ultimate tribute in 1886 by inviting him to succeed Lowell in the Smith Professorship at Harvard. He declined the offer, but the twenty-six years from his Parker House lunch with Lowell to the Harvard invitation formed a success story whose moral was that the expansion of the United States had been matched in literature by an orderly continuity. The West had been won to the East; the East had been bent in the direction of the West.

Howells' critical theme over the same period paralleled his achievement in fiction. He wrote:

> I am in hopes that the communistic era in taste foreshadowed by Burke is approaching, and that it will occur within the lives of men now overawed by the foolish superstition that literature and art are anything but the expression of life, and are to be judged by any other test than that of their fidelity to it.[7]

The test which he was attacking was that which demanded of fiction an idealization of the human condition, which asked of the writer that he lift his readers out of the commonplace by presenting them with models of love, duty, and heroism. Such models, everybody admitted, did not exist except as ideals, but this was all the more reason why they must be brought into being in fiction. Literature, according to those Howells attacked, was best when it freed itself from the mire of experience and held aloft the beautiful prize, regardless of the prize's lack of relation to the realities of the contest. Ugliness is too much with us in everyday life; fiction should ennoble us by showing us a purer world. In response to this view, Howells' insistence on the simple, the natural, and the honest was, to a large class of readers, merely an insistence on the plain, the dull, and the unedifying.

Howells too, as has been seen, had his ideals, but they were the starting points, the principles which sinewed American life and were to be discovered in a minute scrutiny of it, not the vaguely impossible ends which were to be pursued regardless of the realities. If daily experience had to be falsified in order for the writer to strike a lofty tone, then he should not attempt that tone. Indeed, so committed was Howells to his sense of the American present that even as he rejected the tinsel optimism of the hundred and one tales of lovers who had loved as none had ever loved before, he rejected as unsuitable for the American novelist the tragic note which was struck in the work of Dostoevski. "Very few American novelists have been led out to be shot, or finally exiled to the rigors of a winter at Duluth," [8] he pointed out. This meant that, though they should not romanticize the realities, still American novelists could concern themselves with "the more smiling aspects of life, which are the more American, and seek the universal in the individual rather than the social interests." [9]

If his remark that the smiling aspects of life were the typically American ones seemed a tempting of the gods, Howells nevertheless had a twenty-six-year professional career to point to as evidence of the validity of his contention. Reporting on his visit to Florence in a book published in 1886, he carried his provocation of the fates to its farthest point: "Poor, splendid, stupid, glorious past! I stood at the windows of the people's palace and looked out on the space in the rear where those culprits used to disturb the signory at their meals, and thanked Heaven that I was of the nineteenth century." [10] So much for the romance that longed for days of yore and conveniently forgot the bestiality of man to man, the grime that gathered on the collar of lace. Plain, unchivalric America of 1886 was less colorful on the surface, Howells felt, but had far more of worth to express, if only the writer could liberate that expression from the resisting commonplace materials in which it resided.

The gods did not wait long to strike back and show Howells that nineteenth-century America was not so different from the Florence he rejected as dead. In May 1886, after police had broken up an Anarcho-Communist meeting in Haymarket Square, Chicago, a bomb exploded, fatally wounding seven policemen and injuring seventy others. Public indignation quickly ignited into a blind demand for vengeance, and that summer eight men were tried for the murders, although there was no evidence linking them with the bomb itself. They were known to be radical thinkers, and this was sufficient for an enraged populace. Seven were sentenced to death and one to fifteen years in prison.

Howells was horrified at a public that could so rapidly convert a demand for punishment into a disregard for due process in a rage for serving up scapegoats. When you scratched the seemingly coarse modern American, this was not what you were supposed to find, and Howells threw himself into a fight to demonstrate that good sense would prevail in the nineteenth century. His name headed a petition for commutation of sentences, and he worked without stint to line up all responsible forces in society to back that petition. As a result of his effort, two death sentences were commuted to life terms, but on November 11, 1887, within three weeks of the Chickering Hall readings, four men were executed because a murderous bomb had gone off in Chicago and they were known to have been discontented with the organization of American society.

There were reasons, then, why William Dean Howells was not in the best psychological state to join the comfortable assembly at Chickering Hall. On November 18 he wrote his sister:

The last two months have been full of heartache and horror for me, on account of the civic murder created last Friday at Chicago. You may have seen in the papers that I had taken part in petitioning for clemency for the Anarchists, whom I thought unfairly tried, and most unjustly condemned. Annie, it's all been an atrocious piece of frenzy and cruelty, for which we must stand ashamed forever before history. But it's no use. I can't write about it. Some day I hope to do justice to these irreparably wronged men.[11]

The "social interests" which two years earlier he had dismissed as unsuitable subject matter for the American novelist because life in the United States was not centered on such concerns, now pressed in upon him as in crying need of exposition.

These interests were to come to the fore in his fiction with the publication of *Annie Kilburn* (1888), but the material for them lay dormant in the work completed before the Haymarket executions, *The Minister's Charge* (1887). When Howells turned to an explicit treatment of social materials, then, he was turning to a more intense development of subject matter which already abounded in the periphery of his novels.

The Minister's Charge is about the social and moral development of Lemuel Barker, a New England country boy who comes to Boston with the mistaken impression that the polite words of routine encouragement his verse received from a Boston minister who visited his part of the country on a summer vacation are a genuine mandate for him to come to the city and conquer its literary world. Once in the city, he is quickly disabused of the notion that the minister's words were other than polite conversation, but rather than return home he decides to make his way somehow in the city, and the novel is concerned with how he does this, especially in relation to two young ladies with whom he becomes entangled. The first is a cheap, lower-class flirt whom the green country boy mistakes for an accomplished beauty, much as he had, in the country, mistaken the minister's kindness for genuine encouragement. The second is a girl from a good family, one above him in every social respect, with whom he falls in love, but only after he has committed himself to the shoddy Statira. As a parallel to his refusing to flee the city once he realizes the falsity of his hopes for a poetic triumph, he refuses to accept a number of opportunities to abandon his disastrous commitment to Statira, even though he realizes the immensity of his blunder. The novel, then, is on the same theme as is *The Rise of Silas Lapham*—the sturdy morality which underlies the American rustic and which enables him to rise above social and financial disaster.

In *The Minister's Charge,* however, Howells makes use of some aspects of American urban life which had not entered into his earlier novels. Even though he employs them for specific scenic and narrative rather than for thematic effects, a mere listing of them indicates his movement from his old center of interest. They form a catalogue of topics which were to be expressly developed by the young writers of the nineties: Lemuel Barker is forced to live in a series of flophouses and to try his chances as a horse-car conductor, like Dreiser's Hurstwood; he ascends in life by means of a series of vistas that are opened to him, as happened with Dreiser's Carrie; his memory of the farm as a horror of drudgery rather than as a rural retreat foreshadows Garland's theme; the description of shopgirls and of the poisoning to which they are exposed at the box factory opens in fiction topics to be further developed by Dreiser and by Frank Norris; and the ambiguous nature of young Barker's apprenticeship, with the price he must pay for achieving dubious cultural possessions, announces what was to be so brilliantly elaborated in Frederic's *The Damnation of Theron Ware*. Thus, though in *The Minister's Charge* he was concerned with a variation on a familiar theme, the context in which Howells set that theme revealed that even before Haymarket he was recording the facts of a different America. But only the facts; the implications were the same—the "smiling" was the chief aspect of American life.

In the same year that saw the publication of *Annie Kilburn,* Howells also published *April Hopes,* a strangely wooden book when read as the love story it professes to be, but a rather extraordinary work when viewed, as it deserves to be, as a documentary. The use of the word when applied to the period is an anachronism, yet nothing better expresses what Howells achieves. He is concerned with the typical American free-will marriage in the middle class, and he documents one such marriage from the summer meeting, through the courtship, the squabbles, and the conflicting interests of the parents, to the ceremony itself. He begins by giving a sense of the charm of young love and, as the obstacles to its course begin to appear, a sense of its strength in overcoming them. But as these obstacles, not the least of which are the personalities of the young lovers themselves, mount higher and higher and still are overcome, the reader is no longer led to regard the conquering power of love as an unmixed blessing. This is not a romance in which love conquers all. The farther one gets into the affair, the sillier the girl seems and the weaker the man appears, so that what looked like a promising couple now appears to be two people who are not very well suited, and the reader rather hopes that they will not marry. Convention as much as free will, however, carries them to a point from which they cannot turn back, so that, although one can say they marry for love, as is done in America, still this also means there is a heavy dose of parental scheming and inter-family distrust. The marriage which closes the book has the seed of success in it, but also the seed of unhappiness, and even, under certain possible stresses, of divorce.

Though Howells' motive for turning to social interests in *Annie Kilburn* was much more stirring, the plain matter of fact was that the talents developed in exposition of themes of the individual's moral worth, as in *The Rise of Silas Lapham* and *The Minister's Charge,* and a technique which had been sharpened by a close observation of middle-class American domestic mores, as in *April Hopes,* could not convert the new social materials into a satisfactory work of fiction. When class differences became theme rather than context, Howells lost the sureness with which he used to describe them. When the basic pattern of an individual's social and matrimonial career as the story frame was set aside in favor of some form of collective action, Howells lost the balanced focus in which he was able to hold a Silas Lapham or a Lemuel Barker.

Annie Kilburn returns to her native New England home after an eleven-year residence in Europe, to see that her village, Hatboro, has been changed into a sprawling American town; that where somebody from a different part of the same state was, when she left, regarded as somewhat alien, now, thanks to the industry which has made the town boom, one-third of the residents are foreign-born. As the town has grown, its cultural life has deteriorated, and Annie re-enters it at a moment when the new laboring class is in conflict with the owners while the old New England families are divided among themselves on what attitude to take.

Howells himself is uncertain of where to go with his new social theme. In the novel he explores a number of ways of achieving in Hatboro a harmony that will be indicative of what he still hopes is the genuine unity of American life, but one after another these ways fail him, and he is too honest to force them. Annie's and other old residents' attempts to help the laborers on a personal level are philanthropic patronizings which emphasize the dividing gulf rather than bridge it. While the self-made man who has no sympathy with workers' grievances can be effectively exposed as a social menace, Howells cannot counterpose to him an articulate working man with a reasonable scheme for social unity. The closest he comes is the Reverend Mr. Peck, a minister who identifies himself with the working class and who preaches a rather ineffectual form of Christian communism. It is based on a vision of the New Jerusalem which is as obstructive to the immediate betterment of actual conditions as is the capitalist's equating of poverty with ineptness. Howells is eventually put to flight by his materials, and he arranges to have Peck killed by a railroad train, thereby attempting to gain from a forced symbol some hint of what he was unable to dramatize in the novel. After that he falls back on a pattern more familiar to him and concentrates increasingly not on Annie's dilemma in the face of the new American disharmony but on her courtship by and marriage to the local doctor.

Annie Kilburn is not a good novel. In a narrow sense it failed because, as Howells found, even sympathetic readers, for want of any other dramatized relation between the classes, took it as a plea for the rich to exercise charity toward the poor. Hamlin Garland wrote a review which reflected this attitude and in exasperation Howells wrote him that "*Annie Kilburn* is from first to last a cry for *justice,* not alms . . . and you and the *Standard* coolly ask me why I do not insist upon justice instead of alms." [12] He told Garland to read the story again, but the re-reading, if Garland undertook it, would probably not have strengthened Howells' claim.

Howells' passion for social justice had overcome his better judgment as a novelist. In *Annie Kilburn* he had attempted the impossible, and in so doing had strangely imitated that class of writers to whom he was most deeply opposed—the romancers. They justified their Never-Never-Land tales of great feats of self-denial and superhuman love by saying that they were needed precisely because such standards were missing from society unless available in fiction. They admitted they were romancing. Howells took something which he urgently believed to be wanting, social justice, a felt harmony among men which made class differences cooperative expressions of the same group will rather than the signs of a basic division of interest, and attempted to show what it was. But he was a realistic novelist, not a romancer, and so Never-Never Land was unavailable to him. The detailed community of Hatboro which he constructed in his usual accomplished fashion no sooner came into existence than, quite naturally, like the hundred towns on which it was modeled, it began to resist any scheme of social harmony offered it, and *Annie Kilburn* trailed off into ineffectuality.

An obvious solution to the dilemma, even if it was an unsatisfactory one for a novelist, would be, of course, to resort to Never-Never Land, and this is precisely what Howells was ultimately driven to in his utopian work, *A Traveler from Altruria* (1894).

But before this, and just after *Annie Kilburn,* he tried one other significant tack, which resulted in *A Hazard of New Fortunes* (1890).

The point of departure for *A Hazard of New Fortunes* is Howells' own experiences in moving from Boston to New York, and he begins by establishing as his persona Basil March, a some-time literary man in Boston who is persuaded to move to New York to join a cooperative venture in fortnightly journalism un-derwritten by a newly rich Middle Westerner, Dryfoos, who hopes, in sponsoring the magazine, to find some profession for his son. The successes and failures of the new journal, with the love affairs, personality conflicts, and domestic arrangements of its staff, gradu-ally become subsidiary to an examination of New York as a con-centrated example of the new and chaotic social structure of late-nineteenth-century America. Here the problems of immigration, social responsibility, sectional differences, the role of the artist, the limitations to be placed on the capitalist, and the needs of the working class are being played out, and Howells follows them closely.

He does not insist on imposing a strong form on this novel, which must be free to deal with the laissez-faire capitalist, the immigrant radical, the reforming society girl, the Christian social worker, the reactionary social climber, the Southern conservative, and the wide-eyed career girl, and to move from editorial offices to middle-class dining rooms to upper-class drawing rooms to revolutionary cafés. Howells is satisfied to document this pano-rama through the consciousness of March, his alter ego. The con-trol, such as it is, comes from the undaring but tolerant humanity of the novelist, whose rage for social justice is tempered by his artist's instincts, so that he can see the pathos in the private life of the vulgar capitalist who publicly destroys men, as he can see the impersonal rigidity of the honest old one-armed radical. He is horrified by the slums, and yet is so much of a sensitive observer that he is fascinated by the color of a great city and unwilling to allow economic injustices to blot out this attractive vibrancy. Thus

A Hazard of New Fortunes brings New York fully into fiction for the first time, even while politely declining to do much more with it than provide a map of its neighborhoods and their problems.

Perhaps it is most accurate to say that *A Hazard of New Fortunes* is a novel about the scope that must be contained in the new American novel rather than the new novel itself. Howells and Basil March are both well into middle age, and just as March's social interests are contained by the fact of his having a family that needs certain comforts, certain supports, and certain guidance, so Howells' writing habits are contained by the fact that he served his apprenticeship and attained his mastery in plots about middle-class morals and manners. He is content in *Hazard* to accept this and to allow the Marches' domestic concerns and the several love affairs in the book to serve as the plot frame on which he can hang the wide range of March's gentle observations. The unity he so vainly sought in the disharmonious community of *Annie Kilburn* is, he realizes, just where he had left it, in the moral consciousness of the intelligent middle-class American. That this is too old-fashioned an answer, Howells admits, for in the novel March passes the problem of getting New York into a viable fiction on to a younger novelist, Kendricks, who, contemplating the task of incorporating the new diversities into one work, fears that "the great American novel, if true, must be incredible." [18]

As for his alter ego March, so for Howells the struggle for a new form was over, and he entered the 1890s content to continue the ways of *A Minister's Charge,* incorporating an increasing amount of social observation into his works, but developing themes of individual rather than social morality. When he could not resist a full-scale development of social matters, he resorted to the utopian form. His novels of the nineties were, in the main, paler in tone than his earlier works, as in his examinations of courtship and marriage he came more and more to see the attractions of celibacy, that is, symbolically, of a retreat from entanglement to a cool zone of simple and upright living. In this he was lending a qualified and Americanized second to the theories of Leo Tolstoi.

Still, a thread of discontent and consequent self-criticism ran through the resigned novels of the nineties. Howells' uneasiness with his compromise broke out now and again. For instance, in one fragile tale of young love seen through the eyes of the equable Basil March, that alter ego complains to his wife:

> "I wish . . . that instead of coming home . . . and telling you about this girl, I had confined my sentimentalizing to that young French-Canadian mother, and her dirty little boy who ate the pea-nut shells. I've no doubt it was really a more tragical case. They looked dreadfully poor and squalid. Why couldn't I have amused my idle fancy with their fortunes—the sort of husband and father they had, their shabby home, the struggles of their life? That is the appeal that a genuine person listens to. Nothing does more to stamp me a *poseur* than the fact that I preferred to bemoan myself for a sulky girl who seemed not to be having a good time." [14]

Howells prudently let go what he found he could not deal with, but the slightness of what remained sometimes rankled.

A contemporary characterization of what Howells had undergone yet failed to achieve in the nineties was offered by Robert Underwood Johnson, the eminent associate editor of the *Century,* who reflected:

> One might have expected that the man who pleaded for the lives of the Chicago anarchists would have done more in fiction to present the claims of the working men and the proletariat. The fact of it is, perhaps, that his sympathy came from the kindness of his heart and from his conclusions in his study, rather than from close contact with the laboring classes in their everyday life. He was not a slum-ming novelist. [15]

No, Howells was not a "slumming" novelist, and the word stands in the context just as strongly when it is fully granted the overtones of leering innuendo so often assigned it in the 1890s. However courageously the established middle-aged author had come around from his old center of interest to attempt to incor-porate into his fiction an America most of those at Chickering

Hall refused to recognize as a subject for literature, he did not see this new America as in the process of other than social transition. In his criticism of the eighties he had defended the implicit code of censorship of sexual material which prevailed in American publishing. Into the nineties he continued in defense of this bulwark; whatever the social shift might be, he did not see that it was related to a shift in mores.

The mounting attack on the code was largely based on the work of writers like Daudet, Goncourt, and Zola. In 1884 Henry James had written Howells:

> They do the only kind of work, to-day, that I respect; and in spite of their ferocious pessimism and their handling of unclean things, they are at least serious and honest. The floods of tepid soap and water which under the name of novels are being vomited forth in England, seem to me, by contrast, to do little honour to our race.[16]

But the French literary freedom with "unclean things" came as the direct outgrowth of a social system designed to mitigate awkwardness. The good living of society and the good talk of the salon in France were based on worldly wisdom and maturity, and the French never considered sacrificing this general maturity to the particular immaturity of any innocent member of the society. They quite simply did not allow that member, the young lady, downstairs. Her childhood years were followed by a relatively secluded adolescence, one in which she was tutored in the feminine arts, including conversation, while the sound of her mother's salon filtered dimly up the stairwell. In the salon, politics, art, and life were discussed; upstairs, novels and gentlemen callers were forbidden.

To have allowed the young lady to enter the salon would have reduced that gathering to an awkward silence. She was ready to come downstairs when a duly arranged marriage had been consummated. The experience of living with a member of the other sex was the unambiguous ticket of entry without which no girl, regardless of age, could be considered a member of adult society.

The consequences for literature were that such a society presented a mature audience for the writer, who could assume that private experience was a matter of public possession. He need not fear the results of his work on innocence for, by definition, innocence was not of the world that counted.[17]

In America the problem of the young girl was solved in a strikingly opposite fashion, for in America she was from infancy totally part of the family. She had accessible to her all the comforts of the living room—intellectual and cultural as well as physical. She developed independence and maturity through living in a world which had always been hospitable to her and treated her as a cultural equal, even though other cultures—as James's *Daisy Miller* illustrates—failed to appreciate the source of her independent behavior. But many foreigners did appreciate her, and travelers' accounts, however carping they may be about other aspects of America, are filled with hymns to the American girl's attractive vibrancy. Rudyard Kipling in 1889, for instance, set down the couplet:

> *Man is fire and woman is tow,*
> *And the devil he comes and begins to blow.*

But he then went on to explain:

In America the tow is soaked in a solution that makes it fireproof, in absolute liberty and large knowledge; consequently accidents do not exceed the regular percentage arranged by the devil for each class and climate under the skies. But the freedom of the young girl has its drawbacks. She is—I say it with all reluctance—irreverent, from her forty-dollar bonnet to the buckles in her eighteen-dollar shoes.[18]

Kipling admiringly watched her consorting as an equal with her brothers' friends on unchaperoned outings and finally paid her the highest homage at his command: he married her.

The zesty attractiveness of the American system of child-rearing is immediately apparent, but it had its other side also. The price paid by society for treating its young people in this fashion was that of keeping itself in a public state of total innocence so that nothing would offend or corrupt the young person. Sexual experience was forced to remain a secret matter; publicly all was virginal because the public submitted to the standard of its youngest member. A writer who assumed a young-girl audience, then, was not writing down to one snowy element of his society but was, quite simply, addressing all the intelligent readers of his society on the only assumption which would gain him an audience.

Howells well realized this state of affairs—it was his bread and butter—and he gloried in it. The American girl was his joyful subject in novel after novel, and he was delighted to pay the price demanded for keeping her as attractive as she appeared to him. "If the novel were written for men and for married women alone, as in continental Europe," he admitted, "it might be altogether different." [10] But it was not, and he found no difficulty in writing for the young-girl reader. After all, he claimed, the essential subject matters were still available:

> It is quite false or quite mistaken to suppose that our novels have left untouched these most important realities of life. They have only not made them their stock in trade; they have kept a true perspective in regard to them; they have relegated them in their pictures of life to the space and place they occupy in life itself, as we know it in England and America.[20]

Clearly, Howells was not a slumming novelist. Life as he knew it in America had little to do with the "sins of the senses" except insofar as it visited them with swift retribution. In the real world, he insisted, these sins "are deadly poison: these do kill." [21]

His contentions received a resounding amen from every editorial office and every other agency of authority in America. In 1895 the American Academy of Medicine, for example, listened to one of its distinguished members deliver a paper in which he said: "That the exercise of the sexual function is necessary to the health of the male at any age is a pure delusion, while before full maturity it is highly injurious." [22] The professor of anatomy went on to insist:

> Men should be taught the sacred duty and true dignity of reproduction; that any attempt to avoid this duty brings its own punishment; that their sexual powers belong not to themselves, but to the race, and every exercise of them must result ultimately in either a pregnancy or syphilis; that they cannot hope to enjoy the privileges and pleasures of manhood and shirk its responsibilities. [23]

Howells gave his full assent to this part of the picture of life in America. He perceived only the dimmest connection between the social upheaval which attracted him and the upheaval in mores which was its inevitable accompaniment. In their private lives, the radicals who appealed to him and served as models for characters in *A Hazard of New Fortunes* also contracted alliances with young ladies who gave them neither babies nor syphilis, [24] but Howells lived apart from these realities. The kindness which had led him to exercise his social sympathies stemmed from a tradition of Ohio decency and Boston propriety that could not contemplate such things. Whatever other changes he was to make with the time, he was unable to abandon this basic stance:

> When I realized what lives some of my [favorite] poets had led, how they were drunkards, and swindlers, and unchaste, and untrue, I lamented over them with a sense of personal disgrace in them, and to this day I have no patience with that code of the world which relaxes itself in behalf of the brilliant and gifted offender; rather he should suffer more blame. The worst of the literature of past times, before an ethical conscience began to inform it, or the advance of the race compelled it to decency, is that it leaves the mind foul with filthy images and base thoughts. . . . I hope the time will come when the beast-man will be so far subdued and tamed in us that the memory of him in literature shall be left to perish; that what is lewd and ribald in the great poets shall be kept out of such editions as are meant for general reading. [25]

In January 1894 the sculptor St. Gaudens wrote to his friend Howells to tell him of a dream that he had had. [26] In it the two friends were together on a barge in the ocean, and Howells stepped to the edge of the awning with a shotgun, aimed, fired, and brought Venus down from the zenith. This meant, St. Gaudens interpreted, that the stars were not millions of miles away but were within Howells' reach. It was a very pretty compliment. Another interpreter might have said that Howells, in opposing swashbuckling romances of unquenchable love on one hand, and in denying the meaningful presence of passion in the lives of his commonplace characters on the other, had, in his resulting novels of middle-class domesticity, torn love from the skies. Just as in the nineties younger novelists were to dash into social areas where Howells felt it difficult to tread, so they would create many a character who, in William Allen White's memorable phrase, knew "that his sweetheart's shoes were not pinned to the bottom of her skirt." [27] While eager to welcome the young men who explored social issues, even to the extent of showing that the oppression of the lower class led to the sexual degradation of their women, Howells was constitutionally incapable of sympathy with the young writer who would suggest that the sexual license emerging as the result of class aspirations in a commercial society was acceptable both in life and in the novel. This is why he was so hospitable to Stephen Crane's *Maggie,* so vehement against Theodore Dreiser's *Sister Carrie.*

In the nineties, though, young writers found a benign and considerate counselor in William Dean Howells. He was of the establishment, yet keenly aware of its shortcomings, and his memory extended to the time, more than thirty years in the past, when he himself had been encouraged by Lowell. Young Hamlin Garland sought him out in Boston, then in New York came to see him with Stephen Crane in tow. Gelett Burgess made his acquaintance and then pulled along Frank Norris. Howells attempted constantly to encourage breadth in the amplification of national letters and he sought out the furtive Chicagoan Henry Blake Fuller or the robust Norwegian H. H. Boyesen when these men did not seek him. His arrival at a city, Kansas City or Cincinnati, was an

invitation for the local writers, especially the young ones, to come
to the hotel and tell him what they were doing. When Henry
Demarest Lloyd failed with four publishers, Howells got Harper's
to publish his *Wealth Against Commonwealth*. He helped Paul
Laurence Dunbar in the same way. And all this while, as he
worked in New York or traveled about the country, he eagerly
took the national pulse and strove for reform. He was distressed
at the treatment of workers during the Homestead strike in 1892,
but pitied "those poor wretches of detectives too";[28] the Populist
demands received a compassionate hearing from him even while
he deplored the pinning of hopes to the sputtering rocket of free
silver; he was outraged that he could not move the Authors'
Club to a formal expression of sympathy with Zola in the Dreyfus
affair; and he was opposed to the jingoism which preceded the
Spanish-American War, and disappointed, in 1898, to realize
that his gloomy predictions were accurate, that "our war for humanity has unmasked itself as a war for coaling stations, and we
are going to keep our booty to punish Spain for putting us to the
trouble of using violence in robbing her." [29] On his travels through
the country he dined with ex-Presidents and then went off to meet
whoever his correspondent in that city thought was the coming
writer—in Chicago, Fuller brought along William Morton Payne
and George Ade. When he went into the rural districts he was
alert to the tone of life and anxious to improve his knowledge of
it through conversations with farm wives and railroad brakemen.
In Marion, Kansas, he was moved by the bleakness of the countryside and wrote his wife that, though many from the farms were
expected to come to hear him lecture, "the thought of taking their
money makes me sick and I shall give it all (except our expenses)
back for some public object." [30] And first, last, and in between
were the writers and their writings. Had his correspondent heard
of the Yiddish writer Abraham Cahan, who produced an extraordinary novel, *Yekl,* in English? He should read the Italian
Giovanni Verga's *The House by the Medlar Tree.* The Spaniard
Pérez Galdós was finally on the right track with *Doña Perfecta;*

although he could afford to be even more realistic. The Frenchman Zola might be indecent, but he was not immoral; one should
read him, he would not deprave one. The man who had written
"more faithfully of the life common to all men, the universal life
which is the most personal life, than any author whom I have
read," [31] was the Russian Leo Tolstoi.

At mid-decade Stephen Crane wrote Howells, saying:

> Every little time I hear from some friend a kind thing you have said
> of me, an interest which you have shown in my work. I have been
> so long conscious of this, that I am grown uncomfortable in not
> being able to express to you my gratitude and so I seize the New
> Year's Day as an opportunity to thank you and tell you how often
> I think of your kind benevolent life.[32]

The filial tone was not a usual one for Crane and was all the
more moving for that. At the decade's close, Howells reported
another filial gesture, this time on the part of Kipling: "In the
dressing room he saw me in a plump elderly man's difficulties
with a new pair of rubbers, and the dear fellow got down on one
knee and put them on for me; he said he always did it for his
father." [33]

William Dean Howells began the last decade of the nineteenth
century by coming to terms with his own limitations in dealing
with the new social subject matter thrust upon the writer by rapid
changes in American life, and he spent that decade in encouragement of younger men who could encompass the new material. But
at the decade's end, perhaps in genuine discouragement at what the
young men had produced, perhaps in rationalization of his own
procedure, he gave over his insistence on unifying America within
the covers of a work of fiction. He wrote:

> In former times we Americans were accused of being curious, over-
> curious, of being insatiable and impertinent questioners of strangers.
> It may be, however, that we are not so, but that the most pene-
> trating difference between us and the English is that they are social
> and we are personal. Their denser life, we will say, satisfies them

with superficial contrasts, while in our thinner and more homogeneous society the contrasts that satisfy are subliminal. This theory
would account for their breadth and our depth without mortifying
the self-love of either, which I should like to spare in our case if
not in theirs. To float and to dive may be equally creditable.[34]

Here he could have his cake and eat it too. The reason why the
American novel could not, at the century's close, express the unity
of American life as, somehow, he had thought to express that unity
when his career began in 1870 was not that the unity did not exist,
but that the homogeneity of life in America provided little to write
about if one were concerned with distinctly national traits. The
ghosts of Washington Irving and James Fenimore Cooper play
about this remark; it is the oldest plaint in American fiction.

Yet Howells could also say: "To put it paradoxically, our life
is too large for our art to be broad. In despair at the immense
scope and variety of the material offered it by American civilization, American fiction must specialize, and, turning distracted from
the superabundance of character, it must burrow far down in a
soul or two." [35] On the level of manners, the United States presented too much of a sameness; on the level of individual careers,
all was too various. James's deep-diving was the answer to the first
problem; an acceptance of local types and a concentration on
them, such as Mark Twain had once practiced, was the answer to
the second. Although neither James nor Twain could be brought
to see the strength of the other, it had been his, Howells', fate to
aid in the discovery and encouragement of both, and it was his
warmest pleasure to be on intimate terms with them throughout
his adult life. Like him, these great contemporaries had entered
the 1890s as established writers with major accomplishments behind them, and, as with him, the continuity of their careers had
been interrupted by those turbulent years. James had gone so far
as to abandon novel-writing for a time in his desperate search for
the audience he had lost, and Twain had begun his slide to a
pessimism that poisoned satire as well as comedy. Howells learned

his own limitations in the same decade and had looked to the young to go beyond them. As the twentieth century arrived, however, he reflected that James, Twain, and he had after all weathered the storm, and, without stinting his hospitality to the young, he nevertheless took his greatest comfort from the reflection that there was no alternative to the paths his friends and he had followed. The nineties revealed how far Howells had come but showed also that he could go no further.

THREE

Literary Absenteeism:

Henry James and Mark Twain

With *Annie Kilburn* behind him and his move to New York just before him, William Dean Howells wrote to Henry James in October 1888:

> I'm not in a very good mood with "America" myself. It seems to be the most grotesquely illogical thing under the sun; and I suppose I love it less because it won't let me love it more. I should hardly like to trust pen and ink with all the audacity of my social ideas; but after fifty years of optimistic content with "civilization" and its ability to come out all right in the end, I now abhor it, and feel that it is coming out all wrong in the end, unless it bases itself anew on a real equality. Meantime I wear a fur-lined overcoat, and live in all the luxury my money can buy.[1]

James was then living in London, and the fact that he had resided out of the country since 1866 was taken by many as an eloquent demonstration of where he stood on the subject of America. Although, encouraged by Howells, he had begun his literary career while living in Cambridge, Massachusetts, and still regarded himself as an American, his London vantage point appeared to release him from the circumstances that were troubling Howells.

In point of fact, however, James was extremely conscious of and affected by the changing pattern of life in the United States, though his point of observation led him to view it in a different manner from Howells. The elements of the changing pattern which drew his attention were the thinning out of the moral vigor which had marked Emerson's America, and the signs of individual freedom still visible in the ways of his swaggering, laissez-faire countrymen. Understandably, his concern with American life was less detailed than Howells', relatively unmarked by month-to-month changes. So it had the merits of the long view as well as the weakness of tempting James to underestimate the force and direction of proletarian complaints.

Speaking of Emerson in 1887, James had said, "We think the better of his audience as we read him, and wonder where else people would have had so much moral attention to give." ? The "better" was at the expense of the New England of James's day, as was clear to anyone who had read his novel of the year before, *The Bostonians.* Here James had looked at a New England conscience grown lean and gone awry since the great days of Abolitionism. The men were no longer associated with it—they were either dead in the Civil War or, presumably, off somewhere making money—and the ladies who accepted the old moral inheritance were bent on spending it in a cheerless drive for female rights which threatened to deaden the physiological differences between themselves and the males even as it obliterated their social differences. Their domestic confinement, James's reactionary hero, Basil Ransome, insisted, was the source of their great power. When they had accepted the fact that they were not the equals of men, then the differential, their power of sexual attractiveness, was a force which enabled them to move society in any direction they desired. Now, to the extent that they achieved an equal role in public activities, they lost rather than gained power, for now they must compete with men rather than influence them. As a result of this loss of feminine power, society was thrown into an imbalance. Its public—which in America means commercial—tendencies were exaggerated.

The large irony which controls *The Bostonians* is James's conscious use of plot resolutions which run counter to actual social conditions, so that although on the level of the particular individuals around whom the novel turns some temporary settlement of the central dilemma is arrived at, the very nature of the settlement reveals that American life was far more disharmonious than it had been. The road to reunion after the Civil War was paved by works of fiction in which the gallant Yankee officer married—and, in so doing, converted—the Southern belle. James plays his story off against this tradition with conscious irony when he has his unreconstructed Confederate veteran win the Yankee maid, not only gain her in marriage but take her away from her prominent position in the reform movement. This particular event, so obviously counter to the trend of the time even though, on a level of private values, so preferable to allowing the heroine, Verena, to continue her process of desexualization in the interests of reform, dramatizes the insolubility of the over-all situation. When the Ransomes of this world succeed in conserving some quality of the life which is fast disappearing, they do so at the risk of a future unhappiness which will result from their having placed themselves athwart the stream of social progress. On the other hand, should the depersonalizing society be allowed to carry one along, as Burrage permits it to do when he, unlike Ransome, offers Verena marriage and her career, then tranquillity is purchased at the expense of a fully realized private relationship. Verena, in tears, flees with Ransome at the close, and the last word is James's: "It is to be feared that with the union, so far from brilliant, into which she was about to enter, these were not the last she was destined to shed." [3]

If America, by comparison with Europe, had little in its tone to recommend it other than the magnificent moral vigor of Emerson's day (a vigor constantly traced to its subsurface center by Howells), and if that vigor was, in the latter decades of the century, being heavily diluted by feminism, by commercialism, and by a journalistic exploitation of personality, what remained to recommend America as a culture, which is to say, as a subject for the literary imagination? James's response was: individual freedom. If the latitude allowed a Verena was, finally, only a latitude within which she could choose her particular form of unhappiness, still she had free play and she could choose love. In *The Reverberator* (1888) a young French aristocrat is immensely attracted by an American girl but is appalled at the lack of refinement in her commercial father, in her acquired tastes, and in her associates. The girl sees nothing wrong, for instance, in her newspaper friend's publication of a private scandal; as her father says, "Well, if folks are immoral you can't keep it out of the papers—and I don't know as you ought to want to." [4] Faced with so beautiful but so tone-deaf an attraction, the Frenchman, Gaston, hesitates, trembling before all that has been revealed to him as distasteful in American life. In this novel, however, we have a voice very like James's, that of Waterlow, the Europeanized American painter, who, we are told, "mixed his colors, as might have been said, with the general sense of France, but his early American immunities and serenities could still swell his sail." [5] Waterlow urges that his French friend go through with the affair: "Ah don't you see wretched youth . . . don't you see that the question of her possibilities is as nothing compared to that of yours? She's the sweetest young thing I ever saw; but even if she happened not be I should still urge you to marry her, in simple self-preservation . . . to save from destruction the last scrap of your independence. That's a much more important matter even than not treating her shabbily. They're [your family are] doing their best to kill you morally—to render you incapable of individual life." [6]

For all its vulgarity, America still had this virtue: it rendered its children capable of individual life. Flask, the insensitive journalist, is at least a free spirit, and the commercial parent, obtuse as he is to so many finer things, has succeeded not only commercially but privately: he has raised a charming daughter. American enterprise, so long as it is extended to all aspects of life, is not so bad after all, when compared with the caste prejudices of an older society.

As the nineties approached, then, and he listened to the laments of Howells and his other American correspondents, James diluted the particular social causes of their alarm in broader treatments of the quality of experience still possible in America. Particular demands for social justice evaporated under his gaze, leaving a residue of effects on the individual. Even in his one full-scale attempt at depicting modern social upheaval, *The Princess Casamassima*

(1886), he had proved himself, in the last analysis, more comfortable with considerations of the quality of private life—with social calls and with good conversation. His revolutionaries are required to fulminate without being furnished with a social philosophy, and the best moments in the novel, such as the Princess's great Sunday when she sees both Muniment and Vetch, while fine in themselves, are really incongruous ways of getting on with a book about a social movement. At the core of the trouble is the simple fact that the Princess isn't convincing. She is everything James could want in another plot, but why she is even insincerely interested in revolutionary activity remains undemonstrated, and her presence is a signal that the author, even as he attempted a social novel, saw significance, finally, only in the quality of private experience.

As for national experience, from a larger point of view James kept insisting that America was not very different from England. In the same month that he received Howells' lament about America, he wrote his brother William:

> I can't look at the English-American world, or feel about them, any more, save as a big Anglo-Saxon total, destined to such an amount of melting together that an insistence on their differences becomes more and more idle and pedantic; and that melting together will come the faster the more one takes it for granted and treats the life of the two countries as continuous or more or less convertible, or at any rate as simply chapters of the same general subject.[7]

And in explaining why American painters lived in England, he said, in the following year, "Furnished apartments are useful to the artist, but a furnished country is still more to his purpose." [8] Residence in England, then, was for James simply a movement into more comfortable quarters within the same community. In his own life, his visits to America, his retention of a number of American correspondents (even though letter-writing was, in his fine phrase, addressed to Howells, "the great fatal, incurable, unpumpable leak of one's poor sinking bark"),[9] his hospitality to

American visitors, all paralleled his remark to William about the Anglo-Saxon total. A reader of his fiction in the same period, however, recognizes that these sentiments are a makeweight, a responding voice in the dialogue James held with himself on the nature of the Anglo-American world, the dominant theme of which was that there was a difference between England and America and it was important.

In "The Modern Warning" (1888) James posed representatives of both countries next to one another: Chasemore, the English suitor for the American girl Agatha; and Grice, her brother, a disagreeable character with demonstrably unsound prejudices against England:

> Both the men had the signs of character and ability. The American was thin, dry, fine, with something in his face which seemed to say that there was more in him of the spirit than of the letter. He looked unfinished and yet somehow he looked mature, though he was not advanced in life. The Englishman had more detail about him, something stippled and retouched, an air of having been more artfully fashioned, in conformity with traditions and models. He wore old clothes which looked new, while his transatlantic brother wore new clothes which looked old.[10]

They were transatlantic brothers, but the American's moral vigor stood in place of refinement, while the Englishman's manner softened to the point of obliterating any show of spirit. The American's youth and crudity, raw as they were, nevertheless were given such full play in his strident country that he was, paradoxically, already mature though unfinished, while the Englishman's sense of his inheritance, while it gave him finish, left him immature since it had protected him from raw exposure. The way they wore their clothes told their stories.

Starting from an initially unfavorable characterization of Grice, James leads the reader to admire Chasemore and to rejoice that Agatha can override her brother's stupid and provincial attitude and accept Chasemore as her husband and England as her residence. But commitment to Chasemore's Tory ways, while it may not be the horror the prejudiced Grice conjures up, does, James shows, involve some loss: a loss of the free and easy, a loss of the tones of Indian summer, a loss even of the heartiness of American vulgarity. Agatha, though she loves Chasemore, cannot strike an adequate balance between what she can keep and what she must give up. She attempts to suppress herself, then to let herself go; but finally, when her brother comes on a visit and brings about a direct confrontation of cultures once more, she commits suicide. The ending is insufficiently prepared, starker than it need be; James has not adequately built the American side so as to strike the necessary balance. Still, "The Modern Warning" is a remarkable story. Here James asks directly what is to be lost by retaining one's American loyalties and yet living in a more comfortable, beautiful, and tranquil setting, and, he answers, something is to be lost, some betrayal inevitably takes place.

While absorbed by these themes, James was growing painfully aware that he was losing his audience. In January 1888 he wrote to Howells, saying that his last two novels had "reduced the desire, and the demand, for my productions to zero," [11] and when, two years later, his large novel *The Tragic Muse* was published, he told William that it was to be his last long novel.

The recognition he craved was not to be his with *The Tragic Muse,* in spite of William's insistence that with the publication of it, of Howells' *A Hazard of New Fortunes,* and of his own *Principles of Psychology,* "the year 1890 will be known as the great epochal year in American literature." [12] That year, however, though it may have marked the opening of a distinct social period in America, marked distinct endings for the authors of the three books William James cited. In *A Hazard,* as has been seen, Howells acknowledged a new era of social upheaval while at the same time announcing that he was not to produce fictions directly about it but would content himself with being a sympathetic observer. The publication of his *Psychology* released William James from the systematic learning to which he had submitted himself to that point in his life. As Ralph Barton Perry pointed out, he discovered that "things give reasons for themselves and can be called 'intelligible'; but in the last analysis they are what they are and refuse to explain *why*." [13] The path beyond is that of faith, and after *Psychology* William James was freed to explore it. Characterizing this turn in William's career, Perry wrote that in the nineties "James was often moved to reaffirm and amplify the faith of his youth." The result was that

> there was a great expansion of his human sympathies and of his political and social activities. This was the decade of the Spanish War and of the Dreyfus case, both of which deeply stirred his moral emotions. His activities in psychical research revived his old sympathy with religious mysticism, and gave him a new hope of justifying it. All of these reasons conspired to make the decade from 1890 to 1900, or more precisely from 1892 to 1902, James's period of reform and evangelism. [14]

So with Henry, also, the completion of what he then considered his last long novel plunged him into a search for a different manner of expression.

The theme of *The Tragic Muse* is again the nature of freedom, but the two worlds in which it is examined are not those of America and Europe, as in *The Reverberator,* or of the upper and lower classes, as in *The Princess Casamassima*; they are the world of art and the world of politics. At a time when he felt his audience was leaving him, James examined the nature of the artist's relation to the public as shown, for example, in Nick Dormer's desire to leave the Parliamentary career for which his entire life had been a conscious preparation, in order to devote himself to painting. In pursuing a public as a candidate for Parliament, Nick insists, he has had to say things which had nothing to do with the truth. He has had, he says, to appeal "to stupidity, to ignorance, to density, to prejudice, to the love of names and phrases, the love of hollow, idiotic words, of shutting the eyes tight and making a noise." [15]

Even if he does not succeed as an artist, he will at least have taken the world in a "free brave personal way." He will have the satisfaction of making of his life, which like all lives consists of personal experiments, an attempt to impress his style on the material of living, rather than the reverse, which is demanded of the public man.

In a parallel plot, even as Nick's fiancée, Julia, labors to make Nick a public man and open for him the highest possibilities of that field, the diplomat Peter Sherringham labors to make a theatrical career for Miriam Rooth. One of the most significant contrasts developed as the two plots are intertwined is that Miriam, the woman of superior histrionic abilities, has no private character whatsoever—she is totally her performance—whereas Julia, the possessor of a character so intense that she gives every promise of being able to create a prime minister, is in public painfully shy. The public life, the life which leads one inevitably into a dependence on an audience, is one which saps freedom and individuality. The private life, in which one is free to experiment with imparting his tone, his style, to the materials experience affords him, offers no audience. Miriam and Nick, the promising tragedian and the promising politician, threaten, if they follow the paths prepared for them, to be privately hollow. A life lived in response to the expectations of society is incompatible with a life led in response to the expectations of art.

Every writer practices some form or other of magic in order to get on with his serious tasks. He talks to himself in two voices and frequently attempts in one voice to exorcise the ghost that has seized his works, while in another voice the ghost itself speaks. One can see this process at work in Henry James when, on one hand, he chooses residence in England and writes to William of the Anglo-Saxon total, while, on the other, the haunting voice in "The Modern Warning" speaks of unhappy differences between England and America. In *The Tragic Muse* a complicated form of this dialogue is constantly taking place, and in some part it contributes to the actual damaging of the novel as a formal composition. Feeling keenly about losing his audience, James in *The Tragic Muse* demonstrates the impossibility of paying serious attention to a public if one is to lead the life of art with requisite freedom and privacy. This is an attempt at exorcism, because James was already haunted by a spirit which demanded that he not only find an audience at all costs, but that he locate it in the one area where the literary man is nakedly at the mercy of the public— the theater. The stronger the ghost's hold on James, the more explicitly does he talk against it, amplifying the anti-artistic conditions of the theater. So a character speaking for him in *The Tragic Muse* says:

> "The *omnium gatherum* of the population of a big commercial city at the hour of the day when their taste is at its lowest, flocking out of hideous hotels and restaurants, gorged with food, stultified with buying and selling and with all the other sordid speculations of the day, squeezed together in a sweltering mass, disappointed in their seats, timing the author, timing the actor, wishing to get their money back on the spot, all before eleven o'clock. Fancy putting the exquisite before such a tribunal as that!" [16]

The magic did not work. James was already possessed by a desire for a huge theatrical success and from 1889 to 1894 he devoted his major energies to playwriting, not just to gain recognition but in the hope of public triumph. He was anxious to learn the conventions of the stage and he taught himself to accept what they said about pleasing the public, even to the extent, as in his dramatization of *The American,* of providing a happy ending where it was totally unwarranted. The worst fate he had predicted for himself in his unsuccessful incantation in *The Tragic Muse* was realized in 1894, when he was forced to recognize, as he was made the object of public hissing and hooting,[17] that he was a singular failure as a playwright. Characteristically, the deeper he floundered in his dramatic years, the more his plays developed the theme of the superiority of art, tradition, and personal service to public life. Even in *Summersoft,* written in 1895 for Ellen Terry as a last attempt at drama, the insufficient hero elects his family tradition as opposed to politics. The one ghost having become palpable and having entered into James and seized his career, another ghost appeared in his works, singing the song of art and mocking at his attempts to gain a large audience.

During and immediately after his theatrical years, James produced the most memorable of his stories of artists, chiding himself constantly with one after another brilliant variation on the theme of doing things well, regardless of whether one is understood or appreciated. He scored the literary grotesqueries of his day which found lady authors taking masculine names so as to widen the range of what they could talk about, while men took female pseudonyms so as to gain the audience of women, who were the chief consumers of popular fiction. The world will lionize an artist but fail to appreciate his art, he warned, and the artist must be prepared to resist the idolizing, which, in effect, ignores what he stands for. To do something is everything; the inevitable frustrations that will accompany its doing really don't count, for they are after all merely the stuff of life, which, unlike the accomplished thing, passes. The good artist does not sell widely. He realizes:

> We are a numerous band, partakers of the same repose, who sit together in the shade of the tree, by the plash of the fountain, with the glare of the desert around us and no great vice that I know of but the habit perhaps of estimating people a little too much by what they think of a certain style.[18]

Out of the desert and back to the plash and shade James came at mid-decade. Between 1896 and 1901 he published *The Other House* (1896), *The Spoils of Poynton* (1897), *What Maisie Knew* (1897), *In the Cage* (1898), *The Awkward Age* (1899), and *The Sacred Fount* (1901), as well as several volumes of stories. The range of achievement in these books is, for James, markedly uneven, for reasons incisively indicated by F. W. Dupee:

> Some of these are among James's best books; others represent him at his most exasperating; and of all his various "periods," that of

the years 1896-1900 is the least readily summarized and appraised. The reason for this unevenness is fairly clear. Having ceased to expect a wide acclaim, he was frankly trying his hand; "difficulty" alone interested him now, as he was later to observe to Howells. Yet the difficulty he courted was not, as often supposed, merely that of a writer endeavoring to tell stories in perversely complicated ways. The imposition of a stricter form on fiction was certainly one of his aims; and it was the one about which his notebooks and his letters were most eloquent. Indeed, to "*face* my problems" signified, in the first instance, to find some means by which to "convert" . . . his play-writing experience to his uses as a novelist so that the exertions and sufferings of those years should not be wasted. Yet the novels themselves show him to have been engaged simultaneously in another difficult enterprise. This was the task of making sense, of wresting a meaning from modern life.[19]

In wresting that meaning, as Dupee shows, James became fascinated with an examination, in story, novelette, and novel, of "the fate of the moral sense in a corrupt or obtuse world." [20]

After 1898 Henry James was settled at Lamb House, and for the next four years he remained in England, omitting his usual travels to friends on the continent or in America. As he arrived at the brilliant achievement of the early years of the new century, he shifted slightly from the thematic concerns characterized by Dupee and began to develop a new note—new in its resonance if not in its pitch. It was sounded in one story after another in *The Soft Side* (1900), and it spoke of the need to live life passionately. The free commitment of interest was not enough; one had to commit everything, to become passionate about what counted, even though this inevitably destroyed one's balance in life. Such a balanced life was a cage, and the only key to full freedom was passion.

In "The Great Condition" an Englishman hesitates to marry an American woman because he is uncertain about her past; it appears such a blank that he fears there may be an awful secret hidden there. She marries another, only for the first to find out that she simply had no past and that he had lost love because at the crucial moment he had not allowed his passion to win over his prejudice. "Paste" is a story which turns on whether a set of pearls is real and, if so, what that fact must reveal about the passion of its owner. The pearls are given up by the heroine and fall into the scheming hands of Mrs. Guy because the heroine has failed to meet the demands of passion which the pearls symbolized. Mrs. Guy, for all her nastiness, is as passionate as her flaming red hair indicates her to be. In "The Abasement of the Northmores" the widow of an exploited man loses her desire for revenge on her husband's exploiter when that man's posthumous writings reveal his shallowness. She contents herself with arranging that after her death her husband's private letters to her, letters of passion, will be published, for this, after all, is the true source of her husband's superiority over his exploiter. In "John Delavoy" we find that it is impossible to care without caring more than enough. Even in the marvelously comic "The Third Person" two timorous old maids learn that the masculine ghost who haunts their house and simultaneously alarms and titillates them so that he must be put to rest, not so much to calm their fears of the supernatural as to restore the harmony between them which is threatened by the jealousy aroused by the ghost's visiting one or another of them, cannot be put to rest by the payment of conscience money but demands of them some more reckless act. The ghost calls for an act of passion.

The Sacred Fount, following the stories in *The Soft Side,* carried the theme further. The narrator of that novel fails to put his passion where his interests are and as a result is blinded to the reality about him. Though passion is, from one point of view, blind, James shows that the deeper blindness, the blindness of the imagination, comes from caring only and not caring more than enough. The central characters of the three great novels which were to follow, *The Wings of the Dove* (1902), *The Ambassadors* (1903), and *The Golden Bowl* (1904), unlike the narrator of *The Sacred Fount,* care more than enough and therefore rise above whatever seeming defeat they encounter because they are the true possessors of the world they inhabit.

In the 1890s Henry James passed through the flames. He began the decade having bid adieu to the social theme in favor of the eminence of the private experience, only, in his own life, to seek out, disastrously, a public career in the theater. He had emerged from this fiasco at mid-decade to experiment widely with his technique in order to realize the lessons his theatrical experience held for him, and he closed the decade on the threshold of one of the most significant achievements in the history of the novel in English. His themes over the decade modulated from freedom to the nature of art to the need for passion, each successive theme retaining the motifs of the earlier ones and building upon them. By the flames of the nineties he was refined as few American artists have ever been refined. But if they made of him a master they also made him increasingly inaccessible to the troubled young writers for whom the activities of the nineties were not tests of maturity but calls to youthful action. He was generously interested in those who would do what he could not or would not do—in Crane, in one direction, in Stevenson, in another—but his career, finally so passionately free and private, was not one which offered the quick lesson, the only one these younger men had the patience to learn.

A large part of the American reading public in the nineties agreed with the critic Henry C. Vedder when he said that James told the Americans that, compared with the Europeans, they were "in all things the least of these—except, perhaps, in native goodness, which doesn't count." [21] Vedder's mean opinion is representative of the wave which in the nineties was engulfing both James's effort to win his way into a haven in which technique and subject became one and Howells' effort to keep a channel open to reality. Vedder had words for Howells also: "Can it be that Mr. Howells gives us in his books a fair representation of life as he has known it? Has his whole experience been of this stale, flat, unprofitable sort? Has he never known anybody who had a soul above buttons?" [22]

Such emphases as Howells and James were placing on reality and on the pre-eminence of technique obscured for many an American reader the all-important moral standard which he believed to be as clear as sunlight and absolutely necessary as an element in his literature. Anything which blurred this standard and suggested that moral decisions were complex was vicious and foreign in origin. He knew that under the guise of realism Zola imposed upon his readers a nauseating mass of corruption, and he knew that another wicked artist, Oscar Wilde, had informed the world that all that mattered was whether a work was well written or ill written. Wilde's insistence on execution, to the point of cynicism about social content, was at the farthest pole from Zola's effort to bring social materials to fiction in a natural form. But this wide difference was brushed aside by the dominant small-town critical voices of the nineties. Zola and Wilde were one, as Vedder put it, because both were immoral, and Howells and James were following behind them in a dangerous fashion:

> A novel is good when it is well written, it is bad if it is ill written, and Mr. James avows that he can see no other distinction. Now one hopes that the American public is ready to admit the truth of this theory of art neither in the case of pictures nor in the case of novels. The sound, healthy sense of the people, uninstructed in art criticism, revolts from the statement that pictures designed to corrupt the morals of youth, pictures that accomplish such corruption, are to be coldly judged as works of art. Novels that have no better purpose than to drag forth to the light and expose to the gaze of the innocent and pure a mass of festering and putrid moral corruption, cannot be admitted to be good, because of any technical skill shown in the work. The eternal distinction between good and evil, between virtue and vice, cannot be obscured by *dilettante* theories of art.[23]

Intelligent readers, it would seem, could scarcely have taken seriously such easy sliding from the pictorial to the literary art, such misassignment of artistic purpose, such coarse-minded reliance on the clarity of moral standards and their relation to art. But they had to. The kind of voice which speaks here was as important an element in the climate of the nineties as was the benign encouragement of young artists by Howells and the rarefied example set them by James. If it was not heard and gauged by the writer, then he in turn would not be heard. Its dominance was not the result of its coarseness and stridency, but the result of its origin. The voice was the voice of a decency which most Americans cherished as their peculiar contribution to the culture of the world. James's deep diving beneath the facts of love to their psychological causes and consequences was a technique conditioned by this voice, as was Howells' reluctance to admit that a shift in morality was accompanying the shift in social structure which he asked the young writers to record. Indeed, had not Howells always kept himself on guard against some of the influences Vedder so strongly opposed?

In the same year that Vedder published his moral denunciations, Howells had suddenly been called back from Europe to tend to his ailing father, and he wrote to his son, who remained in Paris: "Perhaps it was as well I was called home. The poison of Europe was getting into my soul. You must look out for that. They live much more fully than we do. Life here is still for the future—it is a land of Emersons—and I like a little present moment in mine." [24] The Emersons, however, had shrunk to the size of the Vedders, as Howells realized when he admitted he liked a little present moment in his life, and as he revealed when he followed this portion of the letter with a comment which Henry James was to elevate into the central scene of *The Ambassadors*. Without completing the sentence, Howells had exclaimed, "When I think of the Whistler garden!"

Back home, however, Howells dutifully sat down to defend James and other American authors in exile, to keep the channels to them open. He did not believe that their residence abroad was the result of a distaste for America, though "if it would at all help to put an end to that struggle for material prosperity which

has eventuated with us in so many millionaires and so many
tramps, I would be glad to believe that it was driving our literary
men out of the country." [25] It was more accurate, he felt, to explain
it as follows:

> Literary absenteeism, it seems to me, is not peculiarly an American
> vice or an American virtue. It is an expression and a proof of the
> modern sense which enlarges one's country to the bounds of civiliza-
> tion. . . . Absenteeism is not a consequence of "the struggle for ma-
> terial prosperity," not a high disdain of the strife which goes on not
> less in Europe than in America, and must, of course, go on every-
> where as long as competitive conditions endure, but is the result of
> chances and preferences which mean nothing nationally calamitous
> or discreditable.[26]

Ironically, among those cloaked in Howells' defense was his
friend Mark Twain as well as his friend Henry James, for Twain
had spent the greater part of the nineties abroad in an effort to
recover from the immense financial losses he suffered as a result of
making the wrong moves when he played the great American game
of get-rich-quick. The lessons that the nineties slowly and painfully
brought home to Howells and James came on him more swiftly,
like a thunderclap. Whereas the decade had refined James into
another phase and had brought Howells to a realization of his own
limitations and a mother-hen interest in the young who might exceed them, it had battered Twain so severely that his art was never
to recover.

The irony of Twain's prominence as a literary absentee was that
his greatest work, *Huckleberry Finn* (1884), had come as the
combining and culminating point of two native American traditions. On one hand it was related to the local-color story which
aimed at communicating the flavor of one or another region (for
Harriet Beecher Stowe, New England, for Joel Chandler Harris,
the Southeast, for Bret Harte, California) and which achieved its
greatest popularity in the eighties. All too frequently the tales in
this tradition strayed into the sentimental and made themselves
comfortable there, and often they had no more claim to attention

than the observation that the event depicted could have happened in the way that it happened only in the region in which it happened. But the tradition brought with it a striving for accurate dialogue, fresh simile, chiefly through folk images, and concrete detail.

On the other hand, *Huckleberry Finn* grew from Twain's native familiarity with frontier humor and his conscious refinement of its techniques as he practiced, in the years after 1862, the profession of literary comedian in journals and on the lecture stage. For all his obvious differences from James, Twain through this discipline came also to see that in the art of narrative the telling counts more than what is told, for it is, eventually, all that can be told: "The stories are only alligator pears—one merely eats them for the sake of the salad dressing." [27]

The vernacular of Huck, the narrator, harmonizes a symphony of sounds—the throaty drawls of Negroes, the nasal twangings of farm wives, the rasping sibilants of village windbags. With the frontier illiterate's talent for reading more with the ear than with the eye, Huck hears the night come on through the sequences of its characteristic sounds far more than he sees it growing through a change in light, and he senses the life of the river as much by hearing the plash of the raftsman's oar as by seeing the raft itself. He consistently locates himself in terms of what people say and the way they say it. Huck's ear blends the sounds of the book, and his speech becomes an eloquent literary language because his creator had spent years of care practicing tone and practicing timing for the sake of getting his laughs at the right place and in the right volume. By 1884, through variations of tone and timing, Twain was able to achieve the complex literary effects that had commonly been assumed to be inseparable from a formal literary language, and to do so while providing a ceaseless accompaniment of aural delight.

Mark Twain converted the American vernacular into a subtle literary instrument equal to the most arduous demands the literary artist could put upon it. As Walter Blair said, the talk of his char-

acters "had the precision, the imagination of poetic art," [28] and
in the nineties *Huckleberry Finn* was already quietly advancing toward the position that it would enjoy among writers of the twentieth century, a position most dramatically stated by Ernest Hemingway when he said: "It's the best book we've had. All American
writing comes from that. There was nothing before. There has
been nothing as good since." [29]

In the nineties, however, Twain's achievement was something
felt rather than something understood. Howells believed in Twain's
greatness but James could not agree with him as, in the twentieth
century, T. S. Eliot would readily agree with Ernest Hemingway
that *Huckleberry Finn* was a very great book. Twain himself had
come to look at his writings as outside the pale of what so many of
Howells' friends called "literary," and showed no sense of building
on the achievement of *Huckleberry Finn*. Rather, in 1889 he
heralded the arrival of the troublesome decade with *A Connecticut
Yankee in King Arthur's Court,* a book that looked back to *The
Prince and the Pauper* (1882) more than to *Huckleberry Finn.*

The Prince and the Pauper had depicted life in Henry VIII's
England from the point of view of nineteenth-century democratic
egalitarianism. The prince who was a pauper for a time learned
how the other half lives and became more responsible as a result.
His very experiences with the common people were school enough
in which to develop the democratic instincts dormant in him as
they were in all intelligent people. Now Twain was to carry this
one step further by actually introducing a nineteenth-century car-
rier of enlightened ideals into the England of King Arthur. The
Connecticut Yankee stood for the two great elements of contemporary American life, faith in democracy and faith in superior technology. He awoke in a world in which tyranny ruled by imposing
on the ignorance of mankind—an ignorance so abysmal with relation to the mechanical arts that all labor was bestial. Having set
to work with high American efficiency, the Yankee was soon con-
founding his opponents—the vested interests of church, aristoc-

racy, and magic—through the introduction of electricity, and, with the help of leisure time thus purchased, he introduced the principles of democracy to the downtrodden inhabitants of Arthur's England. As he mechanized the country, so he loosened the rule of fear and prepared the way for self-government.

The great humbug of monarchy was, apparently, to fall before the Connecticut Yankee's efforts, just as in 1889 Twain joyfully observed that monarchy had collapsed in Brazil, and confidently predicted that it was doomed in Portugal, Russia, and even England. If in the collapse of monarchy a number of cultural values were to be swept away—a realization which led James's revolutionary, Hyacinth Robinson, to commit suicide rather than fulfill his obligations to his movement—Twain accepted the consequence. If, in short, James balked at social reform because the inheritance of the ages was endangered, Howells' other friend gladly embraced the notion of reform, claiming that the class he stood for lost nothing anyway. Twain wrote in a letter in 1889: "I have always catered for the Belly and the Members, but have been served like the others—criticized from the culture-standard—to my sorrow and pain; because, honestly, I never cared what became of the cultured classes; they could go to the theatre and the opera; they had no use for me and the melodeon." [30] "Me and the melodeon," in the person of Hank Morgan, the Connecticut Yankee, were to show what up-to-date ideas could do.

But Twain lived in a society in which technology, rather than supporting democracy, was, through its monopolistic combinations, destroying it. The humorous demands of his plot were inadequate to check his perception of this condition, and *A Connecticut Yankee* slowly turns from a pleasant social parable into a nightmare, as vested power proves too much for the impulse toward social improvement and technology turns from the providing of benefits to the many to the killing off of its opponents. What started as a comic fantasy closes with hundreds upon hundreds of knights sizzling to death in their armor, electrocuted by the Yankee's ingenious fence, the final flower produced by the planting of technology in the Arthurian world.

As Twain finally treated the problem in *A Connecticut Yankee,* more than culture was lost in the combination of technology and laissez-faire democracy. Lost also was the common man. The fatal note which he struck in 1889 became his burden increasingly in the nineties as his family, in 1891, began a nine-year European residence for the purpose of economy, and as his own investment in financial glory eventuated in bankruptcy in 1894. Still proud enough to want to pay one hundred cents on the dollar to his creditors, and still possessed of an awed conviction that there was an alchemy which would produce great financial wealth, he gratefully placed his business affairs in the hands of Henry Rogers of Standard Oil and set about the discharge of his debts through lecturing and through the production of potboilers. When he stole time from the ardors of paying off, the book he dreamed of writing was an exposé of the damned human race, not a novel which would carry him further along in the tradition of *Tom Sawyer* and *Huckleberry Finn.* Indeed, these works were now associated in his mind with potboiling, and he used their characters in the nineties in such feeble works as *Tom Sawyer Abroad* and *Tom Sawyer, Detective.*

Twain's one attempt at combining the tradition of his great earlier work with his newly deepened bitterness about the way in which the age-old evils of human nature were destroying all the promises made by nineteenth-century America was *Pudd'nhead Wilson* (1894). Here the masterful hand is evident in flashes, but on the whole there is an unresolved discrepancy between the basically pessimistic view of human nature which seems to inform the book, and the plot, which develops in contradiction to it. The oft-quoted epigraphs from Pudd'nhead's Calendar reveal an attitude which finally has not much connection with what goes on in the story. Twain in the nineties was a divided artist, humorous in familiar ways or censorious in tones of deepest pessimism, but unable to combine the two into one satisfactory work. "The fools, the idiots, the pudd'nheads," [31] these made up the large bulk of the human race; let them do whatever the hell they pleased.

In January 1898 Twain wrote to Howells from Vienna, "We *are* a pair of old derelicts drifting around, now, with some of our passengers gone and the sunniness of the others in eclipse." [32] His immediate reference was to their common loss of deeply loved children. But the image was an apt one for two writers who had come to manhood before the Civil War and achieved eminence in the period of optimistic reunification and expansion which followed it, only, in their advanced years, to believe, as Howells said to James, that American civilization was "coming out all wrong in the end." The great threat to their generation had been the sectional conflict that split America apart, and the great triumph of their generation had been reunification. When the storm of social disunion blew up in the 1890s, they were too old to trim their sails to it and too brave to seek a snug harbor. As the twentieth century approached, they drifted like derelicts, Howells beginning to believe that the privacy that James now regarded as an absolute condition of art was necessary, although his social conscience had kept him from it; Twain unconsciously emulating that other derelict, the *Pequod,* and deciding that if he was to go down at least he would take down a little piece of heaven with him, and so discharging what ammunition was left him at the power which had created such a shabby, poor, ridiculous thing as man.

Yet in 1910, more than twenty years after *A Connecticut Yankee, A Hazard of New Fortunes,* and *The Tragic Muse,* still in the foreground of American literature were Mark Twain, seventy-five years of age, William Dean Howells, seventy-three years of age, and Henry James, sixty-seven years of age. Where were their successors, the young men who grew up after the Civil War and who began their careers in the nineties? What had become of the generation broadly encouraged by Howells? What writers of merit were there, in 1910, who in their forties and fifties were now ripe for their maturest work? If the storm had driven James to harbor and made derelicts of Twain and Howells, had it not been withstood by a new kind of craft? Or did the decade of the nineties sink the young even as it dismasted the old?

The Midwestern Imagination

When, in September 1861, the Confederate Army occupied Columbus, Kentucky, so as to control Mississippi River traffic at that point, an obscure brigadier general from Illinois, Ulysses S. Grant, decided on his own initiative to occupy Paducah, Kentucky, and thereby command the mouths of the Tennessee and Cumberland Rivers. He realized that Kentuckians were ambiguous in their attitude toward the war, but his was a military, not a political command, and in his proclamation to the citizens of Paducah explaining his presence he said:

> I am here to defend you against this enemy, and to assert and maintain the authority and the sovereignty of your government and mine. I have nothing to do with opinions. I deal only with armed rebellion and its aiders and abettors. You can pursue your usual avocations without fear or hindrance.[1]

When President Lincoln read the proclamation, he said, "The man who can write like that is fitted to command in the West." [2]

Grant's language was simple, clear, and practical, addressed to the matter at hand and uncomplicated by qualification or dependency. Like its user, it did its job efficiently. The President from the West appreciated it as a natural expression of the character of the man who controlled it and as an indication of his suitability for dealing with Westerners. The mother tongue inherited by these people, chiefly of British stock, had been kept free of literary ornamentation by a life of practical labor, and adorned, when it was adorned, by the racy imagery of their open life or by the felt rhythms of their Bible and their hymnals.

There was something more American about the West, as Howells' literary idols in Boston had told him in 1860, and this something more American extended to the very language available as
a birthright to the people born there. As Howells had carried this
into Boston, where it had been modified even as it had also modified a more bookish literature, so every expectation was that the
American writer born into this clear and natural linguistic inheritance would take up the task where Howells and Twain had
left it. The postwar migration to the West would build up a particularly American culture as it built up the nation's economy.

The Midwest of the child who was born within five years of the
Civil War was a farming section of separated villages whose isolation had hardened belief into certain knowledge. The residents
knew that Protestantism was the true religion, that the Republican
Party, which had saved the Union, had done so as the result of
divine guidance, and that the farmers were the backbone of the
country. If God, in His wisdom, had given certain seeming ad-
vantages to the dwellers in cities, He had done so as a temptation.
The price the cities, swollen with foreigners, paid, as his newspaper
and his preacher made clear, was an alarming dishonesty which
necessitated locks and policemen, and an unhealthy contiguity of
the sexes which came from the absence of a natural surrounding
which clearly divided man's field work from woman's domestic
work. The great crimes were atheism, theft, and adultery, and they
were crimes of the city, not of the country.[3]

The children, girls as well as boys, carried broomsticks with
which they went through the manual of arms taught them by their
veteran fathers, and they grew accustomed to the sight of worn
Union uniforms now serving as the work garments of the hired
hands. If one of these hands came from a different section of the
country, they pressed him for news of what it was like in New York
State or in the Berkshire Hills, and when the wave of migration
cast a German gardener into the village or a Welsh youth into the
hayfield, they arranged their chores so as to work at his side and
hear about the world beyond the sea.

While the city stood for tainted values that were resisted by the village culture, the Midwesterner nevertheless looked beyond his fields for the beautifying of his family's life. He looked past the city to the New England village remembered by him from experience, from books, or from the talk of relatives, and out of these fragments built the rudiments of civilization, constructed a code of gentility, of manners, of proper attitudes. In so doing he was not only avoiding the consequences of the rise of the city but also looking backward in time to a world which no longer existed, because of the decline of the stony New England soil in the face of the competition from his more fertile fields, and because of the rise of factories. This, however, was of no great practical consequence, because the fancied culture he was emulating was but a dim model, which he modified and made native by his own resources. The volume of Longfellow, for example, one child of Illinois sensed, kept alive for her parents "the notion of mannerliness, of the gesture they missed and meant on behalf of their children, to resume." [4] As he performed this function on the open prairies, Longfellow had been transmuted from words to actual substances, to the hair wreaths in the parlor and the wax flowers under glass, and if only a spinster aunt or two emulated him in verse, most ladies felt that they were aspiring to him in the names and patterns of their patchwork quilts and woven coverlets: Tulip Tree, Democrat Rose, Ladies' Chain, Swing in the Center, Washington's Plume.

Although the outdoors was in religious rhetoric the great teacher of the upright life—what kept the country good while the cities went bad—it was too much with the parents in their tasks and the children in their chores to make a significant contribution to their conscious culture. When the shutters were drawn against the night wind and the lamp was kindled, the fields, except as they related to the day's work, were a boring topic of conversation. If the children were to be uplifted, now was the time to read to them from the Bible or from Longfellow; now was the time to talk of a trip taken beyond the borders of the farm. The book-learning acquired at the schoolhouse and furthered by lamplight was not directly applicable to daily life, but then, it was not meant to be, any more than talk about the outdoors was meant to contribute to culture. It was, rather, the arming of the children against the world at large, which might work its spell on them if they were not prepared with their counter-spell, and it was their redemption from a bestiality which, without learning, would surely follow from their open-air drudgery. If the current which carried the model of the New England village to the Midwestern farmhouse also carried Puritanism, that Puritanism, together with other mistrustings, taught a dread of illiteracy and the shame of sinking to the level of beasts as farmers in other lands had done. If the father's oft-repeated tales of the great war brought home the lessons of the divinity of the Republican Party and the glory of patriotism, they also carried some notion of the way in which different kinds of men had worked together and how the plain citizen could rise to conquer his own troubles without the aid of professional soldiers.

Some books, while dangerous, were nevertheless so fixed in the consciousness as important that they raised the problem of how they were to be dealt with—as dealt with they must be if the counter-spell was to work—and yet not surrendered to. What was one to do with Shakespeare, with Tom Paine, with Lord Byron? The answer was provided by one of the oldest customs in the Western village, one developed in response to political and agricultural problems. When something was to be solved, you talked it over; you learned what the other fellow knew and you tried your ideas out on him.

Quilts were sewn and corn was husked while farmers and their children talked over the crops, the weather, and the election. So Tom Paine and Shakespeare were tackled in groups, where the talking-over would guard against whatever evils resided in private submission to their words, while the conversation would adjudicate what was worth while and fix it in the memory. In the seventies Chautauqua lecturers and troupes began to turn up in the villages as an institutionalization of this habit, appearing at those times of the day and year when all members of a servantless society could attend. Then you could hear a poet telling about his work or a painter talking about his picture and you could learn about the world beyond with the dangers and difficulties of direct exposure reduced. Culture, when attacked in groups and when gleaned from the lecturer, need not increase the drain on a stamina already taxed by a day of toil; it became what many held that it should be, a restful broadening of one's character along moral lines accepted by the community.

While the dramatization of *Uncle Tom's Cabin* had made some inroads on the prejudice against playgoing, still the theater was not an acceptable form of entertainment. Preferable was singing, accompanied by jew's-harp, harmonica, banjo, guitar, or melodeon. The melodic legacy of the Civil War was the male quartet and the tenor with hair oil who sang "Juanita." [5] In addition to more substantive matters, Chautauqua supplied professors and doctors of elocution, the most desirable art within the reach of the farm boy, and mail-order houses supplied cardboard mottoes which could be pinned over his cot to keep him up to the mark.

The culture which resulted did not create a reservoir of men like Howells, as many a prewar theorist had predicted it would. Rather, the emphasis on the safety of group learning and on the oral tradition led young men to aspire to group success, to desire to conquer with their tongues rather than with their pens. They accepted the principles of Protestantism, Republicanism, and the nobility of agricultural labor, and practiced the eloquent embroidering of these principles in speech which would provide recreation as well as self-gratulation to their auditors rather than examining the principles critically through writing. When they aspired to leave the district for a life of fame, their goal was the state capital and, ultimately, Washington, not Boston or New York and the offices of the *Atlantic* or *Harper's*. When their sturdy instincts for self-improvement led them to steal time, that time was more often employed in walking off into the woods, there to practice declamation to the birds and to score each day with an "S" for success

carved into a tree, than in going to the garret with pen and paper.
A clear and coherent line ran from the ideas and habits of their
village to success in public life. But success in the field of culture
meant the acquisition of discontinuous attributes. The very instru-
ments of culture, the melodeon and the cardboard motto, were
confections to be placed on top of a life with which they had little
organic connection, since that life, it was admitted, was to be
beautified from outside. The function of literature was to take
one away from oneself into realms of shimmering beauty and ennobling adventure. It was, on the whole, easier to go West to the
Rockies and live that life than it was to go East and try to write of
it. But when the farm boy found himself driven to literary expression, then what came nimbly from his pen was, most frequently,
tales of knights in days of yore or of pioneer lasses braving the
wilds, dramatic idealizations of the virtues on which the politician
based his career.

As these Midwestern children of the Civil War come to manhood, there was an increasing need for them to idealize the home
virtues, for the Republican Party and the nobility of agriculture
were turning out all wrong, even though the men on the farms had
faithfully upheld their principles. The capital which backed the
mortgage for the old homestead was gladly advanced by the local
broker because it was not his; it came from the East, and the more
he advanced, the larger was his income, which was a percentage of
it. In 1890, in the wheat-growing states of Minnesota, Nebraska,
Kansas, North Dakota, and South Dakota, there was more than
one mortgage to a family, and most farms were mortgaged for all
they were worth. The gold reserves began to diminish dangerously
in that year, and the international money market entered a retreat
which ended in an American financial crash in 1893, one that fell
mightily on the overfinanced farmer. Nature lent her grim cooperation to this disastrous state of affairs, supplying adequate rainfall
in only two of the ten years from 1887 to 1897; for five of these
years there was practically no crop at all. Credit was used up.

Hard times had arrived. In the shock, many bewildered farmers followed the pattern of their parents and moved—but this time eastward; in 1891, 18,000 prairie schooners crossed the Missouri River from Nebraska to Iowa. The back-trailing had begun. The financial and physical frontier was closing down.[6]

On June 2, 1895, Governor Altgeld of Illinois, testifying before the Supreme Court in the Debs case, said, "Never has there been so much patriotic talk as in the last twenty-five years, and never were there so many influences at work strangling Republican institutions." He listed the "brood of evils" which had sprung from unleashed capitalism since 1870:

1. The striking down of over one-third of the money of the world, thus crushing the debtor class and paralyzing industry.
2. The growing of that corrupt use of wealth which is undermining our institutions, debauching public officials, shaping legislation and creating judges who do its bidding.
3. Exemption of the rich from taxation.
4. The substitution of government by injunction for government by the Constitution and laws.
5. The striking down of trial by jury.[7]

Governor Altgeld, however, was a radical—had he not pardoned the Haymarket anarchists?—and his criticisms were aimed, ultimately, at a total overhaul of the American system. The country was so great and the basic morality of the now embattled farmer was so sound that surely the whole system could not be in error. Rather, certain evil forces—foreigners, cynical money captains, effete theorists—had taken over a God-inspired system and should be identified and extirpated. What was needed was not so much a problem-by-problem attack, which denied inspiration, as a swift medicine that would set all right again: single tax, or free coinage of silver, or government ownership of railroads.

The belief in a panacea was encouraged not only by a reluctance to admit that so much that was cherished might be at fault (though the Republican Party, the farmer of the Plains now admitted, had

to be defeated), not only by a desperation which did not want to
stop for a thorough overhauling when, surely, some bolt could be
tightened or some cog inserted to set the whole going again, but
by a continuing fundamental belief in one animating design for
human existence. For many that design was still God's plan for
his chosen: live as Christ would have you live, and burn out the
unchosen. For others, shaken by Darwinism, writers like Herbert
Spencer had provided a substitute design, another philosophy of
inevitability which taught that if the hard-working man could but
have his path clear all would come out well in the end. As Richard
Hofstadter has indicated:

> Spencer's philosophy was admirably suited to the American scene.
> It was scientific in derivation and comprehensive in scope. It had
> a reassuring theory of progress based on biology and physics. It was
> large enough to be all things to all men, broad enough to satisfy
> agnostics like Robert Ingersoll and theists like Fiske and Beecher.
> It offered a comprehensive world-view, uniting under one generaliza-
> tion everything in nature from protozoa to politics. Satisfying the
> desire of "advanced thinkers" for a world-system to replace the
> shattered Mosaic cosmogony, it soon gave Spencer a public influ-
> ence that transcended Darwin's. Moreover it was not a technical
> creed for professionals. Presented in language that tyros in philos-
> ophy could understand, it made Spencer the metaphysician of the
> homemade intellectual, and the prophet of the cracker-barrel ag-
> nostic.[8]

Such a system had been the grand rationale for the reckless expansion which had led to the plight of the farmer in the nineties,
but it was broad enough to suggest to some of them that, properly
interpreted, it would lead to their triumph. Those who relinquished
a total faith in the benignity of a God-inspired America did not,
therefore, relinquish the notion that laws govern and forces rule.
If they had learned from the popularizers of Darwin to read the
natural struggle in terms of politics, they had also learned how to
turn around and read their politics in the light of the sanctions of

nature.[9] The old God might be shorn of his whiskers, but the new rationales were still animistic.

When in 1892 there assembled in Saint Louis "the first great labor conference of the United States, and of the world, representing all divisions of urban and rural organized industry," [10] the grieved farmers were in the vast majority and the preamble to the platform adopted was a creation of the imagination which had been nurtured by Longfellow, the Bible, group learning, and professors of elocution. Accepting the fact that something was terribly wrong, the preamble nevertheless stood foursquare for Almighty God and the Republic and spoke of "imported pauperized labor" beating down wages so that matters were "rapidly degenerating to European conditions." [11] A small class called bondholders were responsible for the desperate state of affairs, and they were not American in their loyalties: "A vast conspiracy against mankind has been organized on two continents and is taking possession of the world." There was nothing wrong, basically, with America, and especially with the American farmer, so long as the international parasites could be cleansed from the system; those who proposed to "sacrifice our homes and children upon the altar of Mammon," those who would not do real work yet would eat, those moneychangers must be driven out of the temple for "the salvation of the republic." [12]

Following the platform, which demanded free and unlimited coinage of silver, a graduated income tax, reclamation of alienated land, and government ownership of transportation, telegraph, and telephone services, the resolutions invoked the Civil War and closed by saying: "The men who wore the gray and the men who wore the blue meet here to extinguish the last smoldering embers of civil war in the tears of joy of a united and happy people, and we agree to carry the stars and stripes forward to the highest point of national greatness." [13]

What is striking about the imagination which thus reveals itself is the way in which the serious radical remedies of the platform are cushioned by a preamble that rings the familiar high-flown changes on biblical rhetoric and identifies the unchosen—foreigners and parasites—as the human agencies of trouble, and a series of resolutions that reassert the glory of patriotism in the romantic lyrics of the cardboard motto, written to be sung to the accompaniment of the melodeon: tears of joy extinguish smoldering embers. While the gravest set of social necessities led to the daring demands, the imagination still lingered in an Eden of sentimental patriotism which was threatened only from the outside.

Four years later the same imagination, eloquently represented by William Jennings Bryan, was to gather its biblical indignation together and unleash it once more in a speech which again joined social remedies to an attack on outsiders: "No private character, however pure, no personal popularity, however great, can protect from the avenging wrath of an indignant people a man who will declare that he is in favor of fastening the gold standard upon this country, or who is willing to surrender the right of self-government and place the legislative control of our affairs in the hands of foreign potentates and powers." [14] That man, it turned out, was plain William McKinley, a Civil War veteran from Ohio, but, Bryan reminded his auditors, he was also a man "who was once pleased to think that he looked like Napoleon." [15]

Ignatius Donnelly, who had written the preamble to the 1892 Saint Louis platform, had said there, "From the same prolific womb of governmental injustice we breed two great classes—paupers and millionaires." [16] Three years earlier he had written a fantasy, *Caesar's Column,* which projected that divided state of affairs into a twentieth-century future when, if matters proceeded unchecked, a small capitalistic aristocracy would rule a world of enslaved workers. The book is concerned with the revolutionary movement which overthrows that aristocracy, only to perish in the debacle of greed and lust which follows the sudden emancipation of the great mass of economic slaves. Social criticism is, of course, the purpose of the book, but the melodramatic plot in which it is placed—the love of Gabriel for Estella Washington and

his saving her from becoming the concubine of a vicious plutocrat
—provides an awesome glimpse into the way in which the artifacts
of civilization, unknown on the farm, were equated with viciousness. The house in which Estella, destined for a career as a white
slave, is imprisoned is filled with paintings, books, bronzes, and
jeweled boxes, and these art objects are equated by Donnelly with
her concubinage. They are the trappings of the oppressive rich,
and their absence from the humble home results, by implication,
from the poor man's virtue, not from his poverty. He would no
more gather this collection than he would keep a mistress.

In spite of the oppressive social conditions which render men
brutal in their attempts to gain bread, still the heroine can occupy
a world of romance and reach for a poisoned dagger while ex-
claiming, "Better purity in death than degradation in life." [17] And
in keeping with this tone Gabriel instructs his imprisoned love to
bar her door:

> "If they break it in . . . use your knife on the first man that touches
> you. If they send you food or drink, do not use them. If they at-
> tempt to chloroform you, stop up the pipe with soap. If the worst
> comes to the worst, use the rope ladder. If you manage to go out-
> side the garden gate, call a hack and drive to that address. . . . If
> you are about to be seized, chew up the paper and swallow it. Do
> not in any event destroy yourself . . . until the last desperate ex-
> tremity is reached." [18]

The step from this penny-dreadful carrying-on to the preamble
of 1892 is not a large one. The same imagination is here crying
out for social remedies but nevertheless picturing to itself a world
of heroism, of idealized and beautiful behavior, which is the true
world of personal relations. Social difficulties do affect the conditions in which one must conduct life, so when they are intolerable
they must be rectified. But they do not affect that life itself; they
do not have any consequences for the moral character. There is
a French girl in the book who can hate "with the characteristic
vehemence of her race," [19] but the American girl, Estella, is above

such behavior, and no amount of social oppression will result in her moral degradation. Troubles, even the massive fictional troubles of a world absolutely in the hands of a few lecherous capitalists, are external. They call forth the chivalric behavior of the true-blue American; they do not announce that chivalry is dead.

The fabric of social reality, when it did not seem clearly to be woven from the principles instilled on the farm or to conform to the way men imbued with those principles would act, had to be patched. But its shoddy condition did not result from any short-comings in the principles, nor did it suggest that a special vocabulary was needed to deal with it. The vocabulary of romance was the vocabulary of honestly raised men under stress; it was the vocabulary of their principles intensified, and it was brought into play by Donnelly in Saint Louis in 1892 as it was by Bryan in Chicago in 1896. It assumed that the morality of a rural upbringing was unshakable, and in the face of finer distinctions it responded that these distinctions, differing from its lofty simplicity as the bronzes of the rich differed from the wax flowers under glass, were the result of a vicious worldliness.

A fiction which deals meaningfully with social reality has to retain a flexibility which sees that conditions somehow grow from character and, in turn, affect it. It must shatter the monolith of morality. Even Howells had some difficulty doing this and balked when it came to carrying this flexibility through to the area of sexual behavior. Rural America after the Civil War had established its culture on the stone of a morality justified by the triumph of the Union. Its dark suspicion that there was a connection between riches, art, and sexuality, as exemplified by *Caesar's Column,* was naïve and sullenly defensive. But this suspicion nevertheless revealed a dim perception that realistic fiction denied that the home-bred moral sense was invulnerable to social change. If there was a connection between the daily toil of the farmer who produced all the soil would yield him and the steady decline of prices for his crop, surely the fault couldn't lie with the man who honestly went about earning his bread by the sweat of his brow. This behavior should result in an Eden regained, and, if it did not, something other than the concept of godly toil was at fault. Similarly, the arts should consist of beautiful illustrations of these principles triumphing in a world cleared of external impediments so that virtue unaided could meet unaided vice and give it its certain defeat. If they lingered on social conditions, longer than to expose them as extraneous to the true moral standards which motivate action and which, ideally, triumph, they were providing an aesthetic object totally unacceptable to an imagination which saw social conditions as temporarily discontinuous with the nature of real life. Literature should illustrate the shared values of the rural community. Because it was fictive it could clear away the extraneous. The wax flower overcame the mutability that inhered in the real one, and was preserved under glass so that its ideal attributes would not be damaged by contact with reality but instead would remain intact to serve their decorative function. So the White City at the Columbian Exposition was the society's wax flower and spoke of an immutable dream of a New Jerusalem. So the rhetoric of the 1892 preamble, cushioning the radical demands of the platform, showed that adverse social conditions were not the ideal effects of the way of life which was threatened by them, but that this way of life was internally perfect. Wax flower, White City, preamble, and the melodrama which organized the social criticism of *Caesar's Column* were outgrowths of a culture in which learning was embellishment and counter-spell rather than criticism and liberation. They were products of the Midwestern imagination.

Of all books published in America between 1880 and 1935, that which sold most widely was *In His Steps* (1896), a novel by a Topeka, Kansas, minister, Charles M. Sheldon, about a group of people in a Midwestern town who, under the leadership of their minister, pledge themselves to pursue their careers by asking themselves at each step what Jesus would have done, faced with their daily decisions. Thus the newspaper editor asks himself, "If Christ was editor of a daily paper, do you honestly think he would print three columns and a half of prize fight in it?" [20] and the novelist is brought to admit that his society novel, "written in a style that had proved popular," had "no purpose except to amuse" and, while not positively vicious, nevertheless did not contain a Christian message, but displayed merely the powers which "the social world petted and admired." [21] Sheldon's style was presumably not such as would prove popular, but was, in point of fact, immensely so, with its vague hintings at a "social world" which, unlike that occupied by those who are putting Jesus' precepts to work in daily nineteenth-century life, is unreal. A rich man's house is called "a palace of luxury." The other extreme of the unreal society is approached when the good Christian girl daringly takes a drunken prostitute home in order to redeem her. After this admirable act of charity is credited to her account, however, Sheldon allows the prostitute to die, thereby obviating the need to go into the details of precisely how the heroine is to rehabilitate her. The reality that counts is the Christlike gesture, not the problems which lead to prostitution or other social evils, because all problems, rest assured, will eventually yield before it. *In His Steps* is another example of the imagination which could produce the 1892 preamble and the White City, differing chiefly in its greater simplicity and, perhaps because of this, in its greater popular success.

The language of *In His Steps* is plain talk embellished, and the embellishments act invariably to clog the flow of the book while giving it a specious elevated tone. Plain talk alone would not be in keeping with a theme which asserts a higher reality than social reality. As a result, the book proceeds in such language as this: "The amount of slangy remonstrances hurled at the clerk back of the long counter would have driven any one else to despair. He was used to more or less of it all the time, and consequently hardened to it." [22] More striking even than the wordiness which results from sprucing up "the slang used" so that it comes out "the amount of slangy remonstrances hurled," is the nearly absolute deafness revealed. Words stand like boulders to be scrambled over. They have lost their rhythmic and melodic qualities. What matters is a display of "learning" which will demonstrate that their user, when he rejects "society," does not do so from lack of erudition. He possesses his language as a counter-spell. So "remonstrances" follows bumpingly after "slangy"; and plain "more or less," used colloquially as a noun, is followed later in the sentence by the judicial "consequently." If the Paducah proclamation is the zenith of a particular style, *In His Steps* is the nadir. This far had the relation of words to actions plummeted from 1861 to 1896.

Sheldon and Donnelly were romantic in a relatively unconscious fashion. The worlds they pictured, in which social details were made ultimately unresistant to the idealized display of absolute moral principles, resulted from their beliefs. In the latter part of the nineties, as a reading public faced with a bewildering range of social theories and an inescapable host of social problems turned increasingly to the response of historical fiction, signalized by the immense triumph in 1897 of *Quo Vadis*,[23] a number of young American writers appeared who were prepared by their upbringing to supply the demand. They were conscious romancers, unlike Sheldon and Donnelly, but like them they drew their sureness from intimate acquaintance with the ways of the Middle West. Indiana became the great literary reservoir. Already the home of the nation's most popular poet, James Whitcomb Riley, it became also the home place of the most popular of the romantic novelists: Charles Major, who wrote *When Knighthood Was in Flower* (1898); Maurice Thompson, who wrote *Alice of Old Vincennes* (1900); George Barr McCutcheon, who wrote *Graustark* (1901). Hamlin Garland saw this as "a natural reaction from dusty roads and weedy fence corners."[24] True enough; but it should also be seen that these conscious Midwestern romancers were reacting by embroidering the principles held by the walkers of the dusty roads. Rather than contrasting the principles held with the actual conditions at the weedy fence corner, they moved them to a realm in which their holders could live out their fantasies free of weeds.

Maurice Thompson, lecturing at the Hartford Theological Seminary in 1893, said of realists:

> They boast of holding up a mirror to nature; but they take care to give preference always to ignoble nature. They never hold up their mirror to heroic nature. Have you observed how, as a man becomes a realist, he grows fond of being narrow and of playing with small specialties? Have you thought out the secret force which controls the movement of his so-called realism, and always keeps its votaries sneering at heroic life, while they revel in another sort of life, which fitly to characterize here would be improper? I can tell you what that force is. It is unbelief in ideal standards of human aspiration, and it is impatient scorn of that higher mode of thought which has given the world all the greatest creations of imaginative genius.[25]

He scored *The Kreutzer Sonata, Leaves of Grass,* and *Madame Bovary* as examples of obscene moral taste, and scolded the female reader who claimed that a reading of *Hedda Gabler* had fortified her virtue: "Woman, you have taken Ibsen's arm and have gone with him into vile company. . . . The smack of hell is sweet to your lips, as it was to those of new-made Eve." [26]

The carefully phrased song of Thompson is a modulation on a theme by Sheldon, and, like the un-Christian novelist petted by society in Sheldon's pages, Henry James, in Thompson's words, is "a cleverly trained . . . voice of current social gossip." [27]

The central figure in Thompson's argument is the average man: "Say what we may, the average mind is the triumphant criterion; by it life wins or loses in all that concerns the body of humanity. What does not concern humanity as a body ought not to concern any man." [28] Here speaks the leveling voice of group learning, the approach to the poet through the lecture rather than the poem, the protective reading of Shakespeare by a circle. Howells sought poetry in the commonplace and therefore made what he thought to be the average his subject matter. Thompson, however, takes

the average to be the fantasies of the average mind and dramatizes
these in high adventures told in inflated language.

In *Alice of Old Vincennes* Thompson wrote a popular romance
about Indiana at the time it was passing from French to English
control. He was conscious that he was addressing his story to a
modern man. "Sitting in the liberal geniality of the nineteenth
century's sunset glow," he said in the novel, "we insist upon having
our grumble at the times and manners of our generation." [29] So
he strips away the times and manners and supplies another set
which will more readily yield the heroism inherent in the reader's
attitudes. The nineties had taught Howells to abandon his pride
in nineteenth-century America, but for Thompson they were
glowing, genial, liberal, sunset years.

The novel itself is written in a style heavy with modifiers; few
nouns or verbs escape without adjectival or adverbial companionship. The French are represented as hot blooded and sensual, unable to talk without using their hands, while the English have a
doughty coolness and courage which are admirable. There is no
doubt that the Americans of English stock have the sturdiest
character in the world, though it is amusing to have the French
around and watch the way they talk to excess and drink wine
with their meals. Here, consciously, are all the elements of the
rhetorical appeal of a Populist manifesto.

While they idealized the beliefs of their readers, however,
Thompson and the other romancers of the turn of the century
betrayed the grave lack of confidence in its own ideals which had
overtaken America at century's end. Howells, for all his poking
into certain unpleasant commonplaces, expressed a faith in the
American character which was, somehow, of a continuous piece
with the American of earlier days. But the romancers, while they
idealized the virtues the American fancied himself to possess, had
to ignore social reality, and in so doing they simply gave up the
attempt to document the American character through a description of it in action. Alice, the heroine of the Thompson book,
is a democratic frontier lass, and presumably all the virtues Thomp-

son claims for his readers should be displayed by her. But what validates Alice, what proves that this child of the log cabin is as good as any highborn lady, is not her behavior but the revelation of the fact that she is a Tarleton—she really is a highborn lady. This revelation has its parallel in almost all the romances set in America. While the virtues of democracy are hymned, they are nevertheless no longer capable of demonstration, so that, even while foreign things are scorned, the only way to show that the rural democrat is the equal of the big-city society person or the European aristocrat is to reveal that, in point of fact, by birth he could if he chose take a seat in the best club in New York or could assume a title and an estate in England.

The high point in the unconscious revelation of loss of faith in the democratic character at the century's end was achieved by the most popular of the Indiana fiction writers, Booth Tarkington. He soared to immediate fame with *The Gentleman from Indiana* (1899), a novel about a young man who comes to Carlow, a small town in Indiana, to publish the local paper, and who in this environment performs so heroically in keeping with the values of rural America that ultimately he is triumphantly sent off to Congress.

The people of Carlow are "simple country people, and they know that God is good." [30] They recognize that "there are fat women who rock and rock on piazzas by the sea, and they speak of country people as the 'lower classes,' " [31] but they don't take this seriously. After all, as the cracker-barrel orator says, "I always had a dim sort of feeling that the people out in these parts knew more—had more *sense* and were less artificial, I mean—and were kinder, and tried less to be somebody else, than almost any other people anywhere. And I believe it's so." [32] The novel is about how Carlow manages its troubles with the Ku Klux Klan, and all the evil in the plot originates outside of town at the Klan's strong point, Six Cross Roads, where an inbred and degenerate breed resides. The plot pattern is clear: the rural American virtues as represented by Carlow and embodied in "the gentleman

from Indiana" will triumph over degeneracy as represented by Six
Cross Roads. This is more than the rich Eastern world of fat
women has been able to do when faced with foreign degeneracy.
Tarkington philosophizes:

> There are, here and there, excrescent individuals who, through
> stock decadence, or their inability to comprehend republican con-
> ditions, are not assimilated by the body of the country; but many
> of these are imports, while some are exports. Our foreign-born
> agitators now and then find themselves removed by the police to
> institutions of routine, while the romantic innocents who set up
> crests in the face of an unimpressionable democracy are apt to be
> lured by their own curious ambitions, or those of their women-folk,
> to spend a great part of their time in or about the villas of Albion,
> thus paid for its perfidy; and although the anarchists and bubble-
> hunters make a noise, it is enormously out of proportion to their
> number, which is relatively very small, and neither the imported
> nor the exported article can be taken as characteristic of our coun-
> try. For the American is one who soon fits any place, or into any
> shaped hole in America, where you can set him down.[33]

Well and fine; so much for Howells' anarchists in *Hazard* and
James's Americans abroad. The fantasy may be puerile, but it is
of a piece with its holders.

What is reprehensible is that, as matters turn out, our gentleman is a gentleman and redeems the Indiana virtues not because
of his behavior but because, as is revealed, he was the darling of
his class in an Ivy League college, the cynosure of all eyes at
gatherings of the Four Hundred, a skilled yachtsman, and a catch
desired by the mother of every debutante from Bar Harbor to
Newport. Rural democracy is better than Eastern degeneracy because he, with all the accomplishments of the East, chooses it.
It is incapable of demonstrating that superiority unless it is so
knighted. Indiana's ennoblement comes through the recognition
of it by what it claims most to despise.

In the following year Tarkington published *Monsieur Beaucaire,*
a brief romantic charade about an eighteenth-century French

prince posing as a barber. Thematically it differs little from the earlier novel, for in it the prince insists on having his merits as a man recognized and advances this democratic lesson through showing that, though a barber, he is the equal of any aristocrat in society at dueling, gambling, lovemaking, and observations of the code of honor. But of course he happens to be aristocracy's equal in all these affairs because he really is a prince in breeding and upbringing, and the punishment visited on those who undemocratically snub the supposed barber is that they must live with the realization that they snubbed a prince. The failure of democratic character to be its own reward in *A Gentleman from Indiana* was re-emphasized in the seemingly quite different *Monsieur Beaucaire*. Romance, which flattered the democratic reader, also tacitly admitted that the possibility of a democratic hero had ceased to exist in fiction.

The rise of the romance to a position of dominance in the late nineties and the first decade of the twentieth century marks the final step in the disintegration of faith in the natural abilities of the native American. As social reality yielded steadily to the "outside" forces, romance came more and more to be used as conscious escape. The more clamorously the native virtues were praised, the more desperately they were in need of shoring up, until finally they were validated not through their inherent superiority in action but through recognition by the despised outside world. Romance at the century's end applied a patch to the mortal wound inflicted on the rural ideal by industrial America.

Crushed Yet Complacent:

Hamlin Garland and Henry Blake Fuller

amlin Garland believed himself a part of the tradition of Western literary influence established by Howells and Twain. Born in 1860, he was the son of a Wisconsin farmer who fought in the Civil War, and he was raised on the series of homesteads in Wisconsin, Iowa, and South Dakota that his westering father occupied in his effort to offset the steadily falling crop prices that led to the Populist revolt.[1] During this Western upbringing Garland, through reading and listening to the conversation of his elders, developed a vision of a New England free of the physical hardships of the prairies, and after rude public schooling he sold out his claim and went to Boston to seize the dream. There he kicked around in poverty, reading in the public library, then moved from menial employment to teaching, lecturing, reviewing, and essay-writing. He called on Howells and on Whitman and by mid-1888 was engaged in a career as a writer of local-color stories which, however, unlike most stories of that genre, expressed outrage at the social injustices suffered by the farmer rather than sentimental charm at the folkways practiced in the countryside. In 1891 his stories were gathered into a book, *Main-Travelled Roads,* so titled because the main-traveled road, wrote Garland, "is a long and wearyful" one with a "dull little town at one end and a home of toil at the other. Like the main-travelled road of life it is traversed by many classes of people, but the poor and weary predominate." [2]

Howells recognized the book's achievement with his characteristic vigorous generosity.

If anyone is still at a loss to account for the uprising of the farmers in the West, which is the translation of the Peasants' War into modern and republican terms, let him read *Main-Travelled Roads* and he will begin to understand, unless, indeed, Mr. Garland is painting the exceptional rather than the average. The stories are full of those gaunt, grim, sordid, pathetic, ferocious figures, whom our satirists find so easy to caricature as Hayseeds, and whose blind groping for fairer conditions is so grotesque to the newspapers and menacing to the politicians. They feel that something is wrong, and they know that the wrong is not theirs. The type caught in Mr. Garland's book is not pretty; it is ugly and often ridiculous; but it is heart-breaking in its rude despair.[3]

From this volume Garland went on to other stories and to novels, did battle in the Congress of Authors at the Columbian Exposition on behalf of realistic fiction, settled into the literary society of Chicago, where he was a prominent personality, especially friendly with the novelist Henry Blake Fuller, and then moved on to New York, where he discovered and encouraged Stephen Crane and hobnobbed with Howells and the foremost members of the literary establishment. In the early nineties he began to find his way into the pages of the *Century,* and by the decade's close he was in demand with the new wide-circulation periodicals, such as those of Bok and McClure. When the successful Garland decided finally to purchase a home in his native Wisconsin, he had to scour the state for a man who could build an open-hearth fireplace in it. So completely had the West grown up as he was moving to fame that the fireplace he sought out of nostalgic dedication to a frontier memory was now considered a primitive feature, in every way inferior to the kitchen range and the enclosed heater; the men who could make it had disappeared.

The broad outline of Hamlin Garland's career thus presents the pattern of the country boy who made good in the literary capitals and returned home to take up farming as a recreation. It provides a seeming continuity with the tradition of Howells, however, only so long as it is not furnished with details. When documented, the pattern turns to one of defeat.

Garland's father had not come back to tranquillity after Appomattox. "His war with the South was over, and his fight, his daily running fight with nature and against the injustice of his fellow-men was begun again." [4] The comforts of camp life, where wife and hungry children were out of sight and where Java instead of pea coffee was served, were greater than those of the homestead. When 1892 found him working in South Dakota yet another farm that failed to yield an adequate income, he realized that in the almost thirty years since the war he had worked his way across the "flowery savannah" of the Mississippi Valley, which had dominated his visions, only to come up against the semi-arid valleys of the Rockies, and he turned eastward to Wisconsin in defeat.

His children and the children of his contemporaries now dreamed of Colorado (about which Garland was later to write his most popular romances) rather than the Plains, and of a life of cattle-raising or mining or hunting, rather than farming. They would wester a bit further and stay ahead of the troubles; the land was not played out yet; its promise had simply changed in form and location. If Hamlin Garland did not attach himself to this dream immediately, but came to it later to romanticize it, he did respond overwhelmingly to the accompanying element, the need to escape the grasp of the powers invisible on the farm but nevertheless in control of its desperate realities. Though he read Emerson and Hawthorne, the East he pictured in his imagination came from his father's talk of the great days of anti-slavery sentiment. For him Boston was primarily the home of Garrison and Webster, and when he went there it was in pursuit of a career that would place him in passionate contact with a new species of abolitionism. He found that new species one night in Faneuil Hall—its prophet was Henry George—and he followed it into Populism and in and out of the sporadic flirtations the Democratic Party had with reform. When the hungry farm lad read on in the Boston Public Library after satisfying his curiosity about *Leaves of Grass* (which had been unavailable to him before and which even there was double-starred and lent only to serious students), he spent his hours with Darwin and Spencer, Helmholtz and Haeckel. His few acquaintances in Boston led him to the Boston School of Oratory, where he quickly turned from being student to being teacher. Here in the East was a version of education understandable in terms of his Western background of public learning with its emphasis on the arts of declamation. Though he met a number of the literati of Boston in the eighties, the greatest illuminations came from an actor: "Edwin Booth in one hour taught me more . . . wonders, more of the beauty of the English language than all my instructors and all of my books." [5]

When Garland, like others from the West, came to belles-lettres, he appreciated them not as experiential constructs but as reference works on how to beautify one's ideas in language which would command the respect of an audience. The School of Oratory furthered the "Gems from Literature" tradition of his Western country schoolhouse.

Hamlin Garland's youth had prepared him for a career as a reform orator if he could bring to it the necessary zeal and stamina, or as an essayist and lecturer on the "beauties" of literary masterpieces. It had not equipped him to be a writer of local-color stories, for this was a genre based on a fundamentally tranquil and loving sense of region and developed as a result of conscious literary practice. While it had its bleaker and more critical examples—Garland approvingly reviewed one, Joseph Kirkland's *Zury* (1887)—it was mainly sentimental in effect, though it could be realistically picturesque in detail. It was not pursued, therefore, by social critics but was practiced, in the main, by professional writers who had served their apprenticeships as essayists, or by maiden ladies of independent income who had turned the invidious gossip habit of village life to more genial literary uses. Garland himself did not for a good while consider writing fiction because he knew of no works which used region as the basis for social commentary, and he pursued his aims through essays and lectures, getting a small income from chats on the felicities of the classics and from book reviews.

In 1887, however, he returned to the farm in South Dakota to help out as his father's hired hand, and en route he stopped in Chicago to talk with the lawyer Joseph Kirkland, who had written tellingly of the meanness of life in downstate Illinois. Kirkland told the young man that fiction was the best field for the expression of the ideas which simmered in him, and encouraged him to show the injustices of farm life in stories. The message Garland picked up in Chicago was dramatized when he reached home and found his mother, bleak and worn from her arduous and monotonous tasks and isolated from all comfort and companionship, in a shacklike house in the middle of the winds. He reacted instantly and began sending Kirkland his outraged impressions, not knowing just how they could be pointed into stories, and the kindly lawyer responded with suggestions on how Garland could convert his feelings into fiction. By mid-1888 Hamlin Garland was a writer of local color stories. Some of them, reminiscences of the farm of his boyhood, were misty and a good deal resembled the typical stories in the genre. But others, while they perhaps came out nowhere from the point of view of action, were crude but moving expressions of their author's sense of despair. Both kinds were in the collection *Main-Travelled Roads,* which grew from six stories in the 1891 edition, to twelve stories in that of 1893.

The emotional center of most of these stories is the inhuman condition of the prairie farmer's wife, cut off from community and doomed to a day-in, day-out drudgery from which no emancipation can reasonably be expected. The hopelessness of her condition is particularly illustrated in three of the stories. In "A Good Fellow's Wife" a woman takes over her bankrupt husband's business and even after he strikes it rich and pays off she continues in business, realizing in her money-making power a satisfaction that domestic drudgery never brought her. Now "her love had friendship in it, but less of sex, and no adoration." [6] But she is a town wife; her escape only underlines the dilemma of the farm wife, who shares her defeats but cannot share her triumph. "A Branch Road" deals with a man who has left the farm to make his way in life and now returns to see his childhood sweetheart, who has since married and raised a family on the farm. She is a battered ruin of her former self, made coarse, ugly, and demoralized by the quality of her daily life. Love is now dead between them: he can muster up only pity, she self-pity. The most moving of this group of stories is "A Day's Pleasure," in which a careworn farm wife accompanies her husband on the long dusty ride to town and then, carrying her complaining baby, walks the streets of the town, making that trip only because this empty visit to nobody is better than yet another day alone with her toil. A town wife sees her from her window and immediately senses the desperation and the yearning which have led to the farm wife's aimless walking the streets with a heavy child. She asks her in and entertains her with food and conversation. "The day had been made beautiful by human sympathy," [7] says the author, and that is all there can be to it. Tomorrow the drudgery will begin again, and, in spite of the happy accident of that one day, there is no guarantee that any tomorrow will contain more fulfillment than an aimless, yearning stroll on a dusty sidewalk.

The story in the collection which came to be best known is "Under the Lion's Paw," a tale of the desperation of a farmer who must meet payments which have soared because of the improvements he himself has made upon the land. The banker who holds the mortgage has done nothing, yet will get the profits of the farmer's labor, and in his rage at the situation the farmer determines to murder his creditor as an expression of his contempt for the system. He is recalled from this purpose by the sight of his child, and for her sake again submits to a cycle of toil which can only enrich another. Written as an illustration of the Henry George thesis on unearned increment, the story surpasses its propagandistic intent because Garland fastens its movement to the rhythm of the wheat crop and restrains his elsewhere all too prominent instinct for editorializing in place of dramatizing. This story served Garland as his chief text when he went about the country reading to reform groups.

Main-Travelled Roads was Garland's first and best book, but in its uncertain use of language it revealed the elements of its author's incapacity for the literary work he was pursuing. The lunch served the lonely farm wife in "A Day's Pleasure" is a moving symbol of the human community regularly denied her, but Garland insists on helping out the contrast inherent in the scene by calling it a "dainty luncheon." The false ring of the phrase works against the desired effect, just as, on a larger scale, does the uneven play of narration and dialogue in "A Branch Road" when Garland says of the returned lover, "As he went on his argument rose to the level of Browning's philosophy"—only to offer as a representative statement: "God don't expect a toad to stay in a stump and starve if it can get out." [8] The author's characterization of such homely dialogue is ludicrous not because it debases Browning's philosophy (if one happens to admire it), but because it belittles the ability of his simple tortured characters to represent their own woes and their own dignities in their own words and gestures.

In almost all his work Garland's settings and characters are resistant to the creeds he seeks to lodge with them, so that in his works of social protest he is left stating rather than dramatizing. He was seldom sure of his language. Though he could grasp the vernacular ("Haskins, this is Mr. Butler—no relation to Ben— the hardest-working man in Cedar County"),[9] he distrusted its respectability and betrayed his awe of a genteel culture by constantly resorting to constructions designed to show he was not limited by the life of which he wrote but had mastered a wider experience. So frequently Garland says not that his characters ate, but rather that they "ate of" food; and things are not like other things, they are "like unto" [10] them. After *Main-Travelled Roads,* regardless of what else happens in a Garland fiction, the language constantly betrays the realistic subject matter by coming to its aid with injections of loftiness. When finally, in the mid-nineties, Garland settled into writing romances about life in the Rockies, this was not so much a betrayal of his promise as an acceptance of the themes for which his language was better suited.

Hamlin Garland could see into the emotional center of the injustices he scored, and he could portray it thus:

> Most of the girls were precocious in the direction of marriage, and brought all their little girl allurements to bear with the same purpose which directs the coquetry of a city belle. At sixteen they had beaux, at seventeen many of them actually married, and at eighteen they might often be seen with their husbands, covered with dust, clasping wailing babies in their arms; at twenty they were not infrequently thin and bent in the shoulders, and flat and stiff in the hips, having degenerated into sallow and querulous wives of slovenly, careless husbands.[11]

The life of the farm woman is not betrayed by words like "coquetry," "belle," and "beaux," for this is the stilted diction of her youthful wonder and conveys the pathos of her actual situation. When, however, Garland attempts to illustrate the potential which resides in the farm girl once she is freed of economic hardship, then he cannot get beyond romantic ejaculations. His hero looks at her and says, "You splendid creature!"

After *Main-Travelled Roads* Garland entered upon a divided career, one half that of the reform orator who cried out at the grievances dramatized in "Under the Lion's Paw," the other half that of an ambitious writer seeking wider audiences than those supplied by reform journals such as the *Arena*. The temporary fusion of local color and social comment that had taken place in the heat of his reaction to his mother's forlorn condition, and that he had been helped to shape by Kirkland, disintegrated in the face of a success which called forth both his desire to speak more directly of social problems and his desire to be accepted as more than a tamed peasant by the genteel circle which attracted him. This circle, of whom Richard Watson Gilder, editor of the *Century*, was representative, could offer the kind of recognition which, finally, a writer conditioned as Garland was conditioned needed. The voice of the people was not effective if it spoke for and about them but only to them, because the people did not read such fiction. The seal of approval had to be sought, rather, from out-side sources which were fundamentally inimical to such fiction, but which, on the other hand, stood for the reading public. To resist these sources and continue in the Whitmanesque hope of finding an audience in the simple democratic man who was the true subject of American literature required a self-confidence and a dedication to literature as an art with which the postwar prairie culture did not equip its sons. The typical qualities of the American farmer and mechanic, Whitman told Garland in 1888, are "his good manners, his quiet heroism, his generosity, even his good real grammar." [12] Such a portrayal, as *Main-Travelled Roads* showed, did not meet Garland's reality. He sought out ruder and more de-feated individuals to embody his theme and expressed it in a loftier language for his audience.

From October 1891 to April 1894 Garland pursued a course of writing and lecturing so active that it rarely found him in the same city for longer than a month. The fiction he produced, freed of the temporary circumstances which had fused the stories in *Main-Travelled Roads,* was an elaboration of the faults rather than the merits in the first collection of stories. *A Spoil of Office* (1892), for instance, a novel about a Western man of the people succeed-ing in the great dream of that people, politics, is full of assertions that men working together will find truth, but is singularly lacking in any reality to match these oratorical claims. The heroine, sup-posedly a "new" woman, is actually that oldest fixture of romantic fiction, the shining star. She is totally perfect and absolutely wooden. The hero loves her, realizing that she is from a more cultivated social class, and Garland sees his fascination with her as being in complete coherence with his hero's background. Gar-land, finally, cannot conceive of conduct as being successful unless it finds its reward in the quarter from which it has been excluded.

In his criticism, during the same period, Garland frantically sought to close this gap and find some aesthetic which would permit the literature of protest to triumph in some way other than by being assimilated and modified by the literary establishment. He was fighting himself far more than he was fighting outsiders. When Gilder had requested him in 1890 to rewrite certain "vulgarisms" in his dialogue, reminding him that the *Century* is "being sent into almost every cultivated household in the United States," [13] his response was overenthusiastic:

> I feel the pressure which is brought to bear upon you on these lines, and I am perfectly willing to make compromises to make your predicament less vexatious. I feel that you would not ask me to sacrifice unnecessarily, and I think you must know me well enough to know that everything I do has *lift* in it, that I want to bring beauty and comfort and intelligence into the common American home. All I write or do has that underlying purpose. [14]

And as his mind began to accept this notion rather than that of a fiction of social protest his reforming instincts fought back by entering the polemical arena of literary criticism and battling loudly in lectures and essays against the establishment.

"The study of evolution," Garland declared, "has made the present the most critical and self-analytical of all ages known to us. It has liberated the thought of the individual as never before, and the power of tradition grows fainter year by year." [15] The realistic writer, whom Garland called a veritist, is enlisted in the cause of evolution, and in his stories of life, which are true if not pleasant, he attempts to provoke thought and speed up the process of social self-analysis which will result in the liberation of the individual from a dead past.

To advance this tenuous connection between evolution, social criticism, and realistic literature, Garland felt compelled to smash the confining traditions which, he believed, stunted the new growth. Howells saw that if realism was to be the dominant mode of American literature, the reason was that it was most closely related to American and therefore, in turn, to British literary traditions. But Garland confused tradition, the subsoil of literature, with restraint, the blighting effects of certain social conditions; he felt that to champion veritism was equivalent to shouting that the past is dead and has no bearing on the present. This error, in turn, lured him into another, the assertion that when modern man completes his liberation from the past centralization will end and the future curve of literature will be from the city back to the folk in the countryside:

> Never again will any city dominate American literature; and, in my judgment, there will be no over-topping personalities in art. The average is rising, the peaks will seem to sink. There are other reasons for the revolt against the domination of the East over the whole nation. New York, like Boston, is too near London. It is no longer American. It is losing touch with the people.[16]

Here was literary Populism with a vengeance! Its greatest pathos resided in the fact that Garland's very career at the moment of his enunciating it was giving it the lie.

He argued that the West should aim at being wise rather than cultured, because wisdom was democratic while culture was decadent and aristocratic. When that argument reached its dead end, he turned again to Populist models and asserted, "I might adduce arguments based on the difference in races; I might speculate upon the influence of the Irish, and Jews and Italians upon New York and Boston, and point out the quicker assimilation of the Teutonic races in the West." [17] And all the while he trimmed his work to the requirements of the *Century*. Even in his demands for veritism, his prose gushed unveritistically: "Gardens will bloom where the hot sand now drifts. . . . Cities will rise where now the elk and mountain lions are." [18] His friends smiled; even his critical opponents saw that this great Western bear who was flailing about with such abandon was, really, an amiable creature who would soon be tamed to the comfort of all.

The domestication of Hamlin Garland began in earnest in the Congress on Literature at the World's Columbian Exposition. This Congress was one of many held at the fair—there were Congresses on Commerce and Finance, on Evolution, and on Religion, among others—the theory being that "the gathering of the peoples of the world at a great exposition furnishes an opportunity for association and conference to those who are widely scattered geographically but are united in interests." [19] Here on July 13, 1893, Garland delivered a paper on "Local Color in Fiction" that challenged the assumptions of an earlier paper given by the popular romance writer Mary Hartwell Catherwood, and Eugene Field saw in this confrontation just the right material for his column in the Chicago *Daily News*. Field, an urbane wit, was one of those newspaper saloon pundits who chided society but were grateful for the free amusement it daily afforded; the next great representative of the tradition was to be H. L. Mencken, though Mencken's tone was far more raucous. Field had made delightful contributions to children's literature ("The Gingham Dog and the Calico Cat" is an example) and was an avid student and biographer of Horace and a knowledgeable collector of rare books. In the latter pursuit he had traveled abroad a number of times and was fond of discomfiting the London booksellers with his demand that they locate for him an unexpurgated copy of the poems of Mrs. Felicia Hemans. He would also speak of the need for a "Fireside Hannah More" and wondered aloud whether one could not edit *Pilgrim's Progress* so as to make it safe for children. Eugene Field, in short, saw the gaps and hypocrisies in American society but had made his peace with them, and he was committed, from the vantage point of a column, to enjoying the passing show and helping others also to enjoy it. Now the Garland-Catherwood difference on whether literature should be realistic or romantic presented itself as a ready subject for newspaper fun, and with his sense of how to make the most of an item he took Mrs. Catherwood's side:

> Mr. Garland's heroes sweat and do not wear socks; his heroines eat cold huckleberry pie and are so unfeminine as not to call a cow "he."
>
> Mrs. Catherwood's heroes—and they are the heroes we like—are aggressive, courtly, dashing, picturesque fellows, and her heroines are timid, stanch, beautiful women, and they, too, are our kind of people.

Mr. Garland's in hoc signo is a dung-fork or a butter paddle; Mrs. Catherwood's is a lance or an embroidery needle. Give us the lance and its companion every time.[20]

Field then went on to say how much he liked Garland personally —how civilized the fellow really was when you talked with him— and he artfully explained the discrepancy between the real Garland and Garland the critic by saying that he got all those ridiculous ideas from Howells and the East, not from the West. The humorous reversal of the Garland thesis was a palpable hit, and Field concluded with another:

So we are glad to hear that there is a prospect of Mr. Garland's making his home here in Chicago, where the ramping prairie winds and the swooping lake breezes contribute to the development of the humane fancy. Verily there will be more joy in Chicago over the one Garland that repenteth than over ninety-and-nine Catherwoods that need no repentance.[21]

In a letter printed in the column, Garland responded in good humor, "It certainly is a curious thing to see the lords and ladies who partake of ambrosia and sip nectar making a last desperate stand in the West—the home of Milwaukee beer and Chicago pork," [22] only to be smothered in affection by Mrs. Catherwood's letter: Mr. Garland's "big, sympathetic, manly heart is so burdened with the human struggle of to-day that he will not let himself look away from it." [23] She then aimed her embroidery needle at his weak spot, the denial of tradition, and simplistically followed its political implications from her point of view: "Pulling down, trampling and denying Yesterday and setting up an apotheosis of To-day was what the French revolution vainly tried to do." [24] Field's last word came in the form of a tale about two men in a first-class railway car in Russia bemoaning the life and destiny of the peasants and the land which they saw from their moving window. Finally, after sharing a lunch of pâté de foie gras and Chambertin, they introduced themselves to each other as Leo Tolstoi and Hamlin Garland.

The apostle of veritism was, indeed, living the life predicted for him by Field as he married and made his home in Chicago in 1894. In later years he admitted this and explained his dilemma in a discussion of clothing.[25] The Prince Albert frock coat, he said, was in the West the proper ceremonial garment for the American democrat. Even though it bore a royal name, it was assumed on holiday occasions by judges, professors, senators, doctors of divinity, and all other eminent representatives of republican principles. Its status as the uniform of the Western professional man was bolstered by the fact that it was as useful as it was dignified:

> It clothed with equal charity a man's stomach and his stern. Generous of its skirts, which went far to conceal a wrinkled trousers, it could be worn with a light tie at a formal dinner or with a dark tie at a studio tea, and it was equally appropriate at a funeral or a wedding.[26]

But the Middle West put on company manners for its Columbian Exposition, and guests at its grand occasions dressed in the "livery of privilege," the claw-hammer suit, associated in the Western mind with dukes, monopolistic pirates, and parasitic aesthetes. Invited to the homes of Mrs. Potter Palmer and her circle to meet distinguished guests, and required to escort the ladies in to dinner, should the Western artist conform further by assuming the proper social garb? If he did not, the invitations would cease; they were already dwindling. If he did, then it was good-by to Walt Whitman and John Burroughs, the heroes of the long beard and soft collar, and what they stood for.

In his perplexity, Garland consulted Howells, also telling him that he planned soon to visit England. "My dear fellow," Howells told his disciple, "why don't you make your proposed visit to England, buy your evening suit there and on your return to Chicago plead the inexorability of English social usages?" [27] Garland gratefully did so. The domestication was complete. By way of England the Midwest had reclaimed her own.

The surrender which Garland thus described received a loving and humorous fictional exposition in a story written by his close

Chicago friend, Henry Blake Fuller. In "The Downfall of Abner Joyce" Fuller introduces the reader to a man who has published a collection of short stories under the title of *This Weary World,* and who responds to increasing adulation from Chicago society by emphasizing the gruffness of his proletarian views. He had earned his living as an instructor of elocution, where his allegiances were to "the old-time classical school, to the ideal that still survives, inexpugnably in the rustic breast and even in the national senate; the Roman Forum was never completely absent from his eye, and Daniel Webster remained the undimmed pattern of all that man— man mounted on his legs—should be." [28] With his second book, a novel, Abner widens his acquaintance to a number of reformers outside of his group of Readjusted Taxers and finds himself more frequently in the salons of the rich, debating his ideas with them. He is, says Fuller, "possessed of the fatalistic belief in the efficacy of mere legislation such as dominates the rural townships of the West," [29] and in accompaniment to this he has a lofty distrust of foreign ways, dress coats, wine, society, and the trusts, which occupy his mind as symbols of orgy and spoliation. As the sophisticated Medora Giles, who has been abroad, progresses in her efforts to tame him and make him marriageable, so Abner stoutly assails the hypocrisies of society with his tongue while gradually easing his body into its comforts. He insists that the urban problem is temporary, that the country will continue to be the center of national life, and that any writing which is not about pressing social problems is dabbling. When Abner tells another writer to forget the past, that writer responds, "Good deal harder to forget than never to have learned at all. *That's* easy." [30]

Medora and the felicities of life work together to bring about Abner's downfall, and at the end he accepts her and evening dress. Fuller concludes:

Yes, Abner had brought down, one after another, all the pillars of the temple. But he had dealt out his own fate along with the fate of the rest: crushed yet complacent, he lay among the ruins. The glamour of success and of association with the successful was dazzling him. The pomp and luxury of plutocracy inwrapped him, and he had a sudden sweet shuddering vision of himself dining with still others of the wealthy just because they *were* wealthy, and prominent, and successful. Yes, Abner had made his compromise with the world. He had conformed. He had reached an understanding with the children of Mammon. He—a great, original genius—had become just like other people. His downfall was complete.[31]

The statement that in his downfall Abner had also brought down the pillars of the temple is meant in irony, for this destruction has consisted of his convincing the capitalist that the small reforms in politics which he did support were meaningless, so that the capitalist turned from using his money to fight the bosses to controlling the bosses through bribery; convincing the society ladies that their charities missed the main point of social injustice, so that those ladies abandoned philanthropy altogether; and convincing the romantic novelist that his sketches of life did not look real life in the face, so that the novelist, accepting his limitations, turned entirely from modern life to the successful confection of historical romances.

When the story appeared in 1901, Garland, his marriage a happy one and his career well supported by the magazines, accepted it in good humor, just as he had cheerfully responded to Field's predictions eight years earlier. Fuller was a good friend, and Garland did not mind sitting as his model even for so unflattering a portrait, since at least it was painted with affection and not with bitterness.

In point of fact, Henry Blake Fuller was a man better qualified to express the social ferment of the nineties in fiction than was Garland, although his forays into this area always had the air of exercises for the left hand. Unlike Garland's, his seemed to be a case of would not rather than could not. A balanced and light cynicism stopped him short of ever giving himself over to a career in realism.

His qualifications for that career were, predictably, the reverse of those of Garland, and therefore superior.[32] He was the last male descendant (in him the direct male line ended) of Dr. Samuel Fuller, the Plymouth Plantation physician whom Governor Bradford had sent to Salem to succor the ailing in the newly landed crew of John Endicott in 1628; his grandfather was a cousin of Emerson's unpredictable friend Margaret Fuller. Born into comfortable circumstances in Chicago in 1857, Fuller, after graduating with an extraordinary record from high school, chose to abandon his formal education in favor of learning the banking business. When he was twenty-two he embarked on the sort of education he preferred and took the Grand Tour, in the course of which he perfected his Italian. Back in America, he did some writing, traveled a good deal, did very little work, and then, on the death of his father in 1885, took his position as head of the family and managed its business affairs, which consisted chiefly of real estate. "We of Chicago are sometimes made to bear the reproach that the conditions of our local life draw us towards the sordid and the materialistic," says one of Fuller's characters. "Now, the most vital and typical of our human products is the real-estate agent: is he commonly found tied down by earth-bound prose?" [33] Thus lightly could he view a life given to the management of property, which he spiced with the easy composition of burlesques for humor magazines, and an occasional novel, story, or serious essay. Until his mother's death in 1907, Fuller lived at the family home, and when even writing failed to occupy his spare time he turned to music, composing both words and music for two operettas—never produced—as well as turning *Cyrano de Bergerac* into light opera.

Leisurely and refined, with a nimble wit and a taste for nuance, Henry Blake Fuller sat in his native place as it grew from a village to a city of more than two million, and, when the spirit moved him, attempted to capture something of what he had observed. But the spirit did not always move him in that direction. His first book, the direct result of his love of Italy, is a fictionalized travel work, *The Chevalier of Pensieri-Vani*. It defies criticism. Although it breathes frivolity on almost every page, the book is nevertheless a feat of elegance and precision, and although it first appeared in an edition for which Fuller paid, in 1886, it quickly drew the admiration of Lowell, Howells, and Charles Eliot Norton, and the Century publishing firm took it over. His next work, *The Châtelaine of La Trinité,* was of the same category as *The Chevalier* and retained many of the same characters. Again, it read like the finger exercise of a promising pianist, executed so brilliantly that his school of velocity was better than many another performer's sonatas.

Fuller had also been making attempts at a story of Chicago, and when the Columbian Exposition raised an interest in everything connected with Chicago, including its fiction, he took out his earlier studies and worked them into a novel, *The Cliff-Dwellers* (1893). He said that the question the book dramatized was "Is it better for a young man to marry a girl who has pleasant, well-disposed family connections, yet who is rather flimsy and deficient herself, or for him to marry a girl who is much finer and stronger in herself, yet who has a disadvantageous and even disreputable set of relatives?" [34] The theme was that even in America marriage was less a matter between individuals than it was between families—almost the precise theme that Howells had pursued in *April Hopes.*

But *The Cliff-Dwellers*—the title refers to the skyscraper in which the action takes place and which was a structure then more characteristic of Chicago than of any other city—focused its readers' attention on Chicago, a city prominent in 1893, and Fuller thought that even his warmest admirers lost sight of his theme in praising the manner in which he brought Chicago to literature. They cannot be blamed, for the theme is overshadowed by the setting, the depiction of the society of go-getting Chicago financiers who boast that the United States is like a sailing ship, with Boston as the mizzenmast, New York as the mainmast, and Chicago as the foremast. Their Chicago is a Chicago where "prosperity had drugged patriotism into unconsciousness, and where the bare scaffoldings of materialism felt themselves quite independent of the graces and draperies of culture." [35] Without bitterness, indeed with a sympathetic understanding for these money men with whom he

himself was in weekly business dealings, Fuller peers at their courtships, their marriages, and their avocations, seeing those as chan-
neled by the central impulse in their life, the profit motive. When
the rich Mr. Ogden dies, Fuller writes, "George undertook the
charge of such arrangements as recognized the old New-Englander
as a dead man merely, and McDowell subsequently took charge of
those which recognized him as a dead property-owner. First, the
funeral; afterwards the Probate Court." [36] Here, deftly, is revealed
the great difference between Fuller and Howells, whom he so much
resembled. Money and people in Fuller are inseparable. Money is
the great measure of American life, even of American death. Men
make it; women use it.

In the pages of Henry Blake Fuller money fully enters American
fiction as motive and measure. The courtship plot is not, ultimately,
used as it was by Howells, as a means of examining the morality
which underlies the American pattern of manners. It is, rather, the
starting point for a description of the way in which money does the
talking in American society, whoever may do the actual speaking.
This is why Theodore Dreiser in 1911 asserted that Howells' view
precluded what he considered to be the real throbbing American
life, and went on to say, "If one wanted to put finger on the name of
the man who first recognized this, strove to work true to his ideals
and pioneered the way to a real expression of American life, I
should say put it on the name of Henry B. Fuller." [37] Indeed, the
Chicago of Dreiser's *The Titan* is based on the description of the
layers of society given by Fuller in his second and final novelistic
treatment of that city, *With the Procession* (1895).

This novel is concerned with the last days of David Marshall, a
wealthy Chicagoan who built up his fortune by establishing a
wholesale supply business when the city was little more than an
Indian settlement. His fortune is the typical Chicago mercantile
fortune—not so large as those of the new speculators, but solid—
and his tenure in Chicago makes him old family, entitled to enter
the highest circle of society. But his simplicity and his devotion to
business have made him content with business alone. Now, as he

declines toward death, depicted by Fuller in the image of the shutting down of a mint, the women in his family are preparing to make an entrance into society; they want to go "with the procession." The novel can, then, center on that moment in Chicago when wealth had compensated for the infancy of the city so that it aspired to purchase the culture it had not had time to develop, and how this affected the basic Chicago type, the merchant.

The fundamental nature of Marshall is described thus:

> Why did he go to bed at half-past nine? In order that he might be at the store by half-past seven. Why must he be at the store at half-past seven? Because a very large area to the west and northwest of the town looked to him for supplies of teas, coffees, spices, flour, sugar, baking-powder; because he had always been accustomed to furnish these supplies; because it was the only thing he wanted to do; because it was the only thing he could do; because it was the only thing he was pleased and proud to do; because it was the sole thing which enabled him to look upon himself as a useful, stable, honored member of society.[38]

But his women's aspirations now force him into a society which looks beyond business to refinement, and the aspirations leave this honest soul baffled:

> Art in all its forms was an inexplicable thing; but more inexplicable still was the fact that any man could be so feeble as to yield himself to such trivial matters in a town where money and general success still stood ready to meet any live, practical fellow half-way—a fellow, that was to say, who knew an opportunity when he saw it. The desire of beauty was not an inborn essential of the normal human being. Art was not an integral part of that great frame of things; it was a mere surface decoration, and the artist was but for the adornment of the rich man's triumph—in case the rich man were, on his side, so feeble as to need to have his triumph adorned.[39]

The artists in the society of *With the Procession* bear out Marshall's view of their function. Bingham, the builder (suspiciously like the Burnham who built the Columbian Exposition), likens

Chicago to the Florence of the Medicis, claiming it is now at the point where the rich man who wants to live on in its annals must make his impress by employing the artists to build monuments for it. The recent fair pointed the way. Another character, Brower, points up the artificiality of such a view when he announces one of the principles which govern Fuller's outlook: "This town of ours labors under one peculiar disadvantage: it is the only great city in the world to which all its citizens have come for the one common, avowed object of making money." [40] For him Chicago is not yet ready for art because it is not yet a community, and he directs his efforts toward social work:

> "The thing to teach the public is this: that the general good is a different thing from the sum of the individual goods. Over in the Settlement we are trying to make those new-comers realize that they are a part of the body politic; perhaps we need another settlement to remind some of the original charter-members of the same fact!" [41]

Until the vast social gaps are closed, the city cannot have a meaningful expression in art, and the fair was, as the cynical Truesdale Marshall realizes, an evasion of the problem. The universal expectation seemed to be that the spirit of the White City would magically be transferred to the real Black City close at hand, "over which it was to hover as an enlightenment—through which it might penetrate as an informing force." [42]

With this novel Fuller had just about had his fill of Chicago as subject matter. He returned to it for a last glimpse, now totally satirical, in the three short stories in *Under the Skylights* (1901), one of which was the treatment of Garland's downfall. Another, "Little O'Grady *vs.* the Grindstone," spoofed the connection in Chicago between capital and art by describing the competition for the job of painting murals in the new Grindstone National Bank. The third story, "Dr. Gowdy and the Squash," goes after naturalism in art by giving it its *reductio ad absurdum:* a country boy masters the art of painting squashes, which he then frames, veritistically, in lichen-covered old fence slats with seed glued on them.

Garland hovers in the neighborhood of the target here also, as do other Chicagoans of the day in the fictionalized cast of characters shared by the three stories (Mrs. Potter Palmer is one of the more delightfully realized, in the character of Mrs. Eudoxia Pence). The air of *Under the Skylights,* however, is one of frivolity, of an artist who can stop to laugh and point up an absurdity but who cannot be bothered to criticize. This air even clings lightly to Fuller's two novels, which are forced into happy endings and which, while realistic, nevertheless reach into melodrama from time to time, or into burlesque to prop a sagging character or move a lagging plot. It is as if Fuller were saying: This is the picture I see. It is time to pay it some attention, but far too soon to take it seriously, for to take it seriously would be to ride the hobby-horse of a thesis and I prefer catching the color of these things to stifling them, as did Garland, with an iron law of life. If I were to do something about the situation, I would far sooner work in the settlements and attempt to make a community of Chicago than take the city and its problems seriously in a fiction. Real reform, he might have said, is tending to specific cases, not generalizing about society.

So Fuller abandoned this line of fiction and continued to compose burlesques, closet dramas, and romances, indulging in a consciously impish way a temper which felt deep affinities with Italian culture but which saw the ludicrousness of taking it seriously in Chicago. He signalized his retreat in *The Last Refuge* (1900), another of his fictionalized travel books, this time about a group of world-weary people seeking comfort in Sicily. Their travel is pure escape, the fulfillment of the daydreams of a bachelor real-estate man trapped in Chicago by his inertia. And in the novel a character who is a novelist speaks wistfully for Fuller looking back on his career in the nineties:

"I have lived, in fact, by the seashore without ever venturing into the water. Others have gone in before my eyes, and I have recorded, to the best of my endeavor, the exhilarations they appeared to feel, the dangers they appeared to brave. But as soon as the waves have stolen up to my own toes, I have always stepped back upon the dry sands." [43]

The tone of a life missed is the tone of a Henry James character, and James it was whom Fuller most deeply admired. But whereas James finally submitted himself to the destructive element through his art, Fuller hesitated on the shore, forlornly waiting for life to rise up and take him:

"I have always wished that it might steal up to me with its myriad fingers and drag me out, despite myself, to an exploration of its depths and dangers. Time and again I have hoped it might rush up the beach in one great wave, overwhelming me, hurrying me out, tossing me, buffeting me, destroying me at need, this wonderful sea of life!" [44]

But, of course, it did not rush up and Fuller fidgeted on the fringes of Chicago commerce, on the fringes of Chicago art, on the fringes of Chicago society, and dreamed of a Sicily of repose.

In 1899 Fuller rationalized his failure of commitment by explaining that the notion that every race must express itself in the arts is untenable. Races, like individuals, may be born inarticulate, and he, as an American, was a member of such a race: "Our national genius, however, *is* expressing itself with great fluency, volume, eloquence—in its own way and its own field: politics, finance, invention. The caucus is ours, and the trust; and we shall all doubtless get to heaven on flying-machines of our own contriving." [45] America, he argued, since it has no traditions, no accumulation of interests from the past, has taken life unfurnished and therefore must content itself with human interest, "our interest in one another." [46] The true American art will probably be biography, the expression of this kind of interest. Meanwhile, he concluded, speaking of literature, "Let us refrain from too serious attempts in in a field that heredity and environment and the spirit of the age all combine to make it difficult if not quite impracticable for us to work in." [47]

In the same vein he wrote to Garland upon the publication of the latter's life of Grant, commissioned by McClure, "I have an idea that the sort of book typified by your Grant may come to supersede the novel." [48] The illumination of actual human events, which was the stuff of the new mass-circulation magazine in the last years of the century, appeared to Fuller to be the logical reading for a people who had finally finished occupying their vast vacant land and were ready to turn to culture. Fiction, especially realistic fiction, held no interest for them compared to the human interest exploited in the journals. If they did not indulge fancy by reading romances, they would turn to facts and science by reading *McClure's* or *Munsey's*.

Howells hailed *The Cliff-Dwellers* as the companion to H. H. Boyesen's *The Mammon of Unrighteousness* (1891) in what he thought would be a wave of new novelists to take up the task where he had left it in *A Hazard of New Fortunes*. Boyesen, in reviewing Fuller's book, said, "Every good novel should, in my opinion, have its sociological bearing, should project the fates and doings of its characters against a background, distinctly felt and realized, of the larger civic and social life";[49] *The Cliff-Dwellers,* he felt, did this splendidly. Actually Fuller had gone well beyond Boyesen's heavy-handed condemnation of capitalistic hypocrisy. Boyesen in a vast number of wandering pages finally began dimly to glimpse what Fuller started with as incisive assumptions—that the men are the makers of money and the women the spenders. Boyesen wallows uncomfortably in the trough which Fuller saw it as meaningless to enter: how can reform be rationalized in a world governed by the predatory laws of survival? As Dreiser saw, Fuller brushed aside conventional motivation to get directly at money as the great mover, and he went past attempting to rationalize his Chicago in terms of laws to seeing it in terms of opportunities. He it was, whatever his failures, who opened the world of Frank Cowperwood and Jay Gatsby to fiction.

The paths of Garland and Fuller crossed in Chicago in 1894, when they became friends. Though they were both Midwesterners and had been born within three years of each other, their backgrounds differed greatly, as did their literary achievements. At century's end, however, both had made their peace. The best work of each—for Garland the first batch of stories and for Fuller the Chicago novels—indicated the shortcoming of the other. To reach a major achievement Fuller would have had to develop a controlling social view out of his witty observations of Chicago's faults. To go beyond his early accomplishment Garland would have had to develop the sense that the ills of society could not be cured by any one proposal—single tax or veritistic literature—and that the complexity that made such a cure impossible was the artist's resource, not his enemy. Both retreated, Fuller to fantasies and Garland to romances and journalistic commissions. And both, in 1899, could only view with awe the dedication of James. In that year Fuller wrote of his novelist on the beach, and Garland visited Lamb House to report: "This man lives on the highest plane. No man of his time is nobler in his aspirations as an artist. He has put the best of his life, and in a sense he has put all of his life, into his art." [50] But it was too late for Fuller to relinquish either Chicago or Italy in exchange for being released from his impotent suspension between the two, too late for Garland to correct the error of his upbringing with regard to tradition.

A third person was on hand in Chicago in the nineties to point the moral which Fuller himself had touched upon in *With the Procession*. Jane Addams had come to Chicago from downstate Illinois with both the comfortable material background of Fuller and the knowledge of rural life of Garland. She had from girlhood felt very keenly the chaotic nature of her society and the need for rebuilding. One of her persistent childhood dreams was "that every one in the world was dead excepting myself, and that upon me rested the responsibility of making a wagon wheel." [51] As a result of this recurring vision, the little girl haunted the blacksmith's shop for hours on end to store up this vital information.

Jane Addams first encountered degrading destitution when, touring abroad to finish her formal education, she saw the slums of London. Her shock called instantly to her mind something she had read by a literary man about how he too had been transfixed by the verbal connotations of what he had witnessed, and she reported:

> This is what we were all doing, lumbering our minds with literature that only served to cloud the really vital situation spread before our eyes. It seemed to me too preposterous that in my first view of the horror of East London I should have recalled De Quincey's literary description of the literary suggestions which had once paralyzed him.[52]

Jane Addams sought to shake this verbal paralysis through action, and in the fall of 1889 moved into Hull-House to begin the social settlement work which was to serve as a model in the next century. She regarded herself as an artist who had chosen a new medium: "There was in the earliest undertakings at Hull-House a touch of the artist's enthusiasm when he translates his inner vision through his chosen material into outward form."[53] Though she felt sympathetic toward reformers, she found herself too busy to join often with them because she was engaged in action while they were engaged in talk, and the situation, as she saw it, was yielding not to creeds so much as to deeds. Like the reformer in *With the Procession,* she felt that reform was the performing of duties rather than the insistence upon rights:

> The decade between 1890-1900 was, in Chicago, a period of propaganda as over against constructive social effort; the moment for marching and carrying banners, for stating general principles and making a demonstration, rather than the time for uncovering the situation and providing the legal measures and the civic organization through which new social hopes might make themselves felt.[54]

In the face of this, her generalizing habits yielded in 1890 to the concrete details, and she set to work, just as Theodore Dreiser, whose pauperized boyhood showed him nothing but the concrete details, was to move from them to a literary vocation. Thus the cross-pattern Jane Addams perceived thirty years later when she looked back on the nineties:

> Was the whole decade of discussion an illustration of the striking fact which has been likened to the changing of swords in Hamlet; that the abstract minds at length yield to the inevitable or at least grow less ardent in their propaganda, while the concrete minds, dealing constantly with daily affairs, in the end demonstrate the reality of abstract notions? [55]

Hamlin Garland did not yield to the concrete details and was carried, by his devotion to abstractions like veritism and the single tax, far off the literary mark. Henry Blake Fuller, immensely knowledgeable about the concrete details of mercantile Chicago, refused finally to abstract a pattern which would elevate that world into the field of artistic expression, contenting himself instead with his skillful and minor impressions. In the first years of the new century neither could any longer be taken seriously as an artist. Anchorless, they had accepted the drift of the nineties and allowed it to carry them along, Garland into hack work for the new popular magazines, Fuller into rationalizing that, after all, his was a land of commerce not of art.

The Tinkle of the Little Bell:

Magazines

By midpoint in the decade Hamlin Garland was an accepted writer in respectable journals. He reported:

> Magazine editors were entirely hospitable to me now, for my tales of the Indian and the miner had created a friendlier spirit among their readers. My later themes were, happily, quite outside the controversial belt. Concerned less with the hopeless drudgery, and more with the epic side of western life, I found myself almost popular. My critics . . . were able to praise. . . . Some of them assured me with paternal gravity that I might, by following their suggestions become a happy and moderately successful writer, and this prosperity, you may be sure, was reflected to some degree in the dining room of the old Homestead.[1]

But to stay successful, Garland found, he had to follow the market, and around 1895 that market was increasingly widened not by the *Century, Harper's, Scribner's,* and *Atlantic,* the sanctuaries of culture when he had begun to write, but by *McClure's, Munsey's,* and other magazines based on the literary principle that men as well as women could be made to buy and read magazines if the content was planned so as to catch them. This carried with it the financial corollary that advertising, not the price of the magazine, would be the principal source of income—a source hardly as yet tapped by the established organs of gentility. Though their influence at the start of the nineties was immense, by 1897 the four established publications did not together sell the number of copies *McClure's* did. Moreover, they were dependent, in the main, on subscribers, while the new magazine aimed at the newsstand.

Frank Munsey, a pioneer in the periodical revolution, had concluded early in the nineties that magazines of the *Century* class seemed made for anemics and that their editors lived in an artificial world devoid of human interest. On the other hand, he noted that the Sunday newspapers appealed to everybody and cost five cents as opposed to up to seven times as much for the magazines. "I became convinced that both the price and the magazines were wrong for a wide circulation," he said. "If a magazine should be published at ten cents and made light, bright, and lively, it might be a different story." [2] It was as Munsey had thought, and "light, bright, and lively" came to mean plenty of pictures of actresses and crowned heads. Soon S. S. McClure was in the field, as was John Brisben Walker with the *Cosmopolitan,* and, with variations, Edward Bok with the *Ladies' Home Journal,* as well as a score of others. When the century ended, these men had obliterated the notion that only an educated public would support a magazine and that it should therefore appeal to the discreet and cultivated. The monument built on the rubble of the older journals was the *Saturday Evening Post* of George Horace Lorimer, who took over the weekly in 1899, when it had a circulation of 1800, and made it the first American magazine to pass the million mark. The trick, Lorimer said, was to capture the American public's interest in business and romanticize it. The men would then buy and the women would follow. The English magazine, he felt, aimed at a leisure class, but there was none in America; the magazine must remember that those who read it worked.[3] The *Century* did not bear this in mind and was, in the face of the new competition, doomed.

The breakthrough to a larger, less literate public was made possible by the development of photoengraving. As McClure had realized, "the impregnability of the older magazines . . . was largely due to the costliness of wood-engraving. . . . The *Century Magazine* used, when I was working for it, to spend something like five thousand dollars a month on its engraving alone." [4] But now he could compete in quantity of illustrations because not only was photoengraving itself cheaper than wood engraving, but it enabled him to make pictures from photographs, which were cheap, instead of from drawings, which were expensive. He could have his fifteen-cent magazine, as Walker could have his twelve-and-a-half-center and Munsey his for a dime. This encouraged circulation, as did a conscientious consultation of the wishes of the new reader who never dreamed of subscribing to the *Century,* and even of the non-reader who at least might be interested in the illustrations or in the inside dope on some celebrity's private life.

McClure, Garland reported, put it to him with zest. "Garland, you're on the wrong track. You despise journalism, but the journalist is the man who wins. Now you can write, but you write of people and subjects that only a few care about. Why not take subjects which interest everybody? You would then stand a double chance of winning. Drop your literary pose and come in with us. Use your skill on topics of the day, or stories of big personalities, and you'll make a place for yourself." [5] Garland hooked up with the winning team, admitting that he had been corrupted. Ironically, he had begun with "topics of the day," which he had sincerely if crudely forced into fiction, only to be carried by his instincts and his aspirations into romances which displayed what McClure not too inaccurately characterized as a literary pose. Now he was to return to topics of the day, but with an eye on personalities and the big sensation. His new allegiance rankled:

> The editors of such magazines studied the appetites of the millions and not the tastes of the cultivated few. They justified themselves—whenever they attempted justification—by saying, "We are teaching the myriads to read. We are reaching the sons and daughters of peasants who never read before"; and there was truth in this statement. But the fact remains, editing became more and more a process of purveying, and writing more and more of an appeal to shopgirls, tired business men, and others who demanded easy and exciting reading.[6]

The charitable view might have been that the new magazines were carrying literature to the masses, but the critical view responded that the literature thus spread had all the marks of a commercial exploitation of humanity.

Until 1900, however, the doomed *Century, Scribner's,* and *Harper's* still bore the tone of what most Americans meant when they spoke of culture. Possessed of a well-developed sense of their positions as arbiters of American taste, such editors as Henry Mills Alden of *Harper's* and Richard Watson Gilder of the *Century* were conservative in their literary preferences. Conscious of the remarkable size of their constituency (an impression gained before the rise of such as McClure and maintained in the face of it by the belief that theirs was the readership that counted), they leveled the peaks and valleys of their contributions, so that their pages breathed an air of high-class mediocrity. Sometimes a piece of sentimental banality sank below this level, and often James or Twain or Howells or Hardy would raise some pages of a magazine above it. But the general effect of issue after issue was one of scrupulous avoidance of the startling. If variety was a consideration, then it was to be gained from a sufficiently diverse range of topics, treatment of which the self conscious editors would modulate to the restrained tone of their magazines, rather than from virile or obstreperous material. The magazines were like a gift shop in which the plaster statuettes are of a wide variety of subjects, but are painted in the same colors and proportioned on the same scale.

Explaining his blue-penciling of *Jude the Obscure,* which was appearing as a serial in *Harper's,* Alden told Hardy in 1894:

> My objections are based on purism (not mine, but our readers'), which is undoubtedly more rigid here than in England. Our rule is that the MAGAZINE must contain nothing which could not be read aloud in any family circle. . . . You will see for yourself our difficulty, and we fully appreciate the annoyance you must feel at being called upon to modify work conscientiously done, and which is best as it left your hands, from an artist's point of view.[7]

Frankly, Hardy was told, the artist's point of view is not the editor's point of view, for the editor must take the part of the reader, and the reader is the Methodist minister in Peoria, the schoolmarm in Schenectady, the lawyer's wife in Tucson, the seminary girl in Saint Louis, and the dowager in San Francisco. As Roger Burlingame of *Scribner's* pointed out: "The buyer of a magazine buys a variety of literature. He may buy it for one thing, yet have another, for which he also pays, thrust upon him. The buyer of a book on the other hand knows—or should know —what he is getting in for." [8] The editor accepted the responsibility of being the friend of the unwary and diluted the contents of his periodical to a safe consistency. So Alden wrote to Henry James in 1890 about his translation of Daudet's *Port Tarascon,* which was running in *Harper's,* that since by actual test he, Alden, had discovered that there was a chance one of the chapters might be misunderstood and considered blasphemous, he had omitted it. This was the usual rule with potentially offensive material: "Readers choose their books; but the MAGAZINE is pledged against offence to any of its patrons; and the fact that such offence is based upon the reader's inconsiderateness or ignorance does not atone to him for what seems to him a violence." [9]

This pushed the Burlingame principle a step further; the reader was guarded not only from the offensive but from the potentially offensive, even though the potential resided in his own stupidity rather than in the material he read. Still, readers did get upset, in spite of all precautions taken in the office, and Richard Watson Gilder had to reply to a superintendent of schools incensed by what he had read of *Huckleberry Finn* in the *Century.* Gilder sent the superintendent a copy of a letter he had written to Twain, to show that the magazine asked its authors to bear its standards in mind, and he further pointed out to the outraged subscriber:

Mark Twain is not a giber at religion or morality. He is a good citizen and believes in the best things. Nevertheless there is much of his writing that we would not print for a miscellaneous audience. If you should ever compare the chapters of "Huckleberry Finn," as we printed them, with the same as they appear in the book, you will see the most decided difference. These extracts were carefully edited for a magazine audience with his full consent.[10]

William Dean Howells had developed his literary muscles on the old *Atlantic,* which represented a culture with actual roots in the Boston community, and then had moved on to the homogenized culture of *Harper's.* He had even taken a brief flyer at more popular journalism with the *Cosmopolitan,* and he knew the ins and outs better than most. When he viewed the publishing situation in the light of his ambitions for the next literary generation, he was concerned but not alarmed. He felt that, as he had found elbow room, so the younger writers would, and he wanted them to keep the realities of publication in mind without becoming cynical about either the reading public or the nice old gentlemen with sleeve garters and eye shades whose blue pencils spoke for it.

Magazines, Howells said, were less likely to make a false reputation for a writer than books because their existence was far more dependent on direct public response without intervening factors. But since most magazines commissioned their work, young authors stood a better chance with book publishers, who were satisfied if they could sell 1500 copies of a first novel. If sales went beyond 2000 copies, the publisher was making good money and was willing on the next book to offer the young writer a higher royalty rate than the 10 per cent he gave on the first. Howells cautioned the neophyte to remember that women, not men, read books, and that there was no use in quarreling with them because there was no appeal from their decision. He did not mean that the young writer should try to please the ladies, only that he should not go out of his way to displease them when working up his subject.[11]

He also maintained that while New York was the publishing center of the country, as Boston had been earlier, it nevertheless was not the literary center as Boston had been, for indeed no such center existed any longer. This was a good thing. The author could live in whatever part of the country—or the world, for that matter—interested him. He was better off out of New York with its petty literary factions and its temptations toward a career of commissions. (McClure was one of the chief tempters because he felt that his success had been in great part built on the realization that when he discovered a good topic for mass appeal he was far better off employing a professional writer to handle it than an expert in the field.) Stay where you are, Howells urged, and keep your writing fresh through everyday contact with your material, rather than coming to New York and losing freshness first and then initiative.[12]

The advice was well meant, and the selflessness from which it sprang was appreciated by most of those to whom it was offered. Heeding it, however, was another matter. When Howells had first been approached to join *Harper's Magazine,* he recalled:

> Mr. Harper skilfully led up to what a man might or might not say in the Harper periodicals. There appeared to be very few things: the only one I can remember was that he might not deal, say, with the subject of capital punishment, which the House probably agreed about with Mr. Curtis [George William, editor of *Harper's Weekly*], but at any approach to which it "rang a little bell." [13]

Howells felt that when he took the job there he was put on his conscience, and "I tried to catch the tinkle of the little bell when it was not actually sounded."

His was a responsible and professional attitude. Every periodical has its little bell, which is to say an editorial policy, and in point of fact it is apt to clang far louder in a radical office than in a conservative one. Howells had felt little discomfort with the policy of the *Atlantic* because he could gradually develop its tradition along the lines of the Twain and James material he published there, and he had the same view of magazines like *Harper's*. He wanted to speak to an intelligent middle class, and if he chose to disagree with it or to educate it on social matters he believed that this could be done without offending it. As his view of the use of sexual material in fiction revealed, his disagreements with the establishment were on public matters and could be worked out in the pages of a genteel publication.

Younger writers, however, not only were producing social attacks or fictional criticism of American manners, like Fuller's novels, but were beginning to suggest that social change led to moral change and that the existence of large masses of poor people, besides meaning a large number of Americans were housed uncomfortably and fed badly, also meant that a way of life was developing which had no real attachment to the code on which the genteel magazines were founded. Some of them also suggested that, although the new amorality may have developed as the result of social injustice, it was not entirely clear that it would wither if conditions were improved, because it carried with it a self-awareness and a recognition of opportunities wider than those presented by the home. It was encouraged by industrialization, rapid transportation and communication, and the waning of God's presence in everyday life. For these writers the established magazines seemed to provide no elbow room.

J. Henry Harper, pattering on in a grandfatherly fashion about the family firm, could say:

Now and then a book comes along that is a really powerful work, and yet impossible to print, because its subject-matter really lies beyond the pale of what is justifiable in literature.

The most notable specimen of this class came in several years ago from a small Massachusetts manufacturing city, a 'shoe town,' as the natives call it. It was a most remarkable piece of literary workmanship; there was vital power in every line. But the subject! The story purported to be a narrative of the last week in the lives of two human derelicts—an immoral woman and a "black sheep" English younger son, who had met by chance at the edge of the abyss. That man could write! He himself must have been the "black sheep" to have plumbed as he did the utmost depths of despair and degradation. The pictures of terror were too horrible for a normal mind to enter upon; one instinctively revolted at this glimpse into an actual hell. There was but one thing to do—to skim it over rapidly and get the dreadful thing out of the place. But it was literature, and great literature, too. It was the kind of book that the devil himself might have written, and it came in the ordinary way by express from a dull and decorous New England town.[14]

Like the other old gentlemen who dominated publishing, J. Henry Harper found the distinction between great literature and a publishable work a clear one. But though the black sheep in the shoe town has never been heard from since, a host of other young writers were impatient with the kind of denial he had received. They were eager to liberate American literature and bring it into line with the actualities of life in a commercial civilization.

While the fiction published by the brash new wide-appeal journals was on the whole trashy, their reportorial exposés, which developed into muckraking in the new century (the Lloyd exposé of Standard Oil, which Howells got *Harper's* to publish, is an example), permitted some freedom with new materials and they attracted many a young writer who felt that he was able in such reporting to say what he wanted to say more directly than in fiction. As Ray Stannard Baker recalled, "Everything I saw interested me, and everything that interested me I wrote about—a state of bliss." [15] This state of bliss, however, was built on an acceptance of the principle which guided men like J. Henry Harper —that the difference between life and literature is such that the number of literary subjects is limited, while the range of human experiences is not. This being so, a young man could drop the literary pose and write directly about what was interesting in life, as the new cheap magazines encouraged him to. But the young man who wanted to write of the effect the commercial extravagances exposed by his colleagues had on private behavior and who wanted to do so through the creation of a story which saw life as governed by principles other than those of the publicly proclaimed moral code had no outlet.

Of all the literary guardians, Richard Watson Gilder, genteel poet and editor of the *Century,* most clearly epitomized the suppressing tone of the literary establishment. When Lee attacked Gettysburg, Gilder was in the artillery unit assigned to protect Meade's left flank, and after the Civil War he continued his daily contact with the brutal actualities of life through serving as a newspaper correspondent in Newark. Though he was the son of a minister, war and misery did not come as revelations to him. When he was a boy his father had taken him on visits to slum missions. He remembered a woman with a blackened eye who begged his father to save her, insisting, "They are trying to kill me here." He remembered descending into a damp subcellar to see a man dying on a litter of straw.[16]

When he came to eminence on the *Century,* Gilder did not hesitate to use his influence in supporting his friend Grover Cleveland, in opposing Tammany Hall, in working for civil-service reform, in strengthening the Young Women's Christian Association, in arguing for the establishment of kindergartens in New York, in fighting for more public monuments, and in securing an international copyright bill. The decencies of life which he held sacred he did not believe to be the exclusive property of a limited class, and he worked to extend them to all. But they were sacred. If life as it was lived in the slums violated those decencies, while he was happy to serve on the Tenement Commission, he would not consider publishing fictional treatments of the quality of that life in the *Century*. Such treatments did nothing to beautify life but offended the readers who shared Gilder's ideals by intruding upon them with vulgarities and obscenities.

Gilder, like Harper and Alden, found no difficulty in making a distinction between his interest in life and his interest in literature, as his relations with Walt Whitman indicate. Whitman said:

> You must never forget this of the Gilders, that at a time when most everybody else in their set threw me down they were nobly and unhesitatingly hospitable. The Gilders were without pride and without shame—they just asked me along in the natural way. It was beautiful—beautiful. You know how at one time the church was an

asylum for fugitives—the Church, God's right arm fending the innocent. I was such an innocent and the Gilders took me in.[17]

The old poet, ostracized in the nineties by most eminent literary people, received Christian treatment at Gilder's hands. But he received it as Christian treatment. Gilder wrote in a letter:

> The fact is that the dear old man who stood holding my hand outside of the church at Bryant's funeral, is the one I love—not the . . . ranting theorizer, reagitating (in prosaic and sometimes comical verse) the Emersonian doctrine like a madman; and stripping off his clothes in half-animal and half-religious frenzy.[18]

A manly regard for decency led Gilder to welcome the dear old man even as it led him to reject the strenuous poet.

The code for which Gilder and his colleagues stood, said the professional writer James L. Ford, had to be understood in terms of the tradition of the *New York Ledger*. Under the editorship of Robert Bonner, this was the most widely read weekly paper of the seventies and eighties, a cheap popular journal specializing in oleaginous sentiment. Although it published material by Dickens and Longfellow, its staple fare was the product of hack writers who prepared material specifically for it and each Friday morning brought their things directly to Bonner. They waited in his outer office while he retired behind the frosted glass, to emerge shortly after with either a ten-dollar piece or a rejection. There was no flimflam about Bonner, as those who gathered in the outer office knew, and they passed along news of his prejudices: "Bonner is down on stepmothers! All *Ledger* horses must be called Dobbin, and there is a heavy fine for driving them through a poem or serial faster than a walk, or, at best, a slow trot! Don't write anything about cousins marrying unless you want to have them back on your hands again!"[19] The hack crew from Pfaff's saloon followed these formulas religiously in order to assure the Friday morning gold piece. Such cheap job-work was infinitely below the great periodicals which spoke to the cultured, and yet, as

Ford pointed out, "A truthful portrayal of life among the criminal and vicious classes would be as much out of place in the *Century Magazine* as one depicting the love of a widower for his own cousin, whom he took out to ride behind a horse with a record of 2.53, would have been in the old *Ledger*." [20] This taboo kept professional writers from interesting themselves in the real story of New York, he complained, and he concluded his insider's lament: "I doubt if any system, either literary, political, or social —unless it be negro slavery—has ever had a fairer trial in this country than has that of pruning-hook editing." [21]

As for the new cheap magazines, Ford likened them to mass-producing factories and singled out for particular contempt Edward Bok, whose *Ladies' Home Journal* offered the editor's picture for sale:

> The code of etiquette which governs the conduct of the dime-museum lecturer ordains that no brutally frank or emphatic allusions shall be made to the pictures of the different human "freaks" which are offered for sale. "I believe," says the lecturer, in a tone of complete indifference, as he brings his glowing eulogy of the "Tattooed Queen" to a fitting close, "that the lady has a few of her photographs which she wishes to dispose of." And as the lady has eight of them in each hand, and twenty-two more arranged along the edge of the platform in front of her, even the most sceptical audience is forced to admit that the professor's surmise is correct.
>
> "I believe," says the diffident Mr. Bok, "that there are some fair likenesses of myself for sale on Chestnut Street, and I understand that they cost a quarter a piece."
>
> My readers can depend upon it that what Mr. Bok has to say about the photographs is absolutely true.[22]

The commercialization of literature which Ford's journalistic training led him to describe with cynical amusement was no laughing matter for the reformer John Jay Chapman, who saw in it the same shortcomings as those which enfeebled American politics. The irregularities of personal feeling had been pumice-stoned to a dismal level. Individuality and private opinion had disappeared in favor of a homogenized pap which offended none, but which also enlightened and enriched none. Pruning-hook editing was the result of commercial pressures, but its ultimate horror was, according to Chapman, that in the name of a false morality it wore away the morality of its practitioners. He offered this explanation:

> Suppose that a judge, in order to please a boss, awards Parson Jones' cow to Deacon Brown; does he baldly admit that even to himself? Never. He writes an able opinion in which he befogs his intelligence, and convinces himself that he has arrived at his award by logical steps. In like manner, the revising editor who reads with the eyes of the farmer's daughter begins to lose his own. He is extinguishing some sparks of instructive reality which would offend— and benefit—the farmer's daughter; and he is obliterating a part of his own mind with every stroke of his blue pencil. He is devitalizing literature by erasing personality. He does this in the money interests of a syndicate; but the debasing effect upon character is the same as if it were done at the dictate of the German Emperor.[23]

Somehow a magazine which encouraged what Chapman called personality should come into being, and if the price paid for avoiding commercialization was that it could not be a big magazine, well, then, let it be a little one. The unrest on the part of would-be authors and those in one or another form of publishing who were unhappy with the rules by which they earned their living provided a pool of talent. A little magazine, small in size because its audience was limited by the audacity of its ideas, would not take much capital. But just how one went about it was fuzzy, and nobody ventured a try until the mails from England brought the first copy of such a project, launched by Henry Harland, an American expatriate. The effect was magnetic. *The Yellow Book* galvanized bored illustrators, ambitious story-writers, defeated poets, cynical subeditors, and alert literary jokesters, and overnight every American city had its magazine.

The first issue of *The Yellow Book* appeared in April 1894 and carried in its pages the sense of a dedicated search for fine shades resulting from a refined taste for the unique word or the brilliant expression. It was defiantly elegant, as if it expected its style to offend many, an anticipation symbolized by the slack leer on the face of the Beardsley woman who appeared in the illustrations. Dispassionate analyses of *The Yellow Book* conducted from a fifty-year perspective[24] reveal that it contained little that was daring and rebellious, even for the period, and that it was buttressed by the overwhelming presence of such safe names as Edmund Gosse, William Watson, George Saintsbury, and Henry James. But the color was yellow—something definitely different and individual—and the voluptuous flatness of the Beardsley illustrations which adorned its first four issues contrived to give it an air of *fin-de-siècle* decadence.

The sense of decadence was very much in the consciousness of many American writers and readers in 1894, and they were disappointed not to find its embodiments in the American scene. The fashion was to liken the condition of culture to the age of the century. Even as the nineteenth century, born in rural simplicity, fledged on the battlefields, and fattened in commerce, was now declining in an anarchy of social conflicts, so art had tried everything normal and now was going to have a wicked old age by flirting with the abnormal. Salvation by the ideals of romance had not worked, and salvation by commitment to realism could not be worked; now how about salvation by dedication to the personal peculiarity? Those who were shocked could keep their noses poked in their own coarse affairs; others wanted their decadent delectation.

That the long sigh of weariness with the normal came from young men rather than old was no paradox, for it was they who, youthful as they were, had inherited an aging century that had tried everything but the sinful. Now, baffled by the homogenizing effects of the genteel magazines, and bewildered by the accelerating clash of social interests, a number of them felt that their release was to be achieved by ignoring both the society of Richard Watson Gilder and the society of S. S. McClure, both allegiance to William McKinley and allegiance to Henry George, in a submission to the fancied disintegration of the age and a consequent search for the word, the odor, the musky taste that would enliven the moment. Oscar Wilde's brilliant flight toward debacle was secretly and enviously eyed, and the doings of contemporary French poets were retailed in gossip as if they were a new set of saints' legends. *The Yellow Book* then arrived to suggest the way in which a little naughtiness might be visited on the American landscape.

The Chap-Book began in May 1894. It was the best as well as the first of the self-consciously avant-garde magazines of the period that soon earned the name of "little magazine," and when it went out of business in July 1898 its valedictory address claimed:

> In its earlier days the effort to put the public in touch with the new and curious developments in foreign art and literature brought upon it considerable ridicule and as well won for it much admiration. Its habit of free speech produced a curious movement among the young writers of the country. There was scarcely a village or a town which did not have its little individualistic pamphlet frankly imitating the form and tone of THE CHAP-BOOK.[25]

The claims were almost accurate. Imitators did leap up, as the publishers said, but the original intent was not what the farewell address implied. The magazine had been directly inspired by *The Yellow Book*; two Harvard undergraduates, Herbert S. Stone and Sidney Kimball, who had founded a publishing house dedicated to the new and to a sense of the printed book as an art object in itself, were struck with the notion that a Stone & Kimball house organ might well be modeled on the English periodical.[26]

The Chap-Book, in its first year, was a semi-monthly advertising circular and prospectus for the infant firm and drew its contributions almost exclusively from the Harvard and Boston literati. When the publishers were graduated from Harvard, the periodical moved with the firm to Chicago, where its chief income initially came from Melville Stone, father of Herbert and head of the Associated Press. There it maintained the personal tone it had gained from its frank reflection of the attitudes of its founders and their friends. Over its four-year career it kept a close eye on *The Yellow Book* and its English imitators, and when it struck the decadent tone, which was infrequently, it did so rather by publishing foreign material than by uncovering American talent. Some of its best illustrative material came from reproducing posters such as the very good but far from radical ones that Edward Penfield had done for *Harper's*. The stories it contained were, in the main, models of a commitment withheld; they saw the angularities of farm life or the color of the Italian peasant transferred to the American slums, consciously refusing to get excited about social conditions, but with a restrained willingness to savor the peculiarities thus afforded the observer. The naughtiness seldom went beyond that of Edith Franklin Wyatt when, for instance, she told in fable form the story of the two ambitious daughters of a grafting politician. One married into society and bored herself with charities, concerts, and French lessons, putting herself into a numbed state in which she neither did anything she liked nor remembered what it was she once liked. The other married a pushy parvenu speculator who provided her with a new dress every day and plunged with her into all the philistine pleasures, so that she lived happily ever after.[27]

The use of color, the search for possibilities in typography, and the tasteful arrangement of the crisp page gave *The Chap-Book* a character worthy of imitation, even if the personal note it struck in its contents was, in the main, one of restraint rather than assertion. Such words as "apparel," "comely," "steed," and "ply" abounded, and while their users might have been reaching for the piquantly individual, their context too often reminded one of the costume romances that also reveled in such usages, so that the effect was that of a prose suspended halfway between the romantic and the experimental. *The Chap-Book,* in short, breathed the air of a period piece, even in its own period, and this, of course, was both its limitation and its attraction. Such self-consciousness as that exhibited by *The Chap-Book* and its imitators was but another example of the rage for personality which was coming to the fore at mid-decade, and which by 1895 everybody almost proudly accepted as decadent.

In that year Max Nordau published the English version of his *Degeneration,* which sought to apply the psychological theories of Lombroso to the cultural productions of the age. Nordau announced that degenerates are not always criminals, prostitutes, anarchists, and pronounced lunatics, but often artists and authors, since the same psychological features can be signaled as easily with the pen as with the knife. Society, he maintained, rightly attempted to establish logical order and to fetter depravity, but now, in the twilight of the century, it had lost the energy with which it customarily had done this. Its vitality had been drained off in pursuit of the immense potentials of the new technology and had been sapped by the greater concentration of men in cities. The result was an outbreak of the unhealthy in the arts, an insistence on personality above custom, mysticism above tradition, and impulse above law. Degeneration, said Nordau, was evident alike in Wilde, Zola, Ibsen, and Tolstoi, in César Franck and Richard Wagner. Thus, although he realized that the notion of *fin-de-siècle* had come about as an affected little piece of anthropomorphism, Nordau announced that the end of the nineteenth century was indeed the end of an established order which had lasted thousands of years.

His book was immensely popular; it achieved the distinction of being cited as emphatically by those who had not read it as by those who had. Everybody had to have an opinion of Nordau. Some Americans took him seriously in the "scientific" way in which he hoped to be understood. The militant saints, such as Vedder, were all too willing to seize upon his theory as further evidence that when you scratched an Emile Zola or an Oscar Wilde you found identical filth beneath the skin. But Nordau had two principal effects on young American writers: amused delight that naughtiness could now be subsumed under so august a theory and justified as inevitable; and level-headed disregard of all the theorizing as coming in the end to little more than an elaborate rationale for disliking modern art.

The first effect was felt by young men such as Vance Thompson and James Huneker, for whom a theory that placed artistic genius in the category of antisocial insanity was every bit as welcome as it was to the self-righteous guardians of public morals. They were willing to take up this stance in order to exploit the recklessness it implied in shocking the guardians, for they too were moralists. From this reaction to the notion of modern art as antisocial and decadent would later come, in the new century, such iconoclastic moralists as Huneker's admirer, H. L. Mencken, who believed in the antisocial bases of literary genius, just as did his priggish opponents. Instead of condemning genius for that reason, he attacked the mentality that shared his notion of genius and therefore sought to fetter artistic expression. Another group saw in the claims that decadence was the basis of modern art a begging of the question of the value of the artistic work. Whether that work was any good was for them the all-important question. Where it came from was of relatively little importance. William James was to point out with regard to such theories as Nordau's which cried down religious inspiration by showing its medical bases that "scientific theories are organically conditioned just as much as religious emotions are; and if we only knew the facts intimately enough we should doubtless see 'the liver' determining the dicta of the sturdy atheist as decisively as it does those of the Methodist under conviction anxious about his soul." [28] So what was important, finally, was the value of the dicta rather than whether they stemmed from a diseased liver or a demented mind. And so, finally, what was important about Wilde or Zola, for some, was the value of their work, regardless of its psychological origins.

This latter view is what guided *The Chap-Book* and gave it a tone of literary hospitality. Regardless of the generally uninteresting quality of the stories it published, it still welcomed the new to its pages, and in its notes it attempted to keep its readers aware of the doings of writers as if these were interesting and important things to know. While *The Chap-Book* and its imitators cannot be said to have discovered any important talents who were languishing for want of a publisher in the climate that existed earlier in the decade, still its literary chit-chat, cutting through the fog bank of the genteel journals, called attention to talent wherever it appeared. When *The Chap-Book* expired in 1898, it did so, among other reasons, because *The Bookman* had now come into existence, and though this well-financed and rather conservatively edited periodical was far from a little magazine, it nevertheless accepted the duties of literary hospitality to the young which the little magazines, in their brief mid-decade careers, had insisted upon.

The most significant followers of *The Chap-Book* were *The Philistine, The Lark,* and *M'lle New York.* The first-named was the creation of Elbert Hubbard, who was later in the decade to compose "A Message to Garcia," a work second only to *In His Steps* in its popularity. *The Philistine* was representative of another facet of its publisher's talent for salesmanship and testifies to the initial attractive power of the little-magazine idea in that Hubbard saw in it another way of selling his personality for fun and profit. That he was to capitalize on the format of the little magazine but not its intent was made clear by the title he gave his magazine. One of the few items to be noted to its credit is that it inspired the parody *Bilioustine,* which exposed Hubbard's self-serving prostitution of the new art movement as well as his meretricious imitation of the recently awakened interest in books as beautiful objects, and pursued them with a humorous and malicious vengeance.

The Lark was hatched in San Francisco, and the double meaning of its name was intended. While it would sing at heaven's gate, it would do so as a merry adventure and have fun with the little-magazine movement. Its originator was Gelett Burgess, an eclectic Easterner transplanted to a city which still revels in his characterization of it as Bayside Bohemia. He gained instant attention for his magazine by committing to its pages his versified reflections on the purple cow. Burgess liked the personal note of *The Yellow*

Book and *The Chap-Book,* but was amused at those who spelled decadence with a capital letter and was determined to demolish them. Accordingly, he showed how far someone with imagination and a flair for the absurd could go. *The Lark* was printed on bamboo paper so thin it could take an impression on only one side, and yellow because the Japanese characters had to be soaked from the borders, leaving red and green stains.[29] Launched in May 1895, *The Lark* flew gaily enough for two years, never allowing the joke it was perpetrating to carry it into the realm of total irrelevance and never allowing its more serious contributors to weigh it to earth. When Burgess felt that the lure of the fad magazines was pushing *The Lark* too far in one direction or another, he threw off a satellite in order to keep his monthly free. Thus he attempted *The Phyllida* as an "effort to give scope to literary ideas of the more critical sort, which were too formal to be tolerated" [30] in *The Lark.* And in protecting *The Lark* from the merely zany, he produced perhaps the most delightful of all freak periodicals of the period, *Le Petit Journal des Refusées.* It was printed on discontinued wallpaper designs cut into trapezoid pages.

Burgess summed up his efforts with candid accuracy, and in so doing he spoke for most of the others who edited little magazines for a year or two in the nineties:

> The success of the "Chap Book" incited the little riot of Decadence, and there was a craze for odd sizes and shapes, freak illustrations, wide margins, uncut pages, Janson types, scurrilous abuse and petty jealousies, impossible prose and doggerel rhyme. The movement asserted itself as a revolt against the commonplace; it aimed to overthrow the staid respectability of the larger magazines and to open to younger writers opportunities to be heard before they had obtained recognition from the autocratic editors. It was a wild, hap-hazard exploration. . . . When the history of the Nineteenth Century decandence is written, these tiny eruptions of revolt, these pamphleteering amateurs cannot remain unnoticed, for their outbreak was a symptom of the discontent of the times, a wide-felt protest of emancipation from the dictates of the old literary tribunals. Little

enough good has come of it that one can see at present, but the
sedition is broached, and the next rebellion may have more blood to
spill.[31]

The epitaph is modest and just.

Burgess also provided the standard alphabetical guide to the
movement, which, for all its juvenility, deserves to be rescued and
reprinted as a taste of that flavor of the nineties which was most
perishable:

> *A is for Art of the age-end variety;*
>   *We* Decadents *simply can't get a satiety.*
>
> *B is for Beardsley, the idol supreme,*
>   *Whose drawings are not half so bad as they seem.*
>
> *C is for Chap-Book, the pater familias*
>   *Of magazines started by many a silly ass.*
>
> *D is for Darn it—it's awfully shocking*
>   *Your Dekel-edge Hosiery, Mistress Stocking.*
>
> *E is for Editor; what does it mean?*
>   *Everyone now runs his own magazine.*
>
> *F is for Freak: see the great exposition*
>   *Of freak magazines—5 and 10 cents admission.*
>
> *G is for Goup; I would much rather be*
>   *A nice* Purple Cow *than a* G-O-U-P.
>
> *H is for Humbug attempts to be Horrid!*
>   *(See* Mlle. New York, *she's decidedly torrid.)*
>
> *I am an Idiot, awful result*
>   *Of reading the rot of the* Yellow Book *cult.*
>
> *J is for Janson the Type of the day,*
>   *Some people can't read any other they say.*
>
> *K is for Kimball, assistant of* Stone;
>   *I wonder how he will get on all alone.*
>
> *L is for Lark, and the fellows who planned it*
>   *Say even they cannot but half understand it.*

M is for Magazines recklessly recent.
 I know of but one that is anyway decent.

N stands for Nothing; I wish it had stood for
 A little bit more than the fly-leaf was good for.

O's for Oblivion—ultimate fate
 Of most of the magazines published of late.

P is for Poster; the best one by far
 Is the one that was made for our own P.J.R. (Price 4 bits.)

Q is for Quarrel; Harte, Hubbard and Taber
 To run the Philistine, each other belabor.

R is for Rubbish; are you looking for some?
 Just open the Bauble and put down your thumb.

S is for Stevie Crane, infant precocious.
 Who has written some lines that are simply ferocious.

T is for Thomas B. Mosher of Maine,
 Whose dinkey toy prefaces give me a pain.

U is for Useless and far beneath notice;
 But I don't want to say all of that of the Lotus.

V is for Versification and Verse;
 We thought Chip's was bad but the Olio's worse.

W's for Woman, who editors humor:
 In the new field of letters, perennial bloomer.

X is for Something Unknown—let us say
 How in the world do these magazines pay?

Y is for Young, and I marvelled to learn
 That fifty's the average age of Les Jeunes.

Z is for Zounds! What unspeakable deco-
 rativeness Bradley has furnished for Echo.[32]

The *M'lle New York,* which exemplified "Humbug attempts to be Horrid," was founded in 1895 by the poet Vance Thompson and James Gibbons Huneker, who was at that time broadening out from his activities as music critic to writing about drama and literature as well. To be a successful critic, he admitted, one "can't wait for masterpieces, but must coddle mediocrity. Otherwise an idle pen." [33] As a literary critic, Huneker championed the cause of Edgar Allan Poe, a cherished symbol of the artist's fate in unfeeling America for those who shared Nordau's theories about the artistic temperament but used them as a club on society rather than a shackle on art; was hopeful about the promise of Henry Blake Fuller; and believed that the greatest living novelist was Henry James because of his "exquisite style and cadenced prose." [34] *M'lle New York* was necessary, said Huneker, as "a safety-valve for our rank egotism and radicalism." [35] With this as a side outlet, he could continue to exist professionally as a writer for newspapers and magazines.

M'lle New York made clear at the outset that it accepted all the terrible things that could be whispered about creative people and wore them as a badge of superiority. The public is a "grotesque aggregation of foolish individuals" which only pretends to literary taste.[36] But *M'lle New York* is not concerned with the public: "Her only ambition is to disintegrate some small portion of the public into its original component parts—the aristocracies of birth, wit, learning and art and the joyously vulgar mob." [37] Clearly, the magazine would stand for the aristocratic and gain amusement from the joyously vulgar, but she would have no traffic with the mediocre in-betweens who made up 95 per cent of the reading public. In American letters Poe and Whitman were admired by her for their lives as much as for their writings, and identified as the only two geniuses the country had produced— men whom, therefore, the country disowned with its characteristic stupidity. Gilder was roundly abused, and Howells was treated to habitual indignation.

M'lle New York received its literary ideas directly from France, bypassing the intellectual customs house of England, which seemed to supervise all Continental material which found its way into magazines of the *Century* class. It championed Verlaine and Symbolism even though the native imitations it printed were woefully short of the models. Its prose was consumed with an admiration for Huysmans and, correspondingly, with Satanism, with a yearning to realize the divine through ritual, and with a fascination with Jews, the males of which people were represented (in illustration as well as in language) as repulsive physically yet with an Oriental allure, while the women were irresistible because they were so seductive in their Oriental languor and were so experienced in the perversities which, it was to be assumed, commonly suggested themselves to the insidious mind of the Jewish male.

New York as well as France found its way into the pages of *M'lle New York,* in the delight the magazine took in the variety of races and types in the city. Its expressed attitude, however, was one of scorn for most lower-class immigrants and positive contempt for the Negro, who with the Jew received broad caricature in the illustrations. The mademoiselle who was the symbol of the magazine was young and jaded. She had been in the best drawing rooms of Fifth Avenue and she had taken part in orgies below Fourteenth Street with people who spoke strange tongues; she had drunk champagne on yachts with the Four Hundred, and she had returned to her rooms to smoke hashish and read Verlaine with a male friend who didn't wear a tie. She had, in short, tried everything, and her beautiful body was not so resilient that it could resist the signs of her experience. But a certain slackness of lip, heaviness of eyelid, and looseness of breast were attractions to those who inhabited her fantasy world, offering them the salvation through having touched bottom that was denied them by the Young Girl of Howells, and yet presenting sin in a youthful body which retained a certain trace of innocence.

Moving erratically across the pages of *M'lle New York* were wisps which were to gather into ideas and movements in the 1920s: Mademoiselle herself was big sister to Lady Brett; the attitude toward Howells and Gilder, on the one hand, and Poe and Whitman, on the other, prefigured (before a World War was dreamed of) an iconoclastic re-evaluation of the American literary heritage; and the contempt for all opinions which sought amelioration of social conditions through some form of collective action, while it might at times sound like the last tootings of the laissez-faire spirit, was actually the first piping of the anti-Progressive Nietzscheanism which was to blare forth in the new century. Vance Thompson told the radical huddled over his mug of beer on Fourteenth Street that civilization at best would be organized into a gentlemanly tyranny. As the "poor Christ of the gutter" listens, Thompson explains: "To-day we are ruled by weaklings, rogues, demagogues, vulgarians, shop-keepers—better, I say, the strong man. 'Tis better to be scourged by Attila than to be eaten alive by parasites. *I hear the grinding of the swords, and he shall come*." [38] This political thesis is related to the attitudes held by *M'lle New York* about French and American literature, about the complex racial mixtures living in New York, about salvation. By postponing problems till the advent of the man on horseback, it could have its diatribe without its commitment, and in its aesthetic and ethical principles it had its sensation without the sin. Thus it is not surprising that in its stories and poems *M'lle New York* had its say but did not have a literature. Some twenty years were to pass before capable American writers would catch up with some of the principles of the magazine. When they did, however, it was to do more than mouth them for the delectation of the few in that oldest of all middle-class games, shocking the middle class.

Sedition was broached in the little magazines, as Gelett Burgess had observed, but it was only broached. These periodicals neither discovered, developed, nor consistently published any young writer of outstanding merit, although in the main they were quick to encourage such writers in their notes, reviews, or gossip columns. These writers did exist, but a condition of their existence was their inability to divorce themselves from the mainstream of their commercial culture even while feeling oppressed by it. If they were not to be found in the genteel or mass magazines at the outset of their careers, neither were they clamoring for recognition in the little magazines. They were, rather, on the newspapers, where they contributed to the new myth that the great American novel, when it came, would come from somebody who had chased fire engines, visited the blood-dabbled scene of the ax slaying, and talked with the whores after they had been booked. James had concluded that he must submit totally to the destructive element of art; they had concluded that they must submit totally to the destructive element of urban life. The different roads came out at places that were not so widely separated.

SEVEN

The School in the Cemetery:

Newspapers

In 1895, when the new mass magazines began seriously to challenge the established subscription monthlies, the New York newspaper business also entered a new phase, aimed at an even greater audience.[1] William Randolph Hearst arrived from the West to publish the *Journal,* and, in great part through sedulous imitation of Joseph Pulitzer's techniques and in some part through innovation, he challenged the dominance in circulation of Pulitzer's *World.* The battle that ensued sharpened the techniques which were in the years to come to be imitated by almost every metropolitan daily. Big-name reporters were vigorously recruited at high salaries; color presses were employed to aid in the paper's visual assault on the buyer (bringing with them the colored comic strip); and the telephone and telegraph were lavishly utilized to insure speed of coverage.

While the new competition substantially bettered the income of those reporters who were already established, it marked the end of the school in which they were trained. Even as the prominent space devoted to such men as Richard Harding Davis served to establish the newpaper profession in the eyes of young men as an exciting and rewarding career, the very conditions which afforded Davis and others their prominence destroyed the tradition which had shaped them. On the *World* or the *Journal* the cub reporter was expected chiefly to phone in the news; the writing would be done, in H. L. Mencken's words, by "a homunculus at the end of a telephone wire." The average reporter's observations would be reduced by "literary castrati who never leave the office." [2] Writing with an individual style would be permitted only to columnists who had served their apprenticeships on more personal newspapers; the opportunities for such apprenticeships were increasingly narrowed after the titans, joining battle in New York, provided the models for mass circulation. A New York reporter, foreseeing the death of personal journalism, said: "The fundamental principle of metropolitan journalism is to buy white paper at three cents a pound and sell it at ten cents a pound. And in some quarters it does not matter how much the virgin whiteness of the paper is defiled so long as the defilement sells the paper." [3] He made his cynical observation in true allegiance to the profession in which he had been raised.

The tradition of personal journalism had been established by Charles A. Dana's New York *Sun* and so devotedly echoed in every American city that the experiences of reporters trained in it formed a new mythology. They had been made to wait for their first assignments, and when the assignments came and they threw all of their literary resources into reporting them, they were thunderstruck that their two-column dispatches had been reduced by the editor to a paragraph. This personage, the editor, had few literary passions—he thought Dickens and Balzac, for example, great writers, all others fools—and he rigorously held his staff to a standard which he at the same time announced they were incapable of meeting. Ideally, he wore a green blinder, had a cruel blue pencil, and kept a bottle of whisky in his drawer. He could magically tell the worthy from the dull in an instant; a glance was sufficient to make him consign pages to the wastebasket. But one day the reporter stumbled on a big story—Davis on the Johnstown flood, Dreiser on a train wreck—and this made him. He was now trusted with other big stories, but he was also encouraged to develop in prose his impressions of what was interesting in the daily human scene, of which he was supposed by now to be a trained observer. "I have always felt," said Dana, "that whatever the Divine Providence permitted to occur I was not too proud to report," [4] and by this he meant the daily life of a Chinese laundryman or the wanderings of a lost child as much as great catastrophes or important political events.[5]

The key to human-interest reporting was the reporter; it was his prose that made the difference between what was common and uninteresting in life and what was absorbingly pathetic or humorous in print. In the heyday of personal journalism he was given a chance to develop a style, and as his stories attracted interest he was allowed to vary this style in the direction of peculiar individuality because the paper brought not only news to its readers but the sense of being addressed by familiar personalities.

The personal newspapers that rose after the Civil War had some resemblances to the old prewar American newspaper, rigidly ruled into single columns with small headlines, carrying advertising with the same lack of display accorded stories. This was the kind of paper on which Whitman had worked around New York, on which Howells had worked in rural Ohio, on which Twain had been employed in the West. Local news was the only news, and once that had been exhausted the reporter—and on the country journals there was only one, and he was also editor and printer's helper—was free to fill space with clippings from other journals or with inventions of his own. The route to writing was through apprenticeship as printer's devil. Personal journalism retained some aspects of the reporter's freedom to develop stories of interest and also some sense of apprenticeship, though this was now the apprenticeship of the cub rather than the printer's devil. In a rural area personal gossip was common knowledge, and the new metropolitan journal after the war attempted to carry that interest in private matters into the city. With the great influx of people into metropolitan centers, it argued, it was the medium that gave a sense of community to the newly arrived farm girl, and it was the medium that Americanized the immigrant. To do so it had to tell about people, not just about events. In 1861 an account of a society ball might daringly include the initials of those present; by 1881 not only were their names given, but their clothing was described and fingered and their conversation was reproduced.

Howells and James saw the new journalism as the vulgar and pernicious violator of private experience. The reporters who figured in their novels were men and women who had lost the sense of the subjects of their stories as fellow creatures; they saw them as natural resources to be exploited. James's Henrietta Stackpole is offended when her prying is met with the remark that she has no sense of privacy, because, as she points out, she never writes about herself.⁰ Twain made the new reporter a consistent butt of his humor and his wrath.

The young men born around the time of the war who were attracted into the newspaper business in the nineties would not seriously have disagreed with these views of their profession. They made no claim for the integrity of their publishers or the intelligence of their readers. They recognized that they were contributing to the growing gap between social reality and its public representation by writing for papers which lovingly gave the details of a murder side by side with a piece designed to bolster the constant editorial claim that the United States of America was the most enlightened nation in history. But reared on tales of the Civil War, in towns where politics was dominated by veterans' associations and the landscape was dominated by memorial statuary, they also had an acute sense of the mark their parents' generation had been able to leave on national events, the tone it had given to the national life. As children they had stood at the corner of Main and Elm and every minute or so seen a man pass wearing the veteran's cap of the Grand Army of the Republic. They had felt the sense of lost adventure, of having been born too late for the stirring events which had reached into every village, however remote, and called forth its young people to do battle. For them were left only twice-told anecdotes, soiled uniforms, and stone monuments.

The newspaper, however, promised the young man with a literary leaning that it would put him in touch with the stirring events of his own day. If he could not actually go to war as a participant —though in 1898 he received even that opportunity—he might go as a witness. Heroism demanded its spectators, as Stephen Crane was persistently to note. If it was increasingly difficult to leave one's mark on the national life, at least newspaper work took you behind that unimpressible façade and showed you what supported it. If there were things you couldn't write about, at least newspapers paid you to acquaint yourself with them.

But in spite of its changed condition, newspaper journalism appeared to these young men no more of a permanent career, as they entered it in the eighties and the nineties, than it had earlier appeared to Howells and Twain. Just as the older journalists had found that reaching the top of their profession meant a somnolent life of observation of country doings, so the younger men knew that the top now meant a career as a businessman, for newspapers were increasingly big business. They were, the cubs realized, cemeteries of talent as well as schools, and each city room had its walking corpses. The trick was to get your schooling and then step out before the inevitable living burial. It was worth the risk because where else in America did such a school exist? David Graham Phillips spoke for the generation when he said, "The daily newspaper sustains the same relation to the young writer as the hospital to the medical student. It is the first great school of practical experience." [7]

The acceptance of this outlook—and accepted it was by, among others, Stephen Crane, Harold Frederic, and Theodore Dreiser— was an acceptance of the fact that the young writers' America, unlike the America that confronted them in the pages of the *Century,* was suffering from a complication of social ills. Nobody knew quite how these were to be represented in fiction. A generation which had survived the perils of disunion was either unable to face these problems or unwilling to admit their seriousness. The ills were representatively on display in the big cities, so that Phillips's simile was an apt one: just as medical schools were located in cities so as to provide themselves with the widest possible range of exemplary cases, so work on city newspapers provided the range of experience necessary for a writer who had as yet to fill his reservoir. Even in the old days newspapers had taught writers the variety of life, and if now writers thought of the Great American Novel as a novel rather than as a poem, still, had not Whitman, who thought of his "Song of Myself" in the same way that they thought of their unborn works, taken his material from the same stream?

The suicide sprawls on the bloody floor of the bedroom,
I witness the corpse with its dabbled hair, I note where the pistol has
*   fallen.*

The blab of the pave, tires of carts, sluff of boot-soles, talk of the
*   promenaders,*
The heavy omnibus, the driver with his interrogating thumb, the clank
*   of the shod horses on the granite floor,*
The snow-sleighs, clinking, shouted jokes, pelt of snow-balls,
The hurrahs for popular favorites, the fury of rous'd mobs,
The flap of the curtain'd litter, a sick man inside borne to the hospital,
The meeting of enemies, the sudden oath, the blows and fall,
The excited crowd, the policeman with his star quickly working his
*   passage to the centre of the crowd.*[8]

Was this not to be the stuff of their fiction? Personal journalism encouraged the picturing of such incidents in an individually colorful style.

Still there were dangers clear to any young man who found himself in the full swing of reporting. First of all, the work left him no time for reading or what David Graham Phillips loosely called "the calmer kind of writing." [9] Related to this was the fact that writing done in time stolen from the daily grind bore a near-fatal resemblance in style to the daily assignments. The demands of form were too often answered by the punchy opening and the twist ending; the demands of manner were too often met by the gaudy modifier rather than the right word for what was being modified. If newspapers provided the material for fiction, they also provided a quick, slick way to handle it, a way that could rust out a writer's style.

More pernicious, however, the experience in the more degraded or troubled areas of American life that the reporter's job afforded him had to be carefully edited if not suppressed when he came to write of it. In New York, Jacob Riis told the neophyte *Post* reporter Lincoln Steffens: "There's a strike on the East Side, and there are always clubbed strikers here in this [police] office. I'll tell you what to do while you are learning our ways up here; you hang around this office every morning, watch the broken heads brought in, and as the prisoners are discharged, ask them for their stories. No paper will print them, but you yourself might as well see and hear how strikes are broken by the police." [10] This on labor problems, while on political corruption Brand Whitlock in Chicago said that the moral atmosphere of politics "was a joke among the newspaper men, who had little respect for the men who filled the positions of power and responsibility; the wonder was, indeed, after such association, that they had any respect left for anything in the world." [11] What gnawed further at their sense of respect was that they could not report what they knew. As to which elements in society the paper could draw on for sensational stories, Theodore Dreiser was told by his editor in Pittsburgh: "There's nothing to be said about the rich or religious in a derogatory sense: they're all right in so far as we know. We don't touch on scandals in high life. The big steel men here just about own the place, so we can't." [12]

The harmfulness of this condition from the writer's point of view was not that he came to believe that there are certain things which, however prevalent, are not to be put into the public prints; this was, after all, a lesson quickly learned, however ardently it might be deplored. It was rather that his daily life was conducted in an atmosphere in which semi-truths were consciously constructed and whole truths were systematically suppressed by men who sympathized with the victims of this injustice. This condition encouraged in him the twin defenses of cynicism and sentimentality. The first kept him from allowing his sentimentality to make him vulnerable; the second kept him from allowing his cynicism to cut him off from the human interest that was his stock in trade. Joined to the hard-drinking editor with the green blinder and the blue pencil, in the legend that emerged, was the hard-drinking reporter who could talk with dry wit about the hundred and one stiffs he had seen fished out of the river and shed spontaneous tears over the urchin maimed by a passing omnibus. Both the cynicism and the sentiment marred many a novel or play composed after hours, and it took the stolid genius of a Dreiser or the brilliant genius of a Crane to transcend them. Neither's work is entirely free of this inheritance from the city room, even as the work of both benefited from the experience newspaper life made possible.

Lincoln Steffens said, "What reporters know and don't report is news—not from the newspaper's point of view, but from the sociologists' and the novelists'," [13] and this kind of news formed part of the best literature of the nineties. Some material was so newsworthy that many a newspaperman turned from the difficult task of shaping it into fiction to the more direct presentation of it as a sociological report, enlivened by an application of the techniques of human-interest reporting. The model work of this kind was supplied by Jacob Riis in 1890 with his *How the Other Half Lives,* and was followed by other studies of conditions in the slums of New York. Riis was not entirely clear as to whether inadequate housing, political corruption, child labor, and the other evils visited upon the urban poor were or were not ultimately economic and environmental in origin, but he made clear that the immediate steps to be taken should aim at these areas. While he portrayed convincingly the processes whereby the stale-beer traffic was carried on or children's labor was exploited, he was almost as insensitive to the cultural commitments of the immigrant populations he studied as he was sensitive to the evils they suffered. So, for instance, with regard to religious life he could say, "They stand, these East Side Jews, where the new day that dawned on Calvary left them standing, stubbornly refusing to see the light." [14] With the Italian and Chinese populations he was equally obtuse about customs, because, an immigrant himself from Denmark, he was concerned not only with righting injustices but with Americanizing their victims, and he saw their European habits as obstacles to the latter process even as political corruption blocked the former.

Jacob Riis's work had an obvious effect on the course of reform, one mark of which was his service as adviser to Theodore Roosevelt. But superior news work like his, entering into quasi-sociological books in the nineties, also brought to public recognition a way of life that needed this airing before it could become accessible to literary treatment. It encouraged, for instance, the work of Walter A. Wyckoff, a lecturer in sociology at Princeton, who in July 1891 set out from the Atlantic coast on foot and worked his way to the Pacific as a day laborer, reporting on his experiences in the two volumes of *The Workers, An Experiment in Social Reality* (1897 and 1898). Wyckoff reported that he had assumed that poverty would bring him into vital contact with the poor, but instead it made him an object of unfailing distrust even on the part of the poor. From his position as day laborer he examined the position of the employer of such labor, to whose advantage it is to have a large pool of unemployed from which to draw; the employer argues that unskilled labor, by definition, is performed by those incompetent to do anything else, and that therefore the complaints of the laborers are meaningless, since if they were competent they would have nothing to complain about. To this argument Wyckoff replied:

> All this is to tell us, in effect, that our lives are the hard, barren, hopeless lives that they are because of our own fault, and that our degradation as men is the measure of our bondage as workmen.
>
> This seems to state an ultimate fact, and then, with the habit of much of such thinking, to settle itself peacefully, with an easy conscience, behind the inevitable.
>
> But for us there is no such peace or comfort in the inevitable. And yet, even in this statement of our case, we are not without hope. We are men, and capable of becoming better men. We may be capable of no other than unskilled labor, but why should we be doomed to perform it under the conditions which now degrade us at our work? [15]

In Chicago, in December, Wyckoff was in the army of the un-employed who shuffled the streets by day to keep from being frozen to death and who herded into the basement of the police station by night to sleep on newspapers spread on the floor. He reported on what it meant to realize that you are a superfluous human being, and brought into the open a theme that Howells had fifteen years before believed impossible in America:

Suddenly there dawns upon you an undreamed of significance in the machinery of social restraint. The policeman on the crossing in his slouching uniform bespattered by the oozing slime of the miry streets . . . is the outstretched hand of the law ready to lay hold on you, should you violate in your despair the rules of social order. Behind him you see the patrol wagon and the station-house and the courts of law and the State's prison and enforced labor, the whole elaborate process by means of which society would reassimilate you, an excrement, a non-social being as a transgressor of the law, into the body politic once more, and set you to fulfilling a functional activity as a part of the social organism.

The result, with the means of living which it implies and the link that it gives you to your kind, even if it be the relation of a criminal to society, may become the object of a desire so strong that the shame and punishment involved may lose their deterring force for you.[16]

In reporting like this or like Riis's, the conditions of a new fiction were established. Although the genteel magazines would resist it as offensive and the little magazines would avoid it as extraneous to their concern with the personal tone, works like *Maggie,* or *Mc-Teague* or *Sister Carrie* were not now impossibilities.

Following on Riis's reports on the New York slums came the work of other reporters, such as Hutchins Hapgood, who were interested in the positive contribution that the foreign ways of the immigrants had to make to American culture. Hapgood attended the Yiddish theaters, familiarized himself with the radical foreign-language periodicals, and learned of the existence in New York of a number of writers whose criteria had been formed by Russian fiction.[17] He became the apostle of Abraham Cahan, who had come to America from Eastern Europe in 1882, made his way up in the socialist movement—twice returning to Europe as the American Jewish delegate to international congresses—and had edited Jewish literary magazines as well as a socialist daily.

In 1896 Cahan published his first English novel, *Yekl,* an effectively told story of an Americanized Jewish immigrant from Russia who turns from his old-world trade of blacksmith to being a sewing-machine operator. When he has earned sufficient money, he sends for his wife, whose Russian ghetto mannerisms are now shameful to his sense of himself as an American, and he divorces her to marry a girl who, like himself, has a shabby overlay of Americanism in her ways. His wife goes on to marry a scholarly man and start a corner grocery with the money Yekl must settle on her.

Howells was attracted to this novel as an example of the susceptibility to local-color treatment of a hitherto undiscovered piece of America, but the theme of *Yekl* lies deeper. Cahan is here raising the question of what is gained and what is lost in the process of Americanization, the theme which was to receive definitive treatment in his masterpiece, *The Rise of David Levinsky* (1917). The ring of authenticity in his fiction was overwhelming in comparison with the work of Henry Harland, the young and cultured New Yorker who in the eighties fixed his literary ambitions on mining New York Jewish material. Writing under the pseudonym of Sidney Luska, Harland produced a number of works on this subject, attracting favorable attention from Howells. But they were bad conventional melodramas which carried a factitious appeal through being set in the New York ghetto and therefore promising new material. In 1889 Harland abandoned "Sidney Luska" in favor of London, and in 1894 he founded *The Yellow Book*. Harland's attempts, when measured by Cahan's achievement, reveal the difference between considering immigrant materials as so much exotic background and as contributions to American culture. Increasingly the writers of the nineties were taking the latter point of view and not only writing about the foreign quarters of the big city but warmly inviting foreign-language writers in America, such as Cahan, to cross the linguistic barrier and enter more directly into modern American literature.

So prominently had newspapermen been converting their unpublishable assignments into sociology and fiction that in 1897, when Lincoln Steffens assumed editorial control of the New York *Commercial Advertiser,* he sent out a call for would-be writers to join his staff, not would-be reporters:

> "We" had use for any one who, openly or secretly, hoped to be a poet, a novelist, or an essayist. I could not pay him much in money, but as an offset I promised to give them opportunities to see life as it happened in all the news varieties. No one would be kept long in any department; as soon as a reporter became expert in one branch of work, he would be turned into another.[18]

Recognizing that the varieties of news were the material of American literature, and that newspapermen in the nineties were semicovert novelists, Steffens openly invited those with such ambitions. Personal journalism had made writers of those reporters who had the stamina to withstand the comforts of cynicism and sentimentalism; of the staff Steffens gathered as a result of his appeal to university English professors to send him their most promising writers, not one ambitious novelist or poet achieved anything in belleslettres. Ironically, rather, his policy turned them into reporters, and, like Norman and Hutchins Hapgood, who came from literary aspirations at Harvard, they found their fulfillment in journalism.

In Chicago, where the tradition of personal journalism remained strong through the nineties, the reforming instinct was less apparent in newspapermen's books. In the first half of the decade, while the *News* featured Eugene Field's "Sharps and Flats," the *Record* had George Ade's "Stories of the Streets and of the Town," and the *Journal* regularly carried Finley Peter Dunne's "Mr.

Dooley." With outlets so readily available to them, the talented writers who joined the city's newspapers learned compromise quickly, and nowhere else was the blend of cynicism and sentimentalism so pronounced. The good in a writer was so readily recognized in Chicago that he hardly had time to think, in meeting his daily assignments, that the best in him might be in the process of destruction.

Ade had come to Chicago in 1890, when it was, he said, a mining camp five stories high.[19] With his Indiana youth fresh in him, he quickly identified as his characteristic material stories of other young Midwesterners who, in spite of their residence in the big city, were still country-bred people looking for hometown pleasures. In his stories he chronicled their doings, using as one of his central figures the young clerk Artie, a lower-middle-class version of the man about town. The tales blended sentiment with sharp observation, and although Ade soon learned to turn them on one or another contrivance, they never lost the charm given them by his nearly infallible ear for the vernacular. The language talked by the inhabitants of Crane's *Maggie* is a patently invented lingo when set next to the vernacular of Ade's characters.

If Artie was not the central figure in an Ade story, then it might be one or another of the acquaintances of Doc Horne in the run-down residence hotel where the Doc served as the Chicago equivalent of the autocrat of the breakfast table. Or again it might be Pink Marsh, the Negro bootblack who, caricatured as he was, nevertheless brought to Ade's readers a stronger sense of the existence of another world, a Negro world, in their midst than they had ever had. Always in Ade's work was the attractive sense that life in Chicago was one-fifth the visible big city and four-fifths the careers of the countless thousands from Kentland and Oshkosh who were, to the best of their abilities, working out small-town patterns. "The dentist was in the city, but not of it," observed Ade. "The Indiana part of him insisted that any woman who drank a glass of beer in a public garden thereby degraded herself." [20] Ade saw in the main a life of real hope and real pleasures, so that when he did from time to time let loose a line pregnant with criticism, it was all but unnoticed in the context. Pink Marsh can tell his white customer, "We got mo' rights 'an anybody, but it sutny ain't safe to use 'em," [21] before going on to less troublesome matters; or a human-interest description of a night court might mention in passing "chalky women with their hats pulled forward, who showed a weary and smiling contempt for this familiar process of taxation" [22] and leave the matter at that. He could also note the aesthetic climate, though his instinct was to protect Chicago from foreign influences. Young Chicago artists were drawing "shell-eyed women with worms in their hair," in imitation of Beardsley, but most of them would get over it; "others will have to be cared for. We had something of the same trouble when Oscar Wilde came over here." [23]

Ade was at his best and his most characteristic when, as in "Effie Whittlesey," he told the story of a successful Chicago businessman who does not allow his city-bred wife's chagrin to dissuade him from recognizing that the new servant she has hired is a childhood friend from his small town. He accepts her calling him by his first name because they had been "reared in the democracy of a small community." [24]

Ade's greatest strength was finally his limitation, because something was happening in Chicago that was not explicable in terms of its just being a metropolitan version of the rural community. When, therefore, syndication in 1900 promoted Ade from $65 to $1000 a week and converted him into a gagwriter, he was not at that point lost to the ranks of realistic literature. His compromise had come earlier in his refusal to develop observations that would impede the joke or suggest that the small-town ways were dying. Syndication only intensified the false geniality.

Finley Peter Dunne, born on West Adams Street in Chicago, was the undoubted master of the Chicago columnists. He had graduated from high school last in his class of fifty and had drifted into newspaper work at the age of seventeen, becoming the first reporter to write narrative reports of professional baseball games.

At the age of twenty-one he was a city editor and a political writer, though within a year he was out of this job because of a change of publishers and was back in reporting.

Having grown up in Chicago and knowing its chaotic conditions both from direct experience and from the reflections of them in the city room, Dunne had every inducement to harden into cynicism early in life. Sent to cover a speech by Senator Foraker in 1892, he was amused that the Civil War was still so much with the Senator's generation, and, after recording yet another tiresome display of the bloody shirt, he concluded his report on the address by saying: "Then all the people put on their hats and went out to see what news had come from Gettysburg, where a terrible battle is still raging." [25] But the crust of contempt for his society was kept from forming on Dunne by what one of his biographers rightly describes as "an intensely emotional sympathy for the under-dog, and a love of humanitarian values." [26] These might well have succumbed to his environment had he not had the genius to present them as the spontaneous outpourings of a Chicago Irish bartender, first called Colonel McNeery and then, after 1893, Mr. Dooley. This persona demanded that Dunne convert his opinions into dialect and make them appropriate to their setting, the Archey Road saloon, and the changes worked the magic of draining off the cynicism—although, from time to time, they may have unduly encouraged sentimentalism. Mr. Dooley's observations on Andrew Carnegie as well as the socialists, on William McKinley as well as the anarchists, had something of the flavor of philosophical nihilism. But his evident love for and enjoyment of his fellow creatures, even at their most foolish, and his unconscious misapprehensions of the actual state of affairs, which, of course, led him to shrewder comments on them than if he had understood them in the way the news columns intended him to, kept him genially unbitter.

Finley Peter Dunne, in creating Mr. Dooley, alone among those who contributed to daily journalism had created an art within that field. Though he talked almost exclusively about the political events of his day, in newspapers that would be deposited in trash cans a few hours after they were printed, Mr. Dooley has resisted the march of events because he spoke of his day from as solid a physical setting and in as well-developed a character as those to be found in the novels of his decade. The sociological content of Riis and the dramatic content of Ade combined in Mr. Dooley's Chicago as he spoke of original sin: " 'Twas took out iv me be Father Tuomy with holy wather first an' be me father aftherward with a sthrap";[27] or of the Negro problem: "He'll ayether have to go to th' north an' be a subjick race, or stay in the south an' be an objick lesson." [28] The social Darwinism which penetrated to Mr. Dooley's part of the universe was shrewdly digested: " 'Tis as hard f'r a rich man to enther th' kingdom iv Hiven as it is f'r a poor man to get out iv Purgatory";[29] and he faced the responsibilities of imperialism, brought on by the Spanish War, with aplomb: "Hands acrost th' sea an' into somewan's pocket." [30] The sting was there, but it came from an affable man gently rotating his rag on the hardwood bar, not from a newspaperman born and raised in Chicago and eroded from within by the acid of suppressed criticism. Dunne made Dooley, and Dooley was his salvation.

While Mr. Dooley spoke tellingly on politics and mores, however, it would have been out of character for him to tackle the kinds of problems represented by the unemployed army who slept in the hallways of public buildings or by the houses of prostitution which ran, with immense commercial success, just west and south of the Loop. The city which had been founded purely for business reasons, and whose victims were victims of that ethic, received its direct exposure from a visiting English reformer and journalist, William T. Stead, who in *If Christ Came to Chicago!* (1895) spoke of Chicago's "other half," with whom he had lived in 1894. Stead's wrath at the degradation he found was turned on the upper half of the population, who failed to recognize their connection with the bottom. While he saw the corruption of the political bosses, he also saw that their organizations attempted to meet the human obligations presented by the lower classes and were, in effect, doing the work of the churches. Farmer Jones, the precinct captain, "rough, vulgar, and faulty," nevertheless cares for those in his district in a way in which the materially comfortable do not care for them, and, for better or worse, he is Christ's agent to the gutters. Stead presented the case history of Maggie Darling, a Chicago prostitute, to demonstrate that her fall was not so grievous as the self-righteousness of those who would not allow her to re-enter society, even as a domestic servant. Recognizing the total commitment of the Chicago males to acquiring money, he turned to their leisured and moneyed wives and said, "Those women who have great opportunities only to neglect them, and who have great means only to squander them upon themselves, are more disreputable in the eyes of God and man than the worst harlot on Fourth Avenue." [31] Most important, Stead saw more clearly than any writer before Dreiser the relation of commerce and morality: "The peculiar temptation of a woman is that her virtue is a realizable asset. It costs a man money to indulge his vice, but for a woman it is money into pocket." [32] Carrie and Hurstwood were to act this out.

Melville Stone, publisher of the *Daily News,* then head of Associated Press and supplier of the capital for his son's publishing firm and for *The Chap-Book,* spoke for Chicago when he said of the Stead book, "It was an honest effort, but its author had seen but one side, and it was therefore grotesquely unfair." [33] Though the book had a sensational sale initially, it was difficult to separate out the number who might have agreed with it from the many who obviously bought it because in its first edition Stead included a map of the red-light district with an annotated blacklist of its proprietors. Subsequent editions omitted this list at the request of the news companies, which refused to vend it on trains should it continue to carry the list. As Fuller's character had suggested, if the Black City had problems it would solve them through the contagious contact with the White City of its fantasies, not through systematic consideration of them. While talk went on, Jane Addams settled in at Hull-House.

Will Payne was the best of the Chicago reporters of the nineties who attempted to steal time from their assignments to write novels. In *Jerry the Dreamer* (1896), he followed the career of a rural youth who entered Chicago with a dream of conquest fresh in his mind but found a less genial world than did the characters in the Ade sketches. Jerry did not dream of getting rich; he dreamed rather "of having his say, of making the fluid mass about him feel his individuality." [34] He married without appreciating the limitations placed on his ambitions until his attempts to avoid the restraints of society forced him to decide between his wife and continued pursuit of his dream. He chose the assured if lesser happiness of life with his wife to the isolated achievement of his ideal and he returned to her, content in his defeat. In *The Money Captain* (1898) Payne used his expertise as a business reporter to examine the decent chap caught up in the web of higher finance, and in describing a particularly corrupt political deal he talked of the Greek statue which personified Chicago: "The typical sturdy young lady with her 'I Will' motto regularly despoiled over night and regularly shrieking the fact in the morning; getting up a fine semblance of outraged hysteria over it—although she knew it would happen again the next night." [35]

Payne had all the materials for the novel of social forces which Howells concluded he himself was too old to write, but he fell far shorter, with his wealth of details, than did Howells with his somewhat prissy selectivity. Whereas Howells was finally incapable of contemplating a society in which he could not detect a unifying moral structure—so that when the plot did not reveal it he supplied it, as in *A Hazard of New Fortunes,* in the consciousness of his central character—Payne, freed of this concern, could not distinguish finally the forest from the trees. Corruption is wrong, yet corruption is inevitable, his novels show, and he can neither break the cycle nor penetrate to what it means. His work illustrates the destructiveness of a naïve acceptance of Howells' claims for realism. When you have the fidelity to life without a higher technique (which is to say, a higher motive), you have something which says nothing. As Bernard Duffey put it, Payne reveals a "lack of interest in positing for the Chicago world any explanation broader than its own manifest wickedness." [36] If he was too young to accept Howells' now rather dated concept of the unity in American life, he was not disentangled enough to posit another one, as Norris and Dreiser were to do. By the close of the decade he had given over the effort to make his literature anything more than a source of income.

Payne's career is representative of the final blow the city room was capable of delivering to the literary aspirant. It trained him to think of the novels he wanted to write as realistic, while at the same time inundating him with details of a reality which the newspaper would not describe. He came to believe, therefore, that these details were worth setting down because they were unprintable in a newspaper, and in his novels he responded to this motive without adequately considering the question of what was the meaningful structure of reality which made it worthy of representation in a fictive work. The romance writer knew that his highly rearranged picture of life amused in its melodrama and held up ennobling ideals in its characters.[37] But the newspaper realist, in dismissing these fantasies as puerile and in dreaming of works which would show life as it really is, seldom paused to consider why this was worth the effort. When they won through to an achieved novel, then they too often found themselves without a meaningful content. At least, they felt, they had been faithful to the life they saw; but fidelity is a condition of art, not art itself. If this is what they had to offer, then better Riis than Payne.

Arthur Brisbane explained the secret of his success to a young reporter by pointing to his shelf: "Do you see those books? It is an encyclopedia; there are thirty volumes; I began at the left, have read straight through fifteen volumes, and shall read straight through the rest. There is a little on every subject under the sun. Young man, if you would succeed in journalism, never lose your . . . *superficiality*." [38] Most newspaper novelists were unable to lose it when they turned to fiction or to sociology, and, having survived the twin perils of cynicism and sentimentalism, they were sunk on the reef of realism as its own excuse for being. Mere fidelity to life was superficiality.

The survivors, however, survived as the result of the newspapers that took them in and schooled them, not just in spite of them. In no other profession in America, if not in the world, could the maimed and undersized misfit from Greece via Ireland, England, and France, Lafcadio Hearn, have been held above water and turned loose to express himself than on an American newspaper, and Hearn, who was worth saving, was thus saved in the eighties before he went on to Japan in the nineties. In no other profession in America could the would-be writer bite the hand that fed him and yet come back again for further material support, however slight, as did Crane. In no other profession in America could a baffled and all but mute refugee from poverty and miseducation have his tongue gradually loosened and his mind slowly filled, as did Dreiser. The myth that was to survive well into the next century and lure such as Ernest Hemingway had its foundation in men who insisted on talking to one another about the hypocrisy of the social system even while they were being paid to explain it away, whose faith in the big scoop was not entirely alien to a faith in the power of prose, and who read everything they could lay their hands on and fanned one another's literary aspirations as they sat about the city room on a rainy night. For the writer coming of age in the nineties, the daily metropolitan newspaper was a dwelling place with comforts and risks which matched his aspirations and fears in a way no other institution in America could approach.

The Poles of Violence:

Ambrose Bierce and Richard Harding Davis

In September 1903, in a letter from West Virginia, Ambrose Bierce wrote: "They found a Confederate soldier over there the other day, with his rifle alongside. I'm going over to beg his pardon." [1]

Bierce had been in the Civil War; he had poured the vitriol there acquired into a career of journalism in England in the seventies, then, with an ample supply remaining, he had returned to America to assume in San Francisco the trade of village scold and critic.[2] The Civil War, the years since had taught him, was the most horrible and yet the only unhypocritical event of his life. Having lost what little faith he had had in the issues over which it was fought, he was prepared to apologize to the skeleton in rags in West Virginia who had been his comrade in experience during those four years when America, he realized, had accepted the violently chaotic nature of its civilization and formalized it in war.

Bierce's stronghold in San Francisco was the *Examiner,* William Randolph Hearst's first essay into journalism, and although his bitterness led him to widespread insult and deliberate character assassination, he was, Hearst knew, worth the price of the paper. Bierce's copy might be late, Bierce's copy might never materialize, but Bierce was worth putting up with. The cynicism which was being developed as a thin defensive armor by younger reporters in America was Bierce's by nature—not like the knight's, but like the armadillo's. In a land in which the murderous side of the war was an oral tradition only and in which toughness was tempered with tenderness, there was room for one specimen of unrelieved cynicism, one veteran of the war who would write only of its grotesqueries.

The Pacific Coast was his logical sanctuary, because there daily violence was a living memory. Few young men in San Francisco had missed some experience with firearms—even the somewhat foppish Gelett Burgess had met armed robbers in Southern California, while the poet Joaquin Miller had fought Indians—and the massive influx of Chinese labor further contributed to the feeling that life was a little cheaper there than elsewhere in literate America. California, moreover, while it was technically committed to the North during the war, had not had the emotional commitment to be found east of the Rockies. Many a northern Copperhead sought sanctuary there (this is why the arch-New-Englander Robert Frost had a San Francisco birth), and the state received refugees who fled direct involvement in the war, just as many went East to get into it.

If the late century could tolerate one veteran who would write of the horrors which were otherwise to reside in talk only, San Francisco was the place for him. So many flags had flown over it in the century (Spanish, Mexican, Californian, and even, slightly to the north, Russian) that the Stars and Stripes were not invulnerable; so polyglot was its population when it became part of the United States that white Protestantism had never managed to establish its creeds as the foundation of urban manners, as it had in almost all other major American cities.

The profession which sustained Bierce was newspaper journalism, and he had a fairly free hand as to what he would put into his columns. The American scene appeared to him to have all the senselessness of battle without the glory and the rules, and he attacked with vigor both the wielders of privilege and their victims. Without benefit of Nietzsche, he had arrived at a philosophy that looked with contempt both on the viciousness with which the plunderers plundered and the foolishness with which the plundered allowed themselves to be plundered. Such an attitude, joined to an effective prose, was a valuable commodity for Hearst, who was mounting his career on the steed of reform and who could employ Bierce to make the initial destructive assault on his foes. Indeed, when Bierce finally left San Francisco in 1897, he went to Washington as Hearst's hatchet man. There he engaged Collis P. Huntington and the Southern Pacific Railroad at closer quarters as they lobbied for favorable legislation. This writer bitterly scornful of social concerns was, in practice, more useful to his boss's political ends than were most reforming journalists.

Like the younger men who were lured by the newspaper legend, Bierce held to the dictum that life was the writer's material: "This I *know*: the good writer (supposing him to be born to the trade) is not made by reading, but by observing and experiencing." [3] Unlike the younger writers, however, Bierce turned the dictum into a defensive as well as an offensive weapon. It meant that he, Bierce, had little to learn from other writers, and it also meant that his wartime experiences could be held in suspension within him and made to stand for all the books and all the other experiences life could afford. Accident Bierce defined as "an inevitable occurrence due to the action of immutable natural laws," [4] and in this he was not merely twitting the complacent. He was rationalizing his arrested outlook, so that war, which abounded in violent reversals, became the pattern of life, and everything that occurred outside his window could be accounted for, as were events in war, as the chance happenings of a universe in which moral causation bore no relation to events.

Realism, then, which presented the commonplace in terms of some immediately recognizable causal pattern was contemptible, and Howells became a constant target for Bierce's abuse. He preferred Poe's romances because they relied on the imagination to throw up pictures of the horrors of life, "and the first three essentials of the literary art are imagination, imagination and imagination." [5]

Journalism, which demanded that Bierce look at daily life, was not, he knew, art, and he roundly condemned it. But it did serve a function for Bierce far greater than the one it served for the younger men who engaged in it willingly. Without journalism, Bierce would not have been held to the hither side of sanity and have been compelled day in and day out to face realities, if only again to dismiss them. The newspaper kept Bierce at observation of life in spite of himself, and, like Mencken later, he enjoyed the observation even though, unlike Mencken, he would not admit it. While his war-arrested mind led him to treat the day's news as mere repetitions of the same old story, at least that mind was constantly forced to face up to its repetitive task and so freed of the dangers of self-hypnosis that constantly threatened the imitators of Poe. The passing scene for which he expressed only explicit contempt is captured and enjoyed, for instance, in definitions he wrote, such as this one:

Riches, *n.* a gift from Heaven signifying, "This is my beloved son, in whom I am well pleased."—*John D. Rockefeller*. The reward of toil and virtue.—*J. P. Morgan*. The savings of many in the hands of one—*Eugene Debs*. To these excellent definitions the inspired lexicographer feels that he can add nothing of value.[6]

To preserve his sense of himself as a man of letters temporarily engaged in a base trade, Bierce developed a style which, though with echoes of Bret Harte, also anticipates the school of Mencken. In his reporting, as also in his stories, he employed an extremely formal, literary language—latinate words, periodic sentences, foreign borrowings—and used it to surround the sordid events with which he dealt so as to demonstrate two things central to his outlook. First, he revealed his contempt for what he was treating by exploiting the incongruity of its vocabulary with his syntax and diction. The object of satire was not just attacked, it was, as it were, dangled contemptuously from a cultured hand. Second, he showed his reader that he had a style which was adequate to more than he was at the moment undertaking and that if he but thought it worthwhile he could excel in the literary craft. So in one of his stories the young lover setting out for California is told by his fiancée to succeed soon and hurry back or she will join him. "I can put the

coins in little bags as you dig them out," she says with unconscious humor, after which Bierce characteristically phrases the
"snapper" in the next sentence in a diction so lofty as to ridicule
through the sheer weight of its being lavished on something so
trivial: "This characteristically feminine theory of auriferous de-
posits did not commend itself to the masculine intelligence: it was
Mr. Doman's belief that gold was found in a liquid state." [7]

An entire twentieth-century style of wise-guy journalism may
be found summed up in a typical Bierce sentence. Inversion, lofty
diction, and foreign borrowings consciously clash with slang when
he writes, for instance: "Of this latter aptitude, indeed, he manifested his disapproval by an act which secured him the position of
clerk of the laundry in the State prison, and for her the *sobriquet*
of 'Split-faced Moll.' " [8]

While Bierce was read and admired by many another writer, it
is difficult to see his work as a direct influence on the journalistic
style of later practitioners, few of whom possessed his skill. The
same factors which formed his techniques—the cynicism which
allowed him to live with conditions he felt himself powerless to
affect; his fascination with words and their syntactic combinations
as opposed to straight reporting styles—could have led others to
imitate him unconsciously. But the imitations, conscious or unconscious, lacked Bierce's distinguishing mark, the tone of arrow-
like contempt, because they were assumed as an artificial way of
dismissing the troubles of the world. Bierce's tone was a natural
outgrowth of a personality so shocked by war that it held itself
together only by the compulsive demonstration that meaningless
slaughter contained all the meaning there was.

The Civil War stories which Bierce published in the nineties
reflected this attitude. In "A Son of the Gods" incredible heroism
goes for nought; in "One of the Missing" heroism is mistaken for
suicide; in "Killed at Resaca" the hero is defamed and his heroism
is misrepresented. Grotesque coincidences abound, in contempt of
the natural laws of probability, and, to enforce the unnaturalness
of war, Bierce turns time and again to the slaughter of kin either in

the unconscious fury of war or in the fulfillment of a military duty higher than the normal requirements. The men who respect orders, who are heroic, who are honorable, are glorified, although they always die. Through following the arbitrary military code they respond cleanly to the violence of life, whereas those who view life as essentially tranquil and give in to feelings which they regard as natural are only deluded. In story after story family and feelings lead only to destruction—not the clean death of the hero who accepts the code, but the horrible death of the betrayed man who has misapprehended the conditions of his existence. The only connoisseur of heroism is he who pursues it to death, just as the only gourmet is he who eats the meat; but he must be conscious of what he is about. The most famous of Bierce's stories, "An Occurrence at Owl Creek Bridge," holds up for display a man who pathetically yields to instinct and in imagination flees for home rather than accepting the death that the rules of war require of him. He should have known better, says the snap of the strangling noose.

In peacetime, Bierce felt, the same values apply. Commerce is based on cheating, and cheats and counter-cheats are a peacetime war far more degrading than the real thing. "That is all nonsense about the 'horrors of war,' " he wrote, "in so far as the detestable phrase implies that they are worse than those of peace; they are more striking and impressive that is all." [9] In war what is expedient is what is moral, and, Bierce believed, in life the same is true.

> If man's notions of right and wrong have any other basis than this of expediency; if they originated, or could have originated, in any other way; if actions have in themselves a moral character apart from, and nowise dependent on, their consequences [he wrote]— then all philosophy is a lie and reason a disorder of the mind. [10]

Unlike the younger men fed on tales of heroism and glory, Bierce knew that war is made "not against the bodies of adult males, but against the means of subsistence of a people." [11] This perception explained why no man counted more than another man in war, and the lesson learned in the 1860s Bierce did not feel had to be unlearned as the result of any subsequent peacetime experiences. Life, like war, was impersonal, and the recurrent theme of his art was the way personality went smash in its failure to comprehend this. Better to grasp this fact and run headlong into the inevitable consequences.

But Ambrose Bierce himself hung back from the plunge and, unable to write long fiction because of disbelief in the rational continuity of experience, he interspersed his slashing journalism in the nineties with brief tales and poems of bitter attack on men who would not see what he saw. Still, he knew what all this meant for himself—that a life as cruel as the one he saw rendered art meaningless and that he was better off dead. Perhaps the apology he wanted to make to the Confederate corpse in 1903 was not "I am sorry you are dead," but "I apologize for living." A dream visited him time and again, calling him to face up personally to the quietus he recommended:

I am passing through an open glade in a thinly wooded country. Through the belt of scattered trees that bound the irregular space there are glimpses of cultivated fields and the homes of strange intelligences. It must be near daybreak, for the moon, nearly at full, is low in the west, showing blood-red through the mists with which the landscape is fantastically freaked. The grass about my feet is heavy with dew, and the whole scene is that of a morning in early summer, glimmering in the unfamiliar light of a setting full moon. Near my path is a horse, visibly and audibly cropping the herbage. It lifts its head as I am about to pass, regards me motionless for a moment, then walks towards me. It is milk-white, mild of mien and amiable in look. I say to myself: "This horse is a gentle soul," and pause to caress it. It keeps its eyes fixed upon my own, approaches and speaks to me in a human voice, with human words. This does not surprise, but terrifies, and instantly I return to this our world.[12]

Bierce compulsively caressed death but fled from its actual meaning. In June 1913 he wrote a friend: "I've seen the last—*my* last —of California and of you. Pretty soon I am going away—O very far away. I have in mind a little valley in the heart of the Andes, just wide enough for one. . . . This is my 'last word'—do you think I shall find my Vale of Peace?" [13] The writer who despised life and held war to be the model condition of living, and death the only fulfillment of the hero, nevertheless refused to accept his own conclusions and fled from the pale steed of his dreams. At the age of seventy-two he set out again to find the peace that did not descend upon him at the time of Appomattox; he disappeared into Mexico, never to be heard from again. The white-hot core of Bierce's bitterness was not contempt for humanity, but contempt for a self which would not relinquish the hope of peace in this life.

Ambrose Bierce's bitterness stood at one pole in the range of experience available to the writer coming of age in the nineties. His scorn for collective action, his dismissal of the realistic novel, his admiration for Poe and the role of the imagination in literature, and his immersion of the vernacular in a sea of latinate diction timed to the rhythms of formal syntax, all found followers, or, at the least, unconscious echoers. *M'lle New York,* committed as it was to its notion of what was French, nevertheless perpetuated Bierce's trappings, although the motivation was different, and he became a tempting guide for some writers in the twentieth century. Whenever life was seen as chaos by a writer who was committed to capturing some shred of that chaos as he condemned it, there Bierce stood as a model. His nearly brutal wrath might maim; but his imitators, lacking that wrath, were in danger of posing.

The society which cheerfully rippled on over and past the semi-submerged Bierces was not inarticulate, and the newspaper world which fostered the cynicism of the neo-Bierces also provided the adventures sought by clear-eyed young men who, born too late for the war and coming from comfortable homes, were determined to test their principles amidst danger. If those who dined at Delmonico's were ignorant or indifferent toward those who starved on Third Avenue, if those who gathered at studio teas would have been hard put to stay alive in a tropical forest, the master of life was he who had experienced stark problems of survival in a ravening wilderness and who could stride into the Waldorf, his weather-beaten face proclaiming his experience, and use the correct fork while reluctantly permitting the young ladies to draw from him the story of his most recent adventure. In the face of the postwar commercialization of life, the popular imagination began to construct for itself a hero who could have the best of both worlds; who would be accepted in the drawing rooms of the effete rich because his natural nobility gave him a place there; who could carry the principles of gentlemanliness into the most brutal situations and show that Americans, through birth and training, were adequate to them. That imagination received its hero in the person of Richard Harding Davis, whose adventurous achievements were proof against all the reservations the cynic could produce. He had been the confidant of criminals and he had been presented to the Queen; he had ridden with a man-hunting patrol in the wastes of the Mexican border and he had seen the coronation in Moscow. At the opposite pole from Bierce, he also attracted.

Davis was born in Philadelphia in 1864 into comfortable material and spiritual circumstances. Two years before his birth, his mother, Rebecca Harding Davis, had published a novel, *Margaret Howth,* intended to show the values resident in the vulgar and common American life, and the year before that she had published a realistic story in the *Atlantic.* She was to continue to write novels and stories throughout the century, sometimes lapsing into sentimentality, but always bringing to them her firm conviction that an active Christian morality was adequate to life. Davis's father was an editorial-writer, and the comfortable Episcopal family circle inculcated in the son a sense that the decent thing to do was the Christian thing to do; when you try to help human beings, his mother said, "God makes you happy my darling." [14] The enlightened Christianity of the Davis home made it one of the centers of congenial artistic Philadelphia, where one could expect to meet H. H. Furness and Frances Hodgson Burnett, and where, when they were performing in town, could be found the Barrymores with their pretty little daughter

Ethel, Henry Irving, Ellen Terry, Augustin Daly, Ada Rehan, Joseph Jefferson, John Drew, and Edward Sothern.

Richard attended Episcopal Academy, summered in Newport, visited with his mother's friend Dr. Holmes in Boston, and, after a slow academic start, finally presented himself as a student at Lehigh University. He arrived there with Sunday-school opinions, light-colored gloves, a hat, and a cane, a ready-made target for undergraduate derision, and, to add to his priggish appearance and prim notions, he chose to make overtures of acquaintance with a polite stiffness which savored to his schoolmates of condescension. M. A. DeWolfe Howe, then a sophomore at Lehigh, recalled how amazed he was to get a formal note addressed to him as "Mr. Howe," from somebody who identified himself as Richard H. Davis, Caledonian Tennis Club. All this chap wanted Howe to do was play tennis, a game then still associated with the rich, but the note was phrased like a formal challenge and closed with the hope that an acceptance would be received "at an early date either conditionally or unconditionally." [15] Young Davis, moreover, suggested that an account of their game be written and submitted to both the college and the town newspapers; he seemed to be not only a fool, but an extremely vain one.

The sophomore class did not wait long to express its feelings about the confident dandy who stood out irritatingly from the others in the freshman class. When Davis told them that he "refused" to be hazed because the practice was "blackguardly," some of them took the information as justification for a jubilant assault upon him in the streets of Bethlehem, Pennsylvania. Davis, an assiduous student of fisticuffs, coolly stood them off and was so clearly the victor that at the close of the conflict the police were addressing him as "sir," and the delighted members of the freshman class urged him to represent them on the athletic committee. This, Davis told his class, he could not possibly do, since he would then be behaving in a blackguardly fashion toward the student who had been their original nominee.

Virtue had triumphed in the street fight, to everyone's amazement save Davis's. Because of the fight, "I am now the hero of the hour," he reported home, but went on to say that of course, as everyone at home had told him, this only proved that "one gets taken care of in this world if you do what's the right thing." [16]

The unqualified way in which his son took the doctrines taught him in his nonage alarmed even his father, who began to send him warning notes. If he could not recant what had been said about the follower of Christ as the man who wins in this world's struggles, at least, he felt, he could prepare his son for a disappointment he was now old enough to begin to comprehend, and he told him that many times trying is as good as doing: "I do not know but I think God loves the effort to do as well as the act done." [17]

Davis, however, needed no such cautions because he had no trouble getting done what he wanted to do and would have been surprised if told there was another way to look at life. He drank ginger ale when the others drank beer and was all the more popular for that. He was invited to join a fraternity and promptly declined on the ground that he did not approve of that scheme of undergraduate life. Rather, he founded a club which met Saturday nights, "so as not to interfere with our work," and which devoted itself to "singing, reading, eating, and boxing until midnight." [18]

After graduation Davis spent a year studying political economy at Johns Hopkins, then, in 1886, left to sail to Cuba on the yacht of his friend William W. Thurston, president of Bethlehem Steel. Upon his return he presented himself for employment at the Philadelphia *Press,* where a city editor who thought himself invulnerable to any new example of human folly gagged at the prospect of employing a cub reporter who went about his duties dressed like the Prince of Wales. But, the editor found, that dress was a costume signifying Richard Harding Davis, city reporter. The acolyte also had a slicker and straps to wear when he went out to report the Johnstown Flood and did a superb job, and a pea jacket and old sweater for his role as confidant of a gang of yeggmen whom he betrayed to the police after planning a burglary with them.

Davis went about his job the way a twelve-year-old boy possessed of the Universal Jim Dandy Disguise Kit goes about his games, while a breathless city room waited for the inevitable fall, which never came. He did all the eager things that were good form in Sunday school and excruciatingly bad taste on the paper, but before the expectant eyes of his colleagues he soared from triumph to triumph. Sent out as legman to a veteran reporter on an important story, he told his mother: "When we got back I had all the facts, and what little he had was incorrect—so I said I would dispense with his services and write the story myself. I did it very politely, but it queered the man." [19] Whether or not it queered Davis with his colleagues, he himself did not say. The story was good—even the editor praised it—and he had done his duty.

In Philadelphia, Davis began also to write stories for the magazines, tales of adventure about newspaper work, for the most part. The most celebrated of the early group was "Gallegher," the story of a copy boy who helps capture the crook and then heroically delivers the news in time for a scoop. It was a romance about the invincibility of pluck, but it was nonetheless representative of the way real life was responding to Davis's humorless, clear-eyed pursuit of the virtuous man's duty, in the same way that Bierce's grotesqueries were representative of what he took the pattern of life to be. Davis continued his story-writing after joining the New York *Sun* in 1888, and as his golden luck held and he triumphed in one adventure after another, which he duly reported with all the boyish confidence with which he had intended to write up his freshman tennis match for the delectation of the readers of the Bethlehem *Times,* the popular imagination gratefully followed this living embodiment of the feasibility of principles that so many dissenters were crying down. Davis's perfection extended even to modesty, based on his appreciation of his father's charge that "a man entrusted with such talent should carry himself straighter than others to whom it is denied." [20]

In 1890 *Harper's Weekly* appointed him editor; he was twenty-six years old. As his income increased and his stories about his adventures spread, his career exerted an attraction on all youngsters who dreamed of gaining fame before their youth was spent. Booth Tarkington recalled:

> To the college boy of the early nineties Richard Harding Davis was the "beau ideal of *jeunesse dorée*," a sophisticated heart of gold. He was of that college boy's own age, but already an editor—already publishing books! His stalwart good looks were as familiar to us as were those of our own football captain; we knew his face as we know the face of the President of the United States, but we infinitely preferred Davis's. When the Waldorf was wondrously completed, and we cut an exam. in Cuneiform Inscriptions for an excursion to see the world at lunch in its new magnificence, and Richard Harding Davis came into the Palm Room—then, oh, then, our day was radiant! That was the top of our fortune; we could never have hoped for so much.[21]

During 1892 Davis visited the West and reported glowingly on hobnobbing with Mexican murderers, Texas Rangers, wizened prospectors, and women who smoked and drank in public; went off to England, where he mingled in Oxford undergraduate life and then London social life, throwing in a dash of Bohemia; returned to his summer home on Cape Cod, where Grover Cleveland, Joseph Jefferson, and Richard Watson Gilder were friends and neighbors; then, in the fall, went off to the dedication of the Columbian Exposition in Chicago. In 1893 he was having tea with official British society on Gibraltar, climbing a harem roof in Spain, handling a fakir's snakes in Morocco, and, in general, watching the way the English did things: "If America starts annexing islands," he wrote home in March of that year, "she will need people to tell her how it is generally done and it is generally done, I find, by the English." [22] On the way home he attended the theater in Paris on a night when the leading actress was hissed by a claque organized by her rejected lover. Davis leapt up and called for all Englishmen and Americans there to join him in silencing the hissers in order to give the French an object lesson in Anglo-Saxon fair play. The next year he was driving through the early-morning gray of London in a victoria with Ellen Terry talking softly beside him, and the year after he was cutting his way through the brush of Central and South America. This was exciting enough until the papers arrived with news of trolley riots in Brooklyn, a crisis in France, war in the Balkans, and a revolution in Honolulu. Then Davis realized that that particular year he was not "in it," and he abused his luck.

For to be in it was everything, and the world provided a splendid variety of "it"s. The normal flow of life and the inner workings of man, Davis believed, except when challenged by heightened incidents, are for nought. He may have appeared to his shrewder contemporaries to have been incredibly lucky though hopelessly naïve about virtuous living, and fantastically exhibitionist about everything, but they had not been through the events which obsessed Bierce and enervated the minds of his contemporaries, and they could not help admiring and envying him. Dick Davis was in it, and, from Crane to Hemingway, they wanted in too, in great part as a result of the attraction he exerted. He was in it, for instance, in 1896 and 1897 when he reported the coronation at Moscow, the Millennial Celebration at Budapest, the Spanish-Cuban War, the McKinley inauguration, the Greek-Turkish War, and the Queen's Jubilee. For the wars he had puttees and a pith helmet; for the royal events he had a velvet suit with steel buttons, silk stockings, and pumps with buckles. He strapped on a pistol in Cuba; he strapped on a sword at the Court of St. James's. When, in 1898, Davis and his generation were finally provided with an American war, he could joyously write from Admiral Sampson's flagship, the *New York*: "The other night, we were heading off a steamer and firing six-pounders across her bows, the band was playing the 'star' song from Meistersinger." It was splendid fun; "Wagner and War struck me as the most fin de siècle idea of war that I had ever heard of." [23]

Davis did not remain on the *New York*. He went into the rough country, pursuing adventure and placing himself in dangerous proximity to the fighting so that he could tell how it felt as well as what had happened. But success at this would have been pointless if he could not also have dined with the senior officers. Davis's ultimate appeal came not just from being in it, but from being able to move with ease from such adventures to lunch at the Waldorf. He demonstrated to those of his generation who would listen that their capacity for excitement was matched by the doings in the wide world. But he also demonstrated to an uneasy plutocracy, which was beginning to hear the clamor of protest from below, that their gospel of wealth coming to the virtuous and their public dedication to genteel manners and gentlemanly Christian behavior were indeed justified. Courage and the Sunday-school code, loyalty to chums, resistance to blackguards and their cronies, fair play to all—Dick Davis proved the practicality of these. He demonstrated that an Anglo-Saxon gentleman could face down a murderous half-breed because savagery and bad blood quailed naturally before civilization and breeding. Rudyard Kipling was telling Americans that the nation which won was the nation which knew enough to keep the dead out of the drinking water and which, knowing that, deserved to win. Richard Harding Davis showed that Americans were such a people.

Davis made an immense contribution to the fantasy of the natural superiority of the American, which halfway through the twentieth century still dominated Hollywood. For example, in *Soldiers of Fortune* (1897), which takes place in a Central American country where an American civil engineer is establishing a mining plant with the cooperation of the local authorities, who recognize the civilizing benefits that will be conferred on the natives as a result, the American hero is a bronzed young man who has fought as an officer with the British in the Sudan, been with the Foreign Legion, hacked his way through Brazil, and, as a result of such exploits, is the owner of countless foreign decorations carelessly thrown into his drawer. The novel also has a charming Irish-American gunrunner who contracts revolutions, a disgraced British officer hiding in exile but at the crucial moment redeeming his earlier shame by dying gallantly, and the girl of good blood, daughter of the mining company's president, who is a debutante but who can nevertheless appreciate engineering details, and who can drive a horse through a hailstorm of bullets. This team cannot lose to the discontented revolutionaries who would seize the mine, and it does not.

Davis knew more than this about such situations. In his reporting he had clearly shown that American interference in Central America was as bloody in its methods as was the practice of the native leaders who resented it, and that Wall Street had contracted for riots and executions.[24] But he also carried in his reporting the assumptions of Social Darwinism, that the bare and poor houses in Venezuela were bare and poor not because the people were poor, but because they were indolent. "There is no more interesting question of the present day," he said, "than that of what is to be done with the world's land which is lying unimproved," [25] and he set out to answer it. The natives of unimproved regions were like gangs of barbarians in beautifully furnished houses, and if they didn't live up to their surroundings they were to be turned out in favor of those who would.

Davis is also remembered for his stories of men about town, such as Van Bibber, or of international socialites, such as the Princess Aline. But his fiction's major attraction was its combination of high life and high adventure. The chief romantic impact of a Davis tale of heroism is not what happened to the hero so much as that what happened has been reported to those who count, that after he engineers the revolution, or builds the bridge, or rescues the heiress, he is there on Park Avenue among his equals to tell them about it. This hero represents the adequacy of the genteel principle to any possible crisis that can arise, and, with the aid of Gibson, the illustrator, Davis provided him with a mate: "A tall, fair girl with great bands and masses of hair, with a head rising like a lily from a firm, white throat, set on broad shoulders above a straight back and sloping breast—a tall, beautiful creature, half-girl, half woman, who looked back at him shyly but steadily." [26] As the Spanish-

American War imposed a temporary unity on American life and de-emphasized the social conflicts which served as midwife at the birth of the nineties, so Richard Harding Davis counterbalanced the attraction that the commonplace and the discussion of social injustices might have had for the writers of his generation. He offered a vision of life in which the old ideals could still work, and his sun-bronzed man with his straight-backed mate walked hand in hand into a future which was totally under his control.

Davis was listened to when he countered the myth of the reporter who must work his way up from copy boy. "That is the old time journalist's idea of it," he said—and that is why he is still a reporter at the age of sixty. Davis provided the definitive legend, based on his career, and in so doing contradicted Bierce and those who agreed with him:

> Now, you cannot pay a good reporter for what he does, because he does not work for pay. He works for his paper. He gives his time, his health, his brains, his sleeping hours, and his eating hours, and sometimes his life to get news for it. He thinks the sun rises only that men may have light by which to read it. But if he has been in a newspaper office from his youth up, he finds out before he becomes a reporter that this is not so, and loses his real value. He should come right out of the University where he has been doing "campus notes" for the college weekly, and be pitchforked out into city work without knowing whether the Battery is at Harlem or at Hunter's Point, and with the idea that he is a Moulder of Public Opinions and that the Power of the Press is greater than the Power of Money, and that the few lines he writes are of more value in the Editor's eyes than is the column of advertising on the last page, which they are not. After three years—it is sometimes longer, sometimes not so long—he finds out that he has given his nerves and his youth and his enthusiasm in exchange for a general fund of miscellaneous knowledge, the opportunity of personal encounter with all the greatest and most remarkable men and events that have risen in those three years, and a great fund of resource and patience. He will find that he has crowded the experiences of the lifetime of the ordinary young business man, doctor, or lawyer, or man about town, into three short years; that he has learned to think and

to act quickly, to be patient and unmoved when everyone else has lost his head, actually or figuratively speaking; to write as fast as another man can talk, and to be able to talk with authority on matters on which other men do not venture even to think until they have read what he has written with a copy-boy at his elbow on the night previous.[27]

Although he was only fifty-two when he died in 1916, Richard Harding Davis outlived the legend he helped to promulgate, and he recognized this. Reporting on the World War prior to American entrance, he met the young men who were to be, after the war, a lost generation, and he recognized that, just as his ideals had sent them off to chase after war and get into it before their country did, so being in this new kind of war would kill his ideals for them. As the kind of reporting he represented had kept Crane and Norris and Frederic from stifling under the influence of a view like Bierce's, so shortly before his death he offered a preview of the new man, such as Hemingway, who had found his legend attractive but who was to shed it.

In his story "The Deserter" Davis presents a young American who has served heroically as a volunteer in an English ambulance unit because his country is not yet at war. After fifteen months, however, the volunteer has had enough of slime and mutilation and visits a group of American correspondents to ask them to help in his plans to desert. He is ready now, he says, to go back to America and capitalize on his military experiences by writing about them. If he has been a hero, as they say, he wants now to return home and receive the hero's price in money and adulation rather than to remain and allow death to be the paymaster. The correspondents, men of Davis's generation, still hold to the principles of loyalty and bravery, and they attempt to argue the deserter back to the trenches on these grounds. He sneers at their arguments; he has been to war and knows that it is not like that. So they change their line of argument and appeal to his cynicism, explaining that if he tries to cash in on his heroism before the war is over somebody will discover that he has deserted and he will find all doors closed. This message hits home. The deserter accepts the horrible realization that he must see the war through to its end before he can profit from his part in it, and he leaves the reporters' hotel room to return. To their cheering remarks, he pauses at the door only long enough to reply before disappearing, "Go to hell." Richard Harding Davis died before American troops landed in France.

Ambrose Bierce, formed by armed conflict, saw in his America only a continuation of war without its cleanness and dignity and counseled contempt while privately searching for a vale of peace. Richard Harding Davis, born in Episcopal Philadelphia while Bierce was in battle, saw in his America a superior vitality which God would reward, and counseled confidence while publicly searching for areas of armed combat. They differed, yet their views intersected, and at the point of intersection they stood for the romantic above the commonplace, the violent as representative of rather than different from the deepest values in tranquillity, and the writer as witness for the hero who might very often be himself. Davis experienced Wagner and war and found it *fin-de-siècle*. Bierce sneered at the twilight self-consciousness of the nineties but admitted it manifested itself in important ways. The scientist, he said, is not impressed by *fin-de-siècle* psychology: "He keeps his head —which, by the way, is worth keeping." [28] The scientist in Davis kept his head also (actually and figuratively, as Davis was fond of adding to the phrase) and preceded the soldier into his country's future in Central America or on a Pacific island.

Bierce abused and Davis praised the newspaper office, but each took his place there to indicate where the writer was to hang his hat when he was ready for work. Neither offered a guide to style, to how to impress one's outlook on the material of his art. Both said, however, that that material, treat it as the writer would, was the violence of life, of which war was only the evident epidermis.

Outstripping the Event:

Stephen Crane

Unlike Richard Harding Davis, Stephen Crane accepted fraternities as a part of undergraduate life and swiftly joined Delta Upsilon after entering Lafayette College in September 1890. As a tough talker with nicotine-stained fingers and a reputation as a pool-player and baseball catcher, he should not have objected to hazing as Davis had done, and most likely he didn't in principle. But the sophomores who burst into his room one fall night to subject him to the customary harassments were stopped short by the sight of tough Stevie, green with fear, standing in his nightgown in a corner of the room, a revolver dangling from his limp hand.[1] They left. The degree of his opposition was ludicrous.

Stephen Crane's expectations had a way of outstripping the event. The youngest of the fourteen children of a minister, he knew that his behavior would be observed a little more closely in whatever New Jersey town the family was then living than that of the butcher's boy. He knew also that legend would have him be either Little Lord Fauntleroy or the wildest kid in town. His athletic accomplishments, his constant cigarette, and his persistent inquiries into the life from which his ministerial upbringing ostensibly excluded him were his youthful answers to society. He sought out the notoriety which he assumed would come to the misbehaving preacher's kid with a vehemence that was ridiculously extravagant in view of the nonchalance with which he and other such children were really regarded. Before his community could impose its standards upon him, before his mother, widowed when he was nine, could impose her Methodism on him, before his friends could ex-

plain the terms on which the gang played, Stephen Crane had developed a set of responses that anticipated the reality. These responses were formed in great part from the shreds and patches of
the conventions being imposed upon him: his anti-Methodism assumed gods, angels, and sinful men; his rejection of the boys' world
led to his studious proficiency at baseball and his rigor in cap-
taining the corps at his military preparatory school. But these were
strengthened and increasingly shaped by an inner consciousness
that told him that whatever was accepted was suspect; that there
was an inside story behind every public history.

At Lafayette such convictions built hazing into a monstrous outrage, and he got the revolver out when he heard footsteps in the
hall. He transferred at the end of the term to Syracuse, a school
founded by his mother's late uncle, Jesse Truesdell Peck, Bishop of
the Methodist Church, uncertain yet as to whether it was college
or Lafayette that he found unbearable, and within the year learned
that it was college. He played the smart aleck in class, refusing
to take the things in books seriously because, he implied, he knew
better. His habitual distrust of the arrangements and explanations
by which society perpetuated itself attracted him, rather, to his
brother Townley's newsgathering agency, and in the spring of 1891
he left formal education for journalism. After a brief period of
working for Townley, he made his way into the New York newspapers, where he was unpopular with the other reporters, who
thought that his aloofness was an arty pose. The defensive Crane
might well have armed himself with such a pose, but he was by
nature set apart anyway because, unlike his fellows, he thought
of the real story, the big scoop, not as a piece of news which was
going to come to him from outside but as fiction he would produce
from within. He was too impatient to wait upon daily happenings
to provide him with his materials. His response to them was preparing before they actually occurred. Events were a test of his
consciousness, not its instructor.

In July 1891 Hamlin Garland lectured in Avon-by-the-Sea on
"The Local Novel," and Stephen Crane, the nineteen-year-old New

York *Tribune* correspondent, came up to him afterward to borrow his notes. The sallow and laconic youth did not impress Garland, but the report he wrote of the lecture did, and Garland befriended Crane during his stay at Avon. The acquaintanceship lasted after Crane was fired from the *Tribune* for sarcastically representing a labor parade he had covered as a procession of slaves marching behind the chariots of their monopolistic conquerors, and drifted away from Avon into Bohemian New York. There a variety of newspaper jobs and friendship with a group of art students who, like him, were leading a hand-to-mouth existence on East Twenty-third Street kept Crane slightly above subsistence level. At Syracuse he had begun work on *Maggie,* the story of a New York girl of the streets, before he had had much, if any, opportunity to explore the slums of New York or learn of the actual experiences of a prostitute. He completed the book in the city and, on money borrowed from his brother, had it published in 1893. Nobody bought it, but Crane sent a copy to Garland, who vigorously sought him out and, struck by his paleness and thinness, fed him. Soon after, Garland delivered him to Howells, who, immensely impressed by *Maggie,* administered encouragement and his customary sound advice. Crane was grateful but far quicker to follow leads the older men gave him as to possible publishers for his stories or jobs writing newspaper sketches than suggestions they gave him as to materials or techniques he might employ. Both men hailed him as a brilliant recruit to realism, one who exposed social injustice, and at their urging he joined a breadline, slept in a flophouse, and reported on these incidents. But his mind was elsewhere.

Garland found this out in March 1893, when Crane, shabby as usual, turned up for a meal. Cutting through his guest's apparent nonchalance, Garland demanded to see the papers with which, with a studied unostentatiousness, Crane had crammed the side pockets of his seedy gray ulster. "Upon unrolling the manuscript," Garland wrote, "I found it to be a sheaf of poems written in blue ink upon single sheets of legal cap paper, each poem without blot or correction, almost without punctuation, all beautifully legible, exact and orderly in arrangement." [2] He read the neat hand quickly and with increasing excitement. The verses appeared to be compressed little capsules of symbolic meaning, but, once read, they expanded into all corners of the consciousness. Garland asked if Crane had more, and he answered that he had four or five, pointing to his temple, "up here, all in a little row." [3] He sat down and wrote one off in finished form; they were, he said, on tap and he could draw them off complete. Howells had read some of Emily Dickinson's poems to Crane, and these somewhat resembled hers. Garland thought they also were like the French translations of Japanese poetry then popular among the more rarefied aesthetes.

On another day the bulge in the seedy pocket turned out to be a tale of the Civil War, which, however, stopped abruptly. Garland read what there was and, now convinced that he was talking to nothing less than a full-fledged genius, asked, "Where's the rest of it?" "In hock," Crane told him, to his typist, [4] and Garland sent him off with $15 to redeem the remainder of *The Red Badge of Courage* from captivity. You're going to be rich and famous, he kept telling Crane. His prediction required no great soothsaying powers: the manuscript he had seen took possession of its reader with a swiftness and a confidence unlike anything then being written. Crane did not dispute his coming fame and glory but offered to sell his prospects for $23 in ready cash: "If I had some money to buy a new suit of clothes I'd feel my grip tighten on the future." [5]

On January 6, 1896, *The New York Times,* under the headline STEPHEN CRANE'S TRIUMPH, carried a story by its London man, Harold Frederic, on how that literary capital was ringing in praise of *The Red Badge*. This echoed the acclaim which had begun with the syndicated newspaper appearance of the novel, in abridged form, in 1894, and had become a roar after October 1895, when Appleton's published it in book form. On the strength of Crane's spreading fame, Copeland and Day in 1895 published his little poems in a volume titled *Black Riders,* and that same year the Bacheller Syndicate, which had first printed *The Red Badge,* sent him on a Western trip and on an abortive filibustering expedition to Cuba, which ended in shipwreck.

By January 1896 Crane, though not yet twenty-five years old, was famous enough to be assured of employment by Pulitzer or Hearst as a star reporter. Then he began reaping the crop of malice he had confidently expected when, as an unknown youngster, he had sown the seeds of naughty behavior. If his life with the art students on East Twenty-Third Street now gave rise to fallacious stories of his alcoholism and dope addiction, he was not surprised; indeed, he may have felt some gratification. A neophyte reporter caught up with him one night in New York, where Crane had stopped off after the shipwreck of his filibustering expedition, en route to the Greek War, and where he seemed to be lurking about the perimeter of night life. The cub tried to draw out his idol about his literary career with no success. But when he mentioned that he too was a minister's son, Crane immediately came to life and greeted him as a brother in a very special fraternity. "Have you ever observed," asked Crane, "how the envious laity exult when we are overtaken by misfortune?" [6] And then, the cigarette in his lips marking time to the words, he added, "This is the point of view: The bartender's boy falls from the Waldorf roof. The minister's son falls from a park bench. They both hit the earth with the same velocity, mutilated beyond recognition." [7]

Crane was so convinced of this that his life had been led in anticipation of extreme reactions; he was determined to make good his belief if he had to climb to the roof of the Waldorf to be seen falling off the park bench. When he made enemies of the New York police by defending Dora Clark from their harrying, even though she was a known prostitute, he was acting on his sense of the way society would behave, a sense which he had projected into *Maggie* three years earlier without benefit of queanly associates. When rumor seized upon his gallant efforts on Dora Clark's behalf and concocted legends about his sexual life, he walked unerringly into an actual though less publicized liaison with the madam of a house of assignation, Cora Taylor. He would outstrip the event.

In the copy of *Maggie* which he had presented to Garland in 1893, Crane wrote:

> It is inevitable that you be greatly shocked by this book but continue, please, with all possible courage to the end. For it tries to show that environment is a tremendous thing in the world and frequently shapes lives regardless. If one proves that theory one makes room in Heaven for all sorts of souls (notably an occasional street girl) who are not confidently expected to be there by many excellent people.
>   It is probable that the reader of this small thing may consider the Author to be a bad man, but, obviously, this is of small consequence to
>
>   THE AUTHOR[8]

Before Garland read the book, the twenty-one-year-old author had been telling him what his reaction should be—"shock"—and how this might lead him to feel that the author was a bad man. The inscription reveals that in *Maggie* Crane was attempting to impose his personality on imagined material rather than to organize documentary material into a fiction. For the young author burning to be recognized, *Maggie* had less of an objective existence apart from himself than is ordinarily seen in the relation between novelists and their works. The objective content laid claim to in the inscription, that "environment is a tremendous thing," is qualified by the subjective expectation that "many excellent people" will have their confident beliefs overturned by it. Crane was, in *Maggie,* calling attention to himself, to a reality projected by his will rather than to one observed and ordered.

The shock received by the few early readers of the work, however, was probably no different from the one received today by those unfamiliar with the work of Stephen Crane, and it did not stem from fancying any wickedness in the author. It came, rather, from encountering an imagination so powerful that it could sweep customary fictional devices aside, replacing them with a series of compressed scenes set forth in a style that was somewhat mannered, to be sure, but was nevertheless amazingly effective in its reliance on the simple sentence, vividly put, to carry its meaning.

Here was no recruit to Howells' realism. The world projected by Crane has no topographical or temporal existence. To be sure, the tale opens in Rum Alley and never strays far from it, and Rum Alley is in the slums of New York. But the sense of Rum Alley's being a specific—even if symbolic—piece of a total social structure, like, say, Dickens' Tom-All-Alone's, is missing. Instead we are plunged into selected details of urban squalor and human viciousness, unrelieved by specific addresses, commonplace activities, or basic communicative speech. Crane's characters, gabbling on in a lingo which is, like their setting, chosen only for being extreme, communicate not at all when they talk to one another. There is no literal level of social reality. With regard to the setting, for instance, the reader realizes that there simply isn't enough furniture and crockery available in a habitation like that of the Johnsons to yield the supply necessary for the crunching destruction which is as fixed a feature of that place as the breaking waves are of a beach scene. While *Maggie* is not an allegory, it is a vision of what typically happens rather than a report of what actually happens. The wilderness equivalent of the world of *Maggie* would be a landscape in which all mountains are towering, all streams are rushing, all birds are singing, and all flowers are blooming.

To some extent, the extremes of this world are the inevitable result of the fact that the writer is making it all up. What Hesketh Pearson says of Oscar Wilde's *Lord Arthur Savile's Crime* may easily be applied to Crane's *Maggie*: "His picture of low life . . . has the unreal melodramatic quality one might expect from a youth who is making the most of his first contact with things beyond his normal experience." [9] But the work is the beneficiary as well as the victim of the youth's imagination, and Crane's was powerful. The grotesque setting, though it achieves only uneasy coher-

ence with the social theme, is of a piece with the rest of *Maggie*
viewed as a subjective projection that finds its center in the psyches
of the characters, chiefly Maggie and Jimmie. The longings of
these dumb creatures are represented as images rather than as
ideas. Jimmie stood at street corners, "dreaming blood-red dreams";
he "menaced mankind at the intersections of streets." [10] Maggie's
"dim thoughts were often searching for far away lands where the
little hills sing together in the morning." [11] Not only does Crane
emphasize in this way the irrational, non-verbal sources of their
behavior, but he gains his impression through using particular
kinds of images. In the brief quotations, for instance, Jimmie in his
furious outlook is not dangerous because he overleaps the mark;
instead of threatening anybody in particular, his mute wrath is
drained off into a generalized menacing of "mankind." Maggie's
wistfulness, similarly, does not carry any specific pathos, since it
is directed past things presumably within her ken toward a biblical image of joy, ideal and unattainable.

These images are typical of the ruthless irony dealt out by the
young Crane. He has, as it were, no middle distance. On one hand,
his inarticulate characters exist in a vortex of maiming incidents.
On the other hand, they are not measured in terms of what they
could be under realistically improved conditions, that is, what they
could be if they had more money or if they lived in Scarsdale
rather than Rum Alley. Instead, their condition is contrasted with
hints of romantic, chivalric, or biblical ideals which never had a
real embodiment. What Maggie is is the result not of the action of
her environment on a plastic personality, but rather of the reaction
of that environment to the proposals made to it by her pretensions
and her longings. She, not the environment, is the first mover.
Jimmie and the other characters also have pretensions and fears
which underlie their behavior and which are imperfectly realized
in it rather than being significantly shaped by it. In this kind of
world the flaws in the setting that result from the author's lack of
experience are not damaging, because the setting is an appropriate

symbolic extension of inner chaos; it is of a piece with the characters who inhabit it.

Maggie, however, cannot be read as a consistently subjective performance, although its strengths lie in this area. The youthful Crane was also drawn to the objective view that society has crushing effects on the individual, and the result is that *Maggie,* brief as it is, is an uneven performance. Its undeniable power, though, comes from his not hesitating to brush aside social reality in favor of his vision of what is really happening and from his freeing himself from any concern with the actual or with conscious reflection and relying upon his inner consciousness as the source of his creation. Crane was mining himself, as his inscription to Garland showed when he calls attention to that self and its fancied relation to society far more than he does to a detached work of fiction.

Copeland and Day, the firm that brought out *Black Riders,* published chiefly literature of an esoteric kind,[12] so that its imprint added to the reader's expectation of something novel and strange from Crane. When *The Red Badge* brought him into prominence, the earlier poems, whose brevity made them eminently quotable, were parodied widely. Their aphoristic, unrhymed, and unorthodox conciseness seemed of a piece with the iconoclastic literary efforts generally labeled *fin de siècle.*

Black Riders, like *Maggie,* represents a response to the world prepared before the world had actually put its proposition, but the poems are more coherent in their presentation of a view of life.[13] The irony which was tone in *Maggie,* and was based on the contrast of images of a cosmic nature with the lives of lowly irrational beings, now becomes subject matter. In most of the poems there is a creature and there is the cosmos, with nothing intervening either to give a sense of proportion and power to man or to shield him from the direct thrust of his God. The world is a rudderless ship before stupid winds, and God is silent in response to the spirit that seeks Him, until the spirit announces that there must, then, be no God. At this remark a swift hand, a sword from the sky, strikes him dead.

One poem in *Black Riders* reads:

> *A youth in apparel that glittered*
> *Went to walk in a grim forest.*
> *There he met an assassin*
> *Attired all in garb of old days;*
> *He, scowling through the thickets,*
> *And dagger poised quivering,*
> *Rushed upon the youth.*
> *"Sir," said this latter,*
> *"I am enchanted, believe me,*
> *"To die, thus,*
> *"In this medieval fashion,*
> *"According to the best legends;*
> *"Ah, what joy!"*
> *Then took the wound smiling,*
> *And died, content.*[14]

The glittering youth of the poem is one of Crane's few satisfied characters. The ridiculously unserviceable ideals by which he has been raised and the unrealistic conventions he applies to life have in this case not, after all, proved false. He has his romantic adventure. The episode, to be sure, leads to his death, but he comes to that death satisfied that life is working out according to the pattern he imagined for it.

The poem, of course, can also be saying that anybody committed to false romantic notions is fit only to die, but no other Crane characters are allowed to enjoy an incident which proceeds "according to the best legends." The most notable example of one who wished to enjoy such an incident is Henry Fleming in *The Red Badge of Courage,* and his failure to find war romantic is representative of an important strain in that novel: *The Red Badge,* whatever else it does, debunks.

Maggie and *Black Riders* are Stephen Crane's self-conscious challenge to the genteel religious and ethical pieties that governed his home and dominated the communities in which he was raised.

The Red Badge is his challenge to the culture of those communities. The folklore built on romantic memories of the Civil War was Shakespeare and the *Iliad* for the American village, giving its inhabitants a sense of identity and of shared achievement, and strengthening their confidence in the future of the American people. The war had proved that it was Union forever. The minister's son, with his habitual distrust of the pieties and with no experience whatsoever of war, but with the puerile notion that it was really a different sort of football game, nevertheless projected himself into that event, determined to write a war story. His inexperience, however, gave even him pause, and he consulted the *Century Magazine*'s series, "Battles and Leaders of the Civil War," from which he gained a sense of the details of the Battle of Chancellorsville to serve as a frame for his tale. But he did not go to the books for an impression of what war was like; this was what, to him, was dramatically lacking in the accounts. He would supply this from his imagination.

Although proper names are occasionally used in *The Red Badge*, most prominently at the very beginning and the very end, the tale proceeds, in the main, through the use of epithets—"the youth," "the loud soldier," "the tattered soldier," etc.; thus, even as he deliberately works against a traditional view of the war, Crane (probably unconsciously but still reflecting the original reasons) is using an obsolete fictional device. The eighteenth-century novel and the English drama which preceded it would have used as proper names "Master Youthful," "Mister Loudly," and "Sir Tattery," the names being not only characteristics but indicative of a generalized view of mankind. This tradition is, in turn, related to the earlier one of allegory. Although *The Red Badge,* like *Maggie,* is far from being allegorical, it builds on the trappings of allegory that can be noted in *Maggie*. The landscape, though presented in detail, is now entirely without name; topographically we can be anywhere, so far as Crane identifies places. Although the elapsed time may clearly be traced, the sense of the specific period of the narrative, as opposed to that before and after, is missing. We know that this is the Civil War, we know, on that basis, that we are somewhere in the United States between the years 1861 and 1865; otherwise, within those limits, this can be anywhere, any time, and, the use of epithets for names adds, anybody.

The way in which Crane uses this generalized sense to heighten the specificity of what happens in his tale indicates the growth of his genius in the two years since *Maggie*. Except for his much-debated concluding paragraphs, he is no longer concerned with an environment which has an objective reality apart from his character's consciousness. After the opening view of the army, we close in on Henry and remain with him throughout, so that the test of credibility is placed squarely where it should be, on Crane's ability to inhabit in imagination the inner consciousness of another.

That there is no world apart from Henry Fleming is made clear by Crane throughout, and most dramatically in Henry's conflicting views of nature. He sees it as kind or cruel, depending upon the state of his own feelings. While nature, to be sure, goes its way, sometimes in parallel to what he feels, but mostly in rude contradiction, and is therefore established by Crane as having a definite independent existence; nevertheless, what are constantly kept in focus are Henry's projections and adjustments. If nature is, indeed, separate, that separateness has no meaning except as ironic commentary on the inner workings of the youth.

As Crane had clarified his context since *Maggie,* so he had clarified his view of man. In *Maggie,* Jimmie and his fellow toughs are characterized as "kings, to a certain extent, over the men of untarnished clothes, because these latter dreaded, perhaps, to be either killed or laughed at." [15] As *Maggie* developed, however, it was not entirely clear that there was an order of men exempted from fear and pretension. Now, in *The Red Badge,* these are the all but exclusive sources of behavior. Henry's fear and his pretensions are like scales on a beam, and what happens is a series of tippings of these scales too far in one direction or in another, so that he is compelled to win his way back to a balance again. As John Berryman has pointed out,[16] the pretension fits Henry for irony, not sarcasm, so long as it is balanced by the pathos evoked by his fear. Should his fear gain dominance over his strutting pretension (as it does over the Swede in "The Blue Hotel"), then he is doomed. In following Henry, we follow a pretentious braggart whose fears in combat silence him, but who in the returning inflow of pretension is again operative, ridiculously so in view of his earlier fears, until fear again mounts up and moves the balance.

Before the steady creative vision of Stephen Crane, the causal framework of traditional ethics evaporates, and the youth acts from impulses starker than words. His thoughts are pathetic rationalizations after the fact, never reflections that lead to decisions and deeds. When he talks he utters banalities, and in so doing indirectly reveals his anxious self. That self thrusts its identity forth directly in the uncontrolled gestures produced under violent stress. Therefore, war is the ideal setting for an examination of man, since it provides the tumult which forces out direct expression. Man is the same under more tranquil conditions, but placidity affords him greater opportunity to mask his nature with irrelevant sentiments.

If coherent thought has so little part in the actions of man, then the traditional literary syntax must be replaced by a new one. The major triumph of *The Red Badge of Courage* is Crane's perfection of a stylistic equivalent for the behavior he wishes to present. In a traditional English paragraph the very syntax and diction weave a web of connections, of causes and consequences. But Crane, viewing man as an uneasy juggler of fears and pretensions who acts as they compel him, no longer uses this syntax. The complex sentence with its independent clause and one or more dependent clauses, in the main, gives way to separate images independently and equally represented. Taken together, they may form a pattern, as the dots of the pointillist taken together form colors and shapes which do not inhere in the particular dot, but the creator puts down only the dots and leaves the generalizations to the observer. One who was actually in the war would afterward in memory attempt to impose some coherence on his experience. But Crane, who wasn't, and who projected himself through sheer

imaginative force into the midst of the turmoil, recorded the independent details.[17]

So distrustful is Crane of the intercession of reason between
the observation and its impression upon the reader that he even
refuses to make mental corrections, like those for distance, which
are all but automatic: "Once he saw a tiny battery go dashing
along the line of the horizon," he tells us of Henry. "The tiny
riders were beating the tiny horses." [18] On the other hand, the immediate is inseparable from the coloring given it by the emotions
of the human being in its midst. It is therefore frequently represented in images, because they dominate the literal event. So, when
the youth sees a brigade enter a wood, and then, awaiting the
event, sees the brigade emerge again, we read, "The brigade was
jaunty and seemed to point a proud thumb at the yelling wood." [19]

The Red Badge of Courage is a tour de force requiring the constant adroit presence of its creator, and though there are slips—
especially with regard to the irony, which sometimes turns rusty
when Crane puts into Henry's mind a vocabulary not fittingly his,
in order to mock at his pretensions—its success is overwhelming.
It is a tour de force because, brief as the novel is, without the
presence of its author at every point life would not go on. The
setting, the action, and the style suit one another startlingly, but
their brilliant coherence is the result of the power and consistency
of the imagination which projected them. *The Red Badge* is like
a dream which impresses one as being truer than daily events, but
which requires the dreaming mind and which, unlike daily events,
never develops a life of its own apart from the dreamer.

Just as Crane's view precluded traditional syntactic organization,
it also precluded plotting, which is, after all, a controlling causal
framework. Henry is scared but curious at the outset; in his first
trivial engagement his confidence grows and his pretensions dominate him; in the next engagement the fears win and his pretensions
evaporate, so that he flees; in his flight he receives his red badge,
and with it his pretensions build up to a point where they again
dominate and he can rejoin the community of the camp; and then

in another engagement they remain on top of his fears so that he acts heroically. Does this mean that his character has developed? Well, yes. He has now learned to control a certain degree of fear, and if he is reasonably lucky he will not soon be put into a situation in which the fear will be so amplified that the compensatory swagger he now possesses will be inadequate to check its total seizure of him. The novel closes with a renewed use of proper names omitted since the opening scene, and a return to the same uninformed gossip of the ranks which began the novel. Again somebody says they are going to cross the river and come in behind them. This emphasizes the sense that what has happened is a fragment of what happens time and again; not a complete tale but a chunk which contains in it a picture of the ceaseless vibration that preceded it and will follow it.

At the very close Crane makes Henry's newly acquired cockiness so great that it becomes ambiguous when we remember his shortcomings and his rationalizations: "He had been to touch the great death and found that, after all, it was but the great death." The concluding paragraphs are self-consciously lofty, invoking a vocabulary that strongly contrasts with the banalities just uttered by the tramping soldiers: "He came from hot plowshares to prospects of clover tranquillity, and it was as if hot plowshares were not." [20] Pretension is on the rise again, and, to the extent that the soldiers did indeed act bravely in their last action, it takes a higher flight. In Crane's world, this is character development. Possessed now of such a confidence, Henry Fleming will not again flee, as he once did, "like a rabbit." But he may, of course, at some future date, flee like a lion.

Stephen Crane took the nineties by storm. At a time when writers were lending a half-willing support to the anthropomorphism of twilight notions, he burst forth young, yet fully grown, seemingly owing no allegiance to any tradition. He cut through the problems of American society by dealing with men's nerve ends and with the pathetically pompous idealizations through which they attempt to give their messages importance. Crane darted below and he soared above the daily events of his day, the communal problems and the manners of Americans. He did not evade them; he simply refused to acknowledge them as part of his vision of the world. But this vision, which had been formed without reference to seeming actuality, while it had the strength of untrammeled clarity, was also terminal. Once the seer has set forth his vision, what can he add unless he turns his attention to the commonplace life around him and attempts now to order that according to his view; unless he allows the world to inform and shape his vision as he had at first tried to inform and shape the world? *The Red Badge* was a tour de force also because it was unrepeatable. Once it was finished, there was nowhere for its author to go. Crane's productions up to 1895 seemed to be all but assembled within him; after a period of gestation he produced them. After 1895 he could only go on repeating himself unless he grew through observation of manners, through reflection, and through periods of rest when gestation could take place.

Life did not present him with those opportunities, and he was incapable of making them. The fame and notoriety which rushed in upon him had sent him off to the West and to Mexico, to Florida and to shipwreck, to Greece and to war. In escape from notoriety and in pursuit of the tranquillity necessary for the gestation that would produce a second phase of his work, he settled in 1897, at the age of twenty-six, in England. To his home there came a host of parasites to bask in his fame and subsist at his expense. The financial demands of his way of life were so great that he was unable to afford the time to digest his experiences or to learn from his newly acquired friends: Joseph Conrad, who had nothing but tranquillity as he strove to write and be recognized, and Henry James, who, now at Lamb House, was holding himself steadily to his art. Rather, Crane heeded the counsels of Harold Frederic, *New York Times* correspondent and practical novelist of the Howells school, who urged Crane to an immediate mining of his experiences, not of his imagination, which required refreshment. Thus he produced *Active Service* (1899), a novel about a journalist in love who risks his life during the Greek war, and abandoned stories like "The Monster," in which he was attempting to transmute his boyhood memories into art. In 1896 he had written *The Third Violet,* which much too facilely drew upon his experiences with the art students on East Twenty-third Street, and *Active Service* only compounded the flaws of this work.

Frederic's advice was well intended. He wished to save his friend from the taint of artiness which he fancied he would catch from such as James, and at the same time, through his practical knowledge of the market, help him to understand the point at which his experience and realistic literature intersected. But realism of the Frederic and Howells sort was alien to Crane, and his material when forced into this frame resembled a hollow imitation of Richard Harding Davis. An occasional story after *The Red Badge* indicated that the young man's failing was not in his genius but in the circumstances which pressed him into hasty production. "The Open Boat," "The Monster," "The Bride Comes to Yellow Sky," and "The Blue Hotel" all showed that he was capable of growth. As *The Red Badge* first sounded a note of distrust of rationalizing after the event, a note consistently to be echoed in style and content by Hemingway, so "The Open Boat" introduced another theme which was to dominate the imagination of the writers of the twenties: the positive values to be found in a company of unpretentious men going about their tasks efficiently and with respect for one another. But there was no time to allow the themes to grow. Just as Crane had, to the age of twenty-five, outstripped the event and offered himself in place of it, now events, the adventures he had been sent on by syndicates and newspapers, were, in his writings, replacing Crane himself.

So mercilessly did extraneous demands beat in upon Crane in England that when the Spanish-American War broke out he gratefully ran to it, not this time to gain experience of war, but rather to enlist; his English tranquillity had turned to chaos, and he hoped submitting to another chaos might afford him relief. Conrad saw the destructiveness of Crane's ambition but, unable to check him, mortgaged his unfinished work in order to lend Crane the necessary funds for his trip to America. The United States Navy, however, detected the tuberculosis that would within a few years kill Crane, and declared him physically unfit for the service. He turned again to reporting and hurried off to the fighting as correspondent for Pulitzer's *World*. That he was there determined to regain his control over events was made clear by his behavior. He courted death in order not to become the victim of life. In a long, dirty white raincoat, Crane made a good target for snipers, and he strode about the battle lines, disregarding orders to get down. Richard Harding Davis finally found the way to get him to cover. He shouted, "You're not impressing anyone by doing that, Crane." [21] Immediately the white raincoat collapsed, and Crane came crawling over to the men in cover. He would not be taken for a show-off.

Davis, his golden luck ever with him, was the best correspondent in the war, but Davis himself claimed that Crane was, because he knew that Crane was the best writer there. Still, he was mystified by Crane's dark behavings. In admiration of *The Red Badge* he had adapted certain of Crane's mannerisms to his breezier ends; shocked by Crane's liaison with Cora Taylor, he had nevertheless stuck to his code of fair play and had beaten a man who publicly insinuated that Crane's illness was syphilis.

Thanks to such mothering as Davis's, the war did not kill Crane; nor did the tuberculosis that was fast growing on him. At war's end, still in need of a resting place, Crane disappeared into an underground existence in Havana. He ignored Cora's frantic inquiries—to which she was driven partly by love and partly by pressure from creditors—in an attempt either to discover his death or to gain sufficient time for his powers to recover control of experience. But Cora's anxiety and the publicity about his disappearance broke through to him, and reluctantly he headed north. After dallying in New York, where he enjoyed the companionship of James Huneker and Albert Pinkham Ryder and indulged himself in dreams of buying a ranch in Texas, he surrendered to life and returned in 1899 to his costly manor house in Sussex, Brede Place.

Seriously ill, Crane plunged back into trying to meet his debts, seeing *Active Service* through the press and beginning work on a historical romance, *The O'Ruddy,* an admitted potboiler with which he hoped to make enough money to provide himself with the respite he desperately needed. In the time spared him from this labor he drove himself to produce poems, impressions of the Spanish-American War, and a series of tales, *Whilomville Stories* (1900), which revealed the direction he would have taken if events had given him the opportunity. In these stories, based on his childhood experiences, he now began to apply his vision to the manners of the American village. The stories were savage, too savage, but they showed the durability of his genius.

His body, however, was not durable, and in the spring of 1900, five months before his twenty-ninth birthday, still running to catch up with an opportunity to rest, Stephen Crane died of tuberculosis.

In the year before his death Crane wrote a letter which might have been addressed to his father had he been alive, but which instead was addressed to the Reverend Charles J. Little, who had been his professor of history at Syracuse and was now president of the Garret Bible Institute. Talking about his activities at Brede Place in the third person, Crane said, "He often tells about his fireside the tale of the man who exhorted him—somewhat without accurate knowledge in regard to crime—but with some kindliness and interest—indeed almost affection—that the lad has almost made it a part of his creed of conduct." [22] He let Little know, if the minister did not already know it, that his erstwhile student was now a widely published and successful author. Stephen Crane, picking up the pieces once again in England, was still sufficiently rebellious to patronize his elders, but, more important, he was now sufficiently mature to acknowledge his connection with the kindly Methodist tradition of his family and to send feelers back along the line of his inheritance. He was ready in his art, if not in his actual presence, to return home, as the *Whilomville Stories* also showed.

Crane's Civil War novel had not been concerned with man as a social animal, but his sketches of the Spanish-American War carried a new tone of communal identity. He wrote of the regular army at San Juan:

> I feel that things were often sublime. But they were *differently* sublime. They were not of our shallow and preposterous fictions. They stood out in a simple, majestic commonplace. It was the behaviour of men. In one way, each man was just pegging along at the heels of the man before him, who was pegging along at the heels of still another man, who was pegging along at the heels of still another man who—It was that in the flat and obvious way. In another way it was pageantry, the pageantry of the accomplishment of naked duty. One cannot speak of it—the spectacle of the common man serenely doing his work, his appointed work. It is the one thing in the universe which makes one fling expression to the winds and be satisfied to simply feel.[23]

A human community was challenging his attention, but he had yet to work out a way of talking about it and not falsifying it, as he had worked out a way, earlier, of giving the feeling of battle without falsifying the immediacy. Until then he would rely upon "one cannot speak of it"; expression had to be flung to the winds.

Or he experimented with pathos, as in his account of the wounded troops debarking at Hampton Roads, shamefacedly passing the verandas of the resort hotels where well-dressed women, shocked at their wasted bodies, sobbed as they shuffled by:

> Most of them seemed to be suffering from something which was like stage-fright during the ordeal of this chance but supremely eloquent reception. No sense of excellence—that was it. Evidently they were willing to leave the clacking to all those natural-born major-generals who after the war talked enough to make a great fall in the price of that commodity all over the world.
>
> The episode was closed. And you can depend upon it that I have told you nothing at all, nothing at all, nothing at all.[24]

Richard Harding Davis talked incessantly about what Crane said one could not speak of, and his undaunted heroes stood jauntily amidst admiring smiles rather than stumbling shamefacedly past women in tears. His note rang false. Crane, having condemned the glorification of battle in *The Red Badge,* was attempting the more difficult task of recognizing human values without cheapening them with talk. He differed from Bierce in seeing war as a magnifying glass through which human behavior could be minutely examined rather than as a metaphor of life in general; for Crane the human condition was not one of constant hopelessness. To this extent he shared with Davis a sense of something splendid. In his later sketches he began to move toward the notion that the something splendid was an intensification of the human community rather than what Davis presented it as being, mere deeds of derring-do.

Crane's art, though it shocked some, as he intended it to, nevertheless won the respect of his society and gave him the fame that at first he willingly turned to notoriety. That notoriety, however, made him a marketable commodity and lured him to let out mortgages on his future to so great an extent that the last four years of his life were a furious and futile pursuit to meet his obligations so that his exhausted imagination could again draw breath. Hamlin Garland, throbbing with social sympathies as the decade began, had by its close succumbed to the limitations placed on his imaginative powers by his Midwestern environment and had turned into a hack writer. Crane, on the other hand, at the start of the nineties had a high disregard for collective social action but at their end was hopelessly seeking a respite that would allow him now to turn to the society with which he had been in constant combat and incorporate it into his art. He went down before he had fought his way free to the prospects of "clover tranquillity" that swam before Henry Fleming at the close of *The Red Badge of Courage.* For Crane the nineties had meant only hot plowshares, and he died before the scar could heal.

Overcivilization:

Harold Frederic, the Roosevelt-Adams Outlook, Owen Wister

H arold Frederic, Stephen Crane's earnest admirer and adviser, swapped stories with him about the details of life in a Methodist household in small-city America. Born in Utica, New York, in 1856, Frederic was eighteen months old when his father, a freight conductor, was killed on the New York Central. He was brought up in a religious home amidst the home-front activities of the War, but in a community of devoted Democrats who backed Horatio Seymour against Grant in 1868.[1] When he was sixteen Frederic joined the Adjutant Bacon Corps of Cadets, a group of young men who sought some of the excitement they had missed by being born too late through dressing up in splendid uniforms and turning out to march down Genesee Street on any occasion which afforded the slightest excuse for display. When the Northern New York Annual Conference of the Methodist Church was held in Utica in 1873, Frederic's house was honored as the lodging selected for Bishop Jesse Truesdell Peck, grand-uncle of the two-year-old Stephen Crane.

Utica meant politics to young Frederic: church politics, county politics, state politics, and national politics. In the 1870s both New York senators, Roscoe Conkling and Francis Kernan, were from Utica, and the youthful observer, breaking into service at nineteen on the town's Democratic newspaper, ranged over the villages and farms of the county, noting the way in which the senators in Washington were related to the bosses in the mill towns, and how the bosses, in turn, managed the rural as well as the industrial vote. The map of his native area spoke to him in terms of special interests, votes, religious prejudices, power conflicts, and ethnic clashes. Still buried beneath the public life of Oneida County was the colonial division between Dutch and English, a phenomenon which delighted him, as did the rural craving for an opposition, some resisting force to justify the farmer's sense of himself as an embattled saint. Harold Frederic before he was twenty was a walking treasury of local history and manners. In direct contrast to Stephen Crane's, his imagination was inhabited by his county, and for him humanity revealed its passion in terms of camp meetings, elections, and strikes.

In 1882 Frederic moved up from the county to the state, becoming editor of the Albany *Journal,* the paper which had served so effectively, decades earlier, as Thurlow Weed's means of championing Lincoln and Seward. But the twenty-six-year-old editor soon led the *Journal* into the Democratic camp, bolting the Republican ticket and helping to elect Grover Cleveland to the governorship. He became friendly with the new governor, not only as the result of the support he lent but because of his astute feeling for the ways of upstate voters. In 1884, however, the *Journal* was sold, and Frederic chose to use his friends in power to secure a position which opened wider journalistic opportunities, rather than to follow along the political road. In June of that year he sailed from New York as *The New York Times*'s new London man.

Frederic's quick eye for manners and his highly developed instinct for the newsworthy item soon led to his acceptance by the professional journalists of London. He was a member of the Savage Club until his instinct for news led him to betray his developing literary allegiances. He cabled a volume of Swinburne's poems to his paper before American publication had been arranged, thereby destroying the poet's copyright and causing the club to ask him to withdraw. Frederic was, as the incident showed, basically a news man, closer to that field than to the community of letters. He was uneasy with writing which was at some remove from public realities; he distrusted and despised Henry James. The kind of men he knew best were those in the circle of acquaintances of the brilliant editor Frank Harris, and indeed Harris's many enemies, as they watched Frederic develop into a novelist, whispered that the American was actually writing Harris's fiction. The rumor lingered on after Frederic's death, when, coincidentally, the quality of Harris's work fell off sharply.[2] Within six years of his arrival, Frederic was so adept at threading the paths of English society that he saw his way to augmenting his domestic relations through taking a mistress and maintaining his children by her as well as maintaining his legal wife and children.[3]

Both in his political writings in New York State and in his correspondence for the *Times,* Frederic had opportunity to write a more reflective and discursive prose than was ordinarily expected of the newspaperman. But his journalistic career with its daily deadlines also tempted him into a facility which leaves his reader puzzled whether to admire the reflective power he was able to bring to bear on news items or to deplore the fact that such power was, in the last analysis, curbed to meet the demands of the deadline. In *The New Exodus, A Study of Israel in Russia* (1892), Frederic collected his newspaper pieces on the Czarist oppression of Jews which led to the massive emigration already being felt in New York. He considered his book to be an indictment, "more solemn, more sweeping, more terrible than exists in written language against any other people," [4] yet he managed in it to give a clear picture of the history of the Czarist attitude and well-documented case histories. He also saw a continuity in the experience the persecuted Jews were to undergo in New York. But he did not sufficiently work out the implications of what he sensed; he reflected to a point, then filed the story:

> Whenever men engage in an unhealthy and unnatural competition those with the worst and most dangerous qualities rise to the top, trampling the weaker and softer ones under foot. We have seen something like this in Wall Street, where there are no laws abridging virtuous happiness or making dishonesty the condition of life. In the terrible Jewish Pale the wonder is that any religion, any charity, any rudimentary notion whatever of honesty survived.[5]

This is more than reporting and reveals that Frederic had studied modern sociology such as that of Lester Ward, as well as Russian history, but he is content to make the point generally and vaguely and goes to the rest of his story.

The same qualities mark most of Frederic's fiction. Possessed of an imaginative knowledge of his home county, in which character was inseparable from ethnic, religious, historical, political, and social conditions, he was able to follow Howells' lead in producing a fiction of the commonplace, yet to surpass the dean in rendering a sense of communal density. Not until Faulkner's Yoknapatawpha County did American literature have a region so fully and intimately explored as Frederic's fictionalization of his native area—the land around the invented cities of Tyre, Tecumseh, and Thessaly. In *Seth's Brother's Wife* (1887); *The Lawton Girl* (1890); *In the Valley* (1890), a historical romance about the region in colonial times; *The Damnation of Theron Ware* (1896); and several collections of short stories, Harold Frederic, sitting in London, detached from the immediate political maneuverings of upstate New York, brought into existence a fully articulated human community. The peculiar quality of rural brutality as well as rural speech, the way the political boss Beekman rules the countryside as well as the town, the relation of the best families to the processes of making public policy, the aldermanic view of responsibility, the contrasting social roles played by the Methodist and the Episcopal Churches, the Dutch resentment of the English settlers who had migrated from Massachusetts, and the code of the masculine small-town world as opposed to the public code of sexual morality, all emerge dynamically; they are, in Frederic's pages, so rich a context of action that the American would appear to be comprehensible only in terms of his dwelling place and the multifold allegiances and enmities that he has inherited with it.

The towns on Frederic's map, such as his Thessaly, appear to his imagination as the products of history and are criticized severely out of a genuine love. As a result, their past and their social structure engage the reader to a far greater extent than the actions of any of the characters. Before the Civil War, Thessaly received its tone from agriculture and from its seminary, a seat of Abolitionism. After the war Thessaly was marked by growing industry, falling farm prices, and a quadrupling of the population to 13,000:

> Thessaly had now some two thousand voters, of whom perhaps two-fifths had been born in Europe. It had a saloon for every three hundred and fifty inhabitants, and there was an uneasy sense of connection between these two facts which gave rise to awkward thoughts. The village was fairly well managed by its trustees; the electorate insisted upon nothing save that they should grant licenses liberally, and, this apart, their government did not leave much to be desired. But how would it be when the municipal honours were taken on, when mayor, aldermen and all the other officers of the new city, with enlarged powers of expenditure and legislation, should be voted for?[6]

These are the kinds of details and the kinds of questions which make the fabric of Frederic's creations. He is, in his art, directly the reverse of Crane; everywhere in Frederic man is a communal animal not to be understood except in terms of the community. This is the same man whose nerves were laid bare by Crane, but his anxieties are explored in terms of group aspirations, as, for example, in this paragraph about the cooperative movement in upper New York before the Civil War:

> In those days it was regarded as having in it possibilities of vastly greater things than mere cheese-making. Its success among us had stirred up in men's minds big sanguine notions of co-operation as the answer to all American farm problems—as the gateway through which we were to march into the rural millennium. These high hopes one recalls now with a smile and a sigh. Farmers' wives continued to break down and die under the strain, or to be drafted off to the lunatic asylum; the farmers kept on hanging themselves in their barns, or flying westward before the locust-like cloud of mortgages; the boys and girls turned their steps townward in an ever-increasing host. The millennium never came at all.[7]

As Crane needed, at the time of his death, respite in which to allow his imagination to cope with details of life such as those with which Frederic dealt, so Frederic badly needed a habit of patience and reflection which would allow him to discover the themes inherent in his rich material. Nowhere in *Seth's Brother's Wife, The Lawton Girl,* or *In the Valley* does he trust to his material for form. Rather he adheres to the old plot lines of fallen women, conventional villains, and idealistic young heroes, and once having launched them spends his energies in setting forth the myriad subcultures within the community he is portraying, returning to his plots only occasionally and relying on melodrama or hackneyed conventions to wind them up. The result is novels in which amplitude of context is betrayed by the irrelevance of the action.

Running along as underdeveloped themes of greater interest than the actual plots of *Seth's Brother's Wife* or *The Lawton Girl* are questions about the relation of history to society and the inevitability of the Social Darwinist's thesis as opposed to one of social control. Frederic sees that the political boss, a usually vicious example of the fittest who survives, is also a demonstration that men can control society and that therefore they are not powerless in the grip of impersonal forces. He tentatively explores planned social management here, as he is later and more fully to do in his English novels. Another theme introduced to American literature by Frederic is that of the war as seen through the eyes of a child on the home front. *The Copperhead* (1893) and *Marsena, and Other Stories of the Wartime* (1894) are stories which, typically, are somewhat feeble in plotting, but which present a splendid picture of a Northern village while the men were away at the front, and serve as Yankee equivalents to the tales in Faulkner's *The Unvanquished.* Frederic here preserves the little insignificant details of those trying days which, in their smallness, give balance, proportion, and humanity to an otherwise misrepresented time. For him it is important, for instance, that "the outbreak of the war had started up the universal notion of being photographed." [8]

The Damnation of Theron Ware (1896) was the last of Frederic's New York State novels, and in it alone did he discover a plot which flowed naturally from his materials. It was recognized as worthy by book-buyers, who made it one of the ten best-selling books of the year, and after a submerged existence of half a century, during which it was read by writers but by few others, it is again prominent and seems assured of its deserved place as a minor American masterpiece. Frederic reached *Theron Ware* by way of the three earlier novels on the region. They equipped him with so full a sense of his scene as a representative area of America that he was freed to assume its history and its class structure as symbolic of the national career. He developed from them a plot which was intimately related to the region in which it took place, yet which at every step reverberated as a symbolic tale of America's progress to disunity in the latter half of the nineteenth century.

Theron Ware, the fundamentalist Methodist minister, was still in petticoats when the last shot of the Civil War was fired, but he inherited from that event confirmed convictions that the way of fundamental Protestantism was the sole path of life and that, although he understood little about politics, the Republican Party shared in Methodism's aura of divinity because it was the party of Lincoln and because the Irish voted Democratic. Now in the full vigor of young manhood, he must serve out a term in Octavius, a particularly pinched and mean town in upstate New York, before going to a big-city parish which, all seem to agree, will soon be the reward for his piety and industry in his calling.

Terribly unknowledgeable about the ways of the world, totally unread except in the Bible and fundamentalist manuals, narrow-minded, yet honest, sturdy, and likable in his upright simplicity, he is, in his wife's words, "a good, earnest, simple young servant of the Lord." [9] As he settles into his new parish, however, Theron meets Celia Madden, daughter of the leading Irish citizen, and through her is introduced to the world of *The Yellow Book,* American village version, with its naughty smoking of perfumed cigarettes, its secret playing of Chopin while others are abed, and its private chamber lined in silk. Through her he also meets the learned Catholic priest Father Forbes, and is introduced to a religious belief which can accept the higher criticism and delight in Renan, yet maintain itself in terms of a psychological theory of the need of the masses for religion, based on the relation of Christianity to pagan cults. Also through Celia, he meets Dr. Ledsmar, scientific experimenter and acid-tongued exponent of a post-Darwinian universe.

Before he became acquainted with these ideas and tastes which informed the world beyond the borders of his semi-rural America, Theron's progress had been crude: "He was conscious of having moved along—was it, after all, an advance?—to a point where it was unpleasant to sit at table with the unfragrant hired man, and still worse to encounter the bucolic confusion between the functions of knives and forks." [10] Farm-bred himself, he had entered well into manhood before arriving at this degree of social nicety.

Now in Octavius, however, Theron's new acquaintances accelerate his education, and he sees that the necessary accompaniments to the ideals in which he was raised and which it is his calling to perpetuate are ignorance and bigotry:

> Yes; the former country lout, the narrow zealot, the untutored slave groping about in the dark after silly superstitions, cringing at the scowl of mean [influential parishioners] . . . was dead. There was an end of him, and good riddance. In his place there had been born a Poet . . . a child of light, a lover of beauty and sweet sounds, a recognizable brother to Renan and Chopin.[11]

As the new aestheticism and the new science thus flood in upon him, the reader is pleased with this redemption of a basically likable country lad from the nastiness of small-town prejudices. But even when chronicling Theron's earlier social progress, Frederic had asked, "Was it, after all, an advance?" and now in the report of Theron's sense of his new self the language is too highflown and vague to be trusted: "Born a Poet . . . child of light . . . brother to Renan and Chopin." The old ideality has failed; it cannot continue with influence in an America that has awakened to the implications of the Darwinist philosophy and the new historical and anthropological findings about organized religion.

But, as Theron's awakening shows, neither science nor aestheticism can replace what it has destroyed. Theron and the sympathetic reader, the American devoted to an advancing rush into the future, are tricked. In place of the honest Christian lad we do not have a refined, wise, and articulate adult; we have instead a pitiful creature who has betrayed the conditions of his breeding —his farming background and his idealistic legacy—in exchange for a grab bag of third-hand tastes, ill-digested ideas, and smirkingly cynical opinions about those who nourished and shaped him. Celia Madden can flee to Europe to indulge her taste for the new art; Father Forbes can control his knowledge of the psychological origins of religious feeling so as to be of greater service in his parish, even though he does not share the unqualified beliefs of his parishioners; Dr. Ledsmar can work out the implications of his science in antisocial isolation. But Theron cannot now turn back to the narrow ideals which have been killed, nor can he advance to a more meaningful life on the basis of the rag-tag and supercilious opinions he has purchased in exchange.

The Damnation of Theron Ware symbolizes the loss of innocent purpose in America. Theron, at the close, emerges from a period of disgrace and self-disgust to start life anew in the West. Now politics seems the best field for him, since in politics his ability to manipulate those who cling to the old beliefs, gained from his experience as a preacher, can be joined to his ability to follow the main chance, gained from his newly acquired set of shoddy modern opinions. It will be a thoroughly practical and usually despicable career. But it will not be pursued with any conscious hypocrisy, for the final irony is that Theron's new exuberance will ultimately lead him to believe the hollow phrases he will dole out, even as he earlier believed in his Sunday sermons.

Celia Madden reflects after his fall that what Theron (and the reader) took to be improvement was actually degeneration. This was the nineties' favorite word for its condition, the flag, as Nordau insisted, of its self-obsession. In *The Damnation of Theron Ware,* Harold Frederic created a masterpiece on the American variation of the theme. Since the Civil War his country had moved from a narrow-minded loutishness, which was nevertheless illuminated by an honest devotion to the Christian rural ideal, to a shallow sophistication, unrelated to the needs created by the changes which had destroyed the ideal. Unity and innocence had degenerated into chaos and guilt. The new attitudes were not organic developments of what was worthy in the old, but betrayals of it, foulings of the nest.

The book, then, is dark, but not unrelievedly so, for if Frederic asserts that there is no turning back to the old innocence, he also suggests, though dimly, that there is a use for the new knowledge. In the Soulsbys he presents two characters who, on appearance, are as disagreeable as Theron is initially agreeable. They are professional fund-raisers, employed by the Methodist Conference to extract church funds from pinchpenny rural parishioners through carefully staged appeals. They sing old hymns to new tunes as they prepare the congregation for their appeals; none but the newly awakened Theron knows that one of their tunes is a simplification of a Chopin melody. In their appeals for money they mix the spice of carefully calculated titillation with the unguent of flattery, counting upon the pride and competitiveness of the small-town Methodists while verbally deploring these very traits and seemingly relying upon humility and brotherly love. They learned their tricks in show business, and they are immensely successful.

No characters are more qualified to be contemptuous of the mass and cynical about human ideals. But in point of fact the calculating Soulsbys do have souls. It is they who nurse Theron back from his self-destructive despondency when he realizes how mistaken he has been about his enlightenment, and it is they who outfit him for his trip West. In their experience as entertainers and near confidence men among the uneducated classes of American society they have, like Twain's Duke and Dauphin, learned to manipulate greed and prurience for their own ends, but they have also developed a love for the people. Their manipulations are finally for the good of those manipulated, and if they have bastardized Chopin they have at least introduced his melodies to men who would never otherwise have heard them.

The Soulsbys represent the possibility of social control by a meritocracy of common-sensical people who sympathize with the masses and are knowledgeable enough to translate new intellectual developments into a tongue they can understand. They stand for what can be done on the American scene with the new knowledge that has destroyed innocence, and if they are manipulators of public opinion they at least derive their power to manipulate from intelligence and an identity with the manipulated rather than from a calculating contempt. They foreshadow the advertising man and the mass communicator with his wheedling explanation that without the 95 per cent trash he purveys nobody would get the 5 per cent of quality he offers, but they also foreshadow the social planner. They are Frederic's suggestion, in opposition to Social Darwinism, that men can control the future of their society if they but yield power to the able. The old Jeffersonian ideal must be modified to meet the realities of a world in which anti-social forces are increasingly centralized and must therefore be fought by centralization.

After 1896 Frederic turned more and more to the English scene for his materials. He had in 1894 produced the delightful *Mrs. Albert Grundy, Observations in Philistia,* a witty portrait of middle-class English feminine morality, and he followed *Theron Ware* in 1896 with *March Hares,* a frothy romance which borrows amiably from a number of *fin-de-siècle* fashions, including Oscar Wilde. In his two final works, *Gloria Mundi* (1898) and *The Market-Place* (1899), Frederic stayed with an English setting but now made explicit investigations of the organization of modern society. The first of those novels criticizes a utopian scheme for social improvement based on a modern profit-sharing form of feudalism. The second continues some of the same characters, but in it the Soulsby theme of *Theron Ware* is made the dominant one, and Frederic urges that the immense gap between poverty and wealth will not

be closed until philanthropy unites itself with politics. The beneficiary of philanthropy, in order fully to be benefited, Frederic
argues, must use his vote to grant political power to his benefactor.
The businessman who has triumphed over the wilderness of the
financial world must be encouraged to turn his energies to politics,
and the voters who habitually distrust him should come to learn
that they are safer when they join him and place power in his
hands than when they force him to affect politics indirectly through
pressures. His success in business proves that he can achieve results for his partners, and his philanthropic enterprises suggest that
he is willing to establish a partner relationship with the public,
should they grant him political power.

For Frederic there is no turning back to simple democratic
ideals. Just as Theron Ware, having lost his innocence, must learn
to live with knowledge, so modern man should stop yearning—as
did Ruskin and the pre-Raphaelites, whose inadequacies are attacked in *Gloria Mundi*—for a simpler civilization. Rather, in an
age of technology, the technocrat must be given power. Since he
has gained all he could hope for from his private business activities,
he should be trusted now to improve the condition of his fellow
man rather than be hampered by public distrust, kept from power,
and forced into only partly effective philanthropies.

Harold Frederic, twelve years away from home, turned in his
final years to fictionalized social studies. His trained eye and facile
pen soon allowed him to capture a recognizable picture of English
manners, but he was a foreigner in the land and this deprived his
English novels of the communal density characteristic of those he
had written about upstate New York, as well as of the confident
use of symbols. The English novels reveal that, if Frederic had
escaped the premature death which was to strike down Crane and
Norris also, he would have concerned himself more and more with
explicit political problems. If he had survived into the next decade
—that of Progressivism—he might very well have turned from
fiction altogether. But in October 1898, forty-two years of age,
he died in London.

In 1897 Frederic had wistfully written to Hamlin Garland: "I wanted always to know how Theron Ware struck [Howells] . . . But he never told me. All the same, I'm a Howells man to the end." [12] Ironically, Howells' most notable recognition of Frederic was related to his one historical endeavor, *In the Valley,* and in his contempt for historical fiction Howells had lost sight of the realist who had produced it. *In the Valley* was, he said, "a fresh instance of the fatuity of the historical novel as far as the portrayal of character goes." [13] But *In the Valley,* while it was admittedly a venture into the lucrative field of historical romance, was also an example of how Frederic's realism was advancing in depth beyond Howells', and of the way in which the complex, disunited America in which he grew up demanded of him historical and political explanations before moral judgments could be made.

In the Valley was a romance of the Revolutionary War set in the Mohawk Valley of Frederic's modern American novels and centering on the Battle of Oriskany, at which eight hundred militiamen under Nicholas Herkimer courageously repulsed one arm of the British pincer that was intended to isolate New England. Frederic's intention was to recall the role the Dutch played in making the new nation. Their foils are the English, both the opposing army and the English colonists who joined the Revolution and to whom history unjustly, so Frederic maintained, gave a great deal of the credit owed the Dutch. In exalting the Dutch, Frederic was doing more than rewriting history, however; he was removing the glamour which surrounded the soldier as opposed to the merchant. His Dutchman were solid, peaceful men, dedicated to the arts of commerce and belligerent only in defense of their rights. On the other hand, his narrator says of an Englishman:

> The thick rank blood of centuries of gluttonous, hunting, marauding progenitors, men whose sum of delights lay in working the violent death of some creature—wild beast or human, it mattered little which—warmed in the veins of the young man now, at the prospect of slaughter. The varnish of civilizations melted from his surface; one saw in him only the historic, fierce, blood-letting islander, true

son of the men who for thirty years murdered one another by tens of thousands all over England, nominally for a York or Lancaster, but truly from the utter wantonness of the butcher's instinct, the while we Dutch were discovering oil-painting and perfecting the noble craft of printing with types.[14]

In preferring the merchant to the soldier, Frederic was denying the merits of the gentleman hunter's life and was opposing the movement, exemplified by Theodore Roosevelt—ironically of Dutch descent—which sought to simplify the complexities of modern society with a military-like approach. As his English novels were later to show, Frederic preferred the sedateness and craftiness of the merchant. He was also accepting the atavism which was to serve Frank Norris for his apostrophes and Jack London for his theme, but denying its merits—the varnish of civilization was to be preserved at all costs and among a truly decent people would not be allowed to melt. He was opposing a theory of history which five years later was to receive its most prominent display in Brooks Adams' *Law of Civilization and Decay* (1895), where the poet and the soldier were linked and their times extolled in opposition to the ugliness of the times in which the merchant was dominant. Frederic was advancing a belief in the basic sanity of the merchant, slow to wrath and quick to bargain—a belief that was going to be pushed under in America by the triumph of jingoism, atavism, and muscularity that produced the Spanish-American War. The Gordian knot which he was attacking realistically, examining the individual fibers inextricably woven into modern American society, was attacked with the sword by others who maintained a belief in unity and were willing to demonstrate its reality if they had to go to war to bring it about.

Harold Frederic separated slaughter from civilization, his English characters symbolized the former and his Dutch the latter; Theodore Roosevelt saw a new unity and lumped battle and civilization together, using England as the splendid example. For instance, in urging his countrymen to retain the Philippine Islands

and to civilize them, even if in the process some of the natives had
to be killed, he argued:

> England's rule in India and Egypt has been of great benefit to Eng-
> land, for it has trained up generations of men accustomed to look
> at the larger and loftier side of public life. It has been of even
> greater benefit to India and Egypt. And finally, and most of all, it
> has advanced the cause of civilization.[15]

The violence Roosevelt feared was that of business individualism,
the resource Frederic hoped to harness for social good, not that of
military force, which came as a splendid answer to the confusing
multiplicity which faced the man who attempted a detailed look
at society: "Without force fair dealing usually amounts to nothing. In our history we have had more trouble from the Indian tribes
whom we pampered and petted than from those we wronged." [16]
This form of strenuousness, should it prevail, would leave little
room for the realist who was committed to a far subtler sense of
the social fabric. Indeed, William Dean Howells, William James,
and other intellectual opponents of the brutalizing simplicity of
force received their comeuppance from Roosevelt:

> The timid man, the lazy man, the man who distrusts his country,
> the over-civilized man, who has lost the great fighting, masterful
> virtues, the ignorant man, and the man of dull mind, whose soul is
> incapable of feeling the mighty lift that thrills "stern men with
> empire in their brains"—all these, of course, shrink from seeing the
> nation undertake its new duties.[17]

Civilization was not a good of which one simply could not have too
much; it was, rather, a middle state between ferocity and pusil-
lanimity, and it was possible to be "over-civilized," which is to say,
reluctant to harm others in order to fulfill one's destiny.

What was wrong with a man like Theron Ware, from the Roosevelt point of view, was not that he had swapped his honest simplicity for a set of ideas which he was not fitted to handle. Rather,
he was becoming overcivilized, and a spell of manly head-crack-

ing was necessary to tone up his system. Roosevelt sang this song while McKinley provided the counterpoint which would assuage whatever vestiges of Methodism remained in Theron's nervous system. Explaining how he came to the decision that America should retain the Philippines, McKinley, a devout Methodist, reported to his brethren in the Church:

> I walked the floor of the White House night after night until midnight; and I am not ashamed to tell you, gentlemen, that I went down on my knees and prayed Almighty God for light and guidance more than one night. And one night late it came to me this way— I don't know how it was, but it came: (1) that we could not give them back to Spain—that would be cowardly and dishonorable; (2) that we could not turn them over to France or Germany—our commercial rivals in the Orient—that would be bad business and discreditable; (3) that we could not leave them to themselves— they were unfit for self-government—and they would soon have anarchy and misrule over there worse than Spain was; and (4) that there was nothing left to do but take them all, and educate the Filipinos, and uplift and civilize them, and by God's grace do the very best by them as our fellow-men for whom Christ also died. And then I went to bed, and went to sleep and slept soundly.[18]

The use of England as splendid example symbolized the recovery of the economy during the McKinley administration. In the hard times which led to 1893 the English had been held up, especially by the Democrats, as the source of a great deal of what was wrong in America. Their chief fault, of course, was their refusal to go off the gold standard, but they were also, in the Democratic and Populist imagination, the purveyors of immoral luxuries and the depressors of American agricultural prices on the world market. *Coin's Financial School,* used as campaign literature by Bryan, said: "A war with England would be the most popular war ever waged on the face of the earth. If it is true that she can dictate the money of the world and thereby create worldwide misery, it would be the most just war ever waged by man." [19] But shortly after McKinley's election the European wheat crop failed, so that American farm prices rose. Gold was discovered in the Yukon, loosening the dollar, and the cyanide process for extracting precious metal from low-grade ore was perfected, further increasing the gold supply. Now England became not the logical opponent in a war, but the model of how to keep prosperity dynamic, namely, by waging war against undercivilized people who in their native lands were, in Richard Harding Davis's image, like hoodlums desecrating a magnificently furnished mansion.

After 1895 Brooks Adams, Henry Cabot Lodge, and Theodore Roosevelt all addressed themselves vigorously to maintaining an air of militancy in America which would serve the nation in its new role as competitor for colonies and for international dominance.[20] Adams would be publicist, furnishing the platform of manifest destiny abroad and centralized government at home with a theory of history which demonstrated that civilization was dependent upon the warrior. Lodge would push for the necessary legislation in Congress, and Roosevelt would organize capital and labor into a united front.

This was part of the upswing from the dark days following the crash of 1893, when Brooks Adams' brother Henry had written a letter containing some characteristic complaints about the ills of the day:

> I am myself more than ever at odds with my time. I detest it, and everything that belongs to it, and live only in the wish to see the end of it, with all its infernal Jewry. I want to put every moneylender to death, and to sink Lombard Street and Wall Street under the ocean. Then, perhaps, men of our kind might have some chance of being honorably killed in battle and eaten by our enemies.[21]

"Men of our kind" traditionally had meant for Henry Adams men of disinterested devotion to public policy; men who were statesmen, not politicians; men who drew their income from the land, not from commerce. "Men of our kind" were men of birth, breeding, and taste who saw their times in the context of the past and who gave moral as well as intellectual leadership to society from a sense of duty, not as a means of self-gratification. But, in the chaotic social setting of the panic years, Adams' search for a principle of unity which would order anarchic multiplicity went astray. He had marveled at the White City of the Columbian Exposition and had willed himself to believe that this symbolized an underlying American unity—though it was but the unity of a fantasy—and now in speaking of "men of our kind" he meant warriors. This was a caricature of what he had stood for. He was now attracted to his brother Brooks's theories and accepted the simplicity of force as equivalent to the profound unity he had sought.

The desperate condition which had moved Henry Adams to accept Brooks Adams' *Law of Civilization and Decay* was made clear in a letter he wrote in 1895 to Charles Milnes Gaskell: "The other day I thought I saw myself, but run mad and howling. I took up a book without noticing its title particularly and read a few pages. Then vertigo seized me, for I thought I must be inventing a book in a dream. It was Nordau's *Degeneracy*." [22] Adams found that his pessimistic complaints about the times, original as was his expression of them, were nevertheless part of a fashion. The more he submitted himself to *fin-de-siècle* psychology and allowed his very precise observations to be subsumed under the pessimism of looser thinkers, the more the quick way out attracted him. He came now to accept a dynamism which countered decadence as a desirable principle and he found it in the muscular simplifications which his brother was promulgating and Roosevelt was putting into action. So in February 1900 Adams saw improvement, as he wrote to Brooks: "From the moment of landing in New York, I was conscious of a change of scale. Our people seemed to sling at least twice the weight, twice as rapidly, and with only half the display of effort. There is now almost no sense of effort, for instance, about our great railways; but the sense of energy is overpowering." [23]

The nineties, which closed with the deaths of distinguished young writers such as Frederic, Crane, and Norris, and which had brought a crisis in the careers of masters such as Howells, James, and Twain, while tossing about and subduing lesser talents such as those of Garland and Fuller, had ended by toning up the intellectual pessimists and giving purpose to the undercivilized. As Howells' spirits sank, Henry Adams' rose, and a popular mind ready to receive realistic treatments of society was scarcely formed before it was replaced by an attitude that was committed to life as a martial adventure.

The kind of writer the new strenuousness called for was the Philadelphian who, en route to Wyoming in 1891, had said of the traveling salesmen he encountered on the train: "There is no escaping these fetid commercial bores. Every state in the Union seems to spawn them, and they infest every mile of railroad in operation. Their song is always the same—booms in Kansas City, dead times in Omaha, skinned Yankees in the South, capital moving to Denver." [24] But Owen Wister did discover a landscape in which he could escape all this and project the romance for which the muscular days after 1895 called.

Born in Philadelphia in 1860, Wister grew up in a refined circle in which he was taught to speak French fluently, gained great distinction as a boy pianist, and met a variety of interesting people, such as Henry James, who came to call when he was twelve. His mother was the daughter of Fanny Kemble, the great actress, but this venerable English celebrity said of her grandson that "like most of his country's people, he is deficient, I am sorry to say, in animal spirits." [25] Used to English boys who were well-mannered in society and rowdy out of it, she thought the gifted Owen was unusually tractable and she did not much like it.

Young Wister was sent off to Saint Paul's School and then Harvard, after which he decided to follow his musical bent and spent a year at a conservatory in Paris.[26] But he returned to America and to banking in Boston, now venting his artistic inclinations in a realistic novel, which he showed to Howells in 1884, and which, he was told, was altogether too plain-spoken to be published. In the following year Wister went to Wyoming for his health, and upon his return attended Harvard Law School. He began practice in Philadelphia in 1893, but continued to visit Wyoming and was soon writing stories and sketches about the West. Theodore Roosevelt, another devotee of Wyoming, was so taken by Wister's initial attempts that in 1893 he encouraged him to try to become the Kipling of the West. The man who had been a hopeful composer and was now a reluctant lawyer accepted the commission. Roosevelt's advice was shrewd: if America was to follow the destiny he envisioned for it, then its literature needed a Kipling to sing the hymns of its manliness.

Wister, however, had to make some effort to replace his tractability with animal spirits, because the realistic tendencies he had displayed as a plain-spoken twenty-four-year-old recently returned from France were also encouraged by what he saw in Wyoming. Finally he conquered the realism and produced a literature fit for the followers of Theodore Roosevelt, leaving his realism to smolder in his journals while his fiction spoke of other things. The calling he abandoned is trenchantly indicated in his entry for June 20, 1891:

I begin to conclude from five seasons of observation that life in this negligent irresponsible wilderness tends to turn people shiftless, cruel, and incompetent. I noticed in Wolcott in 1885, and I notice today, a sloth in doing anything and everything, that is born of the deceitful ease with which the makeshift answers here. Did I believe in the efficacy of prayer, I should petition to be the hand that once for all chronicled and laid bare the virtues and the vices of this extraordinary phase of American social progress. Nobody has done it. Nobody has touched anywhere near it. A few have described external sights and incidents, but the grand total thing—its rise, its hysterical unreal prosperity, and its disenchanting downfall. All this and its influence on the various sorts of human character that has been subjected to it has not been hinted at by a single writer that I, at least, have heard of.[27]

This was not to be the stuff of Wister's immensely popular work.

In "The Evolution of the Cow Puncher" Wister stated the assumption on which his portrait of the cowboy was based and which suited that cowboy for the role Roosevelt had assigned him. The cowboy, Wister said, was the nineteenth-century descendant of the Knight of the Round Table and was, in the American West, acting out the deeds of his Saxon ancestors. By consciously adhering to this assumption, Wister could have his cake and eat it too in a way which escaped writers like Booth Tarkington. They had attempted to make democratic heroes out of men in basically sedentary positions, politicians or newspaper men, and in the pinch they lost faith in the ability of speeches or social actions to demonstrate heroism. They shored up their heroes' qualifications by revealing that they were, after all, the American representatives of noble English families, or that they freely chose to live among the folk after having distinguished themselves on the highest levels of society.

Wister, however, by moving to a scene which was relatively modern and typically American, yet which daily called upon the skills of survival so that daring deeds could be displayed with probability, provided the democratic hero who had eluded other writers. Speaking of cowboys, he said:

> Something about them, and the idea of them, smote my American heart, and I have never forgotten it, nor ever shall, as long as I live. In their flesh our natural passions ran tumultuous; but often in their spirit sat hidden a true nobility, and often beneath its unexpected shining their figures took a heroic stature.[28]

The adventures which Wister portrayed were romanticized, but this romanticism was held in check by a sense of humor and a restrained use of realistic details. In story after story he constructed pictures of different kinds of cowboys, illustrative of one or another virtue in their kind of life, and finally, in *The Virginian* (1902), parts of which began appearing in the magazines before the close of the nineties, he selected the best of the traits he had portrayed elsewhere and constructed the ideal cowboy as he roamed Wyoming from 1874 to 1900. He was tall, clear-eyed, and handsome, but not in a picture-book way. He chose his friends for their demonstrated ability to drink, shoot, and do the work of the range, not for their talk—a fluency in which, indeed, marked an incapable man. The Virginian spoke shrewdly but seldom, and everything he did bore the mark of his character and of his modesty. Just as he distrusted talk, so he distrusted an action which obviously called attention to itself, and he therefore frequently preferred doing things by indirection. The chief thread of continuity in the episodes of *The Virginian* is the hero's wooing of the Vermont-bred schoolmarm, and this is a pertinent theme because he is a rough man whose origins are of no particular distinction, and she is the privileged product of Eastern civilization. Her acceptance of him at the end, therefore, comes as an admission by the effete East that the democratic ideal is still fit to dominate national life, and that a man is to be known not by his birth but by his ability. Nevertheless, where there is such ability, it is also implied, there can only be good Saxon blood.

So in *fin-de-siècle* America the knightly warrior type had, after all, survived; and he, not the flashy traveling salesman, not the jaded aesthete, not the agonized, overcivilized intellectual, was the stuff of which the nation was made. Put him and his friends in the Army, as did Roosevelt, and they would take San Juan Hill. Make them recognize their true natures, and a nation of such men would not trust their destiny to businessmen, moralistic hair-splitters, or fancy talkers. They would not put their faith in any persuasion that was not backed up by the six gun, and they would not recognize themselves in a literature which tangled their warrior virtues in a mesh of economic, political, and historical associations.

The Virginian not only brought literary illustration to the Roosevelt-Adams-Lodge thrust that was pummeling the nation into shape after 1895; it provided the archetype of escape fantasy for the new century, in which the notions which had so baffled poor Theron Ware were to be complicated even further. As commerce, politics, and art, as even war increasingly became abstract, how necessary was the Western, the constant reminder that there really is such a thing as being overcivilized, and the constant proclamation that

Americans were bred to be warriors and that after all at a certain point a punch in the nose beats talk.

The decade following 1900 enthroned the new muscularity. That this was a simplification rather than a clarification of the nation's problems was immediately evident in American literature. The years from 1902 to 1912 form the single most dreary decade in the nation's letters, relieved chiefly by the efforts of the expatriate in Lamb House, who had been away from home long enough to believe that Lambert Strether, not the Virginian, was the democratic hero. Theron Ware and Henry Fleming, however, had to bide their time before resuming their careers under the names of George F. Babbitt and Nick Adams.

Being Old-Fashioned:

F. Marion Crawford and John Jay Chapman

As American wealth expanded after the Civil War, more and more Americans visited Europe, and more and more European gallants learned that one way of making their fortunes was to marry American heiresses. Almost every year from the seventies on saw some spectacular union of a European title with an American pocketbook. In the nineties the tempo increased, reaching a peak in 1895, when the Duke of Marlborough took Consuelo Vanderbilt unto himself, while Sir Almeric Paget, Baron Queenborough, claimed Pauline Whitney, Marquis Curzon of Kedleston won the hand of Mary Leiter, and Count Boni de Castellane was joined in wedlock with Anna Gould. As the decade closed, Julia Grant, granddaughter of a President and heiress to the royalties of his immensely successful *Memoirs,* married Prince Michael Cantacuzene of Russia. The White City of the 1893 Columbian Exposition was but one version of the merger of new-world wealth with old-world tradition, and the same year that brought the thousands of foreign visitors to Chicago saw some 90,000 Americans going to Europe.[1]

Among the frequent international visitors were Henry Adams and his good friends Senator Henry Cabot Lodge and family. The Senator appeared to his social acquaintances to be a man more anxious to defeat his opponents than to win arguments, and his attitude in Europe was one of alertness as he related his observations there to fashioning an America which would be the equal of any European nation in most respects and its superior in all important respects. He was heard to say, with regard to *The Lives of the Dukes of Urbino,* that the dukes were "a pack of unmitigated ruffians and blackguards! I would rather read the lives of the Selectmen of Nahant." [2] His wife was one of the most charming women in international society, and his son Bay (George Cabot), tall and handsome with luminous eyes and a musical voice, was everything the accomplished young American should be, able to compete on an equal footing with the finest youth of the aristocracies.

Some Americans, however, had not awaited the flush times after the war to do their traveling, but were already comfortably ensconced abroad, and to their homes came the more privileged of the travelers, such as Adams and Lodge. One such family was that of Luther Terry, the American painter, who had settled in Rome in 1833 and had there married Louisa Ward Crawford, sister of Julia Ward Howe and widow of the Irish-American sculptor Thomas Crawford. Mrs. Terry, the descendant of Rhode Island colonists and the sister of two vigorous Presbyterian ministers, James and Calvin Ward, raised her little Crawfords and her little Terrys multilingually and committed their catechizing to the Episcopal Church, though some of them, when they came of age, chose Roman Catholicism. These children were taken daily by their nursemaid to stroll on the Pincio, where they might encounter and chat with Pio Nono in one or another garden; with their parents they spent the summers in travel in the mountains or wandering by the sea.

One autumn when the Terrys returned to Rome they found the Redshirts in control, and they mourned the passing of the papal supremacy with all the sorrow of the most devout aristocrats, for, although they disapproved of the Pope, they basked in the color of papal functions and the picturesqueness of medieval survivals. They had been presented at Court and had taken part in its life; Redshirt vulgarity was not what they expected from Italy.

While the Terry children were growing up, the Crawford children were ready to leave home, and Frank—Francis Marion, Louisa's oldest son—went off to school in America, for as long as he could take it, while Annie married a Junker and went to live on his estate in Poland. Now the Terrys' summer travels could be varied by visits to Lesnian and indulgences in Prussian hospitality, spiced with observations of the serfs and the village Jews, who sold everything to them from schnapps to farm implements. One summer there was some unpleasantness during the visit: the American financial crash of 1873 had considerably reduced the value of Annie's dowry, and her husband, Baron von Rabé, reproached Louisa Terry on the matter. But this happened also to be the summer when Aunt Julia had come over from Boston, and she counterattacked with all the Yankee fearlessness shown by her husband, Sam Howe, in his reform battles for Greek and Polish independence, carrying off her sister Louisa in triumph.

One of the Terry children, Margaret, had a talent for the piano and was accordingly provided with the best musical education Rome afforded, which included a friendship with Franz Liszt. At the age of fifteen she was permitted to take charge at the tea table, and in this way for the first time came to meet Americans and through them to form some notion of America. Those she met were rigid in their extreme consciousness of social hierarchies in Boston or New York or Philadelphia, and this seemed cold and unreal to the girl. Moreover, very oddly, they spoke only English. In the spring of 1879 Louisa decided that it was time Margaret came to know the land of her citizenship, and since the Crawford daughters were both married, Frank was off in India studying Oriental languages, and young Arthur Terry was safely placed in a German school, where he was being supervised by old family friends, this was the time to go. They were met in New York by Louisa's brother Sam Ward, who had married an Astor, lost her in childbirth, married a Creole with whom he didn't get along, and made and lost three fortunes through going West in the gold-rush days, lobbying in Washington, and speculating in stocks. He entertained them and sent them on their way to visit Louisa's sister Annie, who was living in Northern California, married to Adolphe Mailliard, son of an illegitimate but acknowledged nephew of Napoleon.

From California the mother and daughter went to Boston and Aunt Julia Ward Howe, and there the girl was struck by the intellectual aura which clung about the ladies and the older gentlemen, and dismayed by the absence of interesting young men. Aunt Julia took her visitors to Newport for the season, where young Margaret was alternately bored by the first families —who were turned out nicely in all the externals money could buy, but who never had anything interesting to talk about—and intrigued by the frumpy families on the perimeter, who appeared to be more interesting and to have a better time, but whom one could never really get to meet.

Back in Rome, life was better. The cotillion came right after Christmas, opening the season, which extended to Mardi Gras. After this fête one followed the Lenten season by attending sermons at successive churches, each one, damask-draped and crystal-chandeliered, representing another station of the cross. At that time of year receptions were small; even the teas were modest. But then came Easter, and after that, until it was time for summer travels, there were the picnics in the Campagna.

In 1887 Margaret Terry married her cousin Winthrop Chanler, who was the son of John Winthrop Chanler and Margaret Astor Ward, Uncle Sam Ward's daughter. Winthrop was one of ten children who, after the death of both parents, had been raised by a Protestant committee appointed by their father's will to keep them free of their grandfather Sam Ward's financially debilitating talents and away from any taint of Romanism. Cooped up at Rokeby, the family mansion on the Hudson, the children quarreled frequently about theology and morals, the two topics most commended to them by the committee in charge of their upbringing. When Margaret Terry, who had been converted to Roman Catholicism at the age of eighteen, married Winthrop, she had a chilly initial reception from her numerous in-laws.

The newly married Chanlers made their residence at first in the Astor family house at Thirty-fourth Street and Madison Avenue, where Margaret found the American social season dismal. In the Protestant epic *Paradise Lost,* she had occasion to reflect, Eve left the table after serving the fruit to Adam and the visiting archangel, and let the men have their talk. She was sure that if Dante had described the scene, Eve would have taken part in the conversation.[3] In Italy people liked to know what a woman thought, but in England, and especially in America, they were indifferent. While a woman was expected to try to be soulful and bookish as well as pretty—a reputation for being intellectual, all other things being equal, adding to her social qualifications—still these attainments were to be credited to her account rather than drawn upon by the men.

The Four Hundred had by that time been enthroned by Ward McAllister, who counseled on such arcane matters as ways of using a Newport party as a steppingstone to a New York drawing room,[4] or the necessity for crossing the street in order to avoid meeting a shabby man from a pedigreed family because to cut him would be to insult a powerful family, but to acknowledge him would be to endanger one's position in fashionable society.[5] The Four Hundred, McAllister said, was made up of the swells, who sustain and carry on the activities of society, and the nobs, who are born to their position and therefore can, if they wish, decline to initiate activities and still remain on all lists because of the divine right of their birth. "A nob," said McAllister, "is like a poet—*nascitur non fit*; not so a swell—he creates himself." [6] If one bears this in mind, then he knows that when he plans a dinner the question is not whom he owes dinners to but who is most desirable.[7]

Afternoon receptions in New York society might be enlivened by a professional model in Greek costume surrounded by art students who were paid to sketch her as the social activities flowed on around them, but this was a staged atmosphere.[8] The Four Hundred, Margaret Chanler observed from the very center of that group, would flee in a body from a poet, a painter, a musician, or a clever Frenchman.[9] The New York world she saw, later to be chronicled by Edith Wharton (the Pussy Jones Margaret had met at Newport on her first trip to America), was proper, censorious, and dull. To be sure, the women were well provided for in a way the unfortunate American girls who married abroad were not. One indignant young Italian had told F. Marion Crawford that when his American wife took ill and died he, the husband, had to bear all the expenses of the sickness and burial, and said of his wife's parents, "Did you ever hear of such heartless people, to leave their own child to the mercy of others?" [10] American men had a more proper sense of their wives than that! Still, the Italian had probably brought good talk, good music, and variety into his wife's life; the American brought business, politics, and propriety. Business made him a social dullard. But politics did sometimes make him take fire; talk at its best in America was political. Margaret Chanler enjoyed Henry Cabot Lodge, with his convictions about American destiny; Henry Adams, the very small old gentleman who always went directly to the nursery to visit the children before making his social call, with his pointed complaints about the state of the nation; Teddy Roosevelt, who treated life like a Christmas stocking to be unpacked—"honors and high office were elaborate toys one must learn to understand; a cantankerous opposing Senate was a jack-in-the-box that popped out and made faces at him" [11]—with his pleasure in name-calling.

There were more artistic visitors, such as John LaFarge, but they exuded an aura of tentativeness, as if they had not yet found their medium. This was not surprising to one raised as Margaret Chanler had been. The American artists in Italy in her father's day had also been tentative, made so by the felt inferiority of their equipment in the face of the riches of the alien land in which they settled. Now LaFarge and other American artists were wanderers, depressed by the sterility of art at home and uncertain about what lessons they should learn from art abroad.

One very puzzling visitor was the writer Henry James, who

seemed to talk out of a cloud of dismayed aloofness until Mrs. Chanler referred to her experience of having been raised in Italy. Instantly James came to life, drawing her out about her feelings and pressing her to say whether she now considered herself an American or a European. She could not understand his earnestness, since, she felt, it was quite possible to be both, and so she was. But James, curiously to her, was heavy in his insistence that she must make a decision and not pass the problem on to her children. How odd of him, she thought; troubled by his seriousness, she mentioned his attitude to LaFarge, who smiled. "Dear Henry," he said to her, "he forgets how easy it has become to cross the ocean; the issue that so worries him does not exist." [12]

But the issue did exist, not to be erased by the ease with which the White Star Line made possible a transatlantic crossing. James was carving his masterpieces from that issue, while LaFarge, mistaking mobility for cultivation, was, like most of his contemporaries in the fine arts, manufacturing a bastard art which in its peculiar combinations reflected neither America nor Europe, neither the nineteenth nor the twelfth century. Henry Adams, LaFarge's friend, was trying to mix the two in a more considered fashion, but his very division of them into separate works, *The Education of Henry Adams* and *Mont-Saint-Michel and Chartres,* recognized the complexity of the problem. The fashionable world in America was not attached to a significant art. It responded, rather, to a romance of good breeding which embalmed certain social mannerisms as examples of indelible good taste, inseparable from a gentleman, on either side of the Atlantic, just as the masses responded to the historical romance which invited them to see themselves as kin to the knights of old. Mrs. Chanler's half-brother, F. Marion Crawford, was the chief of the fashionable romancers, and, as in the case of Richard Harding Davis, his excesses were to be accounted for less by the theory that he was daydreaming than by the fact that he had found such an impossible life as he sang of possible for him.

F. Marion Crawford, born in 1854, was reared among Roman luxuries greater than those later enjoyed by the Terry children, until Jay Gould's Black Friday, in 1869, reminded his mother that her income, like herself, was of American origins.[13] The retinue of servants was severely reduced in number, the best wine was now reserved only for special occasions, and a hundred touches of ease and elegance had to yield to economies. Though the family was still comfortable and leisurely in its ways, Crawford never forgot its fall from the opulent world it had inhabited before 1869. It swam before him as a dream of ease which he would bend every effort to recover. He was, after his Roman years, uncomfortable with the sabbatarian rigor of Saint Paul's in Concord, New Hampshire, where he was sent for his schooling. The incredible linguistic facility which he first developed in multilingual Rome served him well when he went out to study in India, where, in addition to gaining some mastery in Sanskrit, he acquired a ready ease in several modern dialects and was able to keep a diary in Urdu. In Allahabad he took a job on an English newspaper and began to experiment with stories, so that, when he returned to America and to stay with his aunt Julia Ward Howe in Boston in 1881, he believed that he was to make a career out of writing. But for Marion Crawford any career was inseparable from making money; he believed in writing, but he saw no reason why it could not be made to support him in the manner of the Crawfords before Black Friday.

Aunt Julia's twenty-four-year-old nephew in Boston was a tamed exotic, able to speak a number of languages and to converse in them about mathematics, philosophy, modern science, and ancient religion. He knew how to work silver and he understood the mysteries of casting a horoscope or reading destinies from the human hand. But he left the American girls uncomfortable. Used to being considered special, they were nevertheless uneasy with his intense idealization of their sex. Did he really believe that a woman wanted only to be removed to a lofty height and constantly praised? Mary Perkins liked him but could not reconcile herself to a life with him, and the suspicion that he was not, for all the charms which put American boys in the shade, the husband for her was confirmed by the hopelessly stilted manner in which he popped the question. He called on her father and asked him! Thomas Handyside Perkins, unprepared for such formalities, could only reply, "If Mary wants to marry you, Mr. Crawford, I shall make no objections." [14] But Mary did not, and Crawford suffered a physical collapse after the rejection. Lying abed, however, he maintained his extreme sense of the distance between the sexes, and although he allowed his cousin Maude to nurse him, she was not permitted to bathe his bare back but was made to apply the cold bandages over his nightclothes.

In 1882 Crawford's novel *Mr. Isaacs* was published. It was the first of a series of more than forty popular cosmopolitan and historical romances which brought him the wealth necessary for the elegance he sought. He traveled widely, adding fluency in Russian, Turkish, Norwegian, and Spanish to his native English and Italian and his acquired Oriental tongues, and speaking French and German without trace of an accent. He belonged to the German Artists' Club in Rome for six months before they found out he was not a German, so flawlessly did he speak the language and imitate the manners of that nation.[15] He was an expert fencer—"the best nonprofessional I have ever met," said his fencing master—and a skillful sailor who was granted a master's license and captained his own boat on transatlantic crossings. He married Elizabeth Berdan and settled his family in Sorrento, but he spent the social season in New York, living in the penthouse of the Macmillan offices on Fifth Avenue, a tribute the publishers were happy to pay to their great and steady source of income.

For all the popularity of his books, his friends said, they never seemed as full of interest as Frank himself; for instance, one New Year's Eve in Rome he entertained in his tower, forty-seven steps up from the Palazzo Altemps, where his guests gathered around the porcelain Franklin stove in the light of church lanterns and, on the stroke of midnight, heard the strains of Palestrina issuing from the darker recesses of the tower. Gradually the sounds took embodiment and they learned that their host had brought in the chanters from the Pope's private chapel as a surprise. Marriage did not end his idealization of femininity; his wife awoke on the morning of her twenty-fifth birthday, for example, to be led from her room on his arm as she walked over flowers scattered to the very doors of the drawing and dining rooms. The house servants and the sailors from his yacht were assembled in the lower hall with the peasant tributes of eggs, cheese, and fruit. After receiving these she was conducted to the presents which her husband had gathered: a piece of carved furniture inlaid with brass arabesques, a clock which chimed the quarter hours, and glass doors with crimson linings; six pieces of lattice-work furniture from Cairo; a settee with four stools covered with Bukhara carpeting; and a mirror in a solid Louis XV silver frame, designed to match a toilet table with silver articles from Constantinople.

The fictional romances which supported Crawford's living romance were produced at the rate of 5000 words a day, every day but Sunday, written rapidly and neatly on foolscap and seldom revised. The novel, Crawford maintained, is an artistic luxury and the novelist a public amuser who should provide his reader with characters "whom they might really like to resemble, acting in scenes in which they themselves would like to take a part." [16] He should aim at the heart, and rather than writing for a specific doctrinal purpose, hold up ideals worthy to be imitated even though inimitable. Crawford had no theoretical opposition to realism, recognizing that if one examined the actual human community one was bound to find and portray at least as much vice as virtue, and he believed Zola to be a great man. But the French wrote for men and mature women, he said; those who wrote in English also wrote for the young. And so he maintained:

What has art to do with truth? Is not truth the imagination's deadly enemy? If the two meet, they must fight to death. It is therefore better, in principle, to keep them apart, and let each survive separately with their uses. Two and two make four, says Truth. Never mind facts, says Art, let us imagine a world in which two and two make five, and see whether we can get anything pleasant, or amusing, out of the supposition. Let us sometime talk about men and women who are unimaginably perfect, and let us find out what they would do with the troubles that make sinners of most of us, and puzzle us, and turn our hair grey.[17]

The absolute division between truth and art was developed by this witty and widely read author into a deliberate, conservative anti-intellectualism. His novels abound in gibes at modern theories, especially those of psychology. "The seekers after explanations are bold with big words which tell us nothing, and call themselves physiological psychologists, or if that definition fails they say they are psychological physiologists," he wrote, "and establish a difference in meaning between one title and the other." Crawford, in this case developing a character in one of his novels, knew better: "But all the Greek words they can spell with Latin letters cannot show us what the human heart is." [18] Thus did he use his own considerable knowledge of Greek and Latin.

Crawford would invoke the hand of fate in his plots, rejecting opposition to this outmoded notion by saying that if he called it "the chemistry of the universe" the skeptics would be satisfied, though it comes to the same thing. Then, to show that he could if he would, he launched into a brief description of the achievements of modern chemistry, only to conclude: "The things that matter are quite different, and the less they have to do with our bodies, the better it is for ourselves." [19]

The values worthy to be imitated but inimitable, which Crawford held to steadily in his novels, whether they were about eloping Italian nuns, impoverished Russian counts, secretly married New York debutantes, or fifteenth-century Venetian glasswork-

ers, were those of the gentleman, the man of heart, honor and conscience, whose every action sparkled with chivalry. The manners
of this man were slightly formal, and he addressed all women as
he would have addressed his mother, knowing that his deference
and intense admiration for his mother were bred in him as a
model of how he should regard her sex. Marriage he considered
not as a contract but as a vow that he believed indissoluble because there was a God who every moment of his life would exact
fidelity to the vow.

Together with his chivalric Christianity, the gentleman harbored
extremely conservative notions. "An individual cannot change the
conditions of the society in which he is obliged to live," he believed, "and must either conform to them or be excluded from
intercourse with his fellows." [20] Such exclusion was a beastly
existence, and the gentleman chose conformity, which meant submission to the institutions of the society: learning to eat decently
in England or to duel in Germany, as well as supporting church,
government, and family in their established forms. In a Crawford
novel socialism, divorce, and atheism are interchangeable. The
enemies from without are those who are discontented with their
stations in life and those unenlightened by Christianity. "What
we call honour," Crawford maintained, "comes to us from chivalry
and knighthood, which grew out of Christian doings when men
believed; and though non-Christian people have their standards of
right and wrong, they have not our sort of honour, nor anything
like it, and cannot in the least understand it." [21] The enemies from
within are those made suddenly rich by commerce: "beings pre-
destined never to enjoy, because they will always be able to buy
what strong men fight for, and will never learn to enjoy what is
really to be had only for money; and the measure of value will
not be in their hand and heads, but in bank-books, out of which
their manners had been bought with mingled affection and van-
ity." [22]

The romances of Crawford, regardless of the time and place in
which they were set, were static illustrations of his version of

the code of honor. The battle between vice and virtue was not as central to his fiction as was the nicety of the distinctions to be made among the virtues in the code. What to do when love and patriotism or honesty and family loyalty clashed? He constructed plots that would bring such virtues into conflict and force a choice —or at least an examination. But because virtues so conceived usually complement one another, he had to strain to concoct situations in which they would not, and his solution usually involved something incredibly brutal and tasteless. In the midst of opulent surroundings—New York mansions, Schwarzwald castles, and Neapolitan villas—a mother is both loving enough to deserve respect, yet cruel enough to drive her daughter to thoughts of suicide; a father is gentleman enough to honor the marriage vows, yet intemperate enough to beat his son into idiocy; a brother is loyal enough to shelter his outcast brother, yet zealous enough to murder his wife when he discovers that she has committed bigamy with that brother.

Crawford's novels seldom contain adventures, for all the exoticism of their settings; they are intensely descriptive as they minutely split the hairs of the code of honor. They were immensely popular because, to be sure, whatever the theme, they contained a great deal of inside information on how a Fifth Avenue drawing room was furnished, or what went on in a dueling corps in Germany, or the best way to picnic on the Bay of Naples—a function since assumed by the Technicolor camera. But they were not popular merely because of this. A generation dismayed at the shift in social values read them avidly because Crawford refused to accept any conflict in values between the new and the old except to dismiss contemptuously those who wanted change, and because he dwelt lovingly on a social code which he was the first to admit was ideal. He worked almost exclusively with the illusion of social stasis, with the notion that there were such things as good breeding and good manners, exemplified by the Christian gentleman, which were totally invulnerable to the operations of the market, the demands of labor unions, or the actions of discontented immigrants.

With the more impressive thinkers of his social circle, including Henry Adams, F. Marion Crawford in the nineties shared the dream of a unity that would withstand the untempered winds of multiplicity. The sale of his romances reveals that there were many who wished to believe in it, if only for the space of time it took to read the serialized chapters in the *Century*. At the same time, as if to confirm Crawford in his escape, his social circle provided an example of the agony and seeming fruitlessness of plunging into the vortex of actual events and attempting to find a moral unity which could control them. In April 1898 Elizabeth Chanler, another of the ten children raised by committee at Rokeby on the Hudson, married John Jay Chapman.

In Ward McAllister's terminology, Chapman was a nob. He was the great-great-grandson of the first Chief Justice of the Supreme Court, whose name he bore; and his father's mother, Maria Weston Chapman, had been an important associate of Garrison and Phillips in the anti-slavery days.[23] He possessed a deeply entrenched religious zeal which drove him, even in boyhood, into exercises designed to test the durability of his devotion to God, and the Saint Paul's School which Crawford found chilling he, at the age of fifteen, found all too ready an arena in which he could practice his devotions. He alarmed even his pious masters by the rigor of his private religious exercises. Owen Wister, his schoolmate, observed that Jack Chapman was a "belated abolitionist." If he was born too late for the Civil War, what his pietistic temperament hungered after was not the roll of drums and the boom of cannons, but the great moral battle with its enthusiasm that would not let up until the issue came to arms. In his youth, and for briefer periods throughout the rest of his life, this enthusiasm, failing to focus on any specific social issues, spent itself in putting his own soul to a harrowing. So steadfastly did he hound himself as a boy that he finally collapsed of a nervous illness. He had to be withdrawn from Saint Paul's and to have his preparation for Harvard completed through private tutors.

At Harvard, Chapman controlled his zeal so far as casual acquaintances could notice, but in 1887, after he had been graduated and while he was pursuing studies in the Law School, it erupted dramatically. Having fancied, on scarcely any evidence whatsoever, that Minna Timmins, a young lady whom he loved—at that time silently—had received insulting advances from a young man (a fellow member of the Porcellian Club), Chapman seriously beat the imagined offender and then, realizing that the beaten man had been the innocent victim of the subjective war raging within himself with regard to his intentions toward Minna Timmins, he returned home after a period of wandering the streets to thrust his arm into the coal fire, burning and mutilating himself. He possessed great powers, but the capacity to yield was not among them, and even the pain of his body was unable to silence the demands of his conscience.

John Jay Chapman married Minna Timmins in 1889, and they settled in New York City, where he quickly identified a more objective field for his belated abolitionism. "In truth," he observed, "the age was tyrannous and said to each man, 'Perish or play the game.'" [91] Chapman intended to do neither. He agreed with the idealists of his circle who saw the shift in values as an object of horror and who were enraged at the rawness with which base desires revealed themselves in the poisonous alliance between business and government. But he refused to retreat into a speculative realm where it would all be explained historically, or to escape into a romantic region in which the importance of change could be ignored. This too was playing the game, every bit as much as if one actively took graft or offered bribes. Rather, through essays, speeches, organizations such as the Good Government Clubs, political efforts on behalf of independent candidates, and fervid interviews with influential members of the privileged class, he hurled himself against Tammany, against the alliance of business and politics, and against the complacent man's attitude that he could do nothing except keep his own hands clean. Chapman attacked persons by name as well as attacking ideas and institutions; he unleashed his cyclone upon offenders regardless of whether they were ward bosses or nobs. He traced and publicized the subsidy of the bosses by the nobs through intermediaries or through the permissiveness of silence. The motto he framed for his speaking and writing was, "What don't bite ain't right."

In the nineties John Jay Chapman made his life an experiment. As Richard Hovey has said: "With him, to study was to attack: not to view, report, and speculate at a distance, but to be involved in actualities." [25] Conducting himself this way, Chapman greatly resembled the nonconforming Henry David Thoreau, who embarrassed even his friends by his determined habit of placing himself athwart his society. Just as Thoreau insistently traced the progress of the tax dollar to where it paid to return a fugitive to slavery or to arm a gun against Mexico, so Chapman traced the normal activities of a business firm to the ultimate purchase of an alderman or silencing of an editor. Just as Thoreau was considered impractical in the extreme, because to insist on moral connections to the extent that he did was to advocate a passive revolution, so Chapman was considered impractical in the extreme, because his similar insistence might paralyze political processes. Thoreau responded with his theory of civil disobedience, proclaiming the moral superiority of the single conscience, and Chapman responded with his theory of practical agitation, urging each man to disengage himself from the corrupt alliance of business and politics by asking questions to which proper names were attached. A man need not attack the Pennsylvania Railroad, but any citizen, learning that the alderman's nephew held a position in the town freight yards, must question it loudly and not accept it as the way of the world. Just as Thoreau said a few honest men in jail would counterbalance all the dishonest men out of it, so Chapman believed that a few honest men loudly and persistently raising questions about what they noted in their communities could counter the corruption of the many dishonest men in power. "Misgovernment in the United States," he affirmed, "is an incident in the history of commerce," [26] and with brilliant originality he made the connection clear.

Writing to Elizabeth Chanler about the prevailing *fin-de-siècle* mentality, Chapman admitted that perhaps

> we are different in some sense from former generations. But the extent to which we are different will take care of itself. It is sane not to worry over it but to deal with the world unconsciously—to trust our own nature—to fight for the right as we feel it, no matter how mistakenly. Until our experiences and beliefs have been through this alembic and come from within, they are crude, they are undigested, they are fictitious. That's why the *fin de siècle* talk makes me irritated.[27]

"Trust our own nature" was an echo of Emerson's self-reliance, as Thoreau's experiment at Walden Pond had been. Chapman's quarrel with Emerson was that by 1840 his New England had lost its virility and that " 'Distrust Nature' was the motto written upon the front of the temple." [28] Since he felt that "the thing we call belief is a mere record left by conduct," [29] he fought *fin-de-siècle* resignation as fictitious and conducted himself actively so as to put his experiences to the test of fighting for the right and to establish them as valid beliefs. The Emerson he liked was the one described to him by Judge Holmes when he was at Harvard: the Judge said that when he was a boy he had given Emerson a paper he wrote in criticism of Plato, and that the sage had returned it with the advice, "If you strike at a King—you must kill him." [30]

Chapman attempted always to strike this way. After the Spanish-American War he saw that the eminence of his fellow nob Theodore Roosevelt held great promise for good government, and he persuaded Roosevelt to run for governor on an independent ticket. Then the Republican party began dealing with Roosevelt, and Roosevelt's political instincts told him that if he played along with the party he would gain power and could do some good, but that if he stayed with Chapman and an independent ticket that scrupulously kept free of all political entanglement, at best he would perish gloriously. He chose to play the game and repudiated the independent nomination. In response Chapman started his periodical, the *Political Nursery,* as an antidote to corrupt compromise. He refused for twenty years to speak to Roosevelt. Having begun the decade with a dedication to reforms, however petty, in his native city, he ended it with an all-out attack on the imperialism which had come as an answer to McKinley's prayerful vigil and the Roosevelt-Adams-Lodge vision of American destiny.

England, Chapman felt, had been a constant delusive source in American thought, misleading Americans to distrust their own writers, even, until English approval gave them value. England, then, was no model to follow into the twentieth century, as the Republican Party was bent on following it, and Chapman's criticisms of that country were consistently maintained even in his private correspondence. Writing to a friend about to travel to England, he advised her about the equipment necessary for an American tourist:

> Adopt a strong tone in seeing the English, read and collect disgraceful episodes in English history—as the forcing of the opium trade on China (the greatest crime in history), the bombarding of Honduras, their conduct during our Civil War. Have these things handy—to use as required in repartee. Never forget to resent an insult—but anyone can do this. But never forget to give an insult. *Resent* the English generally. If you do like any English people, be careful always to say you like them because they are not like English people—and in fact you would take them for Americans. Quarrel also with their accent and ask them to repeat words. Correct their grammar without fail and make memoranda of their ridiculous usages. This sort of treatment they understand and enjoy.[31]

In short, beat them at their own social game. Otherwise, however, Chapman did not want their game. He too saw an American destiny, not one of imperialism, but one of practical independence, related to the individualism of Emerson and Thoreau. He demanded that his age bring forth its individuals and that its literature escape the pumice stone of conformity.

Chapman, by sponsoring his own publications, did escape the pumice stone, and his writings in the nineties—not the least of which were his brilliant letters—charm through the force of their singular sanity. His judgments ring clear in a remarkably virile way, whether he is discussing public policy or accounting for such a cultural phenomenon as the Browning rage:

> If ever a generation had need of a poet—of some one to tell them they might cry and not be ashamed, rejoice and not find the reason in John Stuart Mill; some one who should justify the claims of the spirit which was starving on the religion of humanity—it was the generation for whom Browning wrote.[32]

But as Chapman looked about him he saw grayness—individualism, even a proper sense of class, worn to a uniform color. He saw that the intellectuals actually escaped the grayness no more than did the shopkeepers:

> The intelligent people in America are dull, because they have no contact, no social experience. Their intelligence is a clique and wears a badge. They think they are not affected by the commercialism of the time; but their attitude of mind is precisely that of a lettered class living under tyranny.[33]

Yet he would not go on from there to attack a business age in itself, and, like Brooks Adams, view America as attempting to extricate herself from the historical cycle which had brought inevitable commercialism. He did not take on petulantly about the existence of robber barons:

> Mere financial dishonesty is of very little importance in the history of civilization. Who cares whether Caesar stole or Caesar Borgia cheated? Their intellects stayed clear. The real evil that follows in the wake of a commercial dishonesty so general as ours is the intellectual dishonesty it generates.[34]

And Chapman showed the professors as well as the politicians, the artists as well as the shopkeepers, that they had been affected.

His listeners were relatively few. William James, dismayed at imperialism and indignant at theories which made American destiny a part of historical drift rather than the result of considered action, urged his Harvard colleague George Herbert Palmer to read Jack Chapman's *Practical Agitation*: "The other pole of thought [from Santayana's] and a style all splinters—but a gospel for our rising generation—I hope it will have its effect."[35] Chapman reciprocated, telling Owen Wister that the only man he had "struck yet in the U.S." was William James—"simply the only man who wasn't terrified at ideas, moonstruck at a living thought, but alive himself." [36] Nevertheless he reserved the right to attack James's notion of the will to believe, adhering to his idea that conduct and conduct alone could lead to belief.

John Jay Chapman did not withdraw from the storm of events as did some members of his class, for instance F. Marion Crawford, nor did he play the game as did others, for instance Theodore Roosevelt. In consequence, when Henry Adams in 1900 saw him and Elizabeth Chanler, whom he had married after the death of his first wife, he reported that the Chapmans "I find to be the most ordinary conventional, simple-minded of cranks, about as near our time as they are to the twelfth century." [37] Chapman's reform rhetoric, not Crawford's romancing, was what was old-fashioned in the eyes of the pessimistic little historian. The man who, like Thoreau, threw his moral force against the drift of society was an anachronism in 1900. Within a month of Adams' having seen him, in the spring of 1900, John Jay Chapman, thirty-eight years old, collapsed from a massive nervous ailment which paralyzed him, and his wife removed him to her childhood home, Rokeby. There the man who had been run over by society lay in a darkened room, all sounds about him hushed, and when he arose two years later, although he occasionally practiced on an old target or two, he was changed, and he turned his marvelous style more and more to the service of those who, like his brother-in-law William Astor Chanler, saw the Jews as the greatest threat to the triumph of civilization. Now commercialism in itself became for him a sufficient object of contempt, and his talent for tracing consequences was exercised chiefly on behalf of privilege, though from time to time there was a flash of the old reformer. In the main, however, John Jay Chapman was a different man. The old Jack Chapman had not played the game in the nineties and he had gone under as a result of the experiment he had conducted in that decade. The new century opened to find him in the mansion of the Astors, stretched on a bed of pain, while past his curtained window the Hudson carried its traffic to New York.

Life without Style:

Frank Norris

In 1902, Frank Norris's doctors discovered too late that their patient was suffering from appendicitis. He died, aged thirty-two, in the midst of plans to do research in Europe for the third part of his trilogy, which he thought of as the Epic of the Wheat. The first part, *The Octopus,* had been published in 1901, and the completed second novel, *The Pit,* was brought out the year after his death, as were two collections of pieces which he had published in magazines—some of them seven years earlier—but had not had time to gather together in book form. In 1906, and again in 1909, more Norris pieces were reclaimed from their first journalistic settings and printed as books. In 1914 *Vandover and the Brute,* a novel which he left in rough draft from his initial labors on it some twenty years earlier, was published. Frank Norris was a man in a hurry, and death had cut him down in mid-stride. The disappearance of his handsome, rugged face and his enthusiastic charm from the social circles of San Francisco and the editorial rooms of New York seemed a terrible irrelevance, for he, more than any other man of the day, appeared to be the novelist who would say the big things that the age of Teddy Roosevelt was calling for. More directly than Owen Wister he had assumed the responsibility for a virile literature which was to match the manifest destiny of his country, and he had, in the year of his death, exclaimed:

> Scholarship? Will we never learn that times change and that sauce for the Renaissance goose is *not* sauce for the New Century gander? It is a fine thing, this scholarship, no doubt; but if a man can be content with merely this his scholarship is of as much use and benefit to his contemporaries as his deftness in manicuring his

finger nails. The United States in the year of grace of nineteen hundred and two does not want and does not need Scholars, but Men—Men made in the mould of the Leonard Woods and Theodore Roosevelts.[1]

Norris's hearty contempt for what he called scholarship was part of an over-all impatience with the uneventful in the face of a world which presented him with so much of consequence to do that a retreat to the past appeared suicidal. This impatience led him also to condemn all talk of literary style, since, he asserted, what was important was what was getting itself told, not considerations of how it was told: "It is precisely what I try most to avoid. I detest 'fine writing,' 'rhetoric,' 'elegant English'—tommyrot. Who cares for fine style! Tell your yarn and let your style go to the devil. We don't want literature, we want life." [2] And he maintained a habitual distrust of writers who gathered to talk of their art. In "Dying Fires" he wrote of a California writer who went to New York, there to be corrupted by his involvement with Bohemia and with talk of Pater, Ruskin, and Arnold. In "Travis Hallet's Half Back" he praised the virtues learned in football: a good footballer, a good soldier; a good soldier, a good husband.

Yet Frank Norris was not so uncomplicated as he pretended to be. He had to force himself to the simplifications which, he hoped, would free him from the trammeling complexities of other writers who shared his concern with modern social themes, and he was not always successful in his attempts. As a result his best work is far more disorganized than his worst, because it is best in its fidelity to life's amplitude and complexity, in contradiction to the theories of unity and simplicity that he rhetorically offered as the organizing principles. When he allowed what he professed actually to control what he wrote, the result was the puerility of "Dying Fires" or "Travis Hallet," sometimes repeated at length, as in the novels *Moran of the Lady Letty* and *A Man's Woman*.

Frank Norris fought the variety and complexity of life because he saw little more than delay in yielding to its attraction, and he was in a hurry for fame. Although he was but six years younger than Richard Harding Davis, that golden youth was already famous when Norris began to write. Before he was through college *The Red Badge of Courage* was spreading the fame of a twenty-four-year-old author. Kipling, whom he admired greatly, had also become famous overnight, as it seemed, and therefore, although the method of Zola[3] appeared to Norris most suitable for the materials which attracted him, he was impatient with the pains which had to be taken in order to bring this method off and the difficulties which were subsequently to be encountered in getting the results published. This impatience led him to abandon efforts to publish *McTeague* in 1895, or to revise *Vandover* so that it could be shown to a publisher. Writing was a young man's game, Norris believed; indeed, America as it recovered from 1893 and tumbled on the raucous road to San Juan Hill appeared to be a young man's country, and everything worth doing was a young man's game. The only thing wrong with writing was that it was not life; but then, Norris felt, this could be corrected; the page could be opened and life allowed to pour in without regard for literature:

> The muse of American fiction is . . . a robust, red-armed *bonne femme,* who rough-shoulders her way among men and among affairs, who finds a healthy pleasure in the jostlings of the mob and a hearty delight in the honest, rough-and-tumble, Anglo-Saxon give-and-take knockabout that for us means life. . . . She will lead you far from the studios and the aesthetes, the velvet jackets and the uncut hair, far from the sexless creatures who cultivate their little art of writing as the fancier cultivates his orchids. . . . [She will lead you] straight into a world of Working Men, crude of speech, swift of action, strong of passion, straight to the heart of a new life, on the borders of a new time, and there only will you learn to know the stuff of which must come the American fiction of the future.[4]

The distinction between literature and life which Frank Norris was committed to tearing down was one which bothered him because, coming from the upper middle class, he felt blocked from life. Unlike his eminent successor in a similar variety of chest-thumping, Jack London, Norris was not asserting the claims of life as a result of equipment he fancied he brought to his profession for the first time, or as a defensive measure against the learned, whom he imagined as sneering at his lack of qualifications for membership in the ranks of American authors. Rather, Norris was trying to break through from his inherited position of comfort and genteel taste, which, he felt, offered him only a substitute for life. What, more precisely, that life was from which he had been sheltered as a boy was a question to which he brought several answers. On one hand, it was the life of the lower classes, which he noted in the streets of San Francisco and about which he read in the newspapers when it flared up in a sensational incident. This life, however, he could not, with his background, share, so that, even while emulating Zola in pursuing his researches on it, he also impatiently gave support to a belief that life as opposed to literature meant adventure—going off to war or taking part in dangerous voyages. His city of San Francisco, moreover, tempted him into giving simplified answers to the question of what life, as opposed to literature, was.

Norris had been brought by his parents to live in San Francisco when he was fifteen. Before then his merchant father had conducted a prosperous jewelry business in Chicago, where the family lived, and to which, after several years in California, the father would return, leaving his wife and children in San Francisco, though continuing to support them comfortably. San Francisco in the eighties and nineties was experiencing the problems of social change felt in all American cities, but it supplied them with a particular tone missing in the East. The city still proudly carried the marks of its earlier associations with mining camp and sailing ship, so that its citizens had freer manners. In Chicago too society was extremely fluid, but the new aspirants in that city retained some quality of the Great Plains homestead and pursued their main chance through speculations on one or another produce exchange. The San Francisco speculator had more of the red plush of the Western gaming room about him, and he came, rather than from a farm homestead, from the less disciplined life of the logging cabin, the mining shack, the cattle ranch, or the schooner deck. From any hill in the city he looked out upon the masts of ships clustered at the girdling Embarcadero, and stucco mission architecture and wooden carpenter's Gothic crowded together on his steep streets, presenting a mélange unlike anything to be seen in the rest of America. His equable climate kept him out of doors and unmuffled throughout the year, and his distance from the rest of the country, while it made his culture provincial, also allowed it a confidence in the absence of dominating neighbors.

The city supported three respectable literary journals: *The Overland Monthly, The Argonaut,* and *The Wave;* submitted to the frequent lashings of its grim jester, Ambrose Bierce; followed the incessant bickering of its coterie of poets, headed by the theatrical Joaquin Miller with his Whitmanesque garb, his eye for pretty girls, his vocabulary of Western terms, and his gushing of vaguely Christian sentiments; dwelt fondly on its associations with Robert Louis Stevenson, Mark Twain, and Bret Harte; and nurtured the whimsies of Gelett Burgess and his friends in such larks as *The Lark.* Its climate had attracted settlers from the Mediterranean, and lower-class life was conducted openly and colorfully in the streets; poverty did not have the visual grayness it presented elsewhere. Moreover, the Chinese and the half-breed Spanish-Indian populations occupied the lowest positions in the economic ladder, so that class distinctions bore a superficial resemblance to racial distinctions, as if nature, here in a more temperate climate, was making open decisions that were less understandable in the closer air of Chicago or New York.

Such was the scene of life for the adolescent Benjamin Franklin Norris. The color that attended the pauper Chinese or the exoticism of dress of the roustabouts on the wharf tempted him to the conclusion that real life, the life that a boy such as himself who had been sent to a suburban preparatory school and for a year to a Paris art school did not live, was adventurous. During his four years at the university at Berkeley, Norris was angered at the almost uniform allegiance of his instructors to standards of scholarship that bore no relation to the environment in which the University of California was set. He enjoyed fraternity life and he enjoyed athletics, but what had the mumblings of his instructors to do with his awareness of men being shanghaied in the tenderloin and white girls disappearing into the basements of Chinatown? Like Crane, he too brought a sense of what the real world was to his college, and he was scornful of genteel inquiries into the treasures of the past. His surroundings appeared to him to have sprung up full-blown, without relation to any past. He knew better than the men who wanted him to read eighteenth-century verse.

At Berkeley, Norris began to write of the life of the San Francisco lower classes, but he could not strike a responsive chord in his professors. In 1894, four years after he entered, disregarding his mathematics deficiency, he left without a degree and went off to Harvard and to Lewis Gates's writing class. There he worked happily on the manuscript of *McTeague* and began *Vandover*. By this time, 1895, Crane was famous and Davis was at his pinnacle, and Norris, anticipating great difficulties in getting his Zolaesque work published and also sensing the gap between his material and his own knowledge of life, impatiently seized an opportunity to gain experience. He arranged to write travel letters for *Collier's* and the San Francisco *Chronicle* and went off to South Africa to observe the difficulties which were a few years later to eventuate in the Boer War. Once there, however, Norris's confusion of life and literature betrayed him. So energetically did he associate himself with the Uitlanders in their efforts to make contact with Jameson's Raiders that he was deported by the government as an undesirable visitor. Moreover, he had the chagrin of finding that Richard Harding Davis, whom he had taken as a model, had deflated the Jameson effort. Davis had tackled this particular assignment not by going to South Africa, but by visiting the clubs and counting houses of London, which were the true center of the agitation.[5] Life, Norris's first time out, evaded him.

Back in San Francisco in 1896, he joined the staff of *The Wave* and poured his exuberance into a valuable apprenticeship. Here he had ample opportunity to publish sketches and stories and to discover the relation of his ideas and experiences to the materials which he wished to treat. Here also, whatever his scorn for style might be, he had to face up to how best to say what he wanted to say. If one was not to worry about technique but just to allow life to flow, by what technique did one do this? In his work on *The Wave,* Norris discovered that he had after all learned something of value at Berkeley, not from his English teachers but from the lectures of Joseph LeConte, geologist and popularizer of Darwin, Lamarck, and Lombroso. LeConte had taught that the brute instincts which remain in civilized man are a necessary part of his equipment for the social struggle, which parallels the earlier tooth-and-claw-struggle of primitive man. But it is now a struggle carried on with established rules, and therefore if he yields to the brutality within him rather than harnessing it for the purposes of progress he will regress and be evil. Said LeConte:

> True virtue consists, not in the extirpation of the lower, but in its subjection to the higher. The stronger the lower is, the better, *if only* it be held in subjection. For the higher is nourished and strengthened by its connection with the more robust lower, and the lower is purified, refined, and glorified by its connection with the diviner higher, and by this mutual action the whole plane of being is elevated. It is only by action and reaction on all parts of our complex nature that true virtue is attained.[6]

The "lower" about which LeConte spoke was the sensual cravings of man, and "the higher" was the use of reason and conscience, but he invited the drawing of parallels in the social structure. The lower classes were at a less advanced stage of evolution than the upper, so that what he said of the balance of lower and upper within a virtuous human being also applied to the necessary balance for a healthy society. And San Francisco with its tongs and half-breeds dramatically presented the robust lower that made for a good society so long as the upper compensatorily exerted greater pressure upon it. Moreover, the LeConte theory implied that civilized man was superior to other men, not just in the restraints he imposed upon his brute instincts but in the instincts themselves. Since they had provided the motor power for his rise and were continually kept in training by their interaction with his higher qualities, when let loose in a war or in a personal confrontation they would overwhelm an opponent who had done nothing but indulge his sensual nature. From LeConte, Norris also learned his Lombroso: that the criminal type forms a separate subspecies characterized by atavism, and a swift degeneration to racial type may come about if his nervous system is disturbed.

The LeConte theories, from one point of view, were a hodgepodge of rationalizations erected on the new science in a most unscientific manner in order to explain to the privileged classes why their superiority was natural. Especially in multiracial San Francisco they appealed, with their inherent assumptions of the superiority of the white race and, more particularly, of the Anglo-Saxons within that race. Harold Frederic, who refused to recognize the superiority of the English, nevertheless himself accepted the atavistic underpinnings taken for granted by the popular science of the day, differing chiefly in his preference for the commercial rather than the military type. But Frank Norris saw in the theory a way of approaching the life from which his experience barred him. He too had a brute side, he was more than willing to admit, and if he imaginatively gave it play he would be in a position to know what went on in the life of the people he saw arguing on Polk Street. Moreover, since a constant push and pull between upper and lower within man and between classes was a condition of health, moving both individuals and society to a higher plane, he was relieved, to a great extent, of working out the larger implications of the personal struggle he recorded. A unifying force could be trusted to see that in the long run all conflict was for the best.

The brand of popular Darwinism Frank Norris endorsed was, of course, in complete keeping with the strenuous times after 1895 and the responsibilities Americans began to discover that they had to their less advanced little brown brothers in other lands. Since it could be foisted on society from above by a writer who in using it was by definition accepting a godlike role and was speaking of his characters from a tranquil area in which he perceived the ultimate social good—something that was invisible to them and for which, indeed, they might have to be maimed or killed without in the least understanding why, and therefore without at all enjoying it—the doctrine might lead to a fiction of incredibly bad taste, full of swagger and hollow at the core. But it also freed a writer to plunge with force into the details of personal agony and render what interested him for its own sake, not having to worry about what it all meant. Norris was the full beneficiary of both the literary merits and literary vices that were consequences of popular Darwinism. If his uncritical acceptance of it finally kept him from being a great writer, the genius which was released, once this handle to the world was grasped, brought into American literature not only a new cast of characters but a closer observation and shrewder delineation of the problems they shared with their fellows—not the least of which was sexuality.

Frank Norris's contributions to *The Wave* read, for the most part, like sketches illustrative of LeConte. One story is even called "A Case for Lombroso" and deals with the masochistic cravings of a Spanish girl, which bring out her American lover's sadism, to their common degradation. Here the more civilized of the two had allowed his regressive tendencies to dominate him, and, after experimenting to the extent permissible in an American publication, Norris said: "A Shakespeare could have handled it—a Zola might have worked it out—I dare not go further with it." [7] In "The Wife of Chino" the Anglo-Saxon Lockwood involves himself in a love affair with a married half-breed woman, who finally suggests to him that her husband be killed. Norris comments:

All the baseness of her tribe, all the degraded savagery of a degenerate race, all the capabilities for wrong, for sordid treachery, that lay dormant in her, leaped to life at this unguarded moment, and in that new light, that now at last she had herself let in, stood pitilessly revealed, a loathsome thing, hateful as malevolence itself.[8]

What he is representing in the story is the debased sensuality of a member of a lower race and how it almost tempts a member of a higher race to regress. The racial theory is distasteful, as is the fondness for modifiers, for heaping up words as an equivalent to intensity of feeling, but, even as the theory leads Norris to these pitfalls, it also gives him license to enter where others had not trod. For the story in detail actually amounts to a tale of the primacy of sexual desire over the notions of fair play; Lockwood, the Anglo-Saxon, does go that far, and, if the suggestion of murder recalls him to himself, it does not do so until Norris has examined the strong hold sexual desire takes of him. "A Case for Lombroso" also contains penetrating observations on the strength of sexual desires, and in general the best of Norris's sketches in the years from 1896 to 1898 show that if LeConte's theory led him to pompous explanations it also nerved him to show examples of the regressive part of civilized man overthrowing the restraint of conventions, and to do this with accuracy and verve.

To be sure, many of Norris's contributions to the San Francisco journals did not have the redeeming merit of illuminating hitherto untalked-of facets of common experience. A great deal too much is made of a chipper halfback, a doughty Anglo-Saxon singlehandedly beating back a mob of ratlike Chinese, a young clerk engaging in highway robbery under the influence of alcohol—because, as we learn, his grandfather had been a bandit and under disturbance he reverted to type. But the space demands of *The Wave* forced Norris to an almost daily confrontation of theory and practice, and under the guise of examining regressive tendencies he explored the powerful role of desire in daily activities.

This is why, with all his protestations on behalf of life, and for all his admiration for William Dean Howells, to whom he was presented by Gelett Burgess in 1898, he did not believe himself to be a realist. He preferred the abused term "romance," not as it was employed to describe the genteel abstractions which were opposed to Howells, but as it was used to encompass the abnormal. "Romance, I take it, is the kind of fiction that takes cognizance of variations from the type of normal life," [9] he said, while realism confined itself to normal life. Howells wrote realism; Zola wrote romance; and Norris, while admiring the former, followed the latter. "Realism," wrote Norris, "bows upon the doormat and goes away and says to me, as we link arms on the sidewalk: 'That is life.' And I say it is not." [10] Rather, life is romance, because romance, which modern writers mistakenly assign to the past or to an exotic modern setting, rightly belongs to "the unplumbed depths of the human heart, and the mystery of sex, and the problems of life, and the black, unsearched penetralia of the soul of man." [11] Although Norris made a great deal of environmental influences in his works, they did not function so as to make him a model naturalist. Zola's appeal to him was not chiefly his sense of environment, it was that in examining a human career he did not stop at the doormat of behavior, but penetrated within the habitation to the soul's secrets.

Penetration is what marks the best of Norris's fiction and what gives *McTeague* a power that endures in spite, rather than because of, the piled-up verbiage which marks its more intense moments. This novel, completed at Harvard in 1895 but not published until 1899, examines the degeneration of a crude man from the mines of Placer County who at the outset of the story has attained some degree of civilization and is working on San Francisco's Polk Street as an unlicensed dentist. When not working, he eats and drinks steam beer (San Francisco's characteristic poor man's beverage), then, "gorged" and "crop-full," he slumbers snoringly in his dentist's chair, his uneasy sleep reflecting the uncertainty of his control of the brutal instincts which have been mastered to the extent that he can be a quasi-professional man. McTeague rises socially through his marriage to a middle-class girl, then, through loss of his job, and drink, declines to bestiality, murder, an atavistic return to the mountains, and a melodramatic end in Death Valley.

The story follows a pattern that Norris took from popular science. Without the pattern he would not have possessed a rationale for the details which give the story its strength, though the pattern itself too often makes certain happenings appear forced and puppet-like. The result is that the novel is uneven, now involving one in subplots designed to illuminate but overemphasized and exaggerated, now dropping the rhetoric of degeneration, brilliantly revealing the postures of desire. The gold tooth, the canary in the cage, the routine of life on Polk Street, and other symbols of which Norris was so proud and with which he was so insistent, pale beside the sections in which he pursues the "unsearched penetralia of the soul." While McTeague the dentist, bending over the anesthetized Trina and fighting a war with his instincts as to whether or not to kiss her, is a stagy dramatization of desire versus reason, his habit, once married, of biting his wife's fingers, even crunching them, in an excess of sexual delight, powerfully calls forth all the implications of physical love which cannot be talked about. Trina eventually contracts the poison which leads to her physical degeneration through the cuts on her fingers, but Norris, at his best with her, refrains from stating that her shallow background did not prepare her to withstand the demands of sexual desire. Trina's subsequent psychic deterioration through obsessive greed can be related to her social origins as a well-disciplined member of a thrifty family, but when it costs her a husband these implications are followed by Norris to the scene of her, stripped naked, entering a bed of coins.

Norris's prose too frequently forces, but in notable moments it is confident, even almost understated. For instance, after the murderous McTeague leaves his battered wife in the cloakroom of the kindergarten where she serves as scrubwoman, he writes:

> Trina lay unconscious, just as she had fallen under the last of McTeague's blows, her body twitching with an occasional hiccough

that stirred the pool of blood in which she lay face downward. Towards morning she died with a rapid series of hiccoughs which
sounded like a piece of clockwork running down.[12]

The cute little wife who was like a toy to the newly wedded Mc-
Teague and who worked as a painter of playthings before her
descent through mutilation and greed to a life of cleaning the filth
of others, now in her death expires like a mechanical doll. When
the children arrive for school they note a funny smell, see the cat
acting strangely at the door of the closed room, and in chattering
about this scare the cat. "Then," writes Norris, "the tallest of the
little girls swung the door of the little cloakroom wide open and
they all ran in." [13] The chapter closes here, Norris confidently declining to portray the greater horror he has implied. The reader's
imagination rushes on to see the doll-woman, the former painter of
toys, discovered in her blood pool by kindergarten girls.

Vandover and the Brute, on which Norris worked right after
McTeague, but which he never polished for publication, approaches
the same theme as *McTeague.* In the earlier novel Norris examined
the brute-civilized distinction by opposing McTeague's origin and
end to his temporary achievement of a higher social plane, and by
objectifying the conflict within him in a drama of his relations with
his wife and friend and in two illustrative subplots. The lower in
man was examined in the lower in society. In *Vandover,* however,
Norris internalized the problem and concentrated on one young
member of the upper class and how his sensual cravings eventually
destroyed him. Such a plan of attack on the material inevitably
provided a less dramatic arena for Norris and called more fully
upon his psychological vocabulary. Perhaps it is because he felt
uneasy without an occasion for melodrama and uncertain about
the power of his pen to render psychological tension that he never
completed the work. *Vandover,* moreover, forced him into a degree
of detail which finally contradicted the over-all theory with which
he was so comfortable, and, possibly sensing this, he laid it by. In
this very detail, however, *Vandover,* while not as arranged as *Mc-*

Teague, gives every promise that it would have been a better book if finished.

Most immediately, *Vandover* is closer to his own personal experience than was *McTeague.* The young man about town becomes increasingly aware of the animal within him when he reaches puberty and begins to have sexual experiences with lower-class girls. He begins to pose questions to himself about the standards of a society which permits men to satisfy themselves so long as they go out of their class, but which bars them from such behavior within that class and bars women from such behavior entirely. The daily environment of Vandover, Norris knew well, and there is a plain-spoken, effective balance in the section devoted to the twelve hours of Vandover's life from the Saturday-night social which he spends with girls of his class, to the after-hours debauch with a whore, to breakfast and the Sunday-morning meetings with the girls of his class at church, which is more eloquent on the subject of the quality of life of the young gentleman in the nineties than anything written at the time. Unlike Crane in *Maggie,* Norris wrote of prostitutes he had met, and in doing so communicated the excitement of the man who spends most of his leisure hours in society: "The general conception of women of her class is a painted and broken wreck. Flossie radiated health; her eyes were clear, her nerves steady, her flesh hard and even as a child's. There hung about her an air of cleanliness, of freshness, of good nature, of fine, high spirits." [14] Her profession was suggested not by her looks but by her actions: "As soon as she removed her veil and gloves it was as though she were partially undressed, and her uncovered face and hands seemed to be only portions of her nudity." [15] These are observations perfectly in keeping with the excitement which imperceptibly seizes Vandover; of the suggestive power of normal feminine gestures when removed from the restraining context of polite society.

Having yielded to sexual desire gradually at first, Vandover is soon on an accelerating descent which involves alcohol as well as women and which propels him from his social class to the gutter. Norris's closing scene of Vandover follows him in detail as he procures a job cleaning a furnished slum room for new tenants and sets about his methodical scrubbing of accumulated human leavings.

As an accompaniment to Vandover's descent, Norris conceived of making him the victim of lycanthropy, so that at his lowest moments he would strip naked and gambol about his room on all fours, howling like a wolf. The device is controlled far more tactfully than a mere mention of it can convey, but it is nevertheless objectionable not only in the obviousness with which it attempts to drive home a point in popular evolutionary theory, but also because through it Norris shows a distrust of the more subtle characterization he has given Vandover. For what Norris has managed to suggest, with a finesse untypical of most of his work, is not that the brute in Vandover, once unleashed, finally takes possession and causes his regression to bestiality, but rather that Vandover's mental breakdown results from his having been raised in an environment which maintains the double standard yet cautions against premarital sexual experience as something purely animal. When Vandover sees himself fail in terms of the social principle he has accepted, he begins to punish himself by telling himself that he is after all a beast, until the guilt bred in him holds him totally in its power. When he grovels on all fours, then, although this is offered by Norris as a textbook case of physical and mental degeneration brought on by overindulgence of the senses, Vandover has in point of fact been rendered more subtly and stands as an example of the immense power of society to sow and fertilize the seeds of sexual guilt. No work of Norris's went so deeply into the penetralia which were his professed subjects, but he turned from the complex fiction he had wrought as a beginning novelist with an impatience at the ways in which adhering to experience could impede one.

His days on *The Wave* led Norris to attempt to simplify psychological problems and to dramatize his results. The first of his novels to be published was *Moran of the Lady Letty* (1898), a sophomoric glorification of Anglo-Saxon superiority which reduced even the simplistic parts of LeConte to penny-dreadful proportions. The first paragraph struck a note which Richard Harding Davis had taught the decade, that of framing the wildest adventures with references to the salons whence the true hero emerged and to which he would return, thereby validating the proposition that the gentleman, when forced to combat, is the superior brute as well as the superior man: "This is to be the story of a battle, at least one murder, and several sudden deaths. For that reason it begins with a pink tea and among the mingled odours of many delicate perfumes and the hale, frank smell of Caroline Testout roses." [16] This aspect of the work of Norris and other contemporaries of Richard Harding Davis is so characteristic of the decade that it came for many to be the very quintessence of American *fin de siècle*. Thomas Beer, for example, made the reproduction of its flavor one of the chief objectives of his brilliant study of the nineties. *The Mauve Decade* begins with a line calculated to convey the contrast Norris and so many others delighted in: "They laid Jesse James in his grave and Dante Gabriel Rossetti died immediately." [17]

In *Moran* the reader is led from the peppy enthusiasm of "he had pulled at No. 5 in his 'varsity boat in an Eastern college that was not accustomed to athletic discomfiture";[18] to the thought that "somewhere deep down in the heart of every Anglo-Saxon lies the predatory instinct of his Viking ancestors—an instinct that a thousand years of respectability and tax-paying have not quite succeeded in eliminating";[19] to the inevitable supporting contrast: "The man, the Mongolian, small, wizened, leather-coloured, secretive—a strange, complex creature, steeped in all the obscure mystery of the East, nervous, ill at ease; and the girl, the Anglo-Saxon, daughter of the Northman, huge, blonde, big-boned, frank, outspoken." [20] As he looks at the two, the hero asks himself, "Where else but in California could such abrupt contrasts occur?" [21] They were, in point of fact, to occur time and again in Jack London, in hundreds of comic strips, and in the Saturday-afternoon movie serials. Needless to say, the hero, in playing the brute and in allying himself with Moran, the blonde Valkyrie, discovers his true self and returns to the young ladies of the Caroline Testout roses every inch the confident and modest gentleman.

Norris knew better than that, and yet he refused to acknowledge it, because, while he would have admitted that *Moran* was pure fantasy, he would also have argued that it was only a melodramatic presentation of certain important truths which were offered in a less interesting form by scientists. That actual experience defied such simplification, however, he was brought to realize soon after he completed the work, when he was sent to the Spanish-American War as one of S. S. McClure's correspondents. He was on the *Three Friends* with Crane, who troubled him greatly by not having a physique to match his talent, and whom he characterized as "a young, a very young personage, celebrated the world round by reason of his novel of battle and sudden death." [22] But now he, Norris, was to experience battle and death and to test his views of them as Crane had tested a quite different set earlier in Greece.

And the war really presented Norris with a test. On one hand, he found it incredibly dull, not at all like the titanic clash of upper and lower which he had expected, and certain of his articles, such as those on the distribution of food to the starving civilians, movingly reflect Bierce's claim that war is waged against the means of subsistence of a people rather than against the bodies of men. On the other hand, Norris insisted on hypothesizing the excitement he failed to find in fact, and would not allow experience to destroy his essential romanticism:

> Santiago was ours—was ours, ours, by the sword we had acquired, we, Americans, with no one to help—and the Anglo-Saxon blood of us, the blood of the race that had fought its way out of a swamp in Friesland, conquering and conquering and conquering, on to the westward, the race whose blood instinct is the acquiring of land.[23]

Very noticeably this effusion flows after the fact of Toral's surrender and is unconnected with any actual combat which may have been observed. Experience did not substantially modify Norris's literary outlook, but it did confirm him in his practice of using realistic detail and then, having overleaped the immediate consequences of the details, proclaiming a lofty unifying principle that was somehow guiding them.

McClure had sent Norris to the war, and it was to that office in New York that he returned to take up editorial work in the environment which had encouraged Garland to drop his "literary pose" and use his skill on topics of the day. The McClure outlook was akin to Norris's own impatience with the belle-lettristic, and he carried it with him to Doubleday, Page & Company, the firm which split from McClure in 1899. *McTeague* was published by them, and was followed in the same year by *Blix,* an idealized treatment of Norris's own extremely joyful courtship and marriage, which went a long way toward establishing San Francisco as a perfect setting for love as well as adventure. In the following year Norris produced *A Man's Woman,* which returned with a vengeance to all the banalities of *Moran,* adding to them the new sense of American purpose that McClure's journalism, Page's outlook (he called his journal *World's Work*), and the rise of Roosevelt and Lodge were emphasizing. In that novel the civilized brute is Bennett, a polar explorer, and he is called upon to undertake another expedition by three men who represent "great and highly developed phases of nineteenth century intelligence—science, manufactures, and journalism." They argue:

> We give out a good deal of money . . . every year to public works and one thing or another. We buy pictures by American artists— pictures that we don't want; we found a scholarship now and then; we contribute money to build groups of statuary in the park; we give checks to the finance committees of libraries and museums and all the rest of it, but, for the lives of us, we can feel only a mild interest in the pictures and statues, and museums and colleges, though we go on buying the one and supporting the other, because we think that somehow it is right for us to do it. I'm afraid we are

men more of action than of art, literature, and the like. . . . [When we give out money we want] to see the concrete, substantial return.[24]

They want to put an American on the pole, not to waste more on museums and "all the rest of it," art, literature, "and the like."

The life of the Doubleday editorial office had brought out the worst in Norris, and he knew it. In a letter he admitted that *A Man's Woman* was a slovenly book put together in haste, and announced, "I am going back *definitely* now to the style of *McTeague* and stay with it right along." [25] He had plans for a wheat series, a trilogy of novels, one on the growing, one on the marketing, and one on the consumption of wheat, which would take place respectively on a California ranch, in the Chicago commodities exchange, and in a famine-stricken European village, and would take its form from the magnetic poles of human hunger and the growing wheat. It was to be a laige-scale attempt at epic on the Zola model. Whatever disservice San Francisco did Norris, it finally did him this service: it made him dissatisfied with life in New York and increased his interest in changing his ways, because the wheat series meant that he would have again to go West to do research.

The Octopus (1901) was centered in the San Joaquin Valley and revolved around several actual incidents in the battle the ranchers waged against the demands of the Southern Pacific Railroad, their only route to their customers. Typical of Norris, the novel is powerful in its rendering of observed details—the massive hunting and slaughtering of jack rabbits, or the variety of people and the energy of purpose at the barn dance—but evades the pragmatic consequences of these details in a lofty rhetoric which insists that, contrary to all one has witnessed of the ruthless exploitation of the ranchers by the railroad, nevertheless the railroad also is but an agent, deprived of will, doing what it must in order to serve the higher purpose of bringing bread to a hungry world. Regardless of what men do, the wheat grows under the sun and under the stars, and this natural fact is symbolized and apotheosized as an explanation of the social injustices which are presented in moving detail. In short, the realism of the scene works powerfully to make *The Octopus* a first-rate novel, while the LeContian theory, used as a Zolaesque organizing principle, drags it back into the confusing and the second-rate.

The destructive aspect of the novel, however, does not stem only from Norris's facile acceptance of a theory which defies his observed facts. It is also related to the more complex question of Norris's refusal to separate literature from life. Fundamentally he advances the view of the popular weekly that writing is a kind of modern, consequential action which contributes to the world's work. Norris wanted *The Octopus* to be like a polar expedition, not like "literature and the like."

The incidents of the novel are seen through the eyes of Presley, a poet who comes to live on a San Joaquin ranch in order to gather the materials for a romance of old Spanish California. The railroad first enters his mind only as a commonplace destroyer of the idealizations he wishes to write of: the old West with its "swift, tumultuous life, its truth, its nobility and savagery, its heroism and obscenity." [26] But he becomes, in spite of himself, caught up in the ranchers' struggle with the railroad, and throws away his Milton, Tennyson, and Browning in favor of Mill, Malthus, and Henry George. He now applies himself to a poem on the exploitation of the man of the land; the new "Song of the West" he composes is a song of the people because he sees now he is of the people. But despite its enthusiastic reception and its being widely reprinted in the East, the new poem does not have any effect on conditions, and Presley abandons literature altogether and devotes his verbal powers to political speeches designed to organize the ranchers into unified resistance to the exploiters. When these too fail—because, he realizes, though the ranchers like him he is not one of them and cannot speak for them—he finally resorts to action and throws a bomb at a railroad office. The bomb does no serious damage and has no effect on the ranchers' losing battle. Presley leaves the scene of his friends' crushing economic defeat and his own personal defeat to sail westward from California with the reflection that "forces," not men, had been involved—though murder, the prostitution of an orphaned girl, and destitution were the immediate results—and that the "Truth" will "in the end, prevail, and all things, surely, inevitably, resistlessly work together for good." [27]

Presley's progress from historical romancer to social poet to political rhetorician to activist to silence is not the center of the book, but it is a revealing choric strain which speaks of Norris's ambivalent attitude toward his art. *The Octopus* itself, in parallel with Presley, attempts to capture the flavor of old California, to document the social problems of modern California, to be a muckraking tract against the Southern Pacific Railroad, and to protest so vividly that, in short, it will be like a raw exposure to direct experience. But since Norris is impatient with literature as opposed to life, he dissipates a good deal of his strength in an undisciplined pursuit of the right mode of forcefulness and finally accepts a set of hypostatizations as a substitute for life—Force, Wheat, Truth, etc. His distrust of art in favor of life has, ironically, made him lifeless. One cannot have *no* style, and disregard for style is, as Norris unconsciously shows, in constant danger of being bad style, bad art, and bad life.

The second in the planned trilogy of novels, *The Pit,* published after Norris's death, bears somewhat the same relation to *The Octopus* that *Vandover* does to *McTeague.* The theme is the same, the naturalistic power of the wheat to work out its own ends regardless of the petty doings of men—in this case their transactions in the wheat pit at the Chicago Board of Trade—and again there is a disjunction between the well-realized incidents and the over-all rhetoric with its staged symbols. But in *The Pit* Norris is dealing with a social class similar to the one from which he came, and in examining the marriage of his wheat speculator, Jadwin, he comes closer to an environment he had experienced directly than he did in *The Octopus.* As a result *The Pit,* like *Vandover,* is a much more even production than its immediate predecessor, and if it lacks certain of the dramatic high points of the earlier novel, it nevertheless, in the absence of the adventurous, leads Norris to a psychological penetration missing from *The Octopus*.

The Pit begins by contrasting a night at the opera with a day in the pit. The same men attend both activities, but at night they are spent and somnolent, giving their due meed to the idol of culture erected and maintained, quite properly, they believe, by their ladies. At the opera Jadwin, the virile gambler in wheat, is attracted to Laura, and he courts her with all the get-up-and-go that elevated him from humble origins to a position of influence in the financial world. To show her the nonprofessional side of his life, he explains to her how business principles have served him even in religion. Looking into the condition of Sunday schools, for instance, he had amalgamated competing institutions into "a regular trust, just as if they were iron foundries," and "put the thing on a business basis," [28] with great success. Laura is awed by the almost brutal vigor of her suitor, so out of keeping with the manners of the gentle artist Corthell, who appreciates the finer things as she does. Bearing in mind the advice that "the kind of a man that *men* like—not women—is the kind of a man that makes the best husband," [29] she accepts Jadwin. Corthell, with his well-developed artistic sensibilities in a society in which these are the expected possessions of women, is after all too effeminate. Norris is ambiguous as to whether he himself, in point of fact, believes that nature endorses this cultural view.

While the focal point of the novel is Jadwin's dealings in the pit —at first carried on with immense success, but finally, when he fails to corner the market, leading to all but ruinous consequences —Norris gives a great deal more time to Laura, left at home to devote herself to beauty and culture, than to Jadwin's speculations. And in this concentration he moves from the conventional description of the financier such as Jadwin who, having built and furnished an art gallery for his wife and having established a costly organ in the hall, can leave her in charge of culture and tend to business, to a penetrating treatment of the psychological consequences of this sexual division of interest. Jadwin is a bull in the market, in the vocabulary of finance, but Norris also makes it clear that the bull who rushes about all day goring and dodging in the pit on La Salle Street returns home at night having spilled his vital seed. He is less than his virile self in his marital relations, and Laura slowly drifts toward a liaison with Corthell, whose refined sensibility, she now realizes, does not limit him but, on the contrary, pre-eminently qualifies him as an attractive male.

Thus the vital tension of the novel is not between the bulls and bears in the pit—as Norris frequently seems to claim it is—but between the pit and the opera; between a masculinity that is vital but totally spends itself in business, leaving only a husk of a man for private life, and a masculinity suspected by society because it possesses the characteristics conventionally associated with women, but which leads to a rich private life even though it does nothing to build up the country. Norris obviously begins by admiring Jadwin and distrusting Corthell, but once he has set his Laura going and followed her sexual frustration and unease at being excluded from her husband's vital activities, he faithfully records the attractive powers of Corthell. It is with a disruptive wrench that he rejects the consequences of his subtle study and, upon Jadwin's financial crash, returns him to Laura, the Corthell liaison remaining unconsummated. Jadwin at the end, however, is acceptable as a husband only because he has been gored in the market and is a broken man. Laura, in nursing him in his despondency and in leaving with him for a more modest career in the West, must sacrifice her artistic interests. Though Norris would not follow the implications of the Jadwin-Corthell tension to the very end, he at least pictures the reunited couple at the close rather bleakly: Laura has Jadwin again, but he is drained of the virility which attracted her; he has her again, but she will no longer indulge the tastes which contributed to her glamour. They are a pair of broken people who could not satisfy each other when each pursued his own bent, but who lose their charm and interest in the sacrifices they must make to mutual accommodation.

In *The Pit* it is not finally the beast in man that sinks him so much as it is his being constrained to release his vigor in imaginative business enterprise, leaving the arts of the good life to the female. The American businessman, Norris shows, excludes his wife from his characteristically most forceful moments, leaving her open to seek gratification in lovers, or to pursue art or social work as substitutes for sexual fulfillment. The scenes which develop this theme—the tired Jadwin ludicrously amusing himself by putting the perforated roll of the overture to *Carmen* into the expensive organ and solemnly pumping the melody out in fatigued ecstasy; the frustrated Laura seeking the attention of her exhausted husband by greeting him every night in a new costume, each more exotic than the one before—build into a whole which successfully withstands Norris's compulsive digressions into talk of Forces and his laboring of the wheat theme. *The Pit,* freed of its relation to the projected trilogy, as it may easily be, is the first profound business novel because it rightly examines the psychic consequences of the commercialization of American life. It goes beyond Howells' view of business as just another field in which traditional moral problems may arise and addresses itself to the question of what, indeed, happens to masculinity in America when the male's successful pursuit of his role in accordance with the business ethic drains him of his virility.

Norris penetrated only when, deprived of a setting for high adventure, he fell back on characters of his own class. Thus it is safe to assume that the third novel of the trilogy, *The Wolf,* which was to have been set in Europe, where Norris planned to do research, would again have swung in the direction of *The Octopus,* with a premium placed on hypostatization as opposed to the immediate meaning of individual passions.

In 1902 Roosevelt was in the saddle and American literature had entered on its dreariest decade, with ambitious young writers seeking their outlet in muckraking or in formulations of the new nationalism. Had Norris lived, he might easily have become part of this group. The social realism which in the early nineties seemed in the ascendancy as a result of the immense social disturbances of those days had subsided in the face of an optimism born of boom times and a successful war. Now hypostatization was a national habit—Manifest Destiny, the White Man's Burden, Progressivism, the New Nationalism—which spurned the complexity of detail characteristic of realism, and the somberness of its tone.

Frank Norris contributed equally to the surge of new writing in the nineties and the outlook which cut it short at the close of the decade. More than Frederic, Crane, Chapman, or Garland, he had a foot in the door of the new century and seemed amenable to its aims. He prepared the way for Jack London; yet he also prepared the way for Theodore Dreiser, for, almost in spite of himself, he did follow the gesture to its psychic source, question the sexual code of society, and show that the business psychology had a domestic as well as a commercial harvest.

THIRTEEN

An Abyss of Inequality:

Sarah Orne Jewett, Mary Wilkins Freeman, Kate Chopin

The division between man and woman which Norris depicted so penetratingly in *The Pit* was a subject for increasing observation in the 1890s, though most authors confined themselves to the surface of manners. Henry James approached it as a new topic in his notebook entry for November 26, 1892:

> About which Godkin, as I remember, one day last summer talked to me very emphatically and interestingly—the growing divorce between the American woman (with her comparative leisure, culture, grace, social instincts, artistic ambitions) and the male American immersed in the ferocity of business, with no time for any but the most sordid interests, purely commercial, professional, democratic and political. This divorce is rapidly becoming a gulf—an abyss of inequality, the like of which has never before been seen under the sun.[1]

But the abyss of inequality, while it was used as atmosphere in James's works, never became the direct theme. He learned from *The Tragic Muse* that his strength did not lie in following men as they pursued "sordid interests," and without treating this masculine side he could not very well explore the abyss between it and the feminine side effectively.

The year before, however, he had noted that women, with their free use of leisure, were the chief consumers of novels and therefore were increasingly becoming producers of them. The feminine attitude, now disengaging itself from that of men, was in point of fact coming to be all that the novel was.[2] Girls who came of age in the nineties were keenly aware that, though being a woman was different from being a man, the sexual difference did not necessitate their dependence upon man. Just what the consequences were was unclear, but their own self-awareness appeared to them a fit subject for their writings, and the social changes which brought new themes into the work of their male contemporaries encouraged them to explore the nature of their sex as an independent entity with its own demands and its own capacity to meet on a level of equality whatever standards—moral, professional, domestic—prevailed in the masculine world. Ibsen's plays were establishing among a devoted group the fact that women had desires and abilities every bit as compelling as those of men, and in the nineties a large number of ladies wanted not so much to escape from the doll's house as to avoid entering it. The bane of their mothers' lives, as Mary Austin expressed it, was the notion of the preciousness of women:

> To preserve such achieved preciousness, the woman must renounce any effort on her own behalf, she must seem, at least, to rest entirely on her man's capacity for creating around her an atmosphere of exemption, of untouchability. Always she must seem to serve, not her own need of protection, but the quality of protectiveness in her man. She might even have to renounce property, to claim few rights, and to rest her case on the assumed material competence of men in general. If these failed her by death, in a pioneer society there was always another man; if they failed her by incapacity or moral dereliction, she was lost.[3]

The most common form of moral dereliction was drunkenness, and as a result feminism developed hand in hand with the Women's Christian Temperance Union. This was an object of ridicule in the nineties and of absolute wrath in the next century, when it resulted in the Volstead Act. But it was not, as scoffers would have it, the result of a prurient love of depriving one's neighbor of his joys. It grew directly out of the vulnerability of women who found themselves and their children completely at the mercy of a drunken husband and father. He held the property and could dissipate it, reducing them to poverty and shame, and he determined the times of copulation and thereby could add to his wife's burden. Moreover, popular notions of atavism in the nineties held that the children of drunkards, if not abnormal at birth, would develop into hopeless wastrels, so that pregnancy caused by a drunkard was a horrifying psychological as well as economic and physical condition. Legally and morally defenseless before her husband's rights, therefore, many a woman struck, rightly or wrongly, at drink itself. If she had not been frightened by her own husband's taking an extra glass, she had been visited by a tearful neighbor asking if her children might sleep there that night, or she had greeted a bruised serving woman in the morning who had truculently muttered something about "my man."

Although no Women's Christian Anti-Adultery Union was feasible, in effect this tacitly existed also. The easily caricatured manifestation of it, the iron madonna with her nose sniffing the breeze for the slightest hint of scandal, hid the terrible anxiety which resulted from women's having no existence apart from men, so that to lose the attentions of a mate was to be cast into an outer darkness of psychological neglect, social isolation, economic deprivation, and what was hardly to be admitted to oneself, sexual frustration. Divorce was scarcely to be considered. A wife's only means of protection was a prudery league, in which each woman was quick to detect the mote in her neighbor's husband's eye.

Thus two somewhat contradictory feminine types developed in the 1890s. On one hand, there was the comfortable, intelligent woman observed by James and Norris, who was made queen of a country which her husband visited only rarely and in which the laws and customs were in direct contradiction to those of the realm where he held sway, so that the two kingdoms were joined by an abyss rather than a fenceless boundary. On the other hand, there was the anti-drink, anti-fornication gossip whose fortress was her home and who was ever vigilant to destroy whatever might weaken her husband's inclination or ability to contribute to that home,

since in the last analysis, regardless of how much she did, his dereliction could bring it down in ruin. Both types of women reflected
the fact that the sex relation was a function of the economic relation. Many a determined daughter in the nineties sought economic
independence, not just to show that she could compete equally
with men, but to protect the sanctity of her inner nature. Her
dream was to enter into marriage or other relations with men as an
equal party whose demands were to be respected every bit as much
as the demands the male's nature made upon him.

Sister Carrie (1900) was certainly the most trenchant portrayal
of the relationship existing between sexual attraction and economic
dependence, but it was not the first. So pervasive was the idea in
the nineties that it even found its way into the "Ladies' Home
Journal Girls' Library," where the young reader had described for
her the first ball she would attend as a debutante, and was told:
"The occasion becomes an universal exchange, a market in which
wares are offered and accepted or passed by for whatever is more
attractive to the seeker." [4] This, then, was a critical event for the
young lady, who in preparing herself was told to bear in mind
that "the truth is the average man prefers mental repose rather
than mental titillation in the companionship of women." [5] The
thesis put forward in the manual was that the young matron should
be given the leadership of society. The unmarried belle cannot lead
but must watch for her chance, while the older matron is no longer
in touch with the most modern recreations. But the young matron
"is most apt to be she who can control and afford such good things
of life as a desirable country house or a yacht, dinners, balls,
opera-boxes, four-in-hands, perhaps a Pullman car." [6] Here, with
appropriate sugar coating, the author, Constance Cary Harrison,
made clear that among the upper classes a marriageable girl was
a marketable commodity which, if merchandised correctly, could
yield enormous profits.

Mrs. Harrison, born in 1843, was one of the older female
novelists of the nineties. The wife of Burton Harrison, then successful as a New York lawyer after an earlier career as secretary

to Jefferson Davis, she turned out fairly routine society novels, but always with an eye to the changing status of women. Her novels ended, conventionally enough, in happy marriages, but the road to marriage was punctuated by shrewder observations than earlier novelists had permitted themselves on the subject of the marriage market. The suffragette in *A Bachelor Maid* (1894) is an unsympathetic schemer, but she is balanced by two ultra-feminine ladies who accepted their total dependence upon men, but miscalculated, and now find themselves spinsters living in limbo. Mrs. Harrison, never one to offend the public, cautiously advanced the thesis that girls must be educated to a greater degree of independence both because they might not find mates and because, even if they were successful on the marriage market as a result of subduing their instinct for independence, they would nevertheless find it an immense resource once they were safely married. She also had the quiet audacity to chip away at the shrine of American Motherhood, observing of American women: "They are not, as a rule, good housekeepers; and I fear they will become worse ones. They are devoted mothers; but in a high-strung, emotional way, not always best for their children." [7] A treasury of suburban experience in the next century was to verify Mrs. Harrison's observation of the new American mother.

The sacredness of marriage, however, was almost beyond dispute, and as a result novelists who wished to examine the female as an independent person had still to frame their stories so that the marriage altar appeared at the end. Most, like Mrs. Harrison, therefore accepted the century-honored plot patterns and confined their explorations to subplots, passing remarks, or choric commentary. To give themselves some freedom, many dealt with a heroine who had two successive marriages. The first was the crucial one, and the dependence of women upon men was attacked as the marriage's inadequacies were detailed. Then, with the novel all but over, the husband would be got rid of by some convenient accidental death, and the conventional demands of plot would be satisfied by the remarriage of the heroine to a man who understood and respected her separateness. Tawdry as this device was—in many cases the more effectively the first part had been executed, the more damning was the second marriage, which could only read like a betrayal of all that went before—it nevertheless provided a cover under which the author could publish her journey into unexplored country. *Sister Carrie* would not have been possible without this intermediate novel of successive marriages, which, in effect if not in art, established the separate claims of the woman. Even so, the novelists were vulnerable. Anti-Ibsenism was strong in its counterattacks, and ironically a great many of these attacks came from women's groups that were responding to the same situation as were the new female novelists. They too recognized the dependence of women on men, but they felt they were protecting women from the havoc immorality could wreak on their homes by scotching any mention of it, including those in novels which glorified the new woman. She might be a model for some, but for them she was the potential homebreaker.

Indeed, Professor Ward Hutchinson informed the American Academy of Medicine at its 1895 meeting in Baltimore, the woman who did not accept economic dependency was the woman who opened the floodgates of vice. The majority of prostitutes, he claimed, were women who had first been engaged in occupations outside the home:

> The woman who works outside of the home or school pays a fearful penalty, either physical, mental, or moral, and often all three. She commits a biologic crime against herself and against the community, and woman labor ought to be forbidden for the same reason that child labor is. Any nation that works its women is damned, and belongs at heart to the Huron-Iroquois confederacy.[8]

While institutionalized science hammered away at the independent woman in this way, established religion remained alert against any suggestion that divorce was a solution to domestic unhappiness. T. DeWitt Talmage, pastor at the Brooklyn Tabernacle, warned in a sermon that "eighty thousand divorces in Paris in one year preceded the worst revolution that France ever saw. It was only the first course in that banquet of hell," [9] while such popular romancers as F. Marion Crawford showed that divorce was but another name for socialism.[10] In Crawford's settings of mansions and castles marriage was not subjected to the stresses of everyday urban life, but the Reverend Mr. Talmage had a city congregation and stood at the crossroads between Howells' country people living in the city and Dreiser's city people who knew no home other than the furnished flat. He warned of the baleful results of residence in a hotel or boarding house:

> The probability is that the wife will have to divide her husband's time with public smoking or reading room, or with some coquettish spider in search of unwary flies; and if you do not entirely lose your husband, it will be because he is divinely protected from the disasters that have whelmed thousands of husbands with as good intentions as yours.[11]

Both attack and counterattack accepted the economic dependence of women, and the horror which Talmage conveyed with the image of loss of husband was as much economic in its essence as was Charlotte Stetso Perkins' insistence in *Women and Economics* that women become financially independent.[12]

In *Patience Sparhawk and Her Times* (1895) Gertrude Atherton took advantage of the successive-marriage plot to have a look at a heroine who not only attracted men in the time-honored way of all heroines, but also realized that when men were attracted to her she found a responsive spark within herself. Into a plot fitted out with every element of what in the next century came to be standard ladies' matinee fare, including a melodramatic finish in the courtroom, she wove a thead of honest examination of the sexuality of women. Granting the public a number of tear-jerking episodes and announcing the over-all thesis that "woman has in her the instinct of dependence on man, transmitted through the ages, and a sexual horror of the arena," [13] the author then in detail showed: that mothers can be drunkards and that their perfectly moral children when they see them in bed with strange men can feel matricidal; that many of the ladies in the WCTU were putting into that movement precisely the same kind of erotic energy that other no less noble women put into loving men; that about half of the upper-class married women, after submitting to their husbands, relieve their ennui in love affairs; and that there are women, such as actresses, who can have a number of love affairs and nevertheless maintain their good looks and even, if they are smart, increase their financial independence.

At a crucial point in the novel Patience tells her father-in-law, "There is only one law for woman to acknowledge, and that is her self-respect," [14] and goes on to deny that even her husband has the right to make her do something to which she does not voluntarily submit. He responds that she is advocating the principles of anarchy, but she insists, "When a man and woman are properly married there is no question of authority or disobedience; but a woman is a common harlot who lives with a man that makes her curse the whole scheme of creation." [15]

In point of fact, Patience's father-in-law was wrong about her anarchism; even the anarchists were not radical enough to accept the female revolution. A number of American anarchist groups refused to associate themselves with Emma Goldman in the nineties because they feared her advocacy of the woman's right to control conception would endanger their work, and she received a cool reception in Paris in 1900 at the International Congress of Anarchism because she had also attended the clandestine meeting of the Neo-Malthusian Congress held there. For all her political activities, Emma Goldman was most vigorous, most radical, and most admirable when she interested herself in the war between the sexes rather than in the war between the classes. She trained herself in midwifery at the Allgemeines Krankenhaus in Vienna, where she also attended the lectures of Sigmund Freud, and her autobiography, which so frequently loses itself in purple prose when she talks of her own love affairs, or in automatic rhetoric when she advances her political views, has a steady, straightforward elo-

quence when she talks of the "fierce, blind struggle of the women
of the poor against frequent pregnancies." [16] The continual dread
of conception, the frantic use of painful devices to achieve mis-
carriage or abortion, and the brooding sense of childbearing as the
curse rather than the blessing of God upon women are reflected
in her pages on the condition of the women of the poor in the
nineties. Only in the actual pain of labor did the mute victims
speak out against their husbands and on behalf of their sex: "Take
him away, don't let the brute come near me—I'll kill him!" [17]

Society, however, was silent on this state of affairs. Society's
agents in the matter, the doctors, pointed out: "The poor have
only themselves to blame; they indulge their appetites too much";
or insisted that children were the only joy the poor had. At best,
some Darwinian comfort would be offered in the medical conjectures that when woman uses her brain more her procreative organs
will function less. [18] Although they were forced to remain silent,
intelligent women in the nineties knew about such matters, and
their determination to write what could be published about the
equal rights of their sex was reinforced by this knowledge. *M'lle
New York* remarked, "The woman who writes is guilty of two sins:
She increases the number of books and decreases the number of
women," [19] but if being a woman meant being silent, she was glad
to decrease that number. To be a serious female author in the
nineties was to be a writer of stories about women and their demands. The woman novelist was trapped by her affiliations to her
sex in precisely the same manner as was the twentieth-century
Negro writer in the 1950s trapped by affiliation to his race. The
condition of women inescapably had to be the material of her art.

Ellen Glasgow was seventeen years old in 1890, when an older
woman, her hostess during a visit for a round of social events at
the University of Virginia, noted her dangerous ignorance and
delicately but painfully explained to her how children were conceived. [20] To this moment Miss Glasgow attributed not only the
awakening of her novelistic instincts but what came to be a corol-

lary to interest in the condition of the American woman, her concern for social history and theories of economics. The novel that was started by this uncomfortable social moment was an awkwardly manufactured book called *The Descendant* (1897), which the young author insisted on setting in New York, a city she knew only from a brief visit, thereby enfeebling an already shaky plot. The book is marred by statement in place of dramatization, and climaxed by a murder committed in response to the theory of atavism rather than to any behavior that might plausibly be expected from the otherwise civilized man whom the author compels to turn murderer. But the polite Virginia girl, serving her apprenticeship in the nineties, would have her say about *la ronde* which society danced:

> Mrs. Van Dam goes smilingly in to dinner on the arm of Bertie Catchings, who supports Callie French, the ballet-dancer, and beams admiringly upon old General Morehead, who has broken the hearts and the reputations of a dozen women in his day, and whose day will not be over until his life is. But as for Callie French herself, why, she blushes if you call her name, and the dozen victims of General Morehead she passes in the gutter and draws her skirts aside.[21]

The novel was published anonymously, and Miss Glasgow resented the suggestion by one reviewer that it was the work of Harold Frederic,[22] although a twenty-four-year-old novice might well have taken this as a compliment. Indeed the basic conception is handled, although more crudely, in the way Frederic handled *The Damnation of Theron Ware*: the reader's conventionalized expectations are built upon at the outset only to be exposed as false to modern life. Akersham, the hero, a radical journalist, enters into a free-love affair with an artist, and the affair keeps pace with his vehement attacks on society. When he meets a purposeful young lady who works among the poor, however, he learns from her that the ideals of duty and religion which he is attacking are all the lower classes have to sustain them in their condition. In destroying these ideals he is making their situation more hellish than it has been, rather than improving it. As he accepts this message and becomes conservative, he turns from the artist to the young social worker, but, Miss Glasgow shows, contrary to the reader's initial expectations, in so doing he has betrayed a splendid free woman who is worth all the meeching do-gooders within society's confines.

In the following year Ellen Glasgow published *Phases of An Inferior Planet* (1898), which repeats many of the faults of the earlier novel: awkward staging of crucial scenes, bad dialogue, and a failure to actualize the New York settings; but which takes a long step forward in character development. Here the young lovers marry early in the novel, and the author concentrates on the disintegration of that marriage; love is not enough to sustain a relationship between a man and a woman in an urban society. After the couple's separation Marianna moves upward in a theatrical career, and Algarcife downward to drunken panhandling, before he is redeemed by religion. To a large extent the careers of Carrie and Hurstwood are here foreshadowed, and the very title, with its strained insistence upon a cosmic continuity that has little to do with petty human actions, also foreshadows Dreiser's chapter headings and often inflated choric comments. But Miss Glasgow keeps within the confines of marriage, and although she hints at a sexual life for Marianna after the separation, she arranges a divorce and a marriage to her lover.

The new theme of the independent woman called for a new plot that would not resistlessly flow to the magnetic terminal of marriage, but the young lady writers of the nineties dared enough when they dared the theme. Their works are marred and sometimes destroyed because they cannot break free of the marriage pattern. To scrap marriage entirely, or to treat it as yet another episode in the continuing development of feminine self-awareness, no more terminal than a birthday party, were the techniques hinted at but not carried out until Kate Chopin and Theodore Dreiser came near obliterating themselves by following their art where society insisted it should not go.

Mary Austin, Gertrude Atherton, and Ellen Glasgow were in their twenties in the decade of the nineties, and their concern for the new woman in fiction was shaped by the publishing market in New York. It was the male writers, not they, who lavished attention on the abyss between the cultured woman and her commercial husband. But in one exceptional case in the nineties the cultured woman was the author and not the subject. Sarah Orne Jewett never married. Her masterpiece, *The Country of the Pointed Firs* (1896), came from New England and radiated the dull late-summer glow of sun on pine needles. Her Maine residence and her Boston affiliations made her an inheritor of the values of the masculine world which had passed, rather than the curator of a separate set of values, because, as James had noted in *The Bostonians* and as Margaret Terry had observed in her visits to Aunt Julia, the great tradition of the New England awakening at mid-century had passed into the hands of women. There scarcely seemed to be a young man left in Boston.

In South Berwick, Maine, Sarah Jewett had been raised in close companionship with her father, the area's doctor, and with the members of his and his parents' generation. "I look upon that generation as the one to which I really belong," she said, "I who was brought up with grandfathers and grand-uncles and aunts for my best playmates." [23] When she said, on September 3, 1897, "This is my birthday and I am always nine years old," [24] she reflected both the respectful yet curious attitude she had toward the older generation which was the subject of her fiction, and her implicit sense of her mind's having opened in the great days of New England letters. Her ninth birthday had been in 1858, eight years after the publication of *The Scarlet Letter,* seven years after the publication of *Moby-Dick,* six years after the publication of *Uncle Tom's Cabin,* five years after the founding of *Putnam's Monthly,* four

years after the publication of *Walden,* three years after the publication of *Leaves of Grass,* two years after the publication of
Emerson's *English Traits,* one year after the founding of the *Atlantic Monthly,* and the year of the publication of *The Courtship
of Miles Standish.* Sarah Jewett in the nineties still shared vicari-
ously in the society of the great, passing her time during her frequent stays in Boston with the daughters of Longfellow, Emerson,
Charles Eliot Norton, Francis Parkman, William Hickling Pres-
cott, and George Ticknor. Her best friend was Annie Fields,
widow of the publisher of Longfellow, Holmes, Lowell, Emerson,
Thoreau, and Hawthorne, and still active as a literary hostess.
With Mrs. Fields she pursued a course of reading which resembled
in tone a religious pilgrimage. When she was down in Maine she
would write about the readings they were undertaking together,
saying of Matthew Arnold, "How much we love him and believe
in him, don't we," [25] or longing to read Burns with Mrs. Fields so
that they could bask together in the "bigness of his affection and
praise." [26]

The ladies of Sarah Jewett's circle were dated, and they brought
half-suppressed smiles to the lips of the young. They were too
precious and the air they breathed was too close for most men.
Harvard undergraduates gleefully passed on the anecdote of Mrs.
Fields at the breakfast table detecting a crumb of toast in the flow-
ing beard of her husband and saying, "Jamie, there is a gazelle in
the garden." [27] But if the ladies were dated, they came from vin-
tage years. As they moved between Bar Harbor, Back Bay, and
Saint Petersburg on the dividends from the modest estates left
them by parents or husbands, and murmured of Wordsworth and
of bluets in the field, they were in a world apart from Populism,
Tammany Hall, and the Pullman strike. Yet so deep was the channel which their traditions had carved that the writings of Sarah
Jewett were no more irrelevant to the nineties than was *Walden* to
the days of the gold rush.

Almost all Sarah Jewett's work is set in her native region and
it is, characteristically, concerned with the activities of a genera-

tion older than hers, although it is set in the present. She deals with older people, their courtships late in life, their attendance at funerals, their pursuit of daily rounds as natural as the activities of a forest flower. Their Maine is a world in which news of the turbulence of the late century arrives drained of urgency by the obstacles it has to cross in getting there, and in which meaning, therefore, must be sought from the customs of the country and private experience rather than from attachment to larger and less personal doings. Occasionally Miss Jewett wrote a story about young people, usually drawing her characters from the Irish or French-Canadian immigrants to be encountered in Maine villages—as if young love, the yearning of adolescence for the cities to the south, and generational differences were characteristics alien to the Maine men and women who occupied the center of her attention. These people mate, live together, and die together in a friendship and felt kinship which is deeper than love. Their marriages are accommodations in response to the needs they recognize they can fill for one another. Otherwise, men and women inhabit separate worlds under the same roof, and though their life is marked by reticence, it is not cheerless. Custom rather than communication makes parallel their paths.

The world Sarah Orne Jewett created was rural and isolated and was therefore a dying one in the 1890s. She was conscious of its impending death, if only in the fact that she dealt chiefly with the old, as if there were no young to inherit their ways from them, but she was more impressed by the significance of this world. The meaning of elderly courtships and spinsterish doings after the funeral is a meaning which expands to fill the entire story and to find itself validated in nature as well as in man; it is all the meaning life can have. The world in which money provides artificial equivalents for what tradition gives to the Maine villager is dimly building just at the margin of many of the stories: if the landmark tree withstands the timber man in this generation, it will certainly yield to the metal light pole in the next. But it does stand, for the space of the story, symbolizing a homely beauty and a courage which are, for Miss Jewett, characteristic of men at their best.

To be sure, there is an immensity of life—social struggles, sexual love, ambitious passions—which never enter Sarah Jewett's pages, but its lack is balanced by the ability of her material to fill the natural world which she creates for it. Her art, learned from the days in which she was nine years old, successfully fuses human gesture and natural setting in a compatible continuum. Man is not, in her pages, a stranger on the land but, as in *Walden,* an organic part of the whole, and his movements, rightly viewed, are as trivial yet as meaningful as the dartings of a perch. This message, to be sure, may be old-fashioned, but it is so only as an isolated notion. When rendered in a style that unifies man and his land-scape it achieves a fresh effect, and Sarah Jewett's leisure for observation combined with her devotion to reading and attentive labors at her desk to form such a style. By 1890 she could write a sketch of a ride taken along a back road and talk about what she saw in this manner:

On a green hillside sloping to the west, near one of the houses, a thin little girl was working away lustily with a big hoe on a patch of land perhaps fifty feet by twenty. There were all sorts of things growing there, as if a child's fancy had made the choice—straight rows of turnips and carrots and beets, a little of everything, one might say; but the only touch of color was from a long border of useful sage in full bloom of dull blue, on the upper side. I am sure this was called Katy's or Becky's *piece* by the elder members of the family. One can imagine how the young creature had planned it in the spring, and persuaded the men to plough and harrow it, and since then had stoutly done all the work herself, and meant to send the harvest of the piece to market, and pocket her honest gains, as they came in, for some great end. She was as thin as a grasshopper, this busy little gardener, and hardly turned to give us a glance, as we drove slowly up the hill close by. The sun will brown and dry her like a spear of grass on that hot slope, but a spark of fine spirit is in the small body, and I wish her a famous crop. I hate to say that the piece looked backward, all except the sage, and that it was a heavy bit of land for the clumsy hoe to pick at. The only puzzle is, what she proposes to do with so long a row of sage. Yet there may be a large family with a downfall of measles yet ahead, and she does not mean to be caught without sage-tea.[28]

Here a glimpse is enough to reveal all to Sarah Jewett; where the child has come from; what her family is like; what will happen after the season; the temper of the land and the temper of its small occupant. The color, the coming dryness, the men who indulged the child, the measles yet to strike fall into place as independent yet coherent elements of a scene fully realized. The glance that could see all this and the style that could hold the harmony of nature and its human inhabitant were the possessions of a superior writer. They speak of the strength of the tradition of Emerson, which late in the century was retained by Miss Jewett, as the heat of an August day lingers past sunset.

The Country of the Pointed Firs is the most sustained of the works which mark the the high point of Sarah Jewett's art. Although it lacks something of the breadth contained in pieces like the sketch of the girl, its confident movement is deep. The sketches which make up the book are framed by the return of the narrator for a summerlong visit to the Maine fishing village of Dunnet Landing and her participation in the routine activities of her hostess, the sixty-eight-year-old Mrs. Todd, who for the most part occupies the center of the book. When Mrs. Todd does yield her position, it is to her eighty-seven-year-old mother. The burying ground which overlooks the bay on the Blackett Farm near Dunnet Landing does not contain the graves of those lost at sea, dead out West, or killed in the war; "most of the home graves were those of women." [29] And, for the same reason, most of the sketches are about women.

The great strength of *The Country of the Pointed Firs* is its sane estimate of the limited value of the fact that Dunnet Landing is out of the way and different. No attempt is made to relate it to a wider world. The values maintained there—loyalty, courage, honesty—are right for it. If they are not more widely applicable, this does not reflect the provinciality of Dunnet Landing but rather the loss the world has sustained by changing. A rooted age is indispensable to the life portrayed. Even talk is meaningless unless it proceeds within the channels of a long-shared heritage: "I see so many of these new folks nowadays, that seem to have neither past nor future. Conversation's got to have some root in the past, or else you've got to explain every remark you make, an' it wears a person out." [30] The world of Emerson and Thoreau is still intact in the hands of the elderly ladies who are its keepers, and Miss Jewett can move unselfconsciously from the flora to the residents because time has matched their movements to one another. The narrator, coming from the world of the city, sheds her anxieties in her commitment to Mrs. Todd's back-country interests, but she does not do so to escape life. Rather, in Thoreauvian fashion, she has exchanged anxious living for life, for an acute consciousness of the succession of the minutes and the myriad of things brought to the senses in each hour of the day. Daily life in Dunnet Landing follows a well-established pattern, but, as the narrator appreciates, this commitment to routine frees the inhabitants from care about the future and enables them to get the most from the naural pleasures of the present.

Sarah Orne Jewett had a devoted readership in the nineties, but it was not a large one, and in *The Country of the Pointed Firs* she appeared to have gone as far as she could along the road she had chosen. Twenty years of writing were, it appeared, an apprenticeship for this one modest masterpiece, and once it was achieved, her career was over. She attempted a historical romance in keeping with the tastes of the time, *The Tory Lover* (1901), which offered little promise of development for her in that direction. Then, on her fifty-fourth birthday, September 3, 1902, she suffered an accident, being thrown from her carriage onto her head. The cerebral injuries she sustained put an end to all questions of where her career as a writer was to go after that time.

At the same time that Miss Jewett was exploring the vital meaning still resident in New England rural life, Mary Wilkins Freeman was writing stories and novels of the region. These, however, spoke of "that black atmosphere of suspicion and hatred, which gathers nowhere more easily than a New England town." [31] Her critical pictures of a region which was dying, unlike those of Miss Jewett, suggested not a genial afterglow of great days, but the piercing northern night which had descended on a land now barren. By 1895, the year before *The Country of the Pointed Firs,* Mrs. Freeman was established as the realist most likely to succeed Howells as leader of the school, but, although her writing career was to continue until 1918, she had already achieved her best work.[32]

Mary Wilkins Freeman had not had a particularly happy childhood in the Vermont and Massachusetts towns in which she was raised, and she did not view a life of spinsterhood with the contentment achieved by Sarah Jewett. When, well into middle age, she received the opportunity to marry she took it, and she was grateful that this also allowed her to live in suburban New Jersey rather than in a time-passed New England village. She was well aware of the changing times and considered the developments they brought important. But Mrs. Freeman was quick to criticize what she disliked before she understood it, and to apply the theories of the day to her fiction before she had made them her own. She was far less of an artist than Miss Jewett, and, in her concern for action and its immediate consequences rather than its relation to setting, she was careless in her diction and all too ready to help herself out of difficulties with a forced ending. The New England of her stories and novels does not convey the sense of place carried by Sarah Jewett's Maine; it could be anywhere rural and neglected: flora, speech, customs do not figure strongly in her plots. She depends, rather, upon some dramatic complication, usually the behavior of a character who goes against the grain of the community, and she devotes herself to working this out as a tale rather than following its reverberation as a metaphor of the quality of the life lived, as did Miss Jewett.

But Mrs. Freeman, though she failed to record the harmonies that Sarah Jewett saw, was concerned with rebellion. Her village folk are petty and grudging. They are materialists whose religion confirms their stinginess rather than relieving it, and her sympathetic characters are forced to act against the narrowness of folkways rather than in concert with them as do Miss Jewett's. Spinsterhood is a prison for Mary Freeman, and in place of the ruddy old age of the single woman in Miss Jewett she clearly presents the single state as a frustrated existence, since in it a woman is deprived of what Mrs. Freeman considers to be her birthright—a man. The heroine of the title story in her best collection, *A New England Nun and Other Stories* (1891), is an example of sexual sublimation, and she pursued this theme in its various guises through a number of tales. The hesitant, reticent New England suitors are far from the charming beings they appear to be in Miss Jewett's pages, but they are always, for Mrs. Freeman, preferable to no man at all. Since Mrs. Freeman's villagers set far more store by their possessions than do Miss Jewett's, poverty is a far more important fact in her stories, as it was in her life. For a man, being jobless is what being manless is for a woman, a horrifying state of uselessness and poverty to be avoided at all costs, and Mrs. Freeman's happy endings usually feature a man landing a job or a woman landing a man. Although not so fully realized—episodes too often substituting for the art of the story—Mary Wilkins Freeman's work aims at a range of impressions well beyond Miss Jewett's ken. While today it takes on an artificiality from which Miss Jewett is almost entirely free, its greater popularity in its own day is understandable.

Since Mary Freeman was at odds with the setting about which she wrote, her work is at its best when she has as her central character somebody who has a legitimate complaint about that environment. In following such a character she can achieve a fusion of her contempt with the psychology of the hero or heroine. Her many volumes are laden with near misses; she seems not to have had a sense of her craft and not to have grown with it. But every now and again there is a rewarding hit like the story "Life Everlastin'." Here Mrs. Freeman has found an ideal alter ego, the hardworking, poor but honest woman who is the village agnostic and is therefore simultaneously respected and an outcast. Measured against her gossipy, homely churchgoing sister, this woman is a saint, but her career of going against the mean grain of her village is threatened finally by her accidental detection of the hiding place of a man who has committed a brutal murder. She knows him: he is John Gleason, one of the wastrel hired men whom she has helped out from time to time, but she cannot permit either her loyalty to him or her scorn for the community to allow her to shield him from the consequences of his act, and she reveals his hiding place to the sheriff. Then this woman, betrayed by life into finally acting according to the standards of her petty village, faces the consequences of her own act and, for the first time in twenty-five years, appears in church. Barabbas, not Jesus, sent her there, and the story closes with her saying: "I've made up my mind that I'm goin' to believe in Jesus Christ. I ain't never, but I'm goin' to now, for . . . *I don't see any other way out of it for John Gleason.*" [33]

The elements which make up this stunning story are often present in Mrs. Freeman's other work in the nineties, but they all too seldom combine, and, especially in her novels, they come forth only spasmodically. In her sustained fiction her failure to penetrate to the psychological workings of her central characters is destructive, because, while a metaphoric act may serve as a substitute for analysis in a short story, the novel calls for a closer examination of the person who goes against the grain. So in *Pembroke* (1894) she launches a massive attack on New England religion with its pinched, dehumanized narrowness leading to sexual frustration or illegitimate relations or psychosomatic crippling, but denies the tale the validity it cries for by refusing to give it psychological dimension. A short story might have got by on the symbolic surface actions alone, but the novel buckles for want of foundation.

Later in the decade Mrs. Freeman turned to the naturalistic issues that were engaging Norris, Ellen Glasgow, and others, and in *Jerome, a Poor Man* (1897) presented a hero who shakes his fist at the stars as he questions the school-taught benevolence of the universe. In this novel she herself questioned the system which produced so few rich and so many poor, and again emphasized her favorite theme, that of the partnership of hypocrisy and institutionalized Christianity. But, ever the careless artist, she seemed to have no second thoughts about dissipating the energy she had poured into these sections of her novel, and quite unconcernedly wrote herself out of the real problems she had raised by arranging for a flood, a generous legacy left in a benevolent man's will, and an unexpected change of heart on the part of a central character.

When the times turned against realism, then Mary Freeman turned with them and took a talent which had never realized its capacity to the production of historical romances. Frank Norris, who had admired her early work, complained: "Even with all the sincerity in the world [which he doubted that she showed in her defection to historical romance] she had not the right to imperil the faith of her public, to undermine its confidence in her. . . . It is as if a captain, during action, had deserted to the enemy." [34] Mary Freeman's artistry was a casualty, however, not of the war of romance and realism but of the battle she had fought with her New England upbringing. If the battle provided her with the materials, it also provided her with a fear of being jobless and mateless, and even her considerable talent was powerless to prevent her from pursuing the path that would assure her of money. Another thing Sarah Jewett had during her career that Mary Freeman had not was an estate of some $75,000 invested in United States Steel, the Pennsylvania Railroad, Calumet and Hecla, and other corporations.[35] A man in the nineties might have stuck it out, but no

woman who had seen the world Mary Freeman had was going to
be so foolish.

Both Mary Wilkins Freeman and Sarah Orne Jewett had initially
received hospitable treatment from the magazines because they appeared to be working in the established field of local-color fiction.
This kind of writing, in which the particular customs, landscape,
and diction of a distinctive region were portrayed, most often in
sentimental little stories, was immensely popular during the two
decades after the Civil War, perhaps because, even as they set
out with a fair prospect of destroying their Union, Americans in
the war had discovered one another and so, after it, were receptive
to the charms of their own diversity. At first Mrs. Freeman and
Miss Jewett appealed because of their ability to capture the peculiarities of the rural New England scene. And in 1888, though
the height of popularity of this mode was past, a new local-color
writer began appearing in the pages of the *Atlantic, Century,* and
Harper's. There was something fresh and charming in the tales of
Creole life being submitted by a Saint Louis widow, Kate Chopin,
and Gilder accepted her stories with, he said, "sincere pleasure,"
while Howells asked, on behalf of *Harper's,* for more.[36]

Kate Chopin was born Katharine O'Flaherty in Saint Louis in
1851 and was raised in a family sympathetic to the Confederacy.
Her mother was French, and she learned the language at home
and at her convent school. Then, after a brief period as a belle,
she married the Creole Oscar Chopin when she was nineteen. For
ten years they lived in New Orleans, where he was a cotton factor,
and then, from 1880 to his death in 1882, at the McAlpin Plantation in Cloutierville, which he managed for his family. After he
died, his widow managed the plantation for a year before moving
back to Saint Louis in 1883 with her six children. A woman of
comfortable leisure, Kate Chopin had perfected her French in
Louisiana, and the reading which prompted her to attempt writing
fiction was chiefly in that language. Her admiration for Maupassant especially inspired her to try short stories. For eleven years,

through 1898, she wrote poems, criticisms, and a play, but concentrated mainly on two novels and about one hundred short
stories, almost all of which are set among the Creoles in Nachitoches Parish. The first of her novels, *At Fault* (1890), was not
read; and, stung by its failure, she was so critical of her second
novel that she destroyed it. But her stories were given a modestly
warm reception.

The most popular of Mrs. Chopin's stories, while they make full
use of the charming lilt of Creole English and the easy openness
of Creole manners, concern themselves, as do Maupassant's, with
some central quirk or turn in events which reverses the situation
that was initially presented. In "Desirée's Baby" Desirée commits
infanticide and suicide when her infant shows increasing signs of
being partly Negro; she, a foundling, assumes that she has brought
this shame on her proud Creole husband. After the deaths, however, the husband, who is not entirely unhappy at the convenient
removal of his difficulties, discovers that it is he, not Desirée, who
has Negro blood. So, characteristically, does the Chopin story depend on a twist.

But more important to Kate Chopin's art than such plotting was
her acceptance of the Creole outlook as the ambiance of her tales.
The community about which she wrote was one in which respectable women took wine with their dinner and brandy after it, smoked
cigarettes, played Chopin sonatas, and listened to the men tell
risqué stories. It was, in short, far more French than American,
and Mrs. Chopin reproduced this little world with no specific intent to shock or make a point, as did, for instance, Frederic, who
was straining after a specific effect when he posed his Celia Madden at the piano with a cigarette. Rather, these were for Mrs.
Chopin the conditions of civility, and, since they were so French,
a magazine public accustomed to accepting naughtiness from that
quarter and taking pleasure in it on those terms raised no protest.
But for Mrs. Chopin they were only outward signs of a culture
that was hers and had its inner effects in the moral make-up of her
characters. Though she seldom turned her plot on these facts, she

showed that her women were capable of loving more than one man at a time and were not only attractive but sexually attracted also.

The quality of daily life in Kate Chopin's Nachitoches is genial and kind. People openly like one another, enjoy life, and savor its sensual riches. Their likes and their dislikes are held passionately, so that action bears a close and apparent relation to feeling. In setting a character, Mrs. Chopin writes, "Grégoire loved women. He liked their nearness, their atmosphere; the tones of their voices and the things they said; their ways of moving and turning about; the brushing of their garments when they passed him by pleased him." [37] This open delight in the difference between the sexes was not a mentionable feeling until Mrs. Chopin brought to American literature a setting in which it could be demonstrated with an open geniality.

In almost all her stories, however, Kate Chopin conventionalized the activities of her passionate characters, and even in some cases betrayed them for the sake of exploiting the quaintness of it all. The ambiance of sensuality was rarely permitted to permeate the actions on which the stories turned. But she was obviously growing in that direction. In "Athénaise" she told the story of a romantic goose of a girl who married too soon and, encouraged by a brother with a flair for melodrama, left her husband's plantation to hide in New Orleans for no other reason than that she was not prepared to accept the anti-romantic termination of her youthful yearnings that marriage represented. She came near having an affair in New Orleans, but then, discovering that she was carrying her husband's baby, she returned to him. Thus summarized, the plot, while slightly daring, ends conventionally enough. Mrs. Chopin, however, does not accept the justification which convention would give her ending, but indicates that if the girl returns to her husband because she is pregnant, it is not merely to have a child in a respectable fashion but also because her pregnancy has, biologically as well as mentally, converted her into a woman, and she now feels passionately toward the man with whom she lives. Just as marriage was not a termination for Athénaise,

neither, the reader gathers, will childbirth be. The story is a fragment of life; the wife will go on growing in her attempts to discover
her nature and may very well, at a later date, meet somebody else
in New Orleans. But the return to home and husband is all Mrs.
Chopin here permits herself.

In her unsuccessful first novel, *At Fault,* Kate Chopin used the
successive-marriage plot in a rather wooden fashion to explore the
responsibilities of the sexes toward each other, and it contains
little that should have made it a success. She was trying her hand
at full-length works too soon after beginning to write, and her
characters refuse to take on the life she learned to give them after
a longer apprenticeship in story-writing. The novel is critical of
the dependence of either sex upon the other—a woman is dependent upon a man, her husband, who in turn is dependent upon
another woman, whom he will eventually marry   and finds both
the married woman who is kept in a tidy home by her husband and
the now independent woman who duels with her suitors unacceptable. The first passes her time in petty card playing and in idle
gossip; the second flirts aimlessly between attendance at such
functions as "An Hour with Hegel" or a meeting of the Hospital
Society. The admirable woman, presumably, is the widow who is
successfully managing a plantation; she is making sensible use of
her independence but nevertheless recognizes her sexual need for
a man, while enjoying the self-sufficiency that will allow her to
make a choice on her terms. The novel, however, proceeds by
contrivance rather than psychological analysis, and, since the
theme is the nature of self-fulfillment, analysis is urgently needed.

The stories Kate Chopin wrote after she destroyed her second
novel showed an increasing deftness of style and a greater daring
in relating the open sensuality of her characters to their inner
cravings and their actions. But the editorial policy of the magazines to which she contributed would not have permitted her a full
exploration of such themes, so that, after ten years of writing, she
again turned to the novel form to bring together the Creole environment and the theme of feminine self-awareness which she

had approached tangentially in *At Fault* and stories such as "Athénaise." The result was *The Awakening* (1899), a novel of the first rank.

Like *Madame Bovary, The Awakening* is about the adulterous experiments of a married woman, and while Mrs. Chopin did not have to go to Flaubert for the theme, she obviously was indebted to him for it as well as for the masterful economy of setting and character and the precision of style which she here achieved. Sarah Orne Jewett had also been an admirer of *Madame Bovary* and had defended Flaubert's theme by saying that "a master writer gives everything weight." [38] But she had drawn quite a different moral from the novel. Miss Jewett wrote of Emma Bovary: "She is such a lesson to dwellers in country towns, who drift out of relation to their surroundings, not only social, but the very companionship of nature, unknown to them." [39] Emma Bovary is a foolish, bored woman, while Mrs. Chopin's Edna Pontellier is an intelligent, nervous woman, but Edna's salvation is not to be found in drifting back into relation with her environment. Rather, the questions Mrs. Chopin raises through her are what sort of nature she, twenty-eight years of age, married to a rich man and the mother of two children, possesses, and how her life is related to the dynamics of her inner self. Sarah Jewett counseled sublimation; Kate Chopin pursued self-discovery and counseled not at all.

The novel opens at Grand Isle in the Gulf of Mexico, where Edna and her children are spending the summer in a cottage at a resort managed by the LeBrun family. She is surrounded by other well-to-do women with their families, all of whom spend their languorous days in expectation of, and in resting after, the weekend visits of the husbands, who work in New Orleans. In and out of the field of vision tortured by the constant glare of the sun pass the mothers and their children, a lady in black, solitary and always at her beads, and a pair of young lovers. They suggest the horizons of experience. But there is also the sea:

> The voice of the sea is seductive; never ceasing, whispering, clamoring, murmuring, inviting the soul to wander for a spell in

abysses of solitude; to lose itself in mazes of inward contemplation. The voice of the sea speaks to the soul. The touch of the sea is sensuous, enfolding the body in its soft, close embrace.[40]

The vague suggestions of the sea keep alive in Edna the questions which have forced themselves unwelcomed upon her. She is the wife of a man who loves her and whom she likes and respects. He cares for her fully and handsomely and leaves her with no sound reason for the discontent she feels now when her nature, like something awakening, yearns for some greater fulfillment and tells her that in her husband and children she has assumed a responsibility for which she was not fitted.

The sea reminds her of the sea of grass in Kentucky, where she was born and raised. There at the age of ten she had fancied herself in love with a passing cavalry officer and had indulged in fantasies about him, fantasies so intense that her father's reading of Presbyterian family prayers threatened the romantic childish self she had constructed and, on one memorable day, she ran from the call to prayers in a long flight which led her swimming deeper and deeper into the sea of grass in protection of her infantile passion. Edna as a girl dreamed of men, and she married Léonce Pontellier because he was devoted to her and because her father violently opposed the marriage, Léonce being a Catholic.

Now, at Grand Isle, her Kentucky background, warring with her unfulfilled fantasies, still makes her uneasy with the Creole life to which she is also attracted:

The mother-women seemed to prevail that summer at Grand Isle. It was easy to know them, fluttering about with extended, protecting wings when any harm, real or imaginary, threatened their precious brood. They were women who idolized their children, worshipped their husbands, and esteemed it a holy privilege to efface themselves as individuals and grow wings as ministering angels.[41]

Edna refuses to acknowledge her membership in this group, and yet it is not because the group is smug or contented. Quite the contrary; their mature and easy attitude toward the experiences they have shared goes against something of her father in her:

> A characteristic which distinguished them and which impressed Mrs. Pontellier most forcibly was their entire absence of prudery. Their freedom of expression was at first incomprehensible to her, though she had no difficulty in reconciling it with a lofty chastity which in the Creole woman seems to be inborn and unmistakable.[42]

She is secretly disturbed at the detail in which the women discuss their *accouchements,* the books they read, the droll stories the men tell them. She wants a fulfillment greater than the motherhood they have accepted, and yet she is more prudish than they in the face of sexual experience because her own background has made it a thing more personal.

At one point Edna attempts to explain to Adele, a strikingly beautiful woman and the devoted mother of a flock of children, what she feels toward her two sons. She says, "I would give up the unessential; I would give my money, I would give my life for my children; but I wouldn't give myself. I can't make it more clear; it's only something which I am beginning to comprehend, which is revealing itself to me." [43] Adele doesn't understand her but approvingly notes that she could hardly give more than her life for her children, and Edna, uncertain as to whether she understands her awakening self either, laughs.

The vague yearnings Edna feels fix on Robert LeBrun, a young and handsome Creole; however, when he feels the attraction of Edna, he responds by accepting employment out of the country so as to preserve the code of chastity to which he assumes she, like other women of his class, is committed. After the vacation season Edna returns to the family home in New Orleans, restless and frustrated, feeling she has yet to realize herself. Her fantasies are dominated by the figure of a naked man standing in hopeless resignation by a rock on the seashore. Léonce Pontellier, sympathetically noticing that his wife is not herself, indulges her as best he can, but to the phrase "she is not herself," Mrs. Chopin adds,

"That is, he could not see that she was becoming herself and daily casting aside that fictitious self which we assume like a garment with which to appear before the world." [44]

In New Orleans in the winter Edna's awakening nature strongly turns to sexual desire as she dotes on the memory of Robert LeBrun, and in his absence she allows herself to drift into an affair with Alcée Arobin, a pleasant rake who is one of the few men of her class willing to put aside the code of chastity that surrounds Creole women; besides, he rationalizes, Edna is not really a Creole. The affair is consummated without any great shame on Edna's part, but her distress quickens at the realization that Arobin does not satisfy her and that her nature still calls for more from life.

At this juncture young LeBrun returns from abroad, and when he visits her at her home she forces him to speak of his love for her. But her impetuous forcing of their meeting to a sexual conclusion is interrupted by a call for her to attend Adele in childbirth, and she leaves LeBrun to await her return. At Adele's bedside her obligations as a "mother-woman" flood in upon her, but the thought of Robert waiting for her is sufficient to dam them. When she returns home to find he has left, however, because, as his note explains, he loves her and therefore dares not destroy her life, she is brought to the realization that she is on the brink of a series of lovers: "To-day it is Arobin; to-morrow it will be some one else." [45] It makes no difference to her, and she doesn't feel her husband really matters, but the effect of her affairs on her children frightens her. "The children appeared before her," says Mrs. Chopin, "like antagonists who had overcome her; who had overpowered and sought to drag her into the soul's slavery for the rest of her days." [46] For their sake only she must accept marriage as the termination of her development and must arrest her awakening.

Edna, however, refuses to do this. She fully realizes for the first time what she meant when she said she would give everything for her children, even life, but she would not give herself. On a spring morning before the vacationers have returned, she appears at Grand Isle, leaves her clothing on the beach, and, naked, swims out to give herself to the sea.

The Awakening was the most important piece of fiction about the sexual life of a woman written to date in America, and the first fully to face the fact that marriage, whether in point of fact it closed the range of a woman's sexual experiences or not, was but an episode in her continuous growth. It did not attack the institution of the family, but it rejected the family as the automatic equivalent of feminine self-fulfillment, and on the very eve of the twentieth century it raised the question of what woman was to do with the freedom she struggled toward. The Creole woman's acceptance of maternity as totally adequate to the capacities of her nature carried with it the complements of a fierce chastity, a frankness of speech on sexual matters, a mature ease among men, and a frank and unguilty pleasure in sensual indulgence. But this was not, ultimately, Edna Pontellier's birthright, and she knew it. She was an American woman, raised in the Protestant mistrust of the senses and in the detestation of sexual desire as the root of evil. As a result, the hidden act came for her to be equivalent to the hidden and true self, once her nature awakened in the open surroundings of Creole Louisiana. The new century was to provide just such an awakening for countless American women, and *The Awakening* spoke of painful times ahead on the road to fulfillment.

Kate Chopin sympathized with Edna, but she did not pity her. She rendered her story with a detachment akin to Flaubert's. At one point Edna's doctor says, "Youth is given up to illusions. It seems to be a provision of Nature; a decoy to secure mothers for the race. And Nature takes no account of moral consequences, of arbitrary conditions which we create, and which we feel obliged to maintain at any cost." [47] These appear to be the author's sentiments. Edna Pontellier is trapped between her illusions and the conditions which society arbitrarily establishes to maintain itself, and she is made to pay. Whether girls should be educated free of illusions, if possible, whether society should change the conditions it imposes on women, or whether both are needed, the author does not say; the novel is about what happened to Edna Pontellier.

The Awakening was published by Herbert S. Stone, who had gone on from his partnership with Kimball and the publication of *The Chap-Book* to establish his own house, where he maintained an active interest in uncovering new talent and printing experimental work. The reviews it received, however, were firm in their rejection of Mrs. Chopin's topic. In her own city of Saint Louis the libraries refused to circulate the book, and the Fine Arts Club denied her membership because of it. Kate Chopin was not merely rejected; she was insulted. "She was broken-hearted," her son Felix said,[48] and in the remaining five years of her life she produced only a few pieces, although her friends insisted that she still had a great deal to say.

Kate Chopin, a wise and worldly woman, had refined the craft of fiction in the nineties to the point where it could face her strong inner theme of the female rebellion and see it through to a superb creative work. *The Awakening* was also an awakening of the deepest powers in its author, but, like Edna Pontellier, Kate Chopin learned that her society would not tolerate her questionings. Her tortured silence as the new century arrived was a loss to American letters of the order of the untimely deaths of Crane and Norris. She was alive when the twentieth century began, but she had been struck mute by a society fearful in the face of an uncertain dawn.

In and Out of Laodicea:

The Harvard Poets and Edwin Arlington Robinson

The most popular poet in America in the 1890s was James Whitcomb Riley. His dialect rhymes of life in Indiana were, for the most part, a doggerel equivalent of the local-color tale, and in unabashed sentimentality he turned his back on the serious concerns of the society in favor of comfortable assurances that the enduring things of life still were the wonders of childhood, the love of parents, and the yearnings of youth, and that these were typically American when they occurred in a Christian rural setting. In July 1890 he wrote a letter of advice to the Kentucky poet Madison Cawein, which, although it was intended but for one pair of eyes, gave forth all the commonplaces of his public personality:

> You can't toss a pebble in any quarter of any back township in Kentucky and not hit a poem spang on the top o' the head—a poem that no one has heretofore dreamed was in incipient existence. . . . Then keep 'em all sunny and sweet and wholesome clean to the core; or, if ever tragic, with sound hopes ultimate, if pathetic, my God! with your own tears baptized and made good as mirth. Think how earnestly I mean everything I say. Nothing to encourage falsely. Go among all kinds of people and love 'em whether you want to or not. Get rightly acquainted and the boor's even a gentleman. God gets along with him, it seems. He listens.[1]

Forced as such sentiments are, there were few in Riley's day, and there are fewer today, who, if made to read the popular poetry of the nineties, would not prefer Riley to the work of those whom Edwin Arlington Robinson characterized as the "little sonnet men" and Walt Whitman called "tea-pot poets." Riley at least offered some easy humor and handled his dialect masterfully.

The others were immersed in the notion that poetry was a special language addressed to subjects which were, at their best, deliberately vague because they somehow masked higher truths. They wrote sonnets, odes, and dramatic monologues which they believed to be American extensions of English Victorian poetry. Their lines were sounded with the flatness of a tone-deaf singer, and their themes consistently equated the ideal with the imprecise.

As Henry Adams noted, poetry in America was a "suppressed instinct." Its chief function was ornament. As the century moved into its twilight, poetry was less and less "the natural, favorite expression of society itself," [2] and there seemed no way for it to reattach itself to American life. The agreements which earlier Romantic poets had reached with science now seemed naïve, as technology and commerce revised life with a thoroughness undreamed of by Poe and overpowering to the aged Whitman. And the assertion of native themes seemed false in the face of the urbanization of society and the steep rise in the number of foreigners who contributed to the cacophony of American life.

Little magazines like *The Chap-Book* or *M'lle New York* accepted the impossibility that a meaningful poetry might arise in their time from American themes and traditional techniques, and, committed to a notion of the decadence of the age, reprinted and imitated the French Symbolists. The sober magazines, such as the *Century,* continued the assertion of American Victorianism; they not only published poetry by the "little sonnet men," but were edited by them. In the eye of the hurricane, however, was a group of young men at Harvard who were training themselves in the classical as well as the modern languages, read Whitman with admiration, followed the French Symbolists closely, traveled to France whenever they could, and yet were vitally aware of the new quality of American life and anxious to elevate it into the area of poetic expression. George Santayana and his friends founded the *Harvard Monthly* in 1885, and, under the successive editorships of Mark Howe, Bernard Berenson, Norman Hapgood, William Vaughn Moody, and Robert Morss Lovett, the magazine became, among other things, a platform for discussion of the problems that educated young Americans felt had to be solved before there could be a revival of American poetry. In its pages a dedicated group of ambitious poets did their thinking aloud.

The Harvard at which they were located was a tranquil isle in the sea of American activity, yet it was very much part of that activity and reflected it.[3] The rear-guard resistance of the faculty had finally been broken by President Eliot, and the students were freed of almost all the required courses which had traditionally marked the training of a gentleman and a scholar. Instead, they could choose whatever courses they felt would best fit them for the changing society they were about to enter. The university, in effect, had admitted that it could no longer define education, and threw the burden on the individual, while standing ready to help him realize his ambition.

The elective system, as it reflected changes in society at large, also changed the nature of the collegiate society. No longer were the students members of a democratic community of learning made homogeneous by the fact that they had, in great part, to pursue the same discipline. They were now rid of the fundamental feature of the college which had checked their tendency to draw apart into cliques and had made them come to know their fellow students, even in spite of themselves. As a result, discrepancies in social status were exaggerated, preparatory-school background was emphasized, and, in place of the real community of interest which had prevailed until the nineties, an artificial community was imposed as substitute. In that last decade of the century, to offset the heterogeneity of the elective system, the notion of school spirit, of rooting for the team, of "good old Siwash," took hold on American campuses. It was but a shoddy substitute for community, and it left its damaging mark on the weaker pages of Frank Norris and Stephen Crane as well as on the contemporary American college and the new American society.

Boston society helped exaggerate the class consciousness that was encouraged by the elective system. Traditionally short of young men, this society now became the determiner of status among the student body of the college because of the overtures it made to some and did not make to others. Moreover, the leading young men of Boston who were enrolled at Harvard became the judges of their schoolmates, since society relied upon them to give advance notice of who in the unknown body of students was suited for a week-end at Newport or a coming-out ball. The club system at the college developed as a mirror to the selections of the city across the Charles.

In *Harvard Episodes* (1897) Charles Macomb Flandrau, fresh from the college, presented a series of stories that glorified the undergraduate way of life. Those students who are incompetent socially, feeble intellectually, or doubtful morally meet with gentle-manly snubs such as, we are given to understand, can be tendered and received in good taste only at Harvard. The beau ideal of Harvard men in the nineties was one who, like Flandrau's char-acter Wolcott,

> knew how to spend an enormous allowance sensibly—if selfishly— who, on the whole, preferred to be in training most of the year rather than out of it, who rarely fell below what he called a "gentleman's mark" in any of his studies, and who, as a matter of course, was given every social distinction in the power of the under-graduate world to bestow.[4]

A friend of this paragon remarks, "We're not 'cynical,' and we're not 'blasé,' and whether or not we believe in God is nobody's business. If we don't drool about the things here we care for very much, it's because people who do are indecent; they bore us." [5] The speaker was proud of the fact that Harvard instructed its students in traditional fields with slight regard for the world that they would enter. Petty concerns would come to the students soon enough; let them first associate themselves with lofty ideals that were unavailable and inapplicable except in the classroom. Har-vard, said he, will make you part of all it has to offer if only you have the guts to keep your head up as you follow along the road it provides for you during your four years.

That such a man is an insensitive prig and that he becomes Fitzgerald's Tom Buchanan upon graduation needs no laboring. That he was the occasional associate of his literary classmates and that they shared certain of his ideals, however, must also be appreciated, as we have come to appreciate the way in which F. Scott Fitzgerald shared the world of Tom Buchanan, even though he criticized it.

On the simplest and perhaps the most important level, college was teaching the educated young writer the same lesson that life was teaching the uneducated—that money is an important thing. When George Santayana visited Henry Adams in the impressive house H. H. Richardson had built for him in Washington, he listened politely as Adams, after retailing his earlier experiences as a teacher of history at Harvard, then sadly assured him, "It isn't really possible to teach anything." Santayana was willing to agree that he might be engaged in a vain pursuit, but he also got the impression from his glimpses of Adams's house that "if most things were illusions, having money and spending money were great realities." [6]

The great reality of money, however, was not the gross success reality that presented itself to writers such as Dreiser. It carried with it, rather, a sense of tone, of what you could make of yourself in the spending. Wolcott had spent both sensibly and selfishly, and Henry Adams was doing the same. Money was necessary to enable one to realize the capacities of one's imagination, to paraphrase Henry James's view of the matter. If the Harvard gentleman was neither blasé nor cynical, yet was more than a little disdainful as the result of his social and financial power, so the Harvard writers, as the result of their incipient powers, were also studying detachment. Santayana, when he returned from his studies abroad to take up an instructorship at Harvard, moved into his old club and sought identification with the students rather than the faculty.[7] The latter may have commended themselves to

his intellect, but the former commended themselves to his sense of
tone. He, William Vaughn Moody, Norman Hapgood, and some
five others formed the Laodicean Club at Harvard in the nineties,
"based on the idea that Paul was too hard on the church that was
in Laodicea, when he attacked it for being neither hot nor cold,
and that there was much to say for the balanced attitude of that
seldom-praised institution." [8] The club, with Santayana as pope,
was something of a lark; still it signified the cultivation among the
young literati of a parallel to the socially prominent young man
who stayed in training and scrupulously avoided going beyond a
gentleman's grade in his courses.

Perhaps the chief literary consequence of this attitude was that
it blocked the accessibility of the American poet who most attracted the Harvard writers of the nineties. Walt Whitman was
read and discussed with approving interest by Santayana, Trumbull
Stickney, George Cabot Lodge, and William Vaughn Moody, yet
his barbaric optimism was so unlaodicean that they hesitated to
adapt his techniques for their own ends. Santayana, who scrupulously protected himself by maintaining that he, at Harvard, was
but a Spaniard abroad (though his mother was an American and
he had been brought to the United States at the age of eight and
reared there), used his self-created vantage point to make a penetrating comment on the matter. In the *Harvard Monthly* for May
1890 he published a dialogue on Whitman, the two voices in it
being those of Harvard students. The negative voice insists that
Whitman is, finally, ridiculous because the process of poetry is an
exploitation of sensuous attractions to be found nowhere on the
map. Poetry looks at the history of civilization and creates for it
a unifying ideal, says this voice, suppressing the anti-heroic qualities of man and the anti-poetic objects and names with which he
surrounds himself. It deals traditionally with fables, and if the
poet attempts to reverse this process and explain the fables as
nothing but symbolized history, he degrades the ideal while distort-
ing the facts. Real objects cannot enter into poetry at all because
there is an absolute sense of poetry which resists the chanting of

such names as Wisconsin and Iowa and the description of commonplace facts.

His respondent disagrees, claiming it is not any absolute but
the residue of habit that makes Venus a fit subject for apostrophe
while Oshkosh is unmentionable:

> This beauty has been pointed out so often that we know it by
> heart. But what merit is it to repeat the old tricks, and hum the old
> tunes? You add nothing to the beauty of the world. You see no new
> vision. You are the Author of nothing, but merely an apprentice
> in the old poetic guild, a little poet sucking the honey with which
> great poets have sweetened words. You are inspired by tradition
> and judged by convention.[9]

The real poet must follow after Whitman, this voice urges, and
make the anti-poetic words and objects poetic by fitting them to
his impression so that they are inevitably a part of the communication of it.

This was a fair start, but Santayana characteristically took away
with one hand what he gave with the other. He was an accomplished Laodicean. Almost forty years after writing the essay, he
was still concerned with the failure of the American poets of his
acquaintance in the nineties, and insisted: "Instead of being interested in what they are and what they do and see, they are interested in what they think they would like to be and see and do: it
is a misguided ambition, and, moreover, if realized, fatal, because
it wears out all their energies in trying to bear fruits which are not
of their species." [10] The description is apt, and any reader of the
verses of those brilliant young men and promising poets Stickney
and Lodge, or of the nineteenth-century work of their friend
Moody, is witness to the struggle of an elm to bring forth an olive.

After saying that poets should be interested in what they do
and see, however, Santayana went on to attack art museums, little
theaters, and the other signs of aesthetic America at the turn of
the century, insisting that these were a false veneer. Instead, he
offered the poets the things which he believed were 100-per-cent

American: "football, kindness, and jazz bands." Santayana, as pope, urged a faith in an America of which he claimed to be no part, and then demonstrated the impossibility of the faith by reducing the scope of that America to games. He insisted that the Spanish-American War was a healthy sign of adolescence and that William James was naïvely anti-historical in opposing it on moral grounds, and he claimed that commercial ferocity was the fiber of the nation. He reveled, in short, in an educated tourist's America, which would be spoiled for him should it attempt to create for itself anything more than a mass culture. He both insisted that American poets be American and scrupulously deprived America of everything, art, grace, manners, which it may have had in common with other civilizations; those things, he insisted, were so much better done elsewhere.

Stickney, Lodge, and Moody, however, more closely saw the America which Henry Adams was describing, one which in the name of progress was hurrying toward darkness, and they insisted on viewing it in a broader frame than that offered by Santayana. They felt the contradiction between science as light bringer and science as destroyer of humane values, and their poetry was filled with imagery inspired by the notion of their living at the twilight of the century. The world of their poetry in the nineties is a darkening and chilly sphere, and their search for values is a search for a light-bringer. It is significant that both Stickney and Moody wrote poetic dramas about Prometheus and that Lodge's two dramas, which dealt with Cain and Herakles, were also set in a mythical past and centered on the Promethean theme. All were impressed by the verse of Whitman, but only Lodge experimented much with its forms; his defiant Prometheans after they assert themselves chant somewhat in the manner of "Song of Myself." These poets were held in suspension, unable to commit themselves to the popular America Santayana urged upon them and still get said what they wanted to say about their darkening times, and at the same time unable adequately to broaden out into the use of traditional non-American—in Santayana's sense—materials without losing sight of their specific concerns. Their failure was a stale-mate of two traditions—that of Whitman and that of Victorian English verse—whose conflicts rendered their inheritors powerless to find a way out of the twilight time.

Trumbull Stickney was born in Switzerland in 1874. Although his family returned to New York in 1879, they traveled to Europe so frequently that upon his entrance at Harvard in 1891 he had spent more time in Europe than had Santayana at that point in his career. In 1895 he was graduated with highest classical honors and went immediately to Paris, where he pursued his doctorate in the classics and received it in 1903, the year of his return to Harvard, where he took up an instructorship in Greek. He died of a brain tumor in 1904, before starting on the second year of his appointment.

The image of the earth as a dark habitation possessed Stickney. He resisted surrender to the decadent view which attracted him strongly in Paris only by cultivating assiduously an outlook derived from his classical studies, that of the Stoic. He was keenly aware of the discrepancy between the optimistic proclamations of the Social Darwinists and the actual degrading human conditions which resulted from the applications of the new technology, seeing only a bitter outcome. His observations reinforced the view of history of his friend Henry Adams, whose characteristic pessimism he shared. Since the nature of man's destiny was so bleak, Stickney the Stoic concentrated on the manner in which it was met, insisting on magnanimity even in defeat.

Large philosophical questions about the nature of man and his relation to his destiny absorbed Stickney, and he sought vehicles for their expression in classic myths or in abstractions of his own experience. He could not turn to the anti-poetic of Whitman, be-cause this indeed was linked in his mind with the science and com-merce which had smashed values. As a result he remained trapped within the house of tradition, searching for some way to make its furniture function for modern use. The propriety of his poetic dic-tion, however, not only restrained him, but, in R. P. Blackmur's words, blinded him to the difference "between creative observation and dead observation." [11] A characteristic sonnet reads:

> *Live blindly and upon the hour. The Lord,*
> *Who was the Future, died full long ago.*
> *Knowledge which is the Past is folly. Go,*
> *Poor child, and be not to thyself abhorred.*
> *Around thine earth sun-wingèd winds do blow*
> *And planets roll; a meteor draws his sword;*
> *The rainbow breaks his seven-coloured chord*
> *And the long strips of river-silver flow:*
> *Awake! Give thyself to the lovely hours.*
> *Drinking their lips, catch thou the dream in flight*
> *About their fragile hairs' aërial gold.*
> *Thou art divine, thou livest—as of old*
> *Apollo springing naked to the light,*
> *And all his island shivered into flowers.*[12]

Aside from the discomforts of its "thee-thine" diction, the poem fails, as Lodge's also were to fail, in the vagueness of its ideal and the self-contradiction consequent upon it. The gods are dead in the verse of these poets, and the darkness which prevails is more easily described and made meaningful than the assertions of light and and color, which are but wishful thinking, unattached to reality. The final image of Apollo, coming after silver, gold, and rainbows, and dealing with the shivering of the white light of the sun into all the colors of flowers, is held up as an ultimate goal to be achieved by one who deliberately lives blindly. The fact that to the darkness of the times must be added an even deeper personal blindness before meaning is to be seized destroys the effect of color in the poem, admitting it is but a vague ideal.

The moving sections of Stickney's *Prometheus Pyrphoros* (1900) are those which capture the quality of chilled numbness which exists among men in the darkened world that followed upon Zeus's displeasure. Prometheus, when he brings light, does so like a magnanimous being acting in the face of a hopeless situation, but the specific gift holds out little realizable promise for humanity.

Men may now stir a bit from their torpor, but the meaning of the light resides chiefly in the courage which has purchased it rather than in any distinct possibilities it holds out to those huddled in a dark time.

Stickney, in some of his poems, comes close to seeing his twilight time as a wasteland, in the manner of T. S. Eliot, who entered Harvard shortly after Stickney's death. But he never breaks through to that view, though the year before he died he approximated it in one of his rare poems concerned with the details as well as the themes of the contemporary scene. In "Six O'Clock" Stickney wrote:

> *Now burst above the city's cold twilight*
> *The piercing whistles and the tower clocks:*
> *For day is done. Along the frozen docks*
> *The workmen set their ragged shirts aright.*
> *Thro' factory doors a stream of dingy light*
> *Follows the scrimmage as it quickly flocks*
> *To hut and home among the snow's gray blocks.—*
> *I love you, human labourers. Good night!*
> *Good-night to all the blackened arms that ache!*
> *Good-night to every sick and sweated brow,*
> *To the poor girl that strength and love forsake,*
> *To the poor boy who can do no more! I vow*
> *The victim soon shall shudder at the stake*
> *And fall in blood: we bring him even now.*[13]

The twilight shuffle at day's end prefigures Eliot's modern world, but the social protest rings false, not that Eliot refused to issue such protests but that even within Stickney's context it is a hollow assertion. Again, unable to rest with realized details of God's death, he has nevertheless made them so convincing that no positive assertion can follow them without seeming false. The sonnet is fine through line eight, because the outbreak of love follows genuinely, and the kindest thing the poet can say to those shuffling in the twilight is "Good night." The lines following degenerate, and their hollowness is made clear by the archaic image of the stake. It has no place in the poem; Stickney did not use the past, as Pound and Eliot were to do, as ironic comment on the present, and its intrusion here reflects his almost automatic dependence upon a traditional arsenal, his failure to distinguish between quick and dead observations.

Stickney's close friend, George Cabot Lodge, born in 1873, was at Harvard with him and studied and amused himself in his company in Paris. Lodge's special interest was French and Petrarchan verse. In Paris, while Stickney pursued the classics, he concentrated on the pre-Renaissance poetry of the Romance languages. Lodge's father was the distinguished Senator, and his mother was one of the most attractive women in international society. As with young Henry Adams earlier, his uncertain career took the form of a private secretaryship to his busy political father and membership in his parents' society—activities which he resented even as they attracted him. He was grateful for the outbreak of the Spanish-American War, seizing the opportunity to get away from his family and do something on his own; but the *Dixie,* on board which he was a cadet, was captained by his uncle—even the war was a family affair. After the war and for the last ten years of his life he moved restlessly in society, deploring the habits of Newport yet enjoying the friendship of Edith Wharton, admiring the artistic isolation of Henry James while feeling powerless in his married state and with his parents' social commitments to emulate it. His personal charm was powerful enough to leave its mark on the memoirs of almost everyone who knew him, and led Henry Adams to undertake the pious office of a brief life of him after his death.

In that *Life* Adams identified Lodge's consistent dramatic motive as "the idea of Will, making the universe, but existing only as subject. The Will is God; it is nature; it is all that is; but it is knowable only as ourself." [14] As in Stickney, then, God is dead, and Lodge too is far more convincing in his depiction of this state —although he lacks the fluidity of Stickney—than he is when he takes up its consequences and attempts an assertion. The title poem of his only nineteenth-century collection, *The Song of the*

Wave and Other Poems (1898), lingers about the imprecise symbol of a wave, describing it from sunrise when it begins to mount, through its cresting and its breaking, by moonlight, on the sand. It was, Lodge says, a prodigal which "lavished its largess of strength/In the lust of attainment," [15] and though it died in its fullness and aimed at things too high for it, it presumably represented the exertion of a superior will, which is all that one can hope to do in this life. The poem is typical of a good deal of Lodge's work, which, as Mrs. Chanler ruefully observed about a person she very much liked, did not at all reveal how nice he was.

Lodge dedicated his second volume of poems to Walt Whitman and experimented, with little success, in that poet's vein. The specific eluded Lodge, if eluded is the right word, since, on the other hand, he appeared, for all his admiration of Whitman, to believe that poetry lost strength if it did not keep itself general through talking about general things rather than attempting to permeate the specific with meaning. "A Song for Revolution," for instance, does not protest particular political or economic evils but deplores a generalized complacency and mediocrity, qualities which are not invested in any objects in the poem but are attached to statements about "man." In "The Voyage" Lodge presents an outward movement from the safe, the deceitful, and the slavish into the unknown, which calls up echoes of Melville's voyage metaphor. What Lodge's voyager leaves behind is perceptible and well realized, but where he is going—other than "outward"—and toward what alternative is fuzzy. Out there is some sort of saving rapture, but Lodge is even more ineffectual than Stickney in defining what he believes will break the twilight spell, and much more oppressive than Stickney in his adherence to a dead diction: "sheer height of scorn," "sufficing chords," "dazzled senses," "shrouded spheres," "evanish," and lines such as: "I am urged with germinal ichor whose functional vigour increases." [16]

In his two Promethean works,[17] *Cain* and *Herakles,* Lodge selected heroes who not only, like Prometheus, went against the gods to benefit their race (his Cain opposes an Abel who accepts God's

tyrannical management of man and wishes to transmit this slavish-
ness to posterity), but also proclaimed their emancipation from the
dark times through the slaughter of kin. The imagery as well as
the plots breathes of such murders, so that the poems speak obviously of Lodge's deeper sense of what it meant to be a member of
the Roosevelt-Adams-Lodge circle and still try to be a poet. He
sees the father, Adam, as an evil influence in his upholding of God
and his support of Abel's unquestioning acceptance of the nature
of order, and he sees Herakles as a hero not only in his killing of
his family but in his flat refusal to accept the responsibilities of
political leadership which are thrust upon him by Creon, portrayed
as a despicable time-server. Herakles shuns political power because he does not want to be bound by his fellow man, "the florid
animal." But George Cabot Lodge did not leave his family's
sphere.

The most successful of the young Harvard poets of the nineties
was William Vaughn Moody, the son of an Indiana riverboat captain. He flourished at Harvard because, as his friend at Harvard
and colleague at the University of Chicago, Robert Herrick, explained, "The best field for the very poor is the neighborhood of
the rich, because the rich are almost always more or less helpless
and in need of all sorts of services." [18] Moody followed Stickney's
lead into the classics, and after graduation hung on as an instructor
of English at Harvard until the financial needs of his family in
Indiana made it necessary for him to follow Herrick to the new
University of Chicago, which William Rainey Harper was building in the nineties on money supplied by John D. Rockefeller.
Like Herrick he believed Chicago to be hopelessly vulgar, and he
joined him in sending letters back to Cambridge which read like
underground notes from a political exile to members of his party
in the homeland. Although they were not initially aware of it,
however, Moody and Herrick were among the first artists to be
patronized by an American university, and their presence at Chicago was one of the early intimations that the tradition of the
writer as journalist was to give way to that of the writer as pro-

fessor. As their literary careers progressed, they made increasing demands on their university for free time in which to write, and these demands were granted. Moreover, the publications with which they managed to achieve some financial independence included, like those of many writer-professors to follow in the new century, textbooks for the constantly expanding market of college students.

In spite of their repeated expressions of contempt for soulless Chicago and their nostalgia for the lilacs topping the fences on Brattle Street, in that city both Moody and Herrick were able to achieve their potential to a far greater extent than were Stickney and Lodge. As yet a third Cambridge expatriate at Chicago, Robert Morss Lovett, said, "Harvard is a nourishing mother, but she keeps her children in leading strings till they reach an unseemly age." [19] In Chicago in the nineties Herrick began his career as a writer of realistic fiction, his first three novels focusing on the problem of self-fulfillment faced by the sensitive personality trapped in a commercial civilization, and Chicago supplied Herrick with scenes and metaphors of struggle. In the next century his use of this material was to make him one of the country's principal novelists. Away from the restricting balance of Cambridge Laodiceanism, he developed characters who chose passion as well as those who accepted responsibility, and if he rejected the commercialism of Chicago in his early works, he also spurned the aestheticism of his Harvard acquaintances, symbolized by Berenson (the Erard of *The Gospel of Freedom,* 1898). He concluded:

> They aren't a good deal more interesting . . . than the Chicago lot with their simpler ambitions and manners and cruder expression. On the whole they aren't so good; they are nearer dead: the others have a race to run, and these have only their graves to dig. And if I were going merely to rot . . . I should rather rot with the Philistines and be a good human animal.[20]

Moody too moved to a greater appreciation of the vulgar, and in the early part of the next century his verse was to reflect this in its concern for the contemporary scene and its growing reliance on the vernacular. In the nineties, however, Moody remained pretty much in the Stickney and Lodge pattern except that he reflected less pessimism. His distress with the twilight time came from specific events or objects, such as the war in the Philippines, and he used them, rather than mankind or waves or clouds, to serve as the vehicles of his meaning. His poems after the turn of the century were popular, for a serious poet, and deservedly so, because Moody was the technical as well as the dramatic superior of his Harvard contemporaries. But he achieved his sureness, where they offered only hesitant conjectures, as the result of some oversimplification, and if, like Herrick, he came to appreciate the Philistines as vital, he accepted with them a slick social theory that saw modern life as progressing toward the good. When he came to the Promethean theme, then, Moody identified the fire which benefited man as akin to modern technology.

Nothing more eloquently marks Moody's movement away from the troubled classicist of Cambridge to the popular serious poet of the new century than a portion of a letter to a Harvard friend, written in 1896. It reveals the kind of life which was flooding in on the poet, newly arrived in Chicago, and speaks charmingly of his openness to it:

> Yesterday I was skating on a patch of ice in the park, under a poverty-stricken sky flying a pitiful rag of sunset. Some little muckers were guying a slim raw-boned Irish girl of fifteen, who circled and darted under their banter with complete unconcern. She was in the fledgling state, all legs and arms, tall and adorably awkward, with a huge hat full of rusty feathers, thin skirts tucked up above spindling ankles, and a gay aplomb and swing in the body that was ravishing. We caught hands in mid-flight, and skated for an hour, almost alone and quite silent, while the rag of sunset rotted to pieces. I have had few sensations in life that I would exchange for the warmth of her hand through the ragged glove, and the pathetic curve of the half-formed breast where the back of my wrist touched her body. I came away mystically shaken and elate. It is thus the angels converse. She was something absolutely authentic, new, and

inexpressible, something which only nature could mix for the heart's intoxication, a compound of ragamuffin, pal, mistress, nun, sister, harlequin, outcast, and bird of God.[21]

The professor who could spend the dirty twilight hour of a cold Chicago day in this manner was better equipped to express feelingly the twilight sensations of his era and to give them value than were his contemporaries who remained at Cambridge, locked out of America even while they were locked in it. Moody was the chief of the minor poets, though finally the contemporary reader must approach him also through the diction and technique of a moribund tradition, which muffle when they do not suffocate the form toward which the matter strives.

In the nineties Moody and Herrick constructed for themselves a Harvard-Chicago polarity, and if, as has been suggested, the Midwestern city freed them to feel common life and to experiment with its expression, Harvard nevertheless provided them with a sense of civilization, a standard in terms of which the cheapening ferocity of Chicago could be resisted. Both in the twentieth century became attached, spiritually in Herrick's case, and physically as well as spiritually in Moody's, to New York as the ideal between the poles. They saw it as the city which contained within it the valuable elements of both Cambridge and Chicago. There culture and commerce struck a happier balance, they felt, and Moody avidly pursued that balance in the theater, turning to the production of prose plays, one of which, *The Great Divide,* was so sound a commercial success that it led the gauntly unsuccessful Edwin Arlington Robinson, Moody's friend and frequent correspondent, to misuse some of his power in that medium. Although by the standards of its day Moody's play may have been serious and artistic, it was in point of fact but one bare notch above the flashy, sentimental melodrama which dominated the American stage at that point.

As early as the seventies Ibsenism had begun to work on the

American consciousness, but when the battle over Ibsen was joined in the eighties, to last for the next twenty years, the issue was not playwriting. In the *Harvard Monthly* for November 1891 Hutchins Hapgood noted that Ibsen was still not being discussed as a dramatist, but that he was branded an anarchist and debated in terms of whether you were for or against his variety of social freedom. His chief American opponent, the New York drama critic William Winter, identified Ibsenism as "rank, deadly pessimism," and saw it, as such, as a disease "injurious alike to the Stage and the Public." [22] Within a condemnation so broad, however, there was little consideration of Ibsen's stagecraft. Nor was the Norwegian dramatist much better off with regard to his followers, who accepted the social badge of anarchy and urged his claims against society rather than on behalf of a realistic theater. Anna Morgan, his apostle in Chicago, thought him part and parcel of her feeling for new art, which included a studio with black woodwork and walls covered with a purplish-gray burlap. She did, as part of her new theater movement, produce the first American *Master Builder* in Chicago in 1896, but again Ibsenism betrayed Ibsen's play. Hamlin Garland was tactless enough to say in his speech before the opening curtain that "Ibsen is not on trial today, but the people of Chicago,"[23] and the critics, taking their cue from this, retorted with lavish abuse in their next-day columns.

The most approved method of play construction in the nineties was that of David Belasco and Henry C. DeMille, who, before they wrote a line, tried out the scene on the stage. Belasco would mount to the blocked-out stage and call to DeMille in the orchestra, "Now Henry, give me a speech that begins here," pacing slowly across the stage, "and takes me over here. Then I turn suddenly like this—and see the woman I love." [24] The succession of meretricious pieces which were constructed on this principle absolutely dominated the stage, so that when James A. Herne, Garland's friend, introduced the theme of the straying husband in his *Margaret Fleming,* the wonder was not that he was condemned by most critics, but that some of the more serious ones seized upon the play, in spite of the Belasco claptrap with which his plot was supported, and proclaimed it an important artistic event. In his best-known work, *Shore Acres,* Herne constructed a plot on the hackneyed theme of the tyrannical father turning out a daughter who returns with her babe on the snowy night on which the mortgage is to be foreclosed. But because he paid some attention to New England dialect and to the details of farm life, and made the forces of villainy reside in real-estate speculation, he was hailed as the realist for whom the American stage had been waiting, and the play is, indeed, better than the average for its day. *Shore Acres,* however, was Herne's only commercial success, and in it, in addition to the conventional plot, he had hedged his bet by introducing a sympathetic uncle on the pattern of the stage Yankee and with the added insurance of being a Civil War veteran.

Invisible as Herne's realism may be to contemporary eyes, it represented a threat which, like other deviations from the standard melodramatic fare, was strictly excluded from the American stage by a commercial arrangement far more effective than any critical opposition would have been. During the 1895-1896 theatrical season, the producing firms of Klaw and Erlanger and Hayman and Frohman of New York, and Nixon and Zimmerman of Philadelphia, began to form a syndicate of first-class theaters, all members of which were guaranteed thirty uninterrupted weeks of "attractions." For a company to be part of the guaranteed season in a number of provincial houses, it had to level its presentation down to the average acceptable by those audiences.

James A. Herne and Minnie Maddern Fiske were prominent holdouts, and their precarious financial existence in a series of specially chartered theaters was an eloquent warning against rebellion. Howells deplored the monopoly, correctly saying that it meant business not art, and Herne said, also correctly, that it would lower the standard of the drama and nullify the influence of the theater. But it prevailed. The syndicate controlled the press and rarely had an outright failure, the worst plays being helped to stay alive in New York so that eventually they could in turn go on the road. Outsiders, however, needed a smashing success before they could make money. Norman Hapgood, going from the *Harvard Monthly* to drama criticism on Lincoln Steffens' *Commercial Advertiser,* protested:

> The Syndicate managers . . . do not try to reproduce the successes of Sudermann, Hauptmann, or Ibsen, or to encourage in any way the sterner aspects of the drama in America. They dread anything austere and tragic. It means to them the same as unpleasant or dull. Obviously, therefore, actors are kept from showing talent in some higher lines as surely as are playwrights.[25]

The most striking aspect of Edwin Arlington Robinson's growth as a dramatic poet in a decade so dedicated to the hackneyed in its drama and the time-emptied symbols arranged in conventional forms in its poetry, was that he was of his time. When he disagreed, he did so chiefly through asserting the values he thought were important, rather than through deploring the prevalence of the false. If he learned from Ibsen, he also believed Kipling to be the greatest poet writing in English in his day. For all his admiration for Daudet, Zola, and Henry James, he had also a conservative sense of the worth of the *Century* and was upset when that magazine consented to publish the humorist Bill Nye, who struck him as "a trifle coarse." [26] He admired William Jennings Bryan, seeing a touch of Lincoln in him, but voted for McKinley, even though his family's straitened financial condition was aggravated by the depression of land values in the West in 1893.[27] He liked to be where writing was being talked about, but he balked at discussing with women the French writers he admired. When he had an opportunity to see Julia Marlowe play Shakespeare, he seized it, but he was also in the queue for tickets to the melodrama.[28]

Robinson was born in Head Tide, Maine, in 1869; the family moved while he was still a baby to Gardiner, Maine. There he was raised and educated as if his future would lie in one or another commercial pursuit in Gardiner; he took the terminal rather than the college-preparatory course at high school. Some idea of the culture of the town may be gathered, however, from the fact that this meant he had to be content with Latin alone rather than going on to add Greek. Gardiner was not unlike the time-passed Maine towns of Sarah Orne Jewett's stories, a place still basking in what chill warmth had been left from the days of Emerson, one where there was a class of people for whom the ancient tongues, the practice of writing, and the reading of good books were parts of a natural inheritance in entire keeping with the fact that they were New England villagers. The town judge knew his Horace, the town doctor wrote poetry, and in Gardiner there were also an accomplished scholar in Hebrew, an illustrator of children's stories, several writers of children's books, and a composer of songs. More than any poet of his time, Robinson, in this setting, came to know his American as well as his European predecessors and to draw heavily upon them.[29]

Because his ailing ear required that he reside in the Boston area to receive periodic treatment from specialists, Robinson was allowed by his family to enroll as a special student at Harvard in 1891. He was somewhat older than the average freshman, he was not a regular student, he came with academic deficiencies in his earlier training, and he had no social connections. These handicaps combined to make him somewhat of an outcast, but his two years at Harvard were a heaven compared to life in Gardiner, which he frequently called life in hell. Robinson was sensitive to being excluded, but this feeling was overshadowed by his gratitude for the friends he did have, the opportunity presented him to learn what his imagination yearned after, and the chances he received to be in a community of young and serious writers. The *Advocate* printed his poems and asked for more, and even though the *Monthly,* the more glorious journal, took nothing of his for publication, he accepted without bitterness the fact that it was run by a clique and that the dazzling Moody and his friends were far more accomplished than he. Not until ten years had passed were they to become his friends, his equals, and then, with some shock on their part but nevertheless with manly generosity, his admirers.

The panic of 1893 ended Robinson's two years at Harvard, and he returned to Gardiner to cope with family miseries—illnesses, deaths, psychological deterioration—which kept unfaltering pace with the family's sinking material conditions. He brought home with him from Harvard a good knowledge of French and an appetite for French writers, which he attempted continuously to feed, as well as an expanding list of other literary favorites. His sojourn among the learned never led him seriously to mistrust his feeling that he had been called to be a writer. But in the dark years after his return he attempted a form that seemed feasible commercially—prose sketches after Coppée and somewhat after Hawthorne, sketches which, however, never found a market and were finally destroyed. During these months devoted to prose, the old French poetic forms sang through his head to such an extent that from time to time he had to succumb and put all else aside to work on a poem which would not leave him. Finally, in 1895, he gave up struggling against the verse which invaded him and yielded to it entirely.

There never was the notion in Robinson's head that his verse would some day support him financially, but neither did he ever doubt that he was a poet. James's splendid artistic concentration and his message, in "The Lesson of the Master," came home to Robinson as basic truths, and he resigned himself to a single life as the necessary condition of the long road he had to walk if he was to succeed as an artist.[30] The lesson Whitman and other American predecessors held for him was one of the values resident in the anti-poetic substance of daily American life and the eloquence resident in plain speech. In the daily hellish round of life in Gardiner, he had ample opportunity to test these lessons, so that his acceptance of them was experienced and unrhetorical. At the same time, his genius was moral and dramatic, and he felt the need to objectify his work, not to make it a chant of the asserting self. He saw no contradiction between his loyalty to American speech and commonplace materials and his delight in traditional forms. In his Gardiner isolation he worked to achieve the miracle of dignifying the former through disciplining it to the demands of the latter. His sonnets were precise models of the Petrarchan form in English, though they spoke of common things, and to the extent that he insisted on precisely fulfilling the demands of form—of a villanelle or a ballad or a sonnet—to that extent he insisted on simple speech being made adequate to the form it took. His rhymes are so unforced, his rhythms so speech-like, his diction so simple, the reader notes with surprise that the organic whole which so clearly grows from the seed of itself is, in fact, a fourteen-line Italian sonnet.

In 1896 Robinson published a collection of poems, *The Torrent and the Night Before,* at his own expense: three hundred copies for $52. In the following year he innocently brought out *The Children of the Night* with a notorious vanity publisher, duplicating some of the poems in the earlier volume and adding seventeen. That year, also, he made his way to New York to seek the company of several minor poets he had come to know through correspondence, then returned to Gardiner to assist with the continuing problems of his family. In 1898 his old Harvard friends, impressed by the quality of his poems, secured him a clerical position in the office of President Eliot; however, the atmosphere of utilitarianism which controlled education deadened what delight he had at being back in Cambridge, and he drifted back to Gardiner at the academic year's end. In 1899 he was in New York, now in a cheap furnished room, now out at Yonkers, where an even slummier room could be had even more cheaply, now back in New York, where an opportunity to free-load presented itself. As the decade ended, he was sharking about for subsistence among bad poets, admiring and well-positioned friends, disreputable Bohemians, and plodding wage earners. Close to hunger as he came, and grateful as he was for occasional work and for a good meal and more than one drink, he kept his independence and, convinced in poverty and neglect that he was a poet and a good one, never yielded to a literary circle, a social set, or a job the freedom necessary to him if he was to fulfill himself. But in 1900 the path was still downward to a nadir of hope in 1903, and his resolve was sorely taxed by the opportunities offered him to earn a living outside of poetry.

Robinson's first volumes were more praised than abused by the critics, but this very fact speaks for the feebleness of the condition of verse in his day. Since he too wrote, in the main, in traditional forms, his work found a place in an omnibus review which linked it with other volumes whose pages had the same visual impact on the reader, and he was vaguely petted as another "singer," without, seemingly, being read by the average critic. As he moved about New York at the close of the century, he was awaiting word from Small, Maynard & Company in Boston as to their decision on his first attempt at a long poem, "Captain Craig," and was writing the shorter poems which were eventually to accompany it when it was published in 1902. The Boston publisher's evasive replies to his inquiries were, in point of fact, designed to cover the fact that the manuscript had been lost and that a desperate search was on for it in the offices of the failing firm. As it later turned out, chance had hit upon a metaphor for the condition of poetry in the age, one which Robinson would have shunned for its gross obviousness: the missing manuscript was in a Boston whorehouse, where the Small, Maynard reader had forgotten he had left it.

In the nineties Robinson's handful of friends were the major part of his audience, but after the appearance of *Captain Craig and Other Poems* (1902), although he received ruder treatment than before from the critics, he also began to attract the attention of serious poets and intelligent readers. He had yet a long way to travel before he would be famous, but, when poetry had an immense American revival after 1912, he was present, single, gaunt, bespectacled, and somewhat deaf, to receive the new poets' acknowledgment: he it was who had shown them the way in his reverence for the formal values of the past but his insistence upon the diction, the rhythm, and the content of the present; in his maintenance of humane values, but displayed in objective dramas rather than in self-proclaiming assertions. He was, they said, the first modern American poet. He was the light-bringer, even though in the nineties the darkness was so Stygian his candle hardly penetrated it.

Robinson, like the Harvard poets of his time, accepted the light-dark imagery as basic to his verse and also invested it with a quality of bleakness characteristic of the times. "Oh for a poet—for a beacon bright/To rift this changeless glimmer of dead gray," began an early sonnet, which went on to condemn the "little sonnet-men." [31] In another early poem he announces that Arcady is now a decayed and ruined land, though his dream was "to command/New life into that shrunken clay," [32] ending the poem with an acceptance of failure and an admission that since commerce is triumphant he will turn from art to commerce. But, of course, he did not do so, and in his most eloquent statement on the theme, the sonnet "Dear Friends," he concluded: "So, friends (dear friends), remember, if you will,/The shame I win for singing is all mine,/The gold I miss for dreaming is all yours." [33]

Unlike his contemporaries, however, Robinson had a great deal of success in accomplishing a meaningful movement from dark or gray or dead gods to light and color and life. Perhaps this is because his genius separated him from them in nothing more clearly than in its depriving him of his youth. Not only did he serve out his apprenticeship in greater geographical isolation than did they, not only did he live a celibate's life, but he also had the stamina to deny himself a young man's outlook on the world. His was a dramatic imagination, and, somewhat like Sarah Jewett, he was able to see himself in older people and to check his impatience at the darkness ahead by seeing that it was ahead only because he was young; that, in point of fact, it was behind for many, and, because they had experienced it, it was not all darkness. He could project a drama involving this perception so completely that his assertions of the light glimmering somewhere were validated by the felt experience set forth in the poem, since a life had been lived there, rather than sounding, as in the poems of his contemporaries, like the pronouncements of youthful bravado.

The theme is developed not as credo but as part of an objective drama in "Isaac and Archibald," where the old man tells the boy:

> The shadow calls us, and it frightens us—
> We think; but there's a light behind the stars
> And we old fellows who have dared to live,
> We see it—and we see the other things,
> The other things.[34]

The speaker is one of two old men whom the reader has had rendered for him as part of a total scene that contains a treatment of the oats which may have been harvested too early, the warmth and western breeze of a late August afternoon, the taste of sun-blighted apples, and the aroma of stored cider. The life that had been lived in the poem by Archibald and its relation to this physical world qualify him to make this statement. The poet, a man in his early thirties, has diffused himself into the talk of old men and the wonder of a boy; he speaks from no given time in life. The youth Robinson denied himself is not present to insist; the agelessness he has assumed—not as a fictive costume which clothes his outside, but as the very spiritual condition of his art— impregnates the drama and the quoted lines with meaning. They stand as truth, not as clamor.

The world was growing young as much as it was growing old for Robinson. It is significant that he saw Greek drama and Greek verse not as parables for his own particular dark time, but as poetry, and that he learned craft from them rather than despair. His rendering of Greek verse into English is concerned with the problem of how to keep the ancient tone without relying on archaisms; how, in short, to treat great poetry as all great art should be treated—as contemporary. In this he prefigured Pound, and in this he differed greatly from his more learned friends who fed on the past because it was a greater time when the gods were not yet dead.

No poets of Robinson's generation had less cause for hope and humor, yet none rendered these qualities more convincingly. Characteristically, he constructed an objective drama, and even when it spoke of blighted lives, as in the Tilbury poems, those lives assumed a dignity through the toughness of verse which convinced the reader that they had been lived. Once so invested, regardless of how tragic might have been their end, they spoke of worth. What a wonder, for all its horrors, is life, Robinson shows; or, to paraphrase Wallace Stevens addressing another matter, one might have thought of living, but who could think of all it holds for all the ill it holds.

His remote situation in Maine in the nineties encouraged Robinson, as it encouraged Sarah Jewett, to think of his particular time in connection with the private lives of the unknown rather than with the large events of the day. But, unlike her, he did not use this outlook to retreat into a world but barely connected with modern history. His excursions to Boston and New York disciplined his perception of the similarity between the villagers he knew and the city people he met, so that, for instance, returning to Gardiner to note that the clerks in the village store were now old men, grown colorless in the pursuit of humdrum commerce, he wrote:

> *I did not think that I should find them there*
> *When I came back again; but there they stood,*
> *As in the days they dreamed of when young blood*
> *Was in their cheeks and women called them fair.*[35]

But he could also see the worth in the men that came from their having lived and their continuing to live, that they were "just as human as they ever were." The clerks are made dramatic through being suspended between the pole of respect for their achievement, supremely human even as it is very petty, and the pole of pity for what they have become in terms of what they had dreamed.

The closing sestet of the sonnet broadens the meaning of the clerks by applying it to those who ache with ambition and those who are consumed with their pedigree—people Robinson had observed closely at Harvard. It is firmly supported by the tense image of the clerks which has been established in the octet, and the sonnet closes: "Poets and kings are but the clerks of Time,/ Tiering the same dull webs of discontent,/Clipping the same sad alnage of the years." The conclusion is a serious one, but it is not in the fashionable gloom of a decade feeling its degeneration. If time destroys, it also makes things valuable. The clerks' experience, while it brings that of more pretentious people to a lower level than they presume for themselves, nevertheless also elevates it by relating it to what is meaningful about their lives. In the Tilbury poems Robinson did not write of his village in order to assert that, since it was made up of people, it was a microcosm of the larger world and would serve as its metaphor; rather, he looked at the world for its moral meanings and then dramatized them in the setting familiar to him.

If, after the twentieth-century poetic revival in America, Robinson, while receiving his long overdue honors, nevertheless faded in his appeal, it is because those who succeeded him took up the tasks of his youth in the nineties rather than the tasks of his later years (*Merlin,* and such work), and pursued them free of the groping that was an inevitable accompaniment of his isolation in his formative decade. There was no condescension in their hailing him as a founder, however, even if that acclaim was mingled with a respect for the mere fact of his survival. For Edwin Arlington Robinson, more neglected than his contemporaries who worked in fiction—even to failing to receive the degree of abuse as well as profit that sometimes came to them—not only survived as a person, which was difficult, but consistently moved through the adversities of the nineties as a conscious poet. If the nineties did not listen to him, this may have been as important a feature in his survival as any other, for too often in that decade he who was heard was destroyed.

FIFTEEN

A Decade's Delay:

Theodore Dreiser

Like Edwin Arlington Robinson, Theodore Dreiser, in the early years of the twentieth century, seemed destined to be an author without a public. His first book, *Sister Carrie* (1900), had been all but ignored, but, like Robinson, he survived to emerge after 1912 as a major figure and to be acknowledged by the writers of the twenties as their leading guide. The survival into recognition of Robinson and Dreiser serves, however, to underscore the phenomenal abrasiveness of the nineties rather than to qualify it, for neither man was able to mature steadily and grow by degrees into a wider acceptance. Rather, at the turn of the century, although they avoided the shattering consequences of psychological breakdowns in a way which John Jay Chapman did not, and although they continued to write, as Kate Chopin was unable to do when *The Awakening* was abused and she was insulted, Robinson's spirits sank dangerously low and Dreiser, walking by the river, seriously considered adding his suicide to the untimely deaths of Norris, Crane, and Frederic.

Like Robinson, Dreiser, born in Terre Haute, Indiana, in 1871, developed as a writer in agreement with his culture's values.[1] But he was the product of a culture different from Robinson's, the Midwest, of the divine right of the farmer and the undeniable glory of America, the culture which was to produce in the nineties the Populist platform, *In His Steps,* and a series of cardboard historical romances. His family was constantly threatened by pauperdom, and his German-speaking Roman Catholic father sent him to parochial schools tended by teachers for whom the German tongue was more natural than the English, so that, however debased the diction of the Midwest had become, it was adulterated even further as it flowed in upon him. Words aplenty he came to know, but nothing in his background or his training taught a respect for them. One word was as good as another, if the two meant approximately the same thing, and they were put together into sentences with indifference to the way a thing got said. When he came to write, Dreiser had to pour his entire energy into the material he wished to present and depend upon matter rather than manner for his meanings. Irony and other devices of literary economy were denied him; in their place—in the place of the artful rendering of selected details —he used a barrage of details. His work forever threatens to be stodgy, to be repetitious, to be boring, but it seldom is. Dreiser's genius used his awkward technique not just to achieve what Crane or Frederic could accomplish in briefer span, but as a means of discovering something major which no writer had thus far rendered. His *Sister Carrie* stood as a new creation, speaking of a world which had not existed in fiction before he brought it into being, but which was so formidably convincing that no serious view of reality could henceforth ignore it. Dreiser's technique, for all its shortcomings, succeeds. It is not, as a careless reading may have it seem, a long and awkward means of constructing a work which, when finished, is very much akin to what others would construct by more artful and more economical means.

Unlike Crane, Theodore Dreiser, the nervous, inept poor man's son, had no response prepared for the world that was keeping him in his lowly place. Shut out from money, the love of well-dressed women, the admiration of witty companions, he yearned for these; he did not despise them or see through them to more important values. When his childish fantasies turned to love, they did so in terms of the popular romance. When he dreamed of a girl who had attracted him, he thought of "being able to sit by her in some dreamland of beauty, of walking with her by lovely waters or under the pointed stars, and listening to the night winds and the murmurings of waters and dreaming and dreaming of all beautiful things." [2] These are the vague and hopeless aspirations of Crane's Maggie, who dreams of a love which will transport her to the place where the little hills sing together. Crane, characteristically, contrasts such misty notions with the harsh realities of Maggie's life in order to make an ironic comment on the human condition. But Dreiser was a partaker of Maggie's dream himself. Though he eventually saw its hopelessness, he never lost his sensitivity to its attractive power, and his deluded characters become objects of compassion rather than irony. When he recalled the popular songs, the newspaper poetry, the theatrical fare of the nineties, Dreiser remarked, "The saccharine strength of the sentiment and mush which we could gulp down at that time, and still can and do to this day, is to me beyond belief." But while it was beyond belief, it was not beyond experience, for, he added, "And I was one of those who did the gulping; indeed I was one of the worst." [3]

Dreiser did not allow belief to control experience. In 1893 he discovered Herbert Spencer, and, in that eventful year of panic, he devoured the philosopher of the thousands who never read philosophy. *Sister Carrie* was to carry his transcriptions of Spencer in almost every chapter. But Spencer operated for Dreiser as a choric explanation of experience, a worldly-wise replacement for the Roman Catholicism of his childhood. Intrusive as they may have been in his work, the ideas he took from Spencer never violated experience to make mock of the careers of Carrie and Hurstwood, as Norris's naturalistic views seared his characters. Dreiser's characters are creatures of the memory of his emotions rather than of his ideas. Unlike the principal figures in Norris's *McTeague,* who are drawn in accordance with their author's philosophy of life, Dreiser's people move in response to their author's suffering of life, and philosophical explanation chimes in only after the fact.

As Dreiser, in his autobiographical writings, details the events along the road to *Sister Carrie,* one incredibility follows another. That these things happened need not, in the main, be doubted, but that they happened to the man who was to write that novel seems unbelievable. His total submission to the success psychology, his ability to write for the mass-appeal magazines, his expertise at editing and filling a magazine next to which such journals as *Leslie's* were pillars of wisdom, mark the hack journalist of the nineties who had all sense of quality hammered out of him in his pursuit of buyers. The miracle of this hack career, however, was that if the conditions to which he, for the most part, willingly submitted destroyed his sense of quality, that sense was so scant and shoddy anyway that its total destruction was a blessing. Had Dreiser had the background and confidence of his better-off Indiana colleagues, he could have resisted his total immersion in the banal art of his day and perhaps have risen to the production of another *Alice of Old Vincennes*. Powerless to resist that tide, however, he was scoured by it. When he finally found the leisure to write seriously, he had no technique but was forced to go to the shards of experience and from these work something absolutely new.

Of all the remarkable aspects of Dreiser's recounting of his youthful career in the nineties, none is more remarkable than his ability to make statements like this in all sober good faith: "I have always had a weakness for members of our family regardless of their deserts or mine or what I thought they had done to me." [4] That the conditions of the typical family circle result in an affection which goes beyond a strict estimation of merits is one of the most common facts of experience. Yet it is discovered in wonder by Dreiser as a phenomenon that requires explanation. This is typical of him. So shattering were his childhood and youth that his sense of the common assumptions of American life was destroyed. Because he lacked that sense, because he must construct life from fragments rather than from any whole pieces lying ready to his hand, he gives the same ponderous emphasis to what might be regarded as a cliché as he does to observations which run startlingly against the grain of his society.

Sister Carrie is a disturbing and convincing work not just because Dreiser, after Carrie loses her virginity, asks what it is she had lost, but because he asks it with no seeming sense of the immense traditional value assigned it. It is a fact of experience to be approached wonderingly and in detail, just as is the equally remarkable fact that one is prejudiced in favor of the members of one's own family. In the former case society violently disagreed with Dreiser, in the latter it agreed so completely that its assent was a reflex rather than an opinion. But Dreiser does not distinguish between heresy and commonplace because he does not proceed from any confident sense of his place in his society or his society's place in history. His genius provided him with a total blindness to the foundations available for his constructions and a superhuman strength to dig new ones and erect a work on entirely different principles. His inability to achieve literary effects except through the amassing of details worked hand in hand with his ignorance of the common axioms, and his ponderous rediscovery of some, and his innocent though radical replacement of others. A geometer of genius who had never heard of Euclid would have to gather together his own set of assumptions and begin the confinement of space anew; the result would not be the world familiar to Euclid's followers. So Dreiser begins the confinement of life anew. He is a literary radical in the basic sense of the word, for he plants new roots, not as an act of rebellion, for this argues an understanding of the bases of society, but as an act of creation, as if the society which he portrays had never been portrayed before. And indeed, as *Sister Carrie* demonstrates, it had not.

Throughout *Carrie* the commonplace accompanies the heretical as fresh discovery. A sane, calm, almost naïve wonder sees that Carrie has a reasonable choice to make between continuing her career as a commodity on the unskilled labor market in Chicago and tramping the wind-swept streets, a virgin with cheap boots through which the snow penetrates, or submitting to Drouet's desires and becoming a commodity of somewhat higher price, whose virginity is lost but whose clothes are weatherproof. Dreiser does not urge her to make the choice she does, but with atonal fidelity to her experience he goes on to detail the material comforts and the unfulfilled spiritual longings that follow. In the same detailed manner in which he goes against convention, Dreiser establishes the conditions for his remark that "two persons cannot long dwell

together without coming to an understanding of one another." [5]
He does not see the obviousness of this, and the reader, immersed
in his radical world, soon comes to learn that it is no more obvious
than is the fact that Carrie does not descend to degradation as the
result of her promiscuity.

All assumptions about life *circa* 1900 are abandoned as one
progresses through *Sister Carrie,* and one is not to think even that
the normal trivia of life have taken place outside the rendered
scenes unless Dreiser says that they have. The reason, indeed, that
Dreiser concerns himself in detail with, for instance, Hurstwood's
dealings with tradesmen as he does the couple's marketing is that
unless he does so that marketing has not taken place. The life
Dreiser sees at every step is so different from the life the reader
has commonly had reported to him that Dreiser dare not risk entering into any convention with him. He must, therefore, deny that
things happen unless he says they do, and as a result he presents
the extraordinary and the banal with equal weight, and the latter,
through the context, begins to take on the aura of wonder that
clings about the former. So when, during her first day on the
chorus line, Carrie responds to another girl, who remarks that it is
warm weather, by saying, "Yes; it is," and Dreiser adds that she
says this, "pleased that some one should talk to her," [6] the reader
knows that this means not just that Carrie is happy to have someone on the new job talk to her, but that no one has said anything
to her since the last time she was addressed in the novel.

The whole that results from Dreiser's remarkably detailed manner is a world in which nothing stands between the individual and
the whirl of life. Dreiser looks and looks, wrings his hands, and
looks again, but for all his details does not see families, friendships,
or other forms of community which act as protective screens between the individual and the onslaught of his environment. To look
at matters conventionally and to say that such protections exist is,
for Dreiser, to look at a wilderness and say it is a botanical garden.
Dreiser's predecessors, in the manner of Howells, did just that,
and, projecting their moral boundaries onto the life they observed,

allowed imagined paths and borders to order the wilderness into an artificial garden. But Dreiser, ignorant of these fine lines and experienced in life at the bottom, gazes and gazes, compiles and compiles, yet, for all his detail, denies that the jungle is a garden. And because of the details and the equal weight of heresy and commonplace, he destroys for all the serious writers who were to follow *Sister Carrie* the possibility of ever again assuming the Howellsian garden, ever again labeling their characters and grouping them into communities, except insofar as they make these a part of their creation rather than accepting them as self-evident assumptions.

Dreiser does not like what he sees in *Sister Carrie*. Yet his descriptions of social injustice, such as the trolley strike in which Hurstwood participates as strike-breaker, or of human indignity, such as Carrie's experiences in pursuit of a job or Hurstwood's skid to suicide, have neither the ring of protest nor the detachment of bitter resignation. Rather, his habit of heaping details becomes like the speech of a deeply moved observer, expressing his compassion for what he is witnessing through the very stammer in which he details it. For all the massiveness of his construction, Dreiser also conveys a sense of inarticulateness which is complementary rather than destructive, because it grows as a genuine response to the enormity of the life portrayed rather than as an inability to portray it. Dreiser compiles, compiles, compiles and, at the end cries out awkwardly against what is happening, but in validation of what he has seen to be.

Howells and Garland had admired the note of social protest in *Maggie,* and had encouraged Crane to join breadlines and sleep in flophouses so as to be able to write about the lives of the poor in a way which would impress the society that was ignoring them. Crane did a few such sketches as a result. But Dreiser's portrayal of the same conditions had nothing of specific social protest about it, while he went on to show that the immense social upheaval which resulted in lives like Hurstwood's was inseparable from a code of morality which had very little to do with what was held publicly by society. The result was that Howells, for all the breadth of his hospitality, avoided him. The grand old man was willing to have the horrors of poverty exposed, but he found unspeakable the suggestion that the social shift, which had resulted in an immense labor pool, had also resulted in the destruction of a sense of community for thousands upon thousands of Americans and in the consequent development of patterns of behavior which neither followed the old agrarian Christian code nor were visited with the dire punishments that the code insisted would follow in this life. T. DeWitt Talmage, railing against the sins of the boarding house, was, with all his prurient suggestiveness, closer to the world Dreiser created than was the gentle and admirable Howells.

Sister Carrie left Dreiser isolated and scorned, unable to get on with the writing of his next novel for several years and unable to find a publisher for it until 1911. If *Sister Carrie* had been a screaming protest, if it had overthrown everything that society accepted, it might have had a *succès de scandale*. But it went deeper than that, and, in its reconstruction of society anew from the bottom up, the mark of its honesty was as much its elaboration of commonplaces into newly discovered truths as its rejection of other fundamental tenets, specifically those concerned with marriage and success. This made its acceptance of sex as a marketable commodity repugnant. Constance Cary Harrison had accepted the same thing in the "Ladies' Home Journal Library," save that she had done so by keeping it within the institutions of society. Like the serious poetry of the day, *Sister Carrie* also demonstrated that the gods were dead, but, unlike the poets' contentions, Dreiser's were unacceptable because he went on to show that life continued all the same, without the gods and without a corresponding sense of human community. It was much more pleasurable to accept their death and then titillate oneself with a twilight sense of ennui and perversity than it was to accept the fact that this was mere hypostatization and that babies kept getting born and men kept looking for a way to earn more money.

The panic year of 1893, the year of the great Columbian Exposition, was a central year in forming the Dreiser who wrote *Sister Carrie*. A gangling reporter turned twenty-two, he saw the fair on assignment for his Saint Louis newspaper and admired it with all the awe of the bumpkins who stood around him. It was, he felt, "as though some brooding spirit of beauty, inherent possibly in some directing over soul, had waved a magic wand," and in this landscape of false dream brought temporarily to reality as an inaccurate representation of the society which produced it but an accurate projection of that society's fantasies, the young Dreiser fell in love with the woman he was to marry. Like the fair, though, the marriage was to fade in the realities of the following years.

But the dream held him, and in the next year, after drifting from job to job, he found himself on the Pittsburgh *Despatch,* where the realities of power impinged upon his romance. There his editor told him how a newspaper was run in a town that was just about owned by the big steel men,[7] and there he discovered Herbert Spencer, who replaced his crumbling Roman Catholicism and helped him resist the cynicism to which he was invited by the conditions of his work in a city thronged with immigrants imported by the carload to keep the price of labor low. With his dream evaporating, he read DuMaurier's *Trilby* and was restored again to fantasy; indeed, the romance set him mooning so strongly after his fiancée that he took a leave of absence to visit her. The ugliness of Pittsburgh had threatened his memories of the Columbian Exposition and of the beauty and romance his fiancée represented, but he now hastened away to the rural Missouri hamlet in which she and her family lived and in which she had been raised in response to the romantic ideal within him which Pittsburgh was destroying. But Pittsburgh had done its work, as his report of his visit indicated:

> I had seen Lithuanian and Hungarians in their "courts" and hovels.
> I had seen the girls of that city [Pittsburgh] walking the streets at
> night. This profound faith in God, in goodness, in virtue and duty
> that I saw here in no wise squared with the craft, the cruelty, the

brutality and the envy that I saw everywhere else. The parents were
gracious and God-fearing, but to me they seemed asleep. They did
not know life—could not. These boys and girls, as I soon found,
respected love and marriage and duty and other things which the
idealistic American still clings to.

Outside was all the other life that I had seen of which apparently
these people knew nothing. They were as if suspended in dreams,
lotus eaters, and my beloved was lost in the same romance.[8]

For Theodore Dreiser the return to the idyllic American farm
of modest prosperity, Christian decency, homely beauty, and heart-
felt ideals was not, after all, a return to what was worth while after
a sojourn in hell. It was, rather, an unreal journey among the lotus-
eaters who inhabited a world that could exist only so long as they
continued to drug themselves. For Howells and his generation, the
terrible realities of the city were always measured, somehow, against
the rural ideality of their youth and in those terms found wanting.
Their nostalgia colored their view of the city and restricted their
ability to realize it in their fiction. But Dreiser, after 1894, recognized that the nostalgia for the farm was a dead sentiment and
shook it off with a nearly brutal contempt. What he felt in Missouri
during his visit he remembered when he came to write *Sister Carrie*.
The story opens with the train which is carrying Carrie from rural
Wisconsin to Chicago, and the city, as a force, enters by the third
paragraph. As soon as Carrie arrives in Chicago she begins behaving in response to its rhythm rather than pursuing her country
habits in a different setting. America is changing, say the older
novelists of the nineties, and she must learn to attach her rural
ideals to the new conditions. Changing? America has changed, says
Dreiser, so much so that talk of the old ideals is beside the point.
The city does not mean the old people in a new combination; it
breeds new people. This is the central difference between *Sister
Carrie* and *A Hazard of New Fortunes*. To speak of the new city
in order to reform along the lines of the past, as did Paul Leicester
Ford in his popular *The Honorable Peter Stirling* (1898), was
acceptable and admirable, but to speak of it as a new world, with

its own moral code derived from the commercial emphases of the society which built it, rather than from the patterns followed in the countryside, as did Dreiser, was immoral.

Jane Addams had observed that social and moral conditions in the nineties were shifting so rapidly that those who possessed abstract theories had to abandon them in order to come to grips with experience, while only those who had experience of the city could offer tenable generalizations. She saw herself in the former category, and that is why she went to work at Hull-House. In the latter category was Dreiser, who seemingly had nothing to recommend him for a literary calling other than experience. Although he came to adopt Spencer's principles, whatever tenability one is willing to grant them as they appear in his pages results from the experienced suffering of Carrie and Hurstwood—from the painful details of their lives—rather than from an intellectual acceptance of Dreiser's explicit paraphrases. The disappearance of these paraphrases would not measurably affect the reader's attitude toward the characters.

Experience in place of theory also brought to Jane Addams the central revelation that Dreiser had had in Missouri in 1894, and which he was to make the very air of Carrie's world. "I have heard a drunken man in a maudlin stage, babble of his good country mother and imagine he was driving the cows home," she said, "and I knew that his little son who laughed loud at him, would be drunk earlier in life and would have no such pastoral interlude to his ravings." [9]

The pastoral interlude was, indeed, over, but not in words. *Sister Carrie* lay unread after publication, and Frank Norris, who had accepted it on behalf of Doubleday; who had told another publisher over lunch at the Waldorf Astoria, "Mark my words, the name of Frank Norris isn't going to stand in American literature anything like as high as Dreiser," [10] and who attempted to promote Dreiser through his weekly column of book news in the Chicago *American,* was powerless to affect critical opinion. In 1902 he was dead, and Dreiser was in a numb and depressed silence. Unwilling to go on with his serious fiction and no longer able to exercise his aptitude for hack work, he was attracted to the quietus offered by the night waters of the East River.

Two years later Dreiser had returned to hack work and pulp editing, fighting his way back to a confidence which would enable him to get on with *Jennie Gerhardt*. In the same year, 1904, the National Institute of Arts and Letters decided to elect an American Academy of Arts and Letters from its membership.[11] This Institute had been organized in 1898 by the American Social Science Association, but had soon separated from it. By 1900 its membership list extended to some 250 persons, and while it had an important function as the collective voice of the working artist in America, its membership felt that this political purpose required too broad a basis for entrance to make it also a distinguished body. Accordingly it was decided that the members of the Institute should choose an Academy of thirty from among themselves as a testimonial to those persons' high distinction in the arts. The first seven members of the Academy were selected in December 1904 by secret ballot of all members of the Institute; these seven went on to choose eight more; these fifteen chose five more; and these twenty then selected the remaining ten members of the American Academy of Arts and Letters.

The writers among the first seven were, in the order of number of votes received: William Dean Howells, Edmund Clarence Stedman, Mark Twain, and John Hay. Howells and Twain represented national letters at their best, Stedman was a poet, editor, and anthologist who ruled his genre like a benevolent pope and was one of the few accepted poets to encourage Robinson, and Hay was the ex-secretary of Abraham Lincoln, who was also a historian, poet, novelist, diplomat, and a central maker of foreign policy in the McKinley and Roosevelt administrations. These men elected, in the next eight: Henry James; Henry Adams; Charles Eliot Norton, a Harvard professor; Thomas R. Lounsbury, a Yale professor; Theodore Roosevelt; and Thomas Bailey Aldrich, venerator of the

New England authors of the fifties, writer of popular romances, and dinner-table wit.[12] The remainder of the list of thirty was made up of names less distinguished, in both that and this day, with the exception of William James, who declined to join, perhaps under the mistaken belief that it would involve him in further institutional work. Howells was president from the inception of the Academy, which was soon widened to fifty members, until his death in 1920.

The remarkable fact about the American Academy of Arts and Letters is that so few of its literary members were any more qualified for membership in 1904 than they would have been in 1890. Howells and Twain had by that time done their best work, and the quantity and quality of James's work was impressive by then, though great work still lay ahead of him. Henry Adams's massive history of the Jefferson and Madison administrations was then appearing, and he had previously published a number of serious essays, to which he made no considerable additions in the nineties. Hay's poetry had appeared in the seventies, his novel in the eighties, and his history in 1890; and Aldrich's best-known work, *The Story of a Bad Boy,* had been published in 1870. Had the election been held in 1890, then, these same men would have entered the Academy.

The election, however, took place at the close of 1904, and although, understandably, age adds the dignity without which it is difficult to convert a man into a monument, still it is remarkable that, several years into the twentieth century, American men of letters thought of themselves principally as conveyors of the Indian-summer afterglow of the great mid-century days. Nothing of the turbulence of the nineteenth century's closing, nothing of the shift to the city, of the extension of the limits of sexuality in literature, of the changing social position of women, of a poetry of precision and felt experience, of the fall from the innocence of national isolation, comes forth as we read their names, save insofar as we think of the political roles of Hay and Roosevelt and the pessimism—as eighteenth-century as it was twentieth—of Henry Adams. Reading the Academy list of 1904, we are still in the

Boston offices of the *Atlantic,* and mass circulation is a ridiculous notion. We hear the tinkle of ice in the water pitcher, and the saloon is but an obscene rumor; we listen as committees call on distinguished men, asking them to stand for office, and political bosses are an unreported species; the Civil War has been won, the West is being settled, and unity has descended upon the nation.

Even if younger people had been chosen, however, who, indeed, would there have been to elect from the nineties? Its great books were *The Red Badge of Courage,* but Crane was dead; *The Damnation of Theron Ware* but Frederic was dead; *The Awakening,* but Kate Chopin was in bad taste and, though few noticed, she too was dead at the year's end; *The Country of the Pointed Firs,* but Sarah Orne Jewett was a feeble, infirm woman whose work looked slight; the novels of Frank Norris, but he was dead; and the poems of Edwin Arlington Robinson, but who had read them? None of these writers had been illustrious enough to be invited to the copyright readings in 1887 and few had survived to the point of the Academy elections of 1904, yet they had produced the decade's significant literature. So the grandfathers took their seats in the Academy as they should have done, because, indeed, academies are grandfatherly institutions. These were remarkable grandfathers, however, because, old as they were in age, in a literary sense they were children. They were the last descendants of the great men of the 1850s, and for all their years they still glowed with the evergreen optimism which had withered, almost at birth, from the younger writers who had come of age and been destroyed in the nineties.

In the first decade of the new century American letters experienced a period of dull transition. Even as Theodore Roosevelt preached the strenuous life, national letters were undergoing, in Ambrose Bierce's words, a weak and fluffy time. Robert Herrick rose to continue the Howellsian grind, and Edith Wharton took up the Jamesian task. But most of the exciting writers who should now have been operating in their mature years were dead or ignored. After the forceful eruption of the new writers of the nineties, the calm of a pleasant senility had returned, and 1901 picked up as the next literary year after 1890. But when the flood tide of literature came after 1915, then the new writers turned to Robinson and to Dreiser; then they remembered the works of Crane, Frederic, and Norris; then the early preachments of John Jay Chapman rang true; then the banal Midwest of the early Garland loomed large. They did not take up from where they found themselves, but went back to the nineties, and if they looked on the years from 1901 to 1910 as the last years of the nineteenth century in American letters, they saw that those from 1891 to 1900 were the first ten years of the twentieth.

American literature affords but this one example of a generation —the generation of the nineties—cut off before its time because it had started before its time, and revivified when the slower processes of history had made room for it. The famous lost generation, which owed so much to this truly lost generation of the nineties, was, in point of fact, soon found and avidly accepted. It was found and it did grow because, in great part, the writers of the nineties had borne for it the consequences of the stunting social shock. Though they had not survived the doing, they had begun to habituate America to the fact that internal divisiveness was more than geographical, that a civilization which pursued commerce and technology constructed for itself a morality drawn from commerce and technology, that sexual experience was a fundamental part of the common human condition, not a secret part of established social institutions. When the transforming events of the nineties subsided into the tranquillity of the following ten years, these writers appeared to be part of the temporary disorders which had been thrown off in the now ended spasms of the decade. But these spasms proved in fact to be not the convulsions of rejection but the first strong and sure labor pains of modern American literature.

Notes / Index

Notes

ONE: *Land of Contrasts*

1. Hubert Howe Bancroft, *The Book of the Fair* (Chicago, 1893), p. 41.
2. Montgomery Schuyler, *American Architecture and Other Writings*, ed. by William H. Jordy and Ralph Coe (Cambridge, 1961), vol. I, p. 246.
3. *The Columbian Exposition Album* (Chicago, 1893), p. [98].
4. Karl Baedeker, ed., *The United States with An Excursion into Mexico* (Leipzig, 1893), p. 494.
5. Eugene Field, *Sharps and Flats*, ed. by Slason Thompson (New York, 1900), vol. II, p. 200.
6. Charles H. Dennis, *Eugene Field's Creative Years* (Garden City, N.Y., 1924), p. 215.
7. Baedeker, op. cit., p. xxviii.
8. Ibid.
9. James F. Muirhead, *The Land of Contrasts* (London, 1898), p. 86.
10. Ibid., p. 20.
11. Ibid., p. 156.
12. Ibid., p. 20.
13. Ibid., p. 90.
14. Ibid., p. 201.
15. Ibid., p. 19.
16. Barrett Wendell, *A Literary History of America* (New York, 1900), p. 229.
17. Walt Whitman, *The Complete Poetry and Prose* (New York, 1948), vol. I, p. 41.
18. Walt Whitman, *Leaves of Grass and Selected Prose* (New York, 1950), p. 444.
19. Whitman, *Complete Poetry*, vol. II, p. 210.
20. Ibid., vol. I, p. 472.
21. Arnold T. Schwab, *James Gibbons Huneker* (Stanford, Calif., 1963), p. 81.
22. This fancy is in Claude Bragdon, *More Lives Than One* (New York, 1938), p. 6.
23. L. Frank Tooker, *The Joys and Tribulations of an Editor* (New York, 1923), p. 215.
24. Ibid., p. 216.
25. Whitman, *Complete Poetry*, vol. II, p. 302.
26. Ellen Glasgow, *The Woman Within* (New York, 1954), p. 141.
27. Ibid., pp. 139-40.
28. Henry Adams, "Chicago," *The Education of Henry Adams* (Boston, 1918).
29. Bragdon, op. cit., pp. 143-44.
30. S. C. deSoissons, *A Parisian in America* (Boston, 1896) pp. 170-71.
31. Sherman Paul, *Louis Sullivan* (Englewood Cliffs, N.J., 1962), p. 50.
32. The statistics are taken from Arthur Meier Schlesinger, *The Rise of the City 1878-1898* (New York, 1933), pp. 65ff.

33. William Dean Howells, *Life in Letters,* ed. by Mildred Howells (Garden City, N.Y., 1928), vol. II, p. 40.

T W O : *Literary Hospitality*

1. Details about Howells' life are taken from Edwin H. Cady, *The Realist at War: The Mature Years 1885-1920 of William Dean Howells* (Syracuse, 1958); Everett Carter, *Howells and the Age of Realism* (Philadelphia, 1954); and William Dean Howells, *Life in Letters,* ed. by Mildred Howells (Garden City, N.Y., 1928), 2 vols.; as well as from Howells' work of non-fiction.
2. William Dean Howells, *Literary Friends and Acquaintances* (New York, 1901), p. 56.
3. John Jay Chapman, *Emerson and Other Essays* (New York, 1909), p. 43.
4. Ralph Waldo Emerson, "The American Scholar," *Selections,* ed. by Stephen Whicher (Boston, 1957), p. 78.
5. William Dean Howells, *The Rise of Silas Lapham* (Boston, 1884), p. 111.
6. Ibid., p. 110.
7. William Dean Howells, *Criticism and Fiction* (New York, 1891), p. 8.
8. Ibid., p. 128.
9. Ibid.
10. William Dean Howells, *Tuscan Cities* (Boston, 1886), p. 155.
11. Howells, *Letters,* vol. I, p. 404.
12. Ibid., vol. I, p. 419.
13. William Dean Howells, *A Hazard of New Fortunes* (New York, 1891), vol. II, p. 27.
14. William Dean Howells, *An Open-Eyed Conspiracy* (New York, 1897), p. 87.
15. Robert Underwood Johnson, *Remembered Yesterdays* (Boston, 1923), pp. 355-56.
16. Henry James, *The Letters,* ed. by Percy Lubbock (New York, 1920), vol. I, pp. 104-105.
17. An incisive characterization of the differing systems may be found in the Preface Henry James wrote for his *The Awkward Age.*
18. Rudyard Kipling, *American Notes* (New York, 1891), pp. 29-30.
19. Howells, *Criticism and Fiction,* p. 149.
20. Ibid., p. 156.
21. Ibid., p. 95.
22. Ward Hutchinson, "The Economics of Prostitution," *American Medical-Surgical Bulletin* (August 15, 1895), vol. III, No. 16, p. 978.
23. Ibid., p. 983.
24. See, for example, Emma Goldman, *Living My Life* (New York, 1931).
25. William Dean Howells, *My Literary Passions* (New York, 1895), p. 43.
26. Howells, *Letters,* vol. II, p. 43.
27. William Allen White, "A Reader in the Eighties and Nineties," *The Bookman* (November 1930), vol. LXXII, No. 3, p. 232.
28. Howells, *Letters,* vol. II, p. 25.

29. Ibid., vol. II, p. 95.
30. Ibid., vol. II, p. 113.
31. William Dean Howells, *Prefaces to Contemporaries (1882-1920)*, ed. by George Arms, William M. Gibson, Frederic C. Marston, Jr. (Gainesville, Fla., 1957), p. 3.
32. Howells, *Letters,* vol. II, p. 42.
33. Ibid., vol. II, p. 100.
34. William Dean Howells, *Heroines of Fiction* (New York, 1901), vol. II, p. 264.
35. Ibid., vol. II, p. 261.

THREE : *Literary Absenteeism*

1. William Dean Howells, *Life and Letters,* ed. by Mildred Howells (Garden City, N.Y., 1928), vol. I, p. 417.
2. Henry James, *Partial Portraits* (London, 1888), p. 10.
3. Henry James, *The Bostonians* (New York, 1886), p. 449.
4. Henry James, *The Reverberator* (New York, 1908), p. 159.
5. Ibid., p. 68.
6. Ibid., p. 205.
7. Henry James, *The Letters,* ed. by Percy Lubbock (New York, 1920), vol. I, p. 141.
8. Henry James, *Picture and Text* (New York, 1893), p. 5.
9. James, *Letters,* vol. I, p. 350.
10. Henry James, *The Aspern Papers, Louisa Pallant, The Modern Warning* (London, 1888), pp. 209-10.
11. James, *Letters,* vol. I, p. 135.
12. Ralph Barton Perry, *The Thought and Character of William James* (Boston, 1936), vol. I, p. 415.
13. Ibid., vol. I, p. 452.
14. Ibid., vol. II, p. 208.
15. Henry James, *The Tragic Muse* (London, 1890), vol. I, pp. 98-99.
16. Ibid., vol. I, pp. 66-67.
17. Details of James's life are taken from his letters, from F. W. Dupee, *Henry James* (Garden City, N.Y., 1956), and from Leon Edel, *Henry James* (Phildelphia, 1953-62), 3 vols.
18. Henry James, *Embarrassments* (London, 1896), pp. 194-95.
19. Dupee, op. cit., p. 161.
20. Ibid., p. 162.
21. Henry C. Vedder, *American Writers of To-Day* (Boston, 1894), p. 75.
22. Ibid., p. 54.
23. Ibid., pp. 82-83.
24. Howells, *Letters,* vol. II, p. 52.
25. William Dean Howells, *Literature and Life* (New York, 1902), p. 202.
26. Ibid., p. 205.
27. Albert Bigelow Paine, ed., *Mark Twain's Letters* (New York, 1917), vol. II, pp. 401-402.
28. Walter Blair, *Native American Humor* (New York, 1937), p. 162.
29. Ernest Hemingway, *Green Hills of Africa* (New York, 1935), p. 22.

30. Paine, op. cit., vol. II, p. 558.
31. Ibid., vol. II, p. 690.
32. Ibid., vol. II, p. 656.

F O U R : *The Midwestern Imagination*

1. Hamlin Garland, *Ulysses S. Grant, His Life and Character* (New York, 1920), p. 182.
2. Ibid.
3. The principal sources for this characterization of Midwestern life are: Mary Austin, *Earth Horizon* (Boston, 1932); Theodore Dreiser, *Dawn* (New York, 1931); Clarence Darrow, *The Story of My Life* (New York, 1932); Fred C. Kelly, *George Ade* (Indianapolis, 1947); Norman Hapgood, *The Changing Years* (New York, 1930); Brand Whitlock, *Forty Years of It* (New York, 1925); and the autobiographical writings of Hamlin Garland.
4. Austin, op. cit., pp. 99-100.
5. Kelly, op. cit., p. 25.
6. The facts are taken from John D. Hicks, *The Populist Revolt* (Lincoln, Neb., 1961).
7. Louis Filler, ed., *Late Nineteenth-Century American Liberalism, Representative Selections, 1880-1900* (Indianapolis, 1962), pp. 52-53.
8. Richard Hofstadter, *Social Darwinism in American Thought* (New York, 1959), pp. 31-32.
9. John Dewey advances this interpretation in *The Influence of Darwin on Philosophy* (New York, 1910).
10. Hicks, op. cit., p. 435.
11. Ibid., pp. 436-37.
12. Ibid.
13. Ibid., p. 439.
14. Filler, op. cit., p. 60.
15. Ibid., p. 59.
16. Hicks, op. cit., p. 436.
17. Ignatius Donnelly, *Caesar's Column* (Cambridge, Mass., 1960), p. 60.
18. Ibid., pp. 80-81.
19. Ibid., p. 74.
20. Charles M. Sheldon, *In His Steps* (Chicago, 1937), p. 33.
21. Ibid., p. 155.
22. Ibid., p. 37.
23. Statements about the popularity of books in the nineties are based on the findings of Alice Payne Hackett, *Fifty Years of Best Sellers* (New York, 1945).
24. Hamlin Garland, *Roadside Meetings* (New York, 1930), p. 283.
25. Maurice Thompson, *The Ethics of Literary Art* (Hartford, Conn., 1893), pp. 18-19.
26. Ibid., p. 30.
27. Ibid., p. 80.
28. Ibid., p. 26.

29. Maurice Thompson, *Alice of Old Vincennes* (Indianapolis, 1900), p. 183.
30. Booth Tarkington, *The Gentleman from Indiana* (New York, 1921), p. 342.
31. Ibid., p. 140.
32. Ibid., p. 182.
33. Ibid., p. 411.

FIVE : *Crushed Yet Complacent*

1. The two studies of Garland most frequently consulted were Donald Pizer, *Hamlin Garland's Early Work and Career* (Berkeley, Calif., 1960), and Jean Holloway, *Hamlin Garland, a Biography* (Austin, Texas, 1960). Garland himself speaks at length about his career in a number of works, the most pertinent of which to this discussion are *A Son of the Middle Border* (1917), *A Daughter of the Middle Border* (1921), and *Roadside Meetings* (1930).
2. Hamlin Garland, *Main-Travelled Roads* (New York, 1893), "Preface."
3. William Dean Howells, *Prefaces to Contemporaries 1882-1920*, ed. by George Arms, William C. Gibson, Frederic C. Marston, Jr. (Gainesville, Fla., 1957), p. 38.
4. Garland, *Main-Travelled Roads*, p. 194.
5. Garland, *A Son*, p. 265.
6. Garland, *Main-Travelled Roads*, p. 376.
7. Ibid., p. 259.
8. Ibid., p. 62.
9. Ibid., p. 207.
10. This trope is very prominent in *Wayside Courtships* (New York, 1897).
11. Hamlin Garland, *The Rose of Dutcher's Coolly* (New York, 1899), pp. 70-71.
12. Hamlin Garland, *Roadside Meetings*, p. 136.
13. Holloway, op. cit., p. 50.
14. Ibid., p. 51.
15. Hamlin Garland, *Crumbling Idols* (Chicago, 1894), p. 43.
16. Ibid., p. 154.
17. Ibid., pp. 176-77.
18. Ibid., p. 78.
19. Rossiter Johnson, ed., *A History of the World's Columbian Exposition* (New York, 1898), p. 1.
20. Eugene Field, *Sharps and Flats*, ed. by Slason Thompson (New York, 1900), vol. I, p. 48.
21. Ibid., vol. I, pp. 50-51.
22. Charles H. Dennis, *Eugene Field's Creative Years* (Garden City, N.Y., 1924), p. 130.
23. Ibid., p. 131.
24. Ibid., p. 132.
25. Garland, *A Daughter*, pp. 86-89.
26. Ibid., p. 86.
27. Ibid., p. 88.

28. Henry B. Fuller, *Under the Skylights* (New York, 1901), p. 7.
29. Ibid., p. 23.
30. Ibid., p. 59.
31. Ibid., p. 139.
32. Biographical details are taken from Constance M. Griffin, *Henry Blake Fuller* (Philadelphia, 1939).
33. Henry B. Fuller, *The Cliff-Dwellers* (New York, 1893), p. 105.
34. Griffin, op. cit., pp. 40-41.
35. Fuller, *Cliff-Dwellers,* p. 50.
36. Ibid., p. 107.
37. In an interview in the November 21, 1911, edition of the New York *Sun,* p. 5.
38. Henry B. Fuller, *With the Procession* (New York, 1895), p. 24.
39. Ibid., p. 141.
40. Ibid., p. 248.
41. Ibid.
42. Ibid., p. 87.
43. Henry B. Fuller, *The Last Refuge* (Boston, 1900), pp. 98-99.
44. Ibid., p. 99.
45. Henry B. Fuller, "Art in America," *The Bookman* (November 1899), p. 222.
46. Ibid., p. 220.
47. Ibid., p. 224.
48. Unpublished letter of September 22, 1898, in the "Hamlin Garland Collection" of the University of Southern California.
49. H. H. Boyesen, "Review of *The Cliff-Dwellers,*" *Cosmopolitan* (January 1893), p. 373.
50. Garland, *Roadside Meetings,* p. 463.
51. Jane Addams, *Twenty Years at Hull-House* (New York, 1910), p. 5.
52. Ibid., pp. 70-71.
53. Ibid., p. 133.
54. Ibid., p. 177.
55. Ibid., p. 193.

SIX: *The Tinkle of the Little Bell*

1. Hamlin Garland, *A Daughter of the Middle Border* (New York, 1921), pp. 35-36.
2. Frederick Lewis Allen, *Paul Revere Reynolds* (New York, 1944), p. 36.
3. Isaac F. Marcosson, *Adventures in Interviewing* (New York, 1923), pp. 60-61.
4. S. S. McClure, *My Autobiography* (New York, 1914), pp. 207-208.
5. Garland, *Roadside Meetings,* p. 342.
6. Ibid., pp. 341-42.
7. J. Henry Harper, *The House of Harper* (New York, 1912), p. 530.
8. Roger Burlingame, *Of Making Many Books* (New York, 1946), p. 83.
9. Harper, op. cit., p. 620.
10. Richard Watson Gilder, *Letters,* ed. by Rosamond Gilder (Boston, 1916), p. 399.

11. William Dean Howells, "The Man of Literature as a Man of Business," in Howells, *Literature and Life* (New York, 1902).
12. William Dean Howells, "American Literary Centers," ibid.
13. Harper, op. cit., p. 321.
14. Ibid., p. 273.
15. Peter Lyon, *Success Story, The Life and Times of S. S. McClure* (New York, 1963), p. 151.
16. Gilder, op. cit., p. 17.
17. Ibid., p. 66.
18. Ibid., p. 411.
19. James L. Ford, *The Literary Shop* (New York, 1899), pp. 24-25.
20. Ibid., p. 67.
21. Ibid., p. 173.
22. Ibid., pp. 158-59.
23. John Jay Chapman, *Practical Agitation* (New York, 1900), p. 93.
24. For example, Hesketh Pearson, *The Life of Oscar Wilde* (London, 1954).
25. *The Chap-Book,* July 15, 1898.
26. A model book on the history of a publishing house is Sidney Kramer, *A History of Stone & Kimball* (Chicago, 1940).
27. Edith Franklin Wyatt, "The Wolf in Sheep's Clothing," *New Stories from The Chap-Book* (Chicago, 1898).
28. William James, *The Varieties of Religious Experience* (New York, 1902), p. 14.
29. Gelett Burgess, *Bayside Bohemia* (San Francisco, 1954) is a useful source of information as is also Joseph M. Backus, "Gelett Burgess: A Biography," unpublished dissertation (University of California, Berkeley, 1961).
30. Burgess, op. cit., p. 37.
31. Gelett Burgess, *Epilark* (May 1897).
32. "Anne Southampton Bliss" [Gelett Burgess], "Our Clubbing List," *Le Petit Journal des Refusées,* Summer 1896.
33. James Gibbons Huneker, *Steeplejack* (New York, 1920), vol. II, p. 122.
34. Arnold T. Schwab, *James Gibbons Huneker* (Stanford, Calif., 1963), p. 82.
35. Huneker, op. cit., vol. II, p. 190.
36. "Foreword," *M'lle New York,* August 1895.
37. Ibid.
38. Ibid., December 1898.

SEVEN: *The School in the Cemetery*

1. For many of the details of the shift from personal journalism, I am indebted to an unpublished study by Wayne Luckmann.
2. H. L. Mencken, *Newspaper Days, 1899-1906* (New York, 1945), p. x.
3. Quoted in *The Dial,* August 16, 1893, p. 80.
4. Charles A. Dana, *The Art of Newspaper Making* (New York, 1895), p. 12.
5. Frank Luther Mott, *American Journalism* (New York, 1950), p. 376.

6. Henrietta Stackpole in *The Portrait of a Lady*.
7. Isaac F. Marcosson, *David Graham Phillips and His Times* (New York, 1932), p. 219.
8. From stanza eight.
9. Marcosson, op. cit., p. 208.
10. Lincoln Steffens, *Autobiography* (New York, 1931), pp. 206-207.
11. Brand Whitlock, *Forty Years of It* (New York, 1925), p. 96.
12. Theodore Dreiser, *A Book about Myself* (London, 1929), p. 406.
13. Steffens, op. cit., p. 223.
14. Jacob A. Riis, *How the Other Half Lives* (New York, 1890), p. 112.
15. Walter A. Wyckoff, *The Workers . . . The East* (New York, 1897), pp. 67-68.
16. Walter A. Wyckoff, *The Workers . . . The West* (New York, 1898), pp. 77-78.
17. His reports are gathered in Hutchins Hapgood, *The Spirit of the Ghetto* (New York, 1902).
18. Steffens, op. cit., p. 314.
19. George Ade, *Single Blessedness and Other Observations* (Garden City, N.Y., 1922), p. 56.
20. George Ade, *Doc' Horne* (New York, 1906), p. 179.
21. George Ade, *Pink Marsh* (Chicago, 1897), p. 120.
22. Ade, *Doc' Horne*, p. 268.
23. George Ade, *Stories of the Streets and of the Town From the Chicago Record 1893-1900*, ed. by Franklin J. Meine (Chicago, 1941), p. 152.
24. Ibid.
25. Elmer Ellis, *Mr. Dooley's America, A Life of Finley Peter Dunne* (New York, 1941), p. 46.
26. Ibid., p. 95.
27. Finley Peter Dunne, *Mr. Dooley's Philosophy* (New York, 1900), p. 19.
28. Ibid., p. 217.
29. Ibid., p. 260.
30. Ellis, op. cit., p. 117.
31. William T. Stead, *If Christ Came to Chicago!* (Chicago, 1894), p. 121.
32. Ibid., p. 255.
33. Melville E. Stone, *Fifty Years a Journalist* (Garden City, N.Y., 1929), p. 202.
34. Will Payne, *Jerry the Dreamer* (New York, 1896), p. 172.
35. Will Payne, *The Money Captain* (Chicago, 1898), pp. 112-13.
36. Bernard Duffey, *The Chicago Renaissance in American Letters* (East Lansing, Mich., 1954), pp. 104-105.
37. Romances appealed to some newsmen as get-rich-quick schemes, and another Chicago reporter of the nineties, George Barr McCutcheon, realized the scheme in *Graustark* (1900).
38. Norman Hapgood, *The Changing Years* (New York, 1930), p. 122.

EIGHT : *The Poles of Violence*

1. Ambrose Bierce, *The Letters*, ed. by Bertha Clark Pope (San Francisco, 1922), p. 75.

2. Arthur McEwen's phrase in Paul Fatout, *Ambrose Bierce, The Devil's Lexicographer* (Norman, Okla., 1951), p. 210.
3. Bierce, op. cit., p. 9.
4. Ambrose Bierce, *Collected Writings* (New York, 1946), p. 192.
5. Ibid., p. 314.
6. Ibid., p. 348.
7. Ibid., pp. 151-52.
8. Ibid., p. 152.
9. Ambrose Bierce, *The Collected Works* (New York, 1911), vol. X, p. 351.
10. Bierce, *Writings*, p. 268.
11. Bierce, *Works*, vol. X, p. 339.
12. Ibid., pp. 132-33.
13. Letter of June 27, 1913, to Blanche Partington in "The Blanche Partington Collection" of the Bancroft Library, University of California, Berkeley.
14. Richard Harding Davis, *Adventures and Letters*, ed. by Charles Belmont Davis (New York, 1917), p. 18.
15. M. A. DeWolfe Howe, *A Venture in Remembrance* (Boston, 1941), pp. 65-66.
16. Davis, op. cit., pp. 25-26.
17. Ibid., p. 32.
18. Ibid., p. 29.
19. Ibid., pp. 39-40.
20. Ibid., p. 56.
21. Ibid., pp. 58-59.
22. Ibid., p. 119.
23. Ibid., p. 230.
24. Richard Harding Davis, *Three Gringos in Venezuela and Central America* (New York, 1896).
25. Ibid., p. 147.
26. Richard Harding Davis, *From "Gallegher" to "The Deserter,"* ed. by Roger Burlingame (New York, 1927), p. 173.
27. Richard Harding Davis, *Cinderella and Other Stories* (New York, 1896), pp. 120-21.
28. Bierce, *Works*, vol. IX, p. 141.

NINE : *Outstripping the Event*

1. Unless otherwise noted, details of Crane's life are taken from Edwin H. Cady, *Stephen Crane* (New York, 1962). Thomas Beer's *Stephen Crane* (New York, 1923) was a consistent source of pleasures and suggestions, but not of facts.
2. Hamlin Garland, *Roadside Meetings* (New York, 1930), p. 193.
3. Ibid., p. 194.
4. Ibid., p. 197.
5. Ibid., p. 199.
6. Robert H. Davis, "Introduction," *The Work of Stephen Crane* (New York, 1925), vol. II, p. xv.
7. Ibid., pp. xv-xvi.

8. Cady, op. cit., p. 108.
9. Hesketh Pearson, *The Life of Oscar Wilde* (London, 1954), p. 133.
10. Stephen Crane, *The Red Badge of Courage and Other Writings,* ed. by Richard Chase (Boston, 1960), p. 12.
11. Ibid., p. 18.
12. Amy Lowell, "Introduction," *The Work,* vol. VI, p. ix.
13. A most useful study is: Daniel G. Hoffman, *The Poetry of Stephen Crane* (New York, 1957).
14. Crane, *The Work,* vol. VI, p. 59.
15. Crane, *Red Badge and Other Writings,* p. 12.
16. John Berryman, *Stephen Crane* (New York, 1950).
17. For suggestions on Crane's style I am indebted to an unpublished essay by Lee E. Siegel, "Impressionism and Irony in *The Red Badge of Courage.*"
18. Crane, *Red Badge and Other Writings,* p. 147.
19. Ibid., p. 219.
20. Ibid., pp. 230-31.
21. Cady, op. cit., p. 64.
22. Stephen Crane, *Letters,* ed. by Robert Stallman and Lillian Gilkes (New York, 1960), p. 209.
23. Crane, *The Work,* vol. IX, p. 238.
24. Ibid., p. 258.

TEN : *Overcivilization*

1. Details of Frederic's life are taken from Thomas F. O'Donnell and Hoyt C. Franchere, *Harold Frederic* (New York, 1961).
2. Grant Richards, *Memories of a Misspent Youth* (London, 1932), pp. 240-41.
3. Lillian Gilkes, *Cora Crane* (Bloomington, Ind., 1960), pp. 161ff.
4. Harold Frederic, *The New Exodus, A Study of Israel in Russia* (New York, 1892), p. 2.
5. Ibid., p. 32.
6. Harold Frederic, *The Lawton Girl* (New York, 1890), pp. 146-47.
7. Harold Frederic, *The Copperhead and Other Stories* (London, 1893), pp. 13-14.
8. Harold Frederic, *Marsena and Other Stories of the Wartime* (New York, 1894), p. 10.
9. Harold Frederic, *The Damnation of Theron Ware* (Chicago, 1896), p. 305.
10. Ibid., p. 26.
11. Ibid., p. 308.
12. Unpublished letter dated May 12, 1897, in "Hamlin Garland Collection" of the Library of the University of Southern California.
13. O'Donnell and Franchere, op. cit., p. 88.
14. Harold Frederic, *In the Valley* (New York, 1890), p. 237.
15. Theodore Roosevelt, *The Strenuous Life* (London, 1902), pp. 18-19.
16. Ibid., pp. 31-32.
17. Ibid., p. 7.

18. James Ford Rhodes, *The McKinley and Roosevelt Administrations, 1897-1909* (New York, 1923), pp. 106-107.
19. Ibid., p. 23.
20. Arthur F. Beringause, *Brooks Adams* (New York, 1955), p. 143.
21. *Letters of Henry Adams,* ed. by W. C. Ford (Boston, 1938), vol. II, p. 35.
22. Ibid., p. 72
23. Ibid., p. 264.
24. Fanny Kemble Wister, ed., *Owen Wister Out West, His Journals and Letters* (Chicago, 1958), p. 97.
25. Ibid., p. 7.
26. Details of Owen Wister's life are taken from Francis K. W. Stokes, *My Father, Owen Wister* (Laramie, Wyo., 1952).
27. Wister, op. cit., pp. 112-13.
28. Owen Wister, *The Virginian* (New York, 1902), p. 33.

E L E V E N : *Being Old-Fashioned*

1. Facts in this paragraph taken from James D. Hart, *The Popular Book* (New York, 1950), pp. 181-82.
2. Mrs. Winthrop Chanler, *Roman Spring* (Boston, 1934), p. 197. This book is drawn upon widely in this chapter not only for details in Mrs. Chanler's life, but also for the descriptions of international society.
3. Ibid., p. 237.
4. Ward McAllister, *Society as I Have Found It* (New York, 1890), pp. 118-19.
5. Ibid., pp. 245-46.
6. Ibid.
7. Ibid., p. 257.
8. *The Daily Tatler* (November 11, 1896), p. 4.
9. Chanler, op. cit., p. 238.
10. Maude Howe Elliott, *My Cousin, F. Marion Crawford* (New York, 1934), p. 242.
11. Chanler, op. cit., p. 195.
12. Ibid., p. 304.
13. Details of Crawford's life are taken from the Elliott book.
14. Elliott, op. cit., p. 92.
15. Details from Elliott and from Chanler, op. cit., pp. 151-52.
16. F. Marion Crawford, *The Novel, What It Is* (New York, 1908), p. 23. First edition, 1893.
17. F. Marion Crawford, *A Rose of Yesterday* (New York, 1906), pp. 216-17. First edition, 1897.
18. F. Marion Crawford, *Greifenstein* (London, 1889), p. 141.
19. Crawford, *A Rose,* p. 34.
20. Crawford, *Greifenstein,* pp. 33-34.
21. Crawford, *A Rose,* p. 202.
22. Ibid., p. 67.
23. Details of Chapman's life are taken from Richard B. Hovey, *John Jay Chapman—An American Mind* (New York, 1959).

24. Ibid., p. 60.
25. Ibid., p. 90.
26. John Jay Chapman, *Causes and Consequences* (New York, 1909), p. 3.
27. M. A. DeWolfe Howe, *John Jay Chapman and His Letters* (New York, 1937), p. 106.
28. John Jay Chapman, *Emerson and Other Essays* (New York, 1909), p. 62.
29. Chapman, *Causes*, p. 92.
30. Howe, op. cit., p. 120.
31. Ibid., p. 93.
32. Chapman, *Emerson*, p. 193.
33. Chapman, *Causes*, p. 40.
34. Ibid., p. 66.
35. Hovey, op. cit., p. 91.
36. Ibid., p. 75.
37. *Letters of Henry Adams*, ed. by W. C. Ford (Boston, 1938), vol. II, p. 275.

TWELVE: *Life without Style*

1. Frank Norris [*Works*] (Garden City, N.Y., 1928), vol. VII, p. 202.
2. Franklin Walker, *Frank Norris* (Garden City, N.Y., 1932), pp. 55-56.
3. Lars Ahnebrink, *The Influence of Emile Zola on Frank Norris*, "Essays and Studies in American Language and Literature" (Upsala, 1947).
4. Norris, op. cit., vol. VII, p. 159.
5. Richard Harding Davis, *Dr. Jameson's Raiders* (New York, 1897).
6. Donald Pizer, "Evolutionary Ethical Dualism in Frank Norris' *Vandover and the Brute* and *McTeague*," *Publications of the Modern Language Association* (December 1961), vol. LXXVI, No. 5, p. 554. I am indebted, in general, to the analysis presented here.
7. Norris, op. cit., vol. X, p. 42.
8. Ibid., vol. IV, pp. 201-202.
9. Ibid., vol. VII, p. 164.
10. Ibid., p. 165.
11. Ibid., pp. 167-68.
12. Ibid., vol. VIII, p. 320.
13. Ibid., p. 321.
14. Ibid., vol. V, p. 44.
15. Ibid.
16. Ibid., vol. III, p. 177.
17. Thomas Beer, *The Mauve Decade* (Garden City, N.Y., 1926), p. 17.
18. Norris, op. cit., vol. III, p. 179.
19. Ibid., p. 214.
20. Ibid, p. 251.
21. Ibid.
22. Walker, op. cit., p. 178.
23. Ibid., p. 199.
24. Norris, op. cit., vol. VI, p. 232.
25. Walker, op. cit., p. 252.

26. Norris, op. cit., vol. I, p. 58.
27. Ibid., vol. II, p. 361.
28. Ibid., vol. IX, p. 116.
29. Ibid., p. 67.

THIRTEEN: *An Abyss of Inequality*

1. Henry James, *The Notebooks,* ed. by F. O. Matthiessen and Kenneth B. Murdock (New York, 1947), p. 129.
2. Henry James, *Essays in London and Elsewhere* (London, 1893), p. 265.
3. Mary Austin, *Earth Horizon* (Boston, 1932), p. 141.
4. Constance Cary Harrison, *The Well-Bred Girl in Society* (Philadelphia, 1898), p. 10.
5. Ibid., p. 54.
6. Ibid., p. 174.
7. Constance Cary Harrison, *A Bachelor Maid* (New York, 1894), p. 164.
8. Ward Hutchinson, "The Economics of Prostitution," *American Medical-Surgical Bulletin* (August 15, 1895), vol. VIII, p. 981.
9. T. DeWitt Talmage, *The Marriage Ring* (New York, 1896), p. 60.
10. Most notably, *A Rose for Yesterday.*
11. Talmage, op. cit., p. 125.
12. Charlotte Stetso Perkins, *Women and Economics* (Boston, 1900).
13. Gertrude Atherton, *Patience Sparhawk and Her Times* (London, 1897), p. 239.
14. Ibid., p. 327.
15. Ibid.
16. Emma Goldman, *Living My Life* (New York, 1931), vol. I, p. 185.
17. Ibid., p. 186.
18. Ibid., p. 187.
19. *M'lle New York,* December 1898.
20. Ellen Glasgow, *The Woman Within* (New York, 1954), p. 78.
21. Ellen Glasgow, *The Descendant* (New York, 1900), p. 87.
22. Glasgow, *Woman Within,* p. 121.
23. F. O. Matthiessen, *Sarah Orne Jewett* (Boston, 1929), p. 30.
24. Sarah Orne Jewett, *Letters,* ed. by Annie Fields (Boston, 1911), p. 125.
25. Ibid., p. 54.
26. Ibid., p. 51.
27. M. A. DeWolfe Howe, *A Venture in Remembrance* (Boston, 1941), p. 156.
28. Sarah Orne Jewett, *Strangers and Wayfarers* (Boston, 1890), pp. 260-62.
29. Sarah Orne Jewett, *The Country of the Pointed Firs* (Boston, 1896), p. 159.
30. Ibid., p. 97.
31. Mary E. Wilkins Freeman, *Madelon* (New York, 1896), p. 334.
32. For facts about Mrs. Freeman's life, I have relied upon Edward Foster, *Mary E. Wilkins Freeman* (New York, 1956).
33. Mary E. Wilkins Freeman, *A New England Nun and Other Stories* (New York, 1920), p. 362.

34. Frank Norris [*Works*] (Garden City, N.Y., 1928), vol. VII, p. 150.
35. John Eldridge Frost, *Sarah Orne Jewett* (Kittery Point, Me., 1960), p. 124.
36. These and other biographical details are taken from Per E. Seyersted, "Kate Chopin: An Important St. Louis Writer Reconsidered," *Missouri Historical Society Bulletin*, XIX (January 1963), pp. 89-114.
37. Kate Chopin, *Bayou Folk* (Boston, 1894), p. 86.
38. Jewett, *Letters*, p. 82.
39. Ibid., pp. 82-83.
40. Kate Chopin, *The Awakening* (Chicago, 1899), p. 34.
41. Ibid., p. 19.
42. Ibid., p. 23.
43. Ibid., p. 122.
44. Ibid., pp. 147-48.
45. Ibid., p. 299.
46. Ibid., p. 300.
47. Ibid., pp. 291-92.
48. Seyersted, op. cit., p. 91.

FOURTEEN: *In and Out of Laodicea*

1. James Whitcomb Riley, *Letters*, ed. by William Lyon Phelps (Indianapolis, 1930), p. 102.
2. [Henry Adams], *The Life of George Cabot Lodge* (Boston, 1911), p. 9.
3. Facts about the Harvard of the day are based on Samuel Eliot Morison, *The Development of Harvard University Since the Administration of President Eliot, 1869–1929* (Cambridge, Mass., 1930), and *Three Centuries of Harvard, 1636–1936* (Cambridge, Mass., 1936).
4. Charles Macomb Flandrau, *Harvard Episodes* (Boston, 1897), p. 97.
5. Ibid., p. 182.
6. George Santayana, *Persons and Places* (New York, 1944), p. 234.
7. Fictionally treated in the story "A Dead Issue," in *Harvard Episodes*.
8. Norman Hapgood, *The Changing Years* (New York, 1930), p. 44.
9. *Harvard Monthly*, May 1890, p. 89.
10. *The Letters of George Santayana*, ed. by Daniel Cory (New York, 1955), p. 225.
11. R. P. Blackmur, "Stickney's Poetry," *Poetry* (June 1933), vol. XLII, p. 159.
12. Trumbull Stickney, *Poems* (Boston, 1905), p. 91.
13. Ibid., p. 208.
14. Adams, op. cit., p. 109.
15. George Cabot Lodge, *Poems and Dramas* (Boston, 1911), vol. I, p. 9.
16. From "The Gates of Life," ibid., p. 32.
17. An extended essay on this theme in Stickney, Lodge, and Moody is Thomas Riggs, Jr., "Prometheus 1900," *American Literature* (January 1951), vol. XXII, pp. 399-423.
18. Robert Herrick, "Myself," unpublished autobiographic manuscript in the "Robert Herrick Papers" at the Library of the University of Chicago.
19. Blake Nevius, *Robert Herrick* (Berkeley, Calif., 1962), p. 63.

20. Robert Herrick, *The Gospel of Freedom* (New York, 1898), p. 264.
21. *Some Letters of William Vaughn Moody*, ed. by Daniel Gregory Mason (Boston, 1913), pp. 52-53.
22. Moses J. Montrose and John Mason Brown, eds., *The American Theatre as Seen by Its Critics* (New York, 1934), p. 94.
23. Anna Morgan, *My Chicago* (Chicago, 1918), p. 45.
24. Daniel Frohman, *Daniel Frohman Presents* (New York, 1935), p. 71.
25. Norman Hapgood, *The Stage in America, 1897-1900* (New York, 1901), p. 35.
26. Denham Sutcliffe, ed., *Untriangulated Stars, Letters of Edwin Arlington Robinson to Harry DeForest Smith, 1890-1915* (Cambridge, Mass., 1947), p. 43.
27. Ibid., p. 261.
28. For the facts of Robinson's life chief reliance has been placed on Hermann Hagedorn, *Edwin Arlington Robinson* (New York, 1938), and Emory Neff, *Edwin Arlington Robinson* (New York, 1948).
29. See Edwin S. Fussell, *Edwin Arlington Robinson, The Literary Background of a Traditional Poet* (Berkeley, Calif., 1954), for a full account.
30. An analysis of the impression of the James story upon Robinson is in Neff, op. cit., pp. 62-64.
31. Edwin Arlington Robinson, *Collected Poems* (New York, Macmillan, 1934), p. 93.
32. Ibid., p. 78.
33. Ibid., p. 84.
34. Ibid., p. 177.
35. Ibid., p. 90.

FIFTEEN: *A Decade's Delay*

1. Facts about Dreiser's life may be located in W. A. Swanberg, *Dreiser* (New York, 1965).
2. Theodore Dreiser, *Dawn* (New York, 1930), p. 461.
3. Theodore Dreiser, *A Book about Myself* (New York, 1922), p. 178.
4. Ibid., p. 313.
5. Theodore Dreiser, *Sister Carrie* (New York, 1911), p. 328.
6. Ibid., p. 353.
7. Dreiser, *Myself*, p. 406.
8. Ibid., p. 426.
9. Jane Addams, *Twenty Years at Hull-House* (New York, 1910), p. 231.
10. Grant Richards, *Author Hunting* (London, 1934), p. 172.
11. A good contemporary account may be found in Robert Underwood Johnson, *Remembered Yesterdays* (Boston, 1923).
12. In his capacity as wit, he attacked James Whitcomb Riley, whom he parodied in a poem, "The Little Boy Blue with a Sickly Spine," which runs: "Ma and me's asked out to dine/And I have dot a sickly spine/But I don't mind a sickly spine/S'long as I'm asked out to dine," (Johnson, op. cit., pp. 363-64). In his capacity as poet, he was, in turn, parodied and attacked in little magazines such as *M'lle New York*.

Index